I0028897

Praise for *Learning API Styles*

Learning API Styles is a must-read for anyone serious about building robust, scalable APIs. From defining APIs and various API design patterns to identifying the trade-offs of the many API communication methods available, this masterful guide contains all you need to know about API design and development.

—*Mark Richards, coauthor of*
Fundamentals of Software Architecture

This book offers an indispensable exploration of modern API development, from low-level protocols to advanced designs. It's a must-have for any developer aiming to understand API fundamentals and make more informed design decisions for reliable systems.

—*William Jamir Silva, senior software engineer*

This book explores the technical underpinnings, the architectural decision points, and the implementation details that a modern developer will need to know to design and implement a web API.

—*Eric Potter, director of Technical Education*

This book provides valuable insights and practical guidance for building and using common API technologies for both beginners and experienced practitioners.

—*Karandeep Johar, software engineering manager, Amplitude*

Learning API Styles

*Understanding the Trade-Offs of Common APIs
and Choosing the Correct Solutions*

Lukasz Dynowski and Marcin Dulak

Foreword by Jacqui Read

O'REILLY®

Learning API Styles

by Lukasz Dynowski and Marcin Dulak

Copyright © 2025 SRP Consultancy and Marcin Dulak. All rights reserved.

Printed in the United States of America.

Published by O'Reilly Media, Inc., 1005 Gravenstein Highway North, Sebastopol, CA 95472.

O'Reilly books may be purchased for educational, business, or sales promotional use. Online editions are also available for most titles (*https://oreilly.com*). For more information, contact our corporate/institutional sales department: 800-998-9938 or *corporate@oreilly.com*.

Acquisitions Editor: Louise Corrigan
Development Editor: Michele Cronin
Production Editor: Clare Laylock
Copyeditor: Krsta Technology Solutions
Proofreader: Sharon Wilkey

Indexer: BIM Creatives, LLC
Cover Designer: Karen Montgomery
Cover Illustrator: Karen Montgomery
Interior Designer: David Futato
Interior Illustrator: Kate Dullea

July 2025:   First Edition

Revision History for the First Edition
2025-07-11:   First Release

See *https://oreilly.com/catalog/errata.csp?isbn=9781098153991* for release details.

The O'Reilly logo is a registered trademark of O'Reilly Media, Inc. *Learning API Styles*, the cover image, and related trade dress are trademarks of O'Reilly Media, Inc.

The views expressed in this work are those of the authors and do not represent the publisher's views. While the publisher and the authors have used good faith efforts to ensure that the information and instructions contained in this work are accurate, the publisher and the authors disclaim all responsibility for errors or omissions, including without limitation responsibility for damages resulting from the use of or reliance on this work. Use of the information and instructions contained in this work is at your own risk. If any code samples or other technology this work contains or describes is subject to open source licenses or the intellectual property rights of others, it is your responsibility to ensure that your use thereof complies with such licenses and/or rights.

978-1-098-15399-1

[LSI]

Table of Contents

Foreword

A software system is not just the definition of its parts but how those parts communicate. The quality of that communication is a huge factor in the system's overall performance. Your communication methods, such as APIs, need to be thoughtfully constructed and governed, built on strong foundations.

This is where *Learning API Styles* comes in. Not only is the content of the book immensely valuable, the way it is structured enables easy and efficient learning.

Learning API Styles starts with important foundational knowledge, an appreciation of API concepts (Chapter 1), including the API lifecycle. Chapter 2, on API design patterns, should be a prerequisite for anyone involved in the design and implementation of any API. Network protocols (Chapter 3) are then built upon with explanations of web protocols (Chapter 4), before introducing the API styles (beginning in Chapter 5) which are based on those protocols.

A hugely important concept for APIs runs throughout this book: security. Lukasz and Marcin say in Chapter 1 that "We perceive security as a force that is present in all phases of the API lifecycle," and I couldn't agree more. An API without security, considered at every stage, provides an easy and tempting target for bad actors.

Look at the news, and you'll see a state government that has allowed anyone access to personal documents, just by knowing a phone number. APIs are the gateways through which numerous businesses lose important data. Carefully designed and implemented security is essential to avoid becoming another newsworthy victim of bad actors. Lukasz and Marcin have woven security into this book like you need to weave it into your API.

This book isn't just theory—it features valuable, practical exercises. You implement the different API styles and, of course, secure them. Practice makes progress. Implementing the API styles will give you a much more thorough understanding of how the styles work, and also their pros and cons.

The concepts in this book are vital to understand before designing, architecting, and implementing an API. Here are just a few.

Multiple API styles exist because no one size fits all. The trade-offs described for each style in this book will enable you to compare the different styles and to choose the best one for your current context.

In *Communication Patterns*, I talk about considering your audience and their needs. Your API has an audience with needs, whether this is an audience internal or external to your company. The shift from *API as glue* to *API as a product*, with an audience and the ability to generate revenue, marked a significant change in how APIs are viewed. The perceived value of APIs increased. This book will enable you and your business to invest effectively in your APIs.

An API provides encapsulation: hiding the complexity of data and functionality behind a user-friendly interface. The customer of the API does not need to know how their requests are handled, only how to make the request and what to expect in return. In the same way that you use security to prevent data leaks, you use design to prevent domain concept leaks. The naming and structure of your data and data values should match your customers' expectations. Speak your customer's language. Do not skip the API naming pattern, or any other design patterns, in Chapter 2.

The API lifecycle is a tricky concept, being iterative not sequential. Each phase is linked to all the other phases, all influencing each other with outputs and feedback. You do not need to complete any phase before starting on the next. The API lifecycle is not about *big up-front design*. Complete *enough* design to move on to implementation, and so on. Vertically slice your API lifecycle to be able to quickly respond to change. The ACED model (*https://oreil.ly/grxkb*) is a useful reference, along with Chapter 1.

Read this book if you want to build a foundation for software systems that communicate effectively, both internally and with other systems.

Get ready to learn API styles from experienced practitioners and start to build your own.

— Jacqui Read
Author of Communication Patterns
Chief architect, The Ministry of Software Design
Co-organizer of DDD London
Winchester, UK, June 2025

Preface

Whether you realize it or not, the presence of APIs is ubiquitous. Without APIs, your smartphone wouldn't be able to get the latest weather forecasts, and ground control mission wouldn't be able to communicate over NASA's deep space network with the crew, or with active satellites orbiting the Earth.

APIs have transformative power, and the finance industry is one example. Nowadays, you don't have to visit a bank in person to run your errands. You can do most things over the web, using a smartphone (mobile application), or over a phone call.

APIs are behind the success of major technological companies like Amazon, Google, Microsoft, OpenAI, Revolut, and Salesforce, generating substantial amounts of revenue via digital channels. APIs are the veins through which data flows, and some technologies like Kubernetes wouldn't work without them.

Application programming interface (API) can have different meanings depending on the context. The term is mainly associated with software, but it can also be applied to hardware. Within the software context, an API can describe a library interface or a network-based API (the most commonly associated term).

We define *API* as an interaction point that allows software components to communicate. The API provides functionality without exposing the underlying system's complexity; it separates system behavior from its implementation details. APIs are primarily used by developers, who programmatically integrate them into the software to enable interoperability within or between systems. The API separates ownership, which allows for better maintenance because what's behind the API is the responsibility of the system that exposes it.

Over the past decades, we've witnessed the rise and expansion of the internet. The internet is a vast, interconnected network of computer systems that allows devices worldwide to communicate with one another. The foundation of this communication is the TCP/IP suite (*https://oreil.ly/9kdrm*), which acts as the language of the network, enabling applications and devices to exchange information.

This book focuses on network-based APIs, which are a group of APIs that software uses to communicate over the network (typically the internet). An API can be thought of as a shared language (governed by protocols, rules, and conventions) that software applications use to exchange data. Like a human who can speak multiple languages, software can utilize many APIs to communicate.

Why We Wrote This Book

Throughout our experience, we've worked with various APIs, including REST, Query, RPC, broker-based systems, and more. Every API style has an ecosystem surrounding it: community, working groups, and sometimes internet giants supporting it.[1] For every style, you may read many books to discover API merits; and believe us, it takes time to master just one style. Yet we can no longer afford to stick to one API style. Sure, you could go far with REST APIs, but only to a point.

This book is a response to a gap we noticed in the IT bookshelves. Namely, recent books on APIs don't provide a detailed overview of various API styles. Moreover, many books about APIs focus on high-level concepts or offer code snippets without providing complete implementations.

The IT industry in the past few years has signaled a need for API skills. In its 2023 "API Trends" report (*https://oreil.ly/Ody1W*), Gartner mentioned that the top API challenges that organizations face were missing key roles, lack of API standards, lack of skills, and security concerns. In 2024, Gartner predicted that 30% of the increase in demand for APIs will come from AI and large language models (LLMs) by 2026.[2]

This book seeks to address some of the aforementioned API challenges and meet the API needs that the IT industry is lacking.

Who Should Read This Book

This book is written for software developers and architects who want to know the trade-offs and implementation details of various API styles. Completing this book will give you an understanding of various APIs from the architecture, implementation, and network perspective. This book is intended for people who want to do the following:

---

1 *Style* is understood as a set of characteristics. See "What Are API Styles?" on page 15 for a summary of the API styles covered in this book.

2 Gartner, "Gartner Predicts More Than 30% of the Increase in Demand for APIs will Come From AI and Tools Using Large Language Models by 2026" (*https://oreil.ly/whm4x*), news release, March 20, 2024.

- Acquire practical skills in designing and implementing APIs securely
- Understand the trade-offs (advantages and disadvantages) of API styles
- Learn about the protocols that enable data exchange in APIs

What's in This Book

In this book, we'll design and implement synchronous and asynchronous APIs in various styles: REST API (Chapter 5), Query API with GraphQL (Chapter 6), Web Feeds API with the Atom protocol (Chapter 7), RPC API with the gRPC framework (Chapter 8), callback API with webhooks (Chapter 9), bidirectional API with Web-Socket (Chapter 10), and broker-based API with RabbitMQ (Chapter 11).

Each style has its benefits and drawbacks to be aware of as a developer or architect. We'll cover the trade-offs of each API style in detail. One additional aspect this book covers, often overlooked, is the role of network protocols in network-based APIs.

What's Not in This Book

This book is not intended for a nontechnical audience. If you fall into this category and you're looking for answers regarding API leadership, strategy, governance, compliance, and management, then consult *APIs: A Strategy Guide* by Daniel Jacobson et al. (O'Reilly, 2011) and *Continuous API Management* by Mehdi Medjaoui et al. (O'Reilly, 2021).

Furthermore, this book doesn't cover topics like API architecture, platforms, and monetization. To learn more about these topics, consult books like *Mastering API Architecture* by James Gough et al. (O'Reilly, 2022) and *API Management: An Architect's Guide to Developing and Managing APIs for Your Organization* by Brajesh De (Apress, 2017).

Weather Forecast Service

To present various API styles, we decided to implement a Weather Forecast Service (WFS). We chose the weather because everyone can intuitively relate to it. Figure P-1 shows an overview of the system, using a C4 context diagram (*https://c4model.com*).

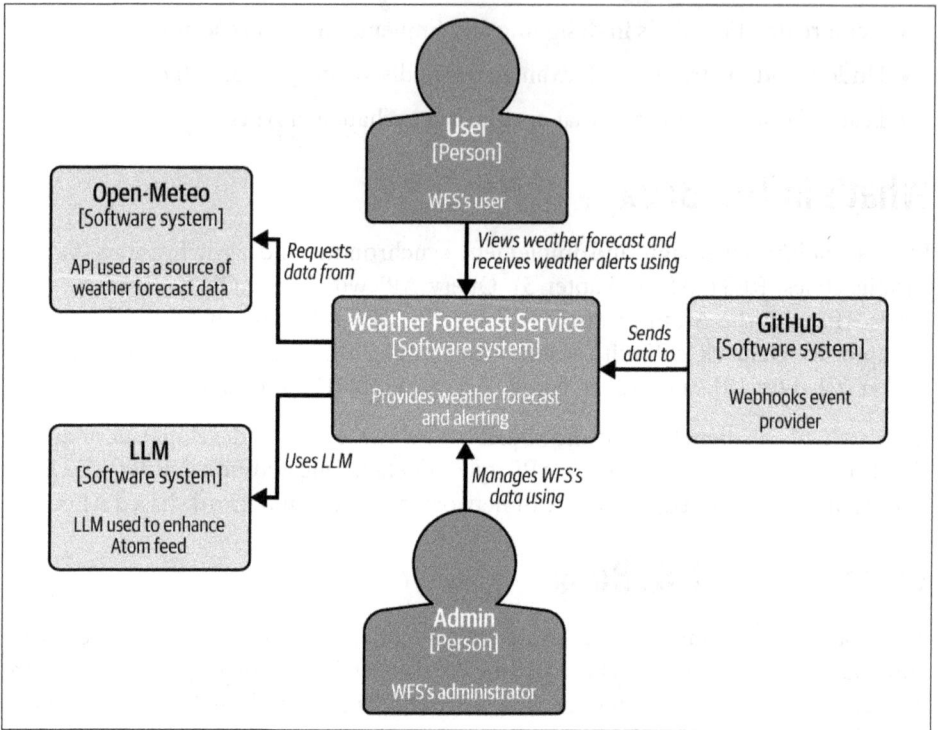

Figure P-1. Weather Forecast Service (WFS) C4 context diagram

The WFS is implemented in the Python programming language, using the Django (*https://www.djangoproject.com*) and Starlette (*https://www.starlette.io*) frameworks. WFS provides two types of information: weather forecasts for up to seven days and historical weather records. You could retrieve weather data using REST, GraphQL, and Atom feeds. Besides the weather data, the WFS offers the functionality of weather alerting using WebSocket and weather information enrichment fetched over gRPC from an LLM. Not all discussed API styles conceptually align with the WFS. As a result, the webhooks and RabbitMQ demo examples aren't related to WFS.

In 2021, GitHub released Codespaces, a cloud-based development environment available to any GitHub user for free (as of now). GitHub Codespaces allowed us to create an environment that you can use to execute the examples described in this book. Furthermore, the environment is Docker-based, which allows you to run the code locally as long as your platform can run Docker containers.

The easiest way to get to work with the code is via GitHub Codespaces. You could also work with code locally, without using GitHub Codespaces, as in Example P-1, later in this preface.

> GitHub Codespaces is free to use with certain limits, currently a few dozen hours. To stay within the free limit, you have to stop Codespaces after finishing working with it.

To work with GitHub Codespaces, you need a GitHub account. If you don't have one yet, use this signup form (*https://oreil.ly/b1dhe*) to create one.

You also need to fork the book's code repository. Visit *https://github.com/ldynia/learning-api-styles* and click the Fork button, as illustrated in Figure P-2.

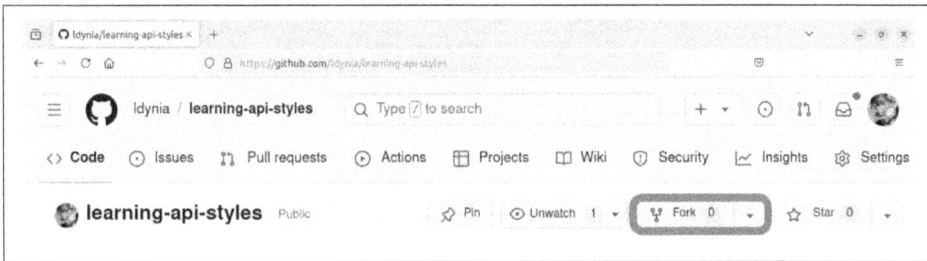

Figure P-2. Book's code repository and Fork button location

Once the repository is forked, the next step is to spin up the environment. For that, you have three options: use a web browser with GitHub Codespaces, use a local integrated development environment (IDE) that supports GitHub Codespaces, or use Docker on your local machine.

The easiest option is to use a web browser. Within the GitHub interface of the forked repository, click the green Code button, then click the Codespaces tab, and last, click the "Create codespace on main" button.

If the preceding steps are successfully executed, you'll have Visual Studio (VS) Code (*https://code.visualstudio.com*) open in the web browser, as shown in Figure P-3. At this point your setup is ready, and you can start executing the code samples included in the book.

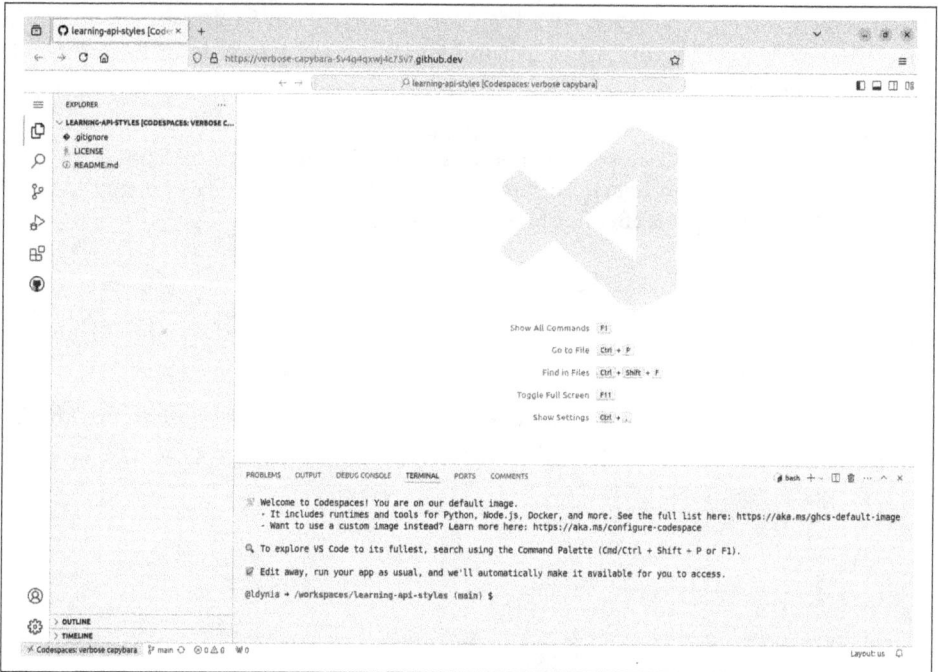

Figure P-3. Book's code repository fork opened remotely in GitHub Codespaces

If you choose to interact with GitHub Codespaces using a web browser, we recommend Google Chrome (*https://www.google.com/chrome*), which may offer the best experience.

Another way of using GitHub Codespaces is from an IDE running locally on your machine. The majority of IDEs support GitHub Codespaces. For example, you can use a locally installed version of VS Code. Open VS Code, click the "Open a Remote Window" button (in the lower-left corner), click the "Connect to Codespace" option, and finally, choose the Codespace to which you want to connect. This process is illustrated in Figure P-4. After connecting to GitHub Codespaces, your setup is ready.

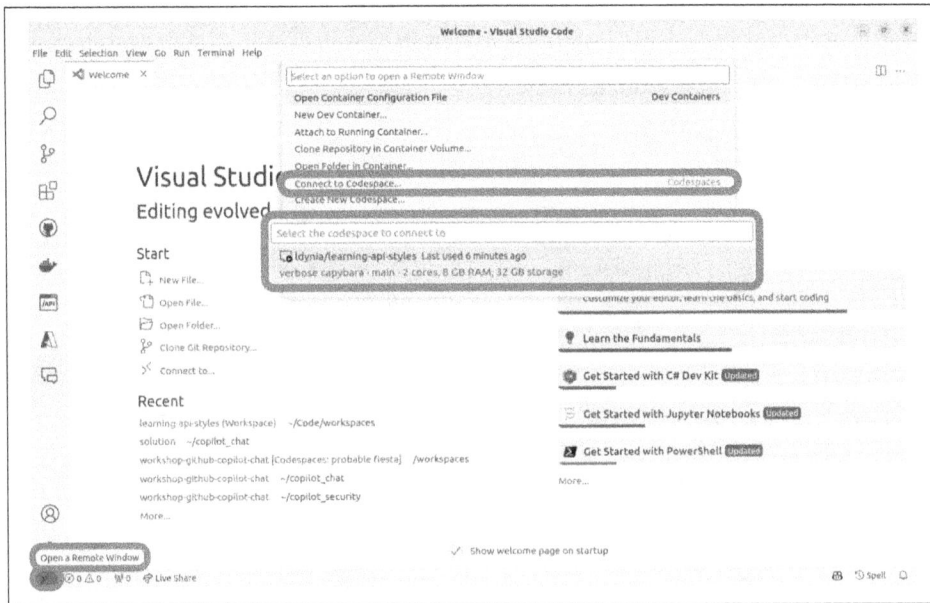

Figure P-4. Process of connecting to GitHub Codespaces using VS Code

If you don't want to work with GitHub Codespaces, you can run the project locally. You can work with a local copy of the book's code repository or your fork of it. The local scenario requires manually provisioning your environment with the necessary software. Besides an IDE, you also need Docker (*https://www.docker.com*) and Docker Compose (*https://oreil.ly/aKCLA*). Example P-1 shows how to clone the book's code repository.

Example P-1. Local clone of book's code repository

```
git clone https://github.com/ldynia/learning-api-styles ❶

code learning-api-styles ❷
```

❶ Clone the book's code repository. You could also clone your fork.

❷ Open the repository with VS Code.

After executing the preceding steps for the local setup, you need to start a dev container.[3] To do that, follow the steps illustrated in Figure P-5. First, click the "Open a

---

3 Dev containers use containers as a base for defining a development environment that can be run locally or remotely. Dev containers are supported by various IDEs, including VS Code, which provides a tutorial (*https://oreil.ly/uWysc*).

Remote Window" button (in the lower-left corner). Then choose the "Reopen in Container" option; this will build the Docker image and provision the dev container. At this point, your local setup is ready.

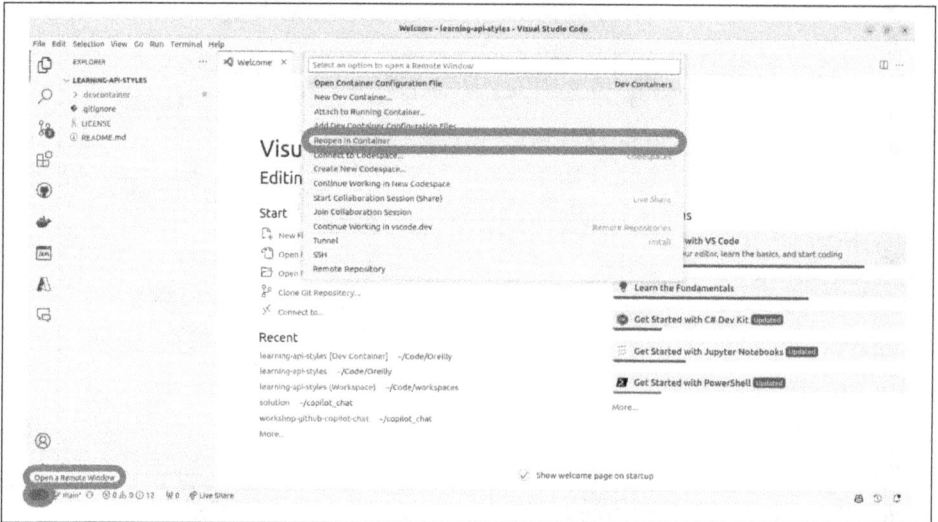

Figure P-5. Local clone of the book's code repository opened in VS Code

Many examples require multiple terminal windows/panes to be open; for that, we suggest installing the `tmux` program (*https://oreil.ly/6N4CI*). Executing the command from Example P-2 allows you to open a terminal window and split it into panes.

Example P-2. tmux session containing three panes

```
tmux new-session \; split-window -v \; split-window -h \; select-pane -U \; ❶
```

❶ The `tmux new-session` command initiates a workspace known as the `tmux` session, which contains multiple panes (windows). The `split-window -v` command splits the window pane vertically, and the following `split-window -h` further splits it horizontally. The last command, `select-pane -U`, selects the upper window pane. The backslashes `\;` are used to separate the individual `tmux` commands, allowing them to be executed sequentially. This ensures that each step is performed in the correct order, resulting in a new `tmux` session with a specific pane layout.

Figure P-6 illustrates the terminal window being split into three panes.

Figure P-6. tmux session containing three panes

Here are tmux shortcuts needed to control terminal panes:

Ctrl + B Shift + "
   Split the pane with horizontal layout.

Ctrl + B Shift + %
   Split the pane with vertical layout.

Ctrl + B + ↑ ↓ ← →
   Move between panes—up, down, left, or right.

Ctrl + B Ctrl + ↑ ↓ ← →
   Resize the window pane up, down, left, or right. Alternatively, you could use the mouse to resize the panes.

Ctrl + B X Y
   Close the pane (alternatively, type the exit command).

If you'd like to learn more about tmux, watch this YouTube tutorial (*https://oreil.ly/upurq*) or use the cheat sheet (*https://tmuxcheatsheet.com*) for a shortcuts reference.

Conventions Used in This Book

The following typographical conventions are used in this book:

Italic
> Indicates new terms, URLs, email addresses, filenames, and file extensions.

`Constant width`
> Used for program listings, as well as within paragraphs to refer to program elements such as variable or function names, databases, data types, environment variables, statements, and keywords.

`Constant width bold`
> Shows commands or other text that should be typed literally by the user.

`Constant width italic`
> Shows text that should be replaced with user-supplied values or by values determined by context.

> This element signifies a tip or suggestion.

> This element signifies a general note.

> This element indicates a warning or caution.

Using Code Examples

Supplemental material (code examples, exercises, etc.) is available for download at *https://learningapistyles.com*.

If you have a technical question or a problem using the code examples, please send email to *support@oreilly.com*.

This book is here to help you get your job done. In general, if example code is offered with this book, you may use it in your programs and documentation. You do not need to contact us for permission unless you're reproducing a significant portion of the code. For example, writing a program that uses several chunks of code from this book does not require permission. Selling or distributing examples from O'Reilly books does require permission. Answering a question by citing this book and quoting example code does not require permission. Incorporating a significant amount of example code from this book into your product's documentation does require permission.

We appreciate, but generally do not require, attribution. An attribution usually includes the title, author, publisher, and ISBN. For example: "*Learning API Styles* by Lukasz Dynowski and Marcin Dulak (O'Reilly). Copyright 2025 SRP Consultancy and Marcin Dulak, 978-1-098-15399-1."

If you feel your use of code examples falls outside fair use or the permission given above, feel free to contact us at *permissions@oreilly.com*.

O'Reilly Online Learning

O'REILLY®   For more than 40 years, *O'Reilly Media* has provided technology and business training, knowledge, and insight to help companies succeed.

Our unique network of experts and innovators share their knowledge and expertise through books, articles, and our online learning platform. O'Reilly's online learning platform gives you on-demand access to live training courses, in-depth learning paths, interactive coding environments, and a vast collection of text and video from O'Reilly and 200+ other publishers. For more information, visit *https://oreilly.com*.

How to Contact Us

Please address comments and questions concerning this book to the publisher:

> O'Reilly Media, Inc.
> 1005 Gravenstein Highway North
> Sebastopol, CA 95472
> 800-889-8969 (in the United States or Canada)
> 707-827-7019 (international or local)
> 707-829-0104 (fax)
> *support@oreilly.com*
> *https://oreilly.com/about/contact.html*

We have a web page for this book, where we list errata, examples, and any additional information. You can access this page at *https://oreil.ly/LearningAPIStyles*.

For news and information about our books and courses, visit *https://oreilly.com*.

Find us on LinkedIn: *https://linkedin.com/company/oreilly-media*.

Watch us on YouTube: *https://youtube.com/oreillymedia*.

Acknowledgments

The concept of writing a book is analogous to the activity of planting and gardening a tree. The tree is an excellent example that demonstrates the process and the formation of knowledge. At the end of the process, with enough care and endurance, you might grow a living object whose fruits are meant to be shared. The following are thanks to everyone who contributed to or influenced this book's formation and made this tree grow.

Both authors would like to thank Troels Ravn Bærentzen and Alexander Zafirov for making it possible for them to meet at work.

We want to thank all technical reviewers whose input populated this tree with new branches, such as Eric Potter, Karamdeep Johar, and others whose acronyms we could not decrypt. In particular, thanks to Marcos Fuentes and William Jamir Silva: your feedback caused a lot of work, but you made this tree blossom.

We'd like to thank Michele Cronin for guiding, removing blockers, linking us with the correct people, and putting up with us for the past two years. Additionally, thanks go to Clare Laylock for the editorial work that started with 3,345 comments to resolve. Thanks to Ben Hurst for trimming the tree (copyediting). Ben, if you wonder what happened to articles (a, an, and the), there is an explanation. We ate them all, sorry! Finally, thanks to anyone in the O'Reilly team who contributed to this book and whom we didn't meet, including artwork people, and so on.

Acknowledgments from Lukasz Dynowski

I want to thank my wife, Juliet, and kids, Camilla and Philip, for giving the much-needed support that allowed me to remain laser-focused on the book. Without your help, this book would not be possible. At the same time, I apologize for not providing the full attention you all deserve, and for experiencing this extrovert living a life of an introvert for too long. Apologies to my kids for being picked last at school and kindergarten, and for the reduced number of play dates. Now it's my turn to give you back the time.

I want to thank Louise Corrigan, who planted the seed of this tree by dropping out of the blue an unexpected email that got my attention and piqued my curiosity.

Thanks to Jacqui Read for writing the foreword. I was afraid to ask for help from a former rival with whom I luckily ended up collaborating. When I saw Jacqui's work at software architectural katas organized by O'Reilly, I knew that it would impact the realms of software architecture. Jacqui rapidly wrote *Communication Patterns* (*https://communicationpatternsbook.com*), which, among other things, teaches how to communicate with diagrams, a skill that so many of us need to acquire.

A tree needs soil to grow. Thanks to Mark Richards for the endorsement, and for being persistent in creating content that continues to educate and inspire me, such as his software architecture Monday lessons (*https://www.developertoarchitect.com/lessons*).

Thanks go to Monty Python, Tim Burton, Pink Floyd, Jean Van Hamme, and Grzegorz Rosiński for Thorgal, and to the "top man" from Indiana Jones. I don't quite know why I mentioned them, but it feels right to do so.

My final thanks go to you for reading this book. If you are familiar with the expression "customer obsession," then two years of our lives were dedicated to "reader obsession." Live long and pull request.

Acknowledgments from Marcin Dulak

I want to thank Alex Schuleit for creating the opportunity to work on this book. My thanks go to Rufus and the other little brothers who enforced breaks from writing by occupying the keyboard or asking for food.

## CHAPTER 1

API Concepts

The term *API* stands for application programming interface. In this book, we focus on a particular type of API—namely, network-based APIs. After examining the history of APIs, you'll be presented with an overview of the APIs covered in the book. The APIs will be compared based on the characteristics that define the API style.

Apart from the differences among various API styles, you'll explore concepts common to all network-based APIs. You'll learn about the reasons APIs are created, including treating them as products and monetizing them. You'll walk through the Software Development Lifecycle (SDLC) process of creating APIs, as well as their governance and management. Understanding these elements will help you identify the API that matches your needs.

Before we explore the specific APIs covered in this book, let's first look at the concept of APIs and their history.

What Is an API?

The term *interface* in application programming interface refers to a point of interaction where entities communicate with each other. An entity can, for example, be a user, a system, or an organization.

Figure 1-1 illustrates an example of an entity-to-entity interface. The image shows an electron microscope picture of a needle and a vinyl record. The needle interfaces with the surface of the vinyl. The grooves are a physical representation of a sound wave engraved into the vinyl. A force acts on the needle and keeps it in the groove, and when the vinyl is put in motion, its effects can be heard.

Figure 1-1. Electron microscope image of a needle and a vinyl record[1]

Here are more examples of interfaces that you may interact with daily:

Human interface device (HID)
> A device that allows a person to interact with and control another device, such as a TV's remote control or a computer's mouse.

Command-line interface (CLI)
> An interface that receives commands from a user through lines of text, and transmits those commands to a computer system.

Graphical user interface (GUI)
> An interface that allows users to interact with computer systems through graphical icons.

Chat interface
> An interface that exposes an application where you can have chat-like conversations.

Brain-computer interface (BCI)
> An interface link that allows for direct communication between the brain and an external device. This interface is alternatively known as the *brain-machine interface.*

---

1 This image is from "Ben Krasnow's "Electron Microscope Slow-Motion Video of Vinyl LP" blog post (*https://oreil.ly/uxWIh*).

APIs are found in various computer systems, such as these:

Software library or framework
The Java Platform, Standard Edition and Java Development Kit (*https://oreil.ly/aMYLg*) is an example library that provides an API for interacting with the operating system, network, and more; the Flask API (*https://oreil.ly/OiLFi*) is an example of a Python web framework.

Computer operating system
Portable Operating System Interface (POSIX) is a set of standards specified by the Institute of Electrical and Electronics Engineers Computer Society (IEEE CS). POSIX defines APIs to ensure compatibility across operating systems (Unix-like and others).

Network-based application
The APIs in this category are designed for applications that communicate over a computer network. Typical interfaces in this category are *web APIs*, which are served by the web server and consumed by the web browser. In this case, the web browser primarily uses the JavaScript web API to interact with the web server.[2] Network-based API applications can operate browserless too. Examples of such applications are command-line tools, mobile apps, and desktop apps.

As you can see, APIs are used across various types of computer systems. The APIs provide specific functionalities and capabilities so that you, as the API user, don't have to implement them from scratch. APIs hide the complexity of the system behind the interface. As a user, you treat an API as an opaque box. Following the API documentation, you provide the inputs and receive the outputs, along with any side effects during this interaction.

Network-Based APIs

In this book, we focus on network-based APIs. A *network-based API* is an interaction point that allows software to communicate over the network (typically, the internet).

Most APIs presented in this book fall into the category of *web APIs*. Web APIs allow software to communicate over the internet and utilize web technologies such as web browsers and protocols like HTTP (for more details about HTTP, see Chapter 4). However, the term *web API* narrows APIs to web-based architectures and technologies. Therefore, we prefer to use the broader term, which is network-based APIs. So, when we mention APIs, we are referring to network-based APIs unless we state otherwise.

---

2 See the browser's JavaScript Web API reference (*https://oreil.ly/LVCGP*).

Let's continue explaining the API acronym, now in the context of network-based applications. Figure 1-2 illustrates components of a typical web application in a client-server architecture.[3]

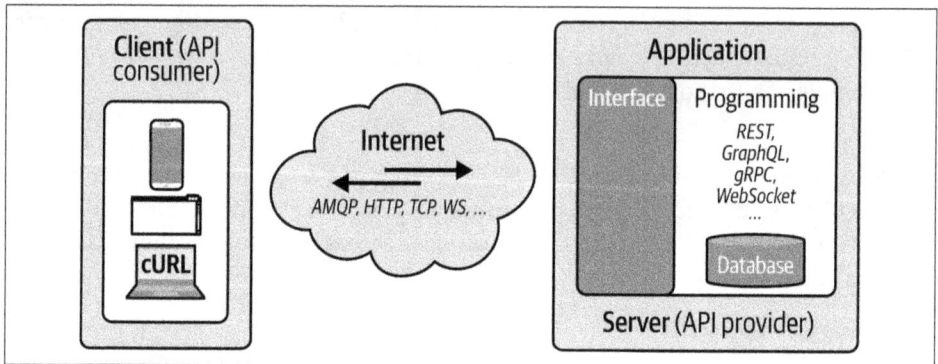

Figure 1-2. Network-based APIs

The following list explains each term of the API acronym:

Application

Although the word *application* appears only on the server side of Figure 1-2, applications exist on both sides of the diagram—namely, both the client and the server. The server application can be treated as an opaque box. In the opaque box, the implementation details are hidden. We know that inputs enter the opaque box, then they go through a set of transformations (usually unknown to an external observer), which lead to expected outputs. In the context of web APIs, the server application is called the *backend*, and the client application is called the *frontend*. The backend application serves data, and the frontend application consumes it.

Programming

Programming consists of providing instructions to a computer to perform tasks. The functionality served by the server application can be thought of as programmed by the client application. Although the term *programming* is present in Figure 1-2 only on the server side, programming happens in applications on both sides: on the client and the server. In this sense, it's a developer who programs (implements) the functionality into the frontend and backend applications by utilizing relevant tools and libraries.

---

3 For the definition of client and server, see "Socket API" on page 78.

Interface

An interface allows systems to communicate and exchange data. The interface is an interaction point where the server application exposes its functionality to the client application that consumes it.

A visual way to think about a network-based API is to imagine a multilane toll bridge connecting two cities, with trucks passing over the bridge, as shown in Figure 1-3.

Figure 1-3. Visual analogy of network-based APIs[4]

In this analogy, cities at both ends of the bridge represent the client and the server applications. The bridge connecting the cities symbolizes the network through which the data flows.

A toll gate through which the truck enters the bridge is the API style. A truck with a cargo (message) entering or leaving the bridge represents a request or response. The address on the cargo symbolizes the API endpoint. The truck and its cargo are validated at the toll gate, ensuring that both the request and the response are correctly formatted and authorized. After the toll gate validation, the truck enters the bridge and adheres to established traffic rules (these rules define network protocols, which you can learn more about in Chapter 3).

---

4 This image was generated using OpenAI's DALL·E.

You can use this analogy to describe the synchronous and asynchronous communication types, defined in "Synchronous and Asynchronous Communication Types" on page 9. For that, consider how a truck delivers its cargo. In synchronous message delivery, a truck delivers the cargo and waits for the acknowledging receipt (confirmation that the cargo was received). Meanwhile, in asynchronous message delivery, a truck departs as soon as it delivers the cargo. The acknowledging receipt is sent back later on a different truck.

Concepts of API Communication

Before we explore network-based APIs in more detail, we still need to explain concepts associated with data exchange over the network: message, transmission modes, and synchronous and asynchronous communication types.

Message

A *message* is a discrete data unit (a self-contained record) sent by a sender to one or many receivers. It typically contains the payload, as well as the metadata that describes the message.

In the Open Systems Interconnection (OSI) model, the term *message* is associated with the application layer protocol (see "TCP/IP and the OSI Model" on page 80). Let's look at a few examples of application layer messages:

HTTP

Example 1-1 shows a typical HTTP/1.1 POST message (for more information about HTTP, see Chapter 4). This message contains the POST request line, followed by three headers and the message body (comment=Hello).

Example 1-1. HTTP message carried by a POST request

```
POST /submit HTTP/1.1
Host: example.com
Content-Type: application/x-www-form-urlencoded
Content-Length: 13

comment=Hello
```

XMPP

Example 1-2 shows an Extensible Messaging and Presence Protocol (XMPP) (*https://oreil.ly/dCqrv*) XML-encoded message (which is a part of the XMPP stream). Note how the XML's attributes are used to describe message metadata.

Example 1-2. XMPP message within an XMPP stream

```
<?xml version='1.0'?>
<stream:stream ...>
  <message from='sender@example.com' to='receiver@example.net' xml:lang='en'>
    <body>Hello</body>
  </message>
</stream:stream>
```

MQTT

Example 1-3 shows a representation of a binary message sent with the MQTT protocol (*https://oreil.ly/5K2et*); the message in MQTT is referred to as a *packet*. An MQTT packet consists of the fixed header, an optional variable header, and the payload. This particular packet (message) describes a PUBLISH control packet type. The variable header contains the topic name (sensor/temperature), and the payload contains data (25.5 C).

Example 1-3. Outline of an MQTT PUBLISH packet

```
Fixed Header:    PUBLISH ...
Variable Header: sensor/temperature
Payload:         25.5 C
```

Transmission Modes

The term *transmission mode* (also referred to as *data transmission mode*) comes from the telecommunication domain and describes how data is shared between communicating parties. Figure 1-4 illustrates three distinct transmission modes that can be used to transfer data between services (or devices) involved in communication. Each communicating party can be in one of three states: *send, receive,* or *send and receive* (simultaneously).

> Transmission modes aren't exclusive to APIs. Any system that needs to exchange information, whether it's a hardware device or software component, implements a suitable transmission mode.

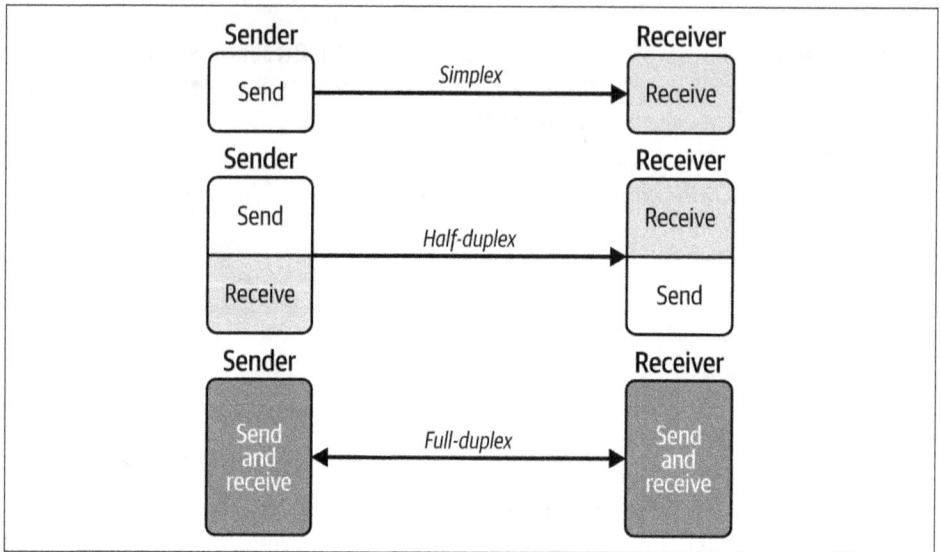

Figure 1-4. Transmission modes

Let's look at the different transmission modes:

Simplex

A one-directional transmission mode. Data flows in only one direction, from the sender to the receiver. For example, a radio or a TV is a device that operates in simplex mode, since you can only receive the data.

Half-duplex/semi-duplex

A bidirectional transmission mode in which data flow happens nonsimultaneously. Data flows in both directions, but in only one direction at a time: from the sender to the receiver. An example of a device that uses half-duplex mode is a walkie-talkie. When communicating using a walkie-talkie, both parties must adhere to a communication protocol (a set of vocabulary like "over" and "out").

Full-duplex/duplex

A bidirectional transmission mode in which data flow happens simultaneously in both directions.[5] A phone is an example of a device that communicates using full-duplex mode. In a phone conversation, you can talk and be heard at the same time.

---

5 A simultaneous, bidirectional transmission can also happen in a dual-simplex mode. This mode uses two separate simplex communication channels, compared to a single channel used by the full-duplex mode.

Synchronous and Asynchronous Communication Types

The word *synchronous* originates from the Greek *syn*, meaning "together," and *chronos*, meaning "time." Therefore, *synchronous communication* requires coordinated timing, while *asynchronous communication* doesn't. For example, synchronous communication in the telecommunication domain involves a shared clock that ensures the receiver can sample and correctly interpret the signal at the rate defined by the sender. This shows that the concept of synchronous and asynchronous communication isn't limited to the request-response model.

Examples of synchronous communication are phone calls and video chats, where participants expect simultaneous engagement. Emails and forum posts are examples of asynchronous communication, where messages are sent and received at different times without needing simultaneous coordination. In asynchronous communication, participants are free to perform other tasks after sending or receiving a message. In technical terms, this means they can perform nonblocking processing. Figure 1-5 illustrates the difference between synchronous and asynchronous communication, where two parties follow a request-response model.

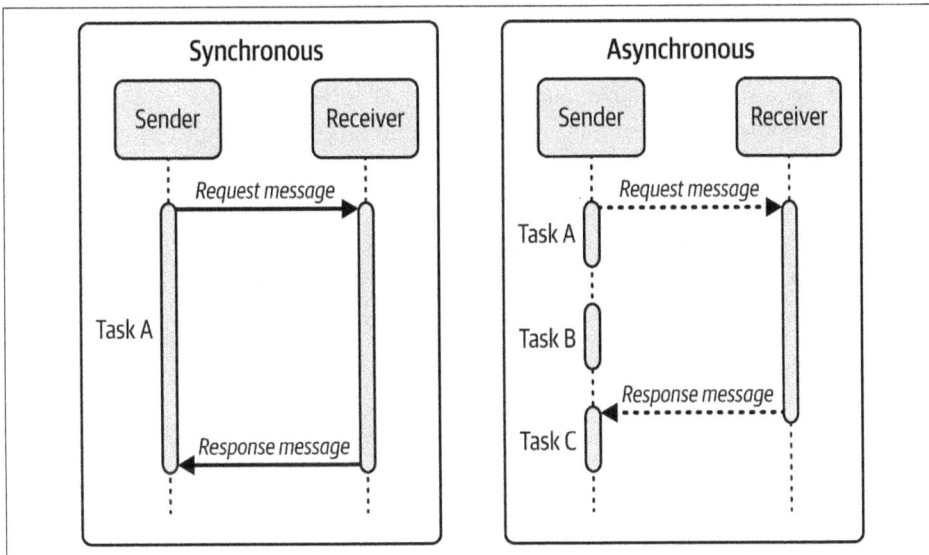

Figure 1-5. Comparison of synchronous and asynchronous communication

In synchronous, request-response communication, a sender sends a message to the receiver and waits for the corresponding response. While waiting for the response, the sender is in a blocked state, meaning the sender cannot proceed (or start a new task) until a response is received. The precondition to successful synchronous communication is that both the sender and the receiver be active and available during the message exchange.

In asynchronous, request-response communication, a sender sends a message to the receiver without being blocked. The sender starts executing other tasks while waiting for a response. In asynchronous communication, the sender and the receiver don't have to be present simultaneously when the communication happens.

The design of a network protocol might determine whether the sender will communicate synchronously or asynchronously. However, if a protocol offers freedom, the sender chooses which communication style to follow. For example, HTTP follows a request-response communication model in which every request has a corresponding response, and because of that, you might assume that, by default, the clients who use HTTP communicate synchronously. However, a JavaScript client sending an HTTP request using the `fetch()` method communicates asynchronously. In contrast, a `curl` client sending the same HTTP request communicates synchronously.

History of APIs

The idea of the API is older than the term itself. Although the term *API* originated in the 1940s, it didn't emerge until the 1960s and 1970s.[6]

In the 1940s, British computer scientists Maurice Wilkes, David Wheeler, and Stanley Gill worked on a modular software library for an early computer called the Electronic Delay Storage Automatic Calculator (EDSAC). The resulting document, the first book on computer programming,[7] contained a notion of using subroutines as standardized interfaces to machines that perform computations. This notion can, in modern terms, be interpreted as an API:

> In order to be able to use a library subroutine, it is not necessary to have an exact knowledge of how it is constructed or of the precise numerical process which it uses, provided that there is available a concise specification of what it does and how it is to be used…. For a subroutine to be useful for inclusion in a library it must be drafted in a sufficiently general form so that it can be used in different contexts without the user having to carry out internal modifications to it.
>
> —*The Preparation of Programs for an Electronic Digital Computer*, 1957

Figure 1-6 shows two images. The top image shows the EDSAC composed of racks responsible for storage, and the input-output units. The rectangle on the right marks the input tape inserted into the tapereader, which is connected to the teleprinter that prints the results. The bottom image shows an operator (programmer) who is using a keyboard to punch a program into a tape by using a tapereader (visible at the center

---

6 Joshua Bloch performed archeological work on the history of APIs, which he presented in "A Brief, Opinionated History of the API" (*https://oreil.ly/hLiqt*) at QCon New York in 2018.

7 Maurice Vincent Wilkes, David John Wheeler, and Stanley Gill, *The Preparation of Programs for an Electronic Digital Computer* (*https://oreil.ly/49YYe*) (Addison-Wesley Press, 1951/1957).

of the image) to mechanically copy the necessary subroutines from the library. The rectangle on the left marks a steel cabinet that contains a library of tapes on which the subroutines were punched.

Figure 1-6. The EDSAC (top) and an operator in the 1950s using a keyboard to punch a program into a tape (bottom)[8]

---

8 Found in *The Preparation of Programs for an Electronic Digital Computer* (*https://oreil.ly/Iw6Do*).

The term *application program interface* (without an "ing" suffix in the word *program*) was used by Ira W. Cotton and Frank S. Greatorex in their 1968 paper, "Data Structures and Techniques for Remote Computer Graphics."[9] The authors use this term to describe an interaction between an application and a computer system. They explain that the system is designed to be hardware-independent, allowing it to adapt to different hardware while keeping the application program interface unchanged.

As computer networks became common in the 1970s and 1980s, programmers wanted to call libraries located not only on their local computers but also on computers located elsewhere. The idea of the API expanded further with the notion of the Remote Procedure Call (see "Remote Procedure Call" on page 244 for details).

In the 1990s, computers continued to operate across different environments, operating systems, and programming languages. The Object Management Group (OMG) (*https://www.omg.org*) defined the Common Object Request Broker Architecture (CORBA) standard (*https://www.corba.org*). CORBA was agnostic to any programming language, and it allowed remotely calling objects and performing operations on these objects despite them being distributed across various systems. CORBA bindings enabled cross-language object interaction, and objects were described in interface definition language (IDL) syntax (*https://oreil.ly/Akrew*).

In 1993, Microsoft's Component Object Model (COM) (*https://oreil.ly/PizNK*) addressed similar problems to CORBA, but for binary programs using application binary interface (ABI) (*https://oreil.ly/qm08x*). Contrary to APIs, which are hardware-independent and define access to programs in source code (high-level), ABI is hardware-dependent. It defines how routines (functions) and data structures are accessed in machine code (low-level), allowing binary programs to communicate.

The year 1998 gave birth to Simple Object Access Protocol (SOAP) (*https://oreil.ly/h5EGt*), a protocol for exchanging XML-formatted messages between web services. SOAP used application layer protocols, mainly Hypertext Transfer Protocol (HTTP) and, less frequently, Simple Mail Transfer Protocol (SMTP).[10] SOAP was criticized for being verbose because its messages were large; for being slow to parse because it didn't use HTTP features; as well as for not defining a standardized interaction model that would enforce a specific way for clients and servers to interact.

---

9 Ira W. Cotton and Frank S. Greatorex, "Data Structures and Techniques for Remote Computer Graphics" (*https://oreil.ly/k4fek*), in *AFIPS '68: Proceedings of the December 9-11, 1968 Fall Joint Computer Conference* (1968).

10 According to Postman's "2023 State of the API Report" (*https://oreil.ly/knMeq*), SOAP is the fourth most used API technology.

In 2000, Roy Thomas Fielding outlined Representational State Transfer (REST) in his Ph.D. dissertation "Architectural Styles and the Design of Network-Based Software Architectures" (*https://oreil.ly/O1rcQ*), describing an idea of a network-based API.

API Mandate

The REST architecture style, introduced by Fielding in 2000, helped in the adoption of network-based APIs on the public internet. Soon after, another document, known as the API mandate, revealed that this trend was also present within enterprises.

As the story goes, around 2002, Amazon CEO Jeff Bezos issued a memo (*https://oreil.ly/YlZ7C*) to his employees (the *API mandate*). The mandate was written in the context of service-oriented architecture (SOA). If we rephrase the original mandate principles in modern terms, they may sound as follows:

1. Service data and functionality are exposed through APIs.
2. Services communicate through APIs only.
3. No other ways of communication apart from network-based APIs are allowed.
4. APIs are implemented using a technology that fits the context.
5. APIs are to be designed so that they are externalizable to public clients.

The beginning of this century, in particular, the 2010s, saw a growth in the use of API technologies; hence we could call this period the "Age of APIs." Here is the timeline of some of the API technologies that appeared during this period: REST (2000), webhooks (2007), WebSocket (2011), GraphQL (2015), and gRPC (2015).

Why APIs?

You might wonder why APIs are important in the first place. We'll answer this question from the perspective of an individual, a developer, and an organization.

There is a common notion that people should invest in developing *soft skills*—job skills that are generic, like time management, communication, or teamwork. Soft skills may lead you to an invitation for a job interview, but an organization is looking for a candidate who can help achieve its goals. Hence, organizations are looking for candidates with particular x, y, and z skills. These could be soft interpersonal skills or hard technical skills. As a candidate, you have an advantage if you possess the skills desired by organizations. Therefore, whether you are a software developer or an architect working with network-based applications, you may want to invest in developing API skills, since they can be transferable across roles and industries.

Gartner's 2023 report titled "API Trends" (*https://oreil.ly/Ody1W*) says that 38% of organizations that responded to Gartner's survey plan to add API developer roles next year.

APIs enable development based on a modular architecture, where components (services) are built and managed as independently as possible. APIs also aid interoperability by ensuring that various systems communicate through a standardized interface. If desired, this enables a transition to an SOA, such as a microservices architecture.

One of the goals of an organization is to generate a profit. In an increasingly online world, understanding that, in certain industries, "every business is a software business"[11] leads to the realization that your organization's online presence will influence profits. APIs can help organizations to grow, connect with internal and external organization services, and facilitate building software through the following:

Creating new revenue streams
Websites like Skyscanner (*https://www.skyscanner.com*) act as API aggregators. These aggregators query airline and hotel offers, primarily through APIs, and make the data searchable. This allows users to choose an airline or hotel that is attractive to them, hence generating new revenue for the airline or hotel. It also generates revenue for the API providers. APIs were reported to bring more than half of the revenue generated by companies like Salesforce, eBay, and Expedia.[12]

Increasing market reach
The video communication platform Zoom (*https://zoom.com*), besides being accessible via the website, is also available on smartphones, tablets, desktops, and smart TVs. Companies that open APIs to mobile devices may potentially reach a large part of the world population.[13]

Accessing the latest technologies
In 2021, GitHub released a tool called GitHub Copilot, based on a Generative Pre-trained Transformer (GPT) model trained on millions of code repositories. With time, GitHub Copilot evolved from a code-completion tool to a coding assistant. OpenAI, by making the model APIs public, allows GitHub (and other companies) to access the updated versions of the model.

---

11 Watts S. Humphrey, *Winning with Software: An Executive Strategy* (Addison-Wesley Professional, 2001).

12 See Bala Iyer and Mohan Subramaniam, "The Strategic Value of APIs" (*https://oreil.ly/k3KXU*), *Harvard Business Review*, January 7, 2015.

13 In 2024, the world population was estimated at 8.1 billion (*https://oreil.ly/FBvVV*), whereas the estimated number of smartphone subscriptions was 7.2 billion (*https://oreil.ly/EHMBT*).

Private, Public, and Partner APIs

APIs can be categorized in many ways, including by API access type:

Private
> These APIs are known as *internal APIs* and are developed internally within an organization. The intended use of these APIs is to exchange data among organizational units.

Public
> These APIs are exposed by an organization to the general public. Services or data exposed by public APIs can be provided for free or monetized by the organization that owns them. For example, Open-Meteo's weather APIs (*https://open-meteo.com*) are free for noncommercial use and paid for commercial use.

Partner
> These APIs are accessible only to the organization that develops them and the organization's partners.

What Are API Styles?

To start thinking about API styles, let's compare them with architectural styles in civil engineering. An architectural style is a set of characteristics, features, methods, materials, structures, and regional and cultural forces that impact the design, function, and appearance of a building. An architectural style is often associated with a time period and has a unique name that encapsulates its characteristics. Hence, you might have heard of buildings being described as Roman, Greek, Renaissance, Baroque, Victorian, or vernacular.

The same way of thinking about architectural style can be applied to software and APIs. Therefore, we define an *API style* as a paradigm that uses patterns, practices, and protocols to design, implement, and expose APIs. Similar to architectural styles, API styles have their purpose and function, and they come and go with time.

The interesting aspect of defining an API style is that each unique style is created from a blend of characteristics (protocols, design constraints, etc.), and some characteristics can dominate the style. One way to explain this is to use an analogy of a music band. A typical band consists of drums, bass, guitar, keyboard, and vocals. With just these five instruments, a band can create music in various styles, such as rock, pop, reggae, and many others. Oftentimes, a band can blend different styles, expanding the spectrum of music styles even further by creating a fusion of pop-rock, funk-rock, or jazz-funk. However, a band often identifies itself with a dominant music style, not a set of instruments used to create it. The same applies to API styles. Even though various API styles can use the same instruments, such as protocols, communication types, principles governing it, or design constraints, what defines an API style is the set of its most dominant characteristics. We may classify API styles as follows:

REST/RESTful

RESTful APIs adhere to six constraints outlined in Roy Fielding's dissertation (*https://oreil.ly/vNPXH*). While many APIs claim to be RESTful, the reality is that they omit the inclusion of hypermedia links, which is a requirement of RESTful API design.[14] REST is described in detail in Chapter 5.

Query-based

The dominant characteristic of a query-based API style is its ability to let clients query the API to return data in a specific shape. A representative technology for this API style is GraphQL (*https://graphql.org*), described in Chapter 6. A GraphQL API exposes an endpoint where clients send queries specifying the fields to be retrieved.

Web feed

The dominant characteristic of this API style is its ability to deliver continuously updated content in a structured format. Well-known examples of this approach are the RSS (Really Simple Syndication, also known as Rich Site Summary) (*https://oreil.ly/wfbrT*) and the Atom (*https://oreil.ly/3X1ib*) standards. Both technologies rely on XML to structure the data and use HTTP as an application protocol. This style is described in Chapter 7.

Remote Procedure Call (RPC)

The dominant characteristic of the RPC API style is the ability to invoke a function (procedure) on a remote server, giving the appearance of local execution. The RPC client makes a call (sends data over a network) to the RPC server that exposes the procedure, and the results of the call (computation) are returned back to the RPC client. A technology (framework) that took the lead in this API style is gRPC (*https://grpc.io*), described in Chapter 8.

---

14 Roy Fielding, "Rest APIs Must Be Hypertext-Driven" (*https://oreil.ly/NJLH1*), *Untangled*, October 20, 2008.

Callback

The dominant characteristic of this API style is a callback mechanism. In this API style, we have two sides: a destination system that creates and handles the callback (receives messages), and the source system that calls the callback (sends messages). Every message sent from the source to the destination system in callback APIs is expected to be acknowledged. A typical technology that uses this API style is webhooks (Chapter 9). Webhooks resemble an event-based API style because the mechanism that triggers the callback is an event; the difference is that webhooks aren't routed through an intermediary like a message broker. Commonly, webhooks are referred to as *HTTP callbacks* because when an event occurs, the source system notifies the destination system by sending a message with an HTTP POST request, acting as a callback mechanism.

Bidirectional

An API implemented in this style allows exchanging the data between client and server in both directions simultaneously (see full-duplex transmission in Figure 1-4). APIs built with the WebSocket protocol (*https://oreil.ly/XzJeg*) or gRPC framework (*https://grpc.io*) belong to this category because both can exchange data between the client and the server in a full-duplex mode. (WebSocket is covered in Chapter 10, and gRPC is covered in Chapter 8.)

Broker-based

APIs implemented in this style are characterized by messages passing through an intermediary known as a *broker*. Broker-based APIs deliver messages by using different protocols. There are many broker-based messaging systems, including Apache ActiveMQ (*https://activemq.apache.org*), Apache Kafka (*https://kafka.apache.org*), and RabbitMQ (*https://www.rabbitmq.com*), which we describe in Chapter 11.

There are many other ways of classifying network-based APIs. For example, the authors of *Continuous API Management* (O'Reilly, 2021) mention five API styles: tunnel, resource, hypermedia, query, and event-based APIs.

Table 1-1 shows distinct features of the API styles. The columns contain the API styles discussed in this book, and the rows contain various style characteristics.

Table 1-1. Selected characteristics of various API styles

	RESTful	Query	Web feed	RPC	Callback	Bidirectional	Broker-based
Technology	REST	GraphQL	Atom	gRPC	Webhook	WebSocket	RabbitMQ
Protocol	HTTP	HTTP[a]	HTTP	HTTP/2	HTTP	WebSocket	AMQP
Communication type	Synchronous	Synchronous	Asynchronous	Synchronous	Asynchronous	Asynchronous	Asynchronous
Binary data support	Yes	Partial	Partial	Yes	Yes	Yes	Yes
Responsiveness	Medium	Medium	Medium	High	Medium	High	High
Development effort	Medium	Medium	Low	High	Low	Medium	High

[a] Besides HTTP, GraphQL can also use the WebSocket protocol.

The factors described in Table 1-1 are defined as follows:

Technology
> An example of a technology that implements the given API style.

Protocol
> The primary network protocol used by the given technology.

Communication type
> The most commonly used communication type for this API style. The communication type can be either Synchronous or Asynchronous (see "Synchronous and Asynchronous Communication Types" on page 9).

Binary data support
> The ability to support the transfer of binary data. A Yes value indicates support by default, No indicates no support, and Partial indicates that binary encoding is supported but requires application-level implementation, such as encoding an image as a Base64 string (*https://oreil.ly/miCop*).

Responsiveness
> The ability of the system to respond in a timely manner as defined in "The Reactive Manifesto" (*https://oreil.ly/zAaMk*). Values are categorized as Low, Medium, and High.

Development effort
> A subjective effort required to build a minimum viable product API of low complexity. Values are categorized as Low, Medium, and High.

API as a Product

The API mandate (see "API Mandate" on page 13) shifted digital organizations' perspective on APIs—from thinking about them as a glue connecting services to seeing them as financial building blocks that can influence revenue. This shift became possible after organizations realized that an API is a product.

API Monetization

Besides being a digital channel for an organization's products and services, APIs can become a source of direct or indirect revenue. Generating revenues from APIs is called *API monetization*. There are several monetization models:

Pay-per-use
> A user pays for API utilization, measured in the number of calls, the amount of data exchanged, or other usage metrics. This model allows for accurate billing and can appeal to users who don't know their exact needs. However, the model requires tools that allow for precise call tracking in order to bill the user, and for the user to see and predict API utilization costs.

Subscription
> In this model, a user pays a fixed subscription fee (monthly or annually). This model offers a predictable revenue from your API. And it is often combined with offerings such as more API calls per month or some advanced features.

Freemium
> This model offers free access to basic offerings of your APIs but charges for advanced features, higher usage, or premium support. The model assumes that you'll be able to grow the user base and is based on the premise of converting a free user to a paying user.

Transaction fee
> A fee is applied to every transaction made via the API. This model is common in e-commerce or financial services APIs. For example, you might charge a percentage of each transaction processed by a payment API.

Revenue sharing
> The revenue for the API is shared between the third-party developer and the API provider. This model is common in affiliate marketing or marketplaces, where third-party developers generate revenue through providers' APIs. For example, a third-party travel booking website integrates with your hotel booking API. Every time a user books a hotel room via the website, you receive a portion of the commission from the booking fee.

To understand *API as a product*, you first need to realize that most organizations treat APIs as an integration technology. This way of thinking results in APIs that have limited value in terms of scope, extensibility, and durability, leading to APIs that are underdesigned. Such an API may be poorly documented and lack design standards, versioning, and security, or extensibility may be an afterthought.

Treating an API like a product means treating it with the same attention as any other asset. The success of APIs developed this way is grounded not only in marketing or design but also in the experience of third-party developers. By addressing their needs, you can increase the adoption of your API. In recent years, developer portals such as Backstage (*https://backstage.io*), Clutch (*https://clutch.sh*), and Cortex (*https://www.cortex.io*) have gained popularity, and products of this type can help in internal API discoverability and management.

Having an API-as-a-product mentality requires you to consider both the API usage and technical factors. As an owner of an API product, you'd like to know the following: Who are the API's power users? What geographical regions are requests coming from? What errors does the API throw? What is the error rate? What is the response time? Therefore, you need to have tools in place that will allow you to monitor APIs and create usage reports.

> If you are interested in a product perspective on API, consult *Building an API Product* by Bruno Pedro (Packt Publishing, 2024).

As with any digital product, you'd like to ensure that the API is secure. Therefore, you need to think about authentication and authorization (see "Encryption, Authentication, and Authorization" on page 70), create policies and rate limits, and be alerted about unusual traffic to your API.

> Be aware that opening your API to the public creates a maintenance responsibility. Having a public API requires following API release and deprecation procedures, such as communication or deprecation timelines, and it's hard to undo past mistakes after the API is released. As a practical example of API deprecation, let's follow Facebook (now Meta), which planned and communicated cutting off third-party developer API access to its Groups API.[15]

---

15 See Mohamed Amr Abouelhassan's "Introducing Facebook Graph API v19.0 and Marketing API v19.0" (*https://oreil.ly/YOxWt*), *Meta*, January 23, 2024.

API Lifecycle

SDLC is a process used to manage a software application during its lifetime, from planning to retirement. Let's be clear that an API is software and should be viewed as such. Therefore, the term *API lifecycle*, used in the context of APIs, is synonymous with SDLC. Even if you're not strictly following the API lifecycle, familiarity with its elements can help guide your approach.

The API lifecycle describes how an API is planned, designed, implemented, tested, deployed, maintained, and retired. Figure 1-7 illustrates its phases.

> Often the phases in the API lifecycle (or SDLC) are interpreted as independent and sequential. The reality is that they all are interconnected and interact with one another. For example, the implementation phase may reveal factors not taken into account during the design phase, leading to changes in the original design. Moreover, we don't indicate the starting phase of the process because it's contextual to the timeline of your project.

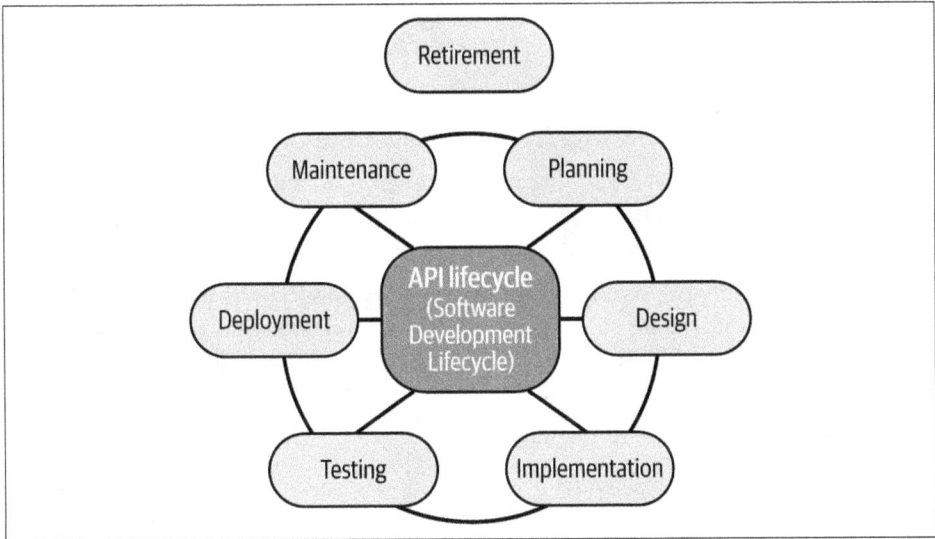

Figure 1-7. API lifecycle

You may notice that two phases (often included) appear to be missing from this lifecycle diagram: security and documentation. Some diagrams describing the API lifecycle show security as a separate phase. This is problematic because it suggests that security awareness is limited to one place. We perceive security as a force that is present in all phases of the API lifecycle.

Some projects also delay creating documentation until the maintenance phase. The idea is that software that has yet to exist in its final form cannot be fully documented, so it's better not to document it at all. This approach has several drawbacks, the most important being that one may never find time to create documentation, as software is never finished until it is retired. A more realistic approach to documentation is to draft at least some of it during all phases of the API lifecycle.

Planning

Developers who adopt a code-first approach often overlook the planning phase, which is important for the success of any project. *Planning* is where decisions and considerations about the API are made.

In addition to defining the project's scope, schedule, goals, deliverables, and deadlines, the planning phase lays the foundation for the API. During this phase, owners, architects, and developers identify organizational objectives, understand the target audience, and formalize the API's functional and nonfunctional requirements. Functional requirements (FRs) capture software functionality, and nonfunctional requirements (NFRs) capture software quality. For example, if you are building a search engine, an FR might be to allow users to send search queries through the API, and an NFR could be that the API must return query results within one second.

Functional and Nonfunctional Requirements

In system design, several types of requirements (*https://oreil.ly/qvpIP*) are created at different phases of the SDLC, such as user, business, regulatory, system, architectural, functional, nonfunctional, and implementation requirements.

However, from the perspective of a designer, the first three phases of the SDLC focus on functional requirements (FRs) and nonfunctional requirements (NFRs). The classification into FRs and NFRs can be helpful for prioritization of design and development efforts, or communicating risks that might originate from a requirement.

Let's look at the definitions of FRs and NFRs:

FRs
> The specific functions, tasks, or behaviors that a system should fulfill. FRs can be described from the user's perspective, where the user performs specific actions on the system, or from the system's perspective, where the system performs specific actions. For example, *User should be able to reset password* or *Service should allow admins to disable user access*.

NFRs

Capabilities and constraints to which the system should adhere. In other words, NFRs describe the quality of the system. They are also known as architecturally significant requirements, software architectural characteristics, or quality attributes. NFRs are said to describe a system's "ilities" (*https://oreil.ly/s85Wq*)—for example, deployability, maintainability, performance, security, and usability. For example, *The system should be fast* or *The system should be available 99.9% of the time.*

The distinction between an FR and NFR can often be fuzzy. For example, the requirement *Service provides timely weather alerts* can be both an FR and an NFR:

- *Service provides weather alerts*; service provides a function.
- *Service provides timely alerts*; service operates in a timely manner.

When facing dilemmas between FRs and NFRs, answer questions such as these:

- Does the requirement provide a function?
- Does the requirement impact system *ilities*?
- Does the requirement force the system or function to operate in a certain way?
- Does the requirement relate to the input or output of the system?

Because the system continues functioning beyond the implementation phase, the impacts of NFRs aren't immediately visible; they take time to appear.

During the planning phase, answer the following questions:

What is the API scope?

Is it private—built within the organization—or is it public—intended to be consumed by external users? Or maybe the API scope is partnered to facilitate collaboration among organizations?

Who are the API user devices?

Are they Internet of Things (IoT) devices, web browsers, mobile phones, AI agents, or other types?

What are the requirements?

Is there a programming language or framework that the designer imposes on the API? Should all API responses be fulfilled within a certain time limit? Is the API dependent on external services?

What is the scale that the API should operate with?

What is the approximate number of users?

What versioning strategy should you use?
> Will you use semantic versioning or other schemes, such as release date?

Are there any constraints for the API?
> Are there regulatory constraints such as the General Data Protection Regulation (GDPR) or Health Insurance Portability and Accountability Act (HIPAA) that might influence the functionality of the API?

Are there already established communication channels for API users?
> Where and how will you provide documentation to API users? Should access to API documentation be unlimited or restricted?

These are just a few questions that need to be answered before implementing the API. Furthermore, when drafting the API in the planning stage, security and compliance should be embedded into the process of formulating the requirements.

Design

In the *design phase*, designers (architects and developers) identify an approach for designing the API, based on an understanding of the API audience, requirements, and constraints extracted from the planning phase. The design phase addresses API functionality not only in terms of what it should provide but also how it should provide it. In this phase, designers make the decisions of whether to integrate the software with third-party solutions, and what technology and tools to choose.

API-First Approach

One method for designing APIs is the *API-first* strategy (*https://oreil.ly/wStKl*). This approach advocates that API development starts first with creating API specifications (gathered from the organization and the API user requirements), and implementation follows next. This approach works well when you have access to the intended users of the API, with whom you can agree on the API shape before it's implemented.

The designer may choose to follow the API-first approach, resulting in the creation of an API specification, written often in a commonly supported API specification format such as OpenAPI (*https://swagger.io*) or AsyncAPI (*https://www.asyncapi.com*). Software tools available to support these formats also help in implementing and testing the API, as well as generating the API documentation.

The subject of API design is further discussed in Chapter 2.

Implementation

The software is forged in the *implementation phase* by transforming the design into code. This is why we also call this phase the *applied architecture phase*.

Requirements extracted from the planning phase and API specifications created in the design phase are turned into code. Recall, however, that learnings from the implementation phase may lead to revisiting and adjusting earlier decisions created in the preceding phases, resulting in changes to the requirements or API specifications.

Note also that it's the implementation that determines the actual system behavior. While the implementation details are meant to be hidden behind interfaces, they can still leak through and become observable.

Interface Versus Implementation

The idea that abstractions fail to hide implementation details, which leads to portability and software complexity problems, was described by Gregor Kiczales in "Towards a New Model of Abstraction in Software Engineering" (*https://oreil.ly/33Qqi*):

> The "abstractions" we manipulate are not, in point of fact, abstract. They are backed by real pieces of code, running on real machines, consuming real energy and taking up real space. To attempt to completely ignore the underlying implementation is like trying to completely ignore the laws of physics; it may be tempting but it won't get us very far.
>
> —Gregor Kiczales, 1992

This idea was popularized as the "Law of Leaky Abstractions" (*https://oreil.ly/mBLLI*):

> All non-trivial abstractions, to some degree, are leaky.
>
> —Joel Spolsky, 2002

Now, the observation that implementation details surface through the API's interface is known as *Hyrum's law* (*https://www.hyrumslaw.com*):

> With a sufficient number of users of an API, it does not matter what you promise in the contract: all observable behaviors of your system will be depended on by somebody.
>
> —Hyrum Wright, 2012

Leaky abstraction leads API users to depend on the system's internal behaviors known as the *implicit interface*. This behavior makes it difficult to modify the APIs.[16]

---

16 This behavior has been satirized by xkcd 1172 (*https://xkcd.com/1172*).

Also the security of the API is affected by the practical choices made during the implementation phase. Encryption, authentication, authorization, and safe programming practices—including input and output validation, among others, described in "API Security" on page 68—are elements of building secure APIs.

Testing

In the *testing phase*, the API is tested for functionality, security, and performance. Developers and the quality assurance (QA) team implement and execute the tests.[17] Testing can happen in parallel with implementation, and learnings from testing may influence other phases, like the design, implementation, or deployment phases.

Testing is part of API development, and depending on what is tested and how, it can be either daunting or exciting. Why is testing so important? Testing helps to create maintainable software, validate system functionality, identify the presence of bugs (but not the absence of bugs), and enable more confidence in refactoring. Tests can be executed manually or automatically if they are part of the continuous integration/ continuous delivery and deployment (CI/CD) pipelines (see "Deployment" on page 30). Running tests in a pipeline allows developers to continuously detect software issues, ensuring the software's ongoing quality.

Integration testing

Integration tests check how components work together, including how software interacts with external services such as databases, filesystems, and third-party APIs. Unlike unit tests, which focus on individual pieces of code in isolation, integration tests ensure that these components collaborate as part of a larger system.

With tools like Docker (*https://www.docker.com*), integration tests have become easier to set up. Docker spins up isolated containers of the required services (e.g., a database, a cache, or a message queue). This allows testing software against running copies of services instead of relying on mocks, making the tests more realistic. If a certain third-party service can't be run locally, you may try to set up a separate testing instance and configure integration tests to interact with it. This way, the tests still interact with a real service in a controlled testing environment, but such a setup may be unreliable, leading to unexpected and nonreproducible test errors.

---

17 Sometimes the API is exposed first to a subset of users, to perform so-called beta testing. This is often a more effective testing method in terms of finding missing features and bugs than letting the developers and QA teams test the software.

If testing using production data is permissible, dump the service's response into a file (e.g., *response.json*) and read the response from the file. Use this file in integration tests, sometimes called *record and replay* tests, to simulate the service, allowing for repeatable tests while avoiding unintended interactions with the live environment.

Contract testing and fuzzing

Another integration testing approach is *contract testing*. This testing originates from work by Robert W. Floyd, who in the late 1960s suggested a method for proving program correctness through assertions. The goal of this, and subsequent methods such as Hoare logic (*https://oreil.ly/DAhnS*) (1969) and design by contract (*https://oreil.ly/KV5BZ*) (1986), was to prove that a program will produce the expected results given the admissible inputs:

> People would write code and make test runs, then find bugs and make patches, then find more bugs and make more patches, and so on until not being able to discover any further errors, yet always living in dread for fear that a new case would turn up on the next day and lead to a new type of failure. We never realized that there might be a way to construct a rigorous proof of validity.
>
> —Donald E. Knuth, 2003

Today, contract testing in the context of APIs is not about providing rigorous proof of validity of fixed API consumers and providers (such as clients and servers in a client-server architecture). Instead, API contract testing is about checking that evolving consumers and providers still behave according to the contract (the API specification). An API specification is often captured in a static form, as a schema that describes the shape of the data, its contents, consumer requests, and provider responses. However, APIs can also include behaviors beyond static schemas. For example, only certain combinations of inputs may be considered valid, or an API may implement rate-limiting, and neither of these may be described in the API specification.

However, similarly to the record and replay method, it may be possible to keep a set of past requests and responses and verify that they, as well as the current implementations of the API consumer and provider, conform to the API specification. Such contract testing can be thought of as regression testing (*https://oreil.ly/wwfCo*), in the sense that it detects whether consumers and providers continue to comply with the API contract. When automated into the development workflow, contract testing can identify contract violations. For example, it could be used to detect whether a change in the provider is incompatible with the supported versions of the consumers, or whether a field that is used only by sunset consumers could be removed.

The contract can be written by the API consumer or provider, respectively called consumer-driven contract (CDC) and provider-driven contract (PDC). In CDC, the consumer defines the service behavior, and the provider's task is to implement the contract in the service API. This approach puts more effort on the provider, since it has to catch up with the consumer's specification. In PDC, the effort is reversed; the provider defines the contract, and the consumer adheres to it.

The limitation of contract testing is that it's often infeasible to capture a sufficiently large set of requests and responses to cover the API contract. Capturing inputs is challenging when adopting a popular *defensive programming* approach (see "Defensive Programming" on page 172), where error handling and recovery are prioritized, leading to a broad scope of inputs and behaviors supported by the API. This is in contrast to an *offensive programming* approach, also called *fail-fast*, where a program stops when provided with incorrect inputs.

Therefore, together with contract testing, API fuzzing is used, where a set of inputs includes random values. The API is expected to handle such inputs gracefully, with the fuzzer exercising a larger part of the API specification.

End-to-end testing

This testing approach mimics a user interacting with the system. The purpose of these tests is to verify that the system works as a whole. End-to-end tests are executed from the API users' perspective and were traditionally performed manually. Tools like Cypress (*https://www.cypress.io*), Playwright (*https://playwright.dev*), and Selenium (*https://www.selenium.dev*) can automate this manual labor. However, when working with these tools, be prepared for a certain amount of test flakiness.[18]

Agile testing quadrants

Testing is a field that can be overwhelming, and as a developer, you'll create many types of tests. To get an overview of the field, you may find the *Agile testing quadrants* diagram in Figure 1-8 useful, which categorizes various testing tools and approaches. The horizontal axis ranges from team support to product critique, while the vertical axis covers user-facing and technology-facing impacts.

---

18 See "Why Playwright Is Less Flaky than Selenium" (*https://oreil.ly/UF0sj*) by Justin Searls.

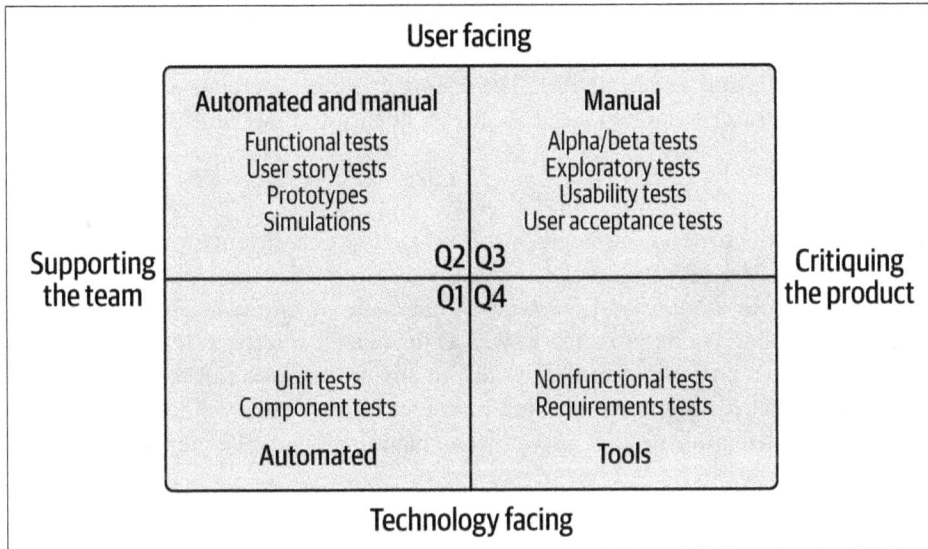

Figure 1-8. Agile testing quadrants

Let's break down the responsibilities of each quadrant:

Q1

Testing in this quadrant is technology-focused and aims to support the development team. Unit and component tests are typically written and automated by developers. Since these tests execute quickly, they provide developers with instant feedback and attract developers' interest.

Q2

Testing in this quadrant is approached from the perspective of the software user and supports the development team. These tests focus on system functionality, ensuring that the system fulfills user objectives. When test automation isn't feasible, manual testing should be considered.

Q3

Testing in this quadrant is user-focused and critiques the product. These tests are designed to identify issues that were missed during development. User Acceptance Tests (UATs) are commonly conducted here, often contributing to an enhanced user experience. However, a drawback of UATs is that they are frequently performed manually.

Q4

Testing in this quadrant is technology-focused and critiques the product. The tests are technical in nature, concentrating on NFRs like security and performance. Specialized tools are often necessary to conduct these tests.

Q1 and Q2 support the development process by ensuring that the product is built according to FRs. Meanwhile, Q3 and Q4 focus on evaluating the product to ensure it meets user needs and satisfies NFRs. The testing quadrant serves as a roadmap, covering the aspects of testing that lead to software quality and maintainability.

Deployment

Deployment is the process of moving a software artifact to the environment in which it will operate. The process usually requires software packaging, configuration, and environment provisioning and is executed manually or automatically. Moving the API artifact (a standalone program, as well as the related specification and documentation) to a target host might sound trivial, but anyone who has worked in operations will confirm that it's more complicated than that. This section will leave you with a few questions that you'll need to answer when planning the deployment of your API.

The first question to answer is: how will the team that manages the API deployment be structured? Will you have a separation between the development and operations teams, or follow the movement called DevOps, which brings these two domains together? DevOps promotes the creation of pipelines where you continuously integrate (build), deliver (release), and deploy your software.

Figure 1-9 shows steps in API deployment, as well as relationships between CI/CD pipelines.[19]

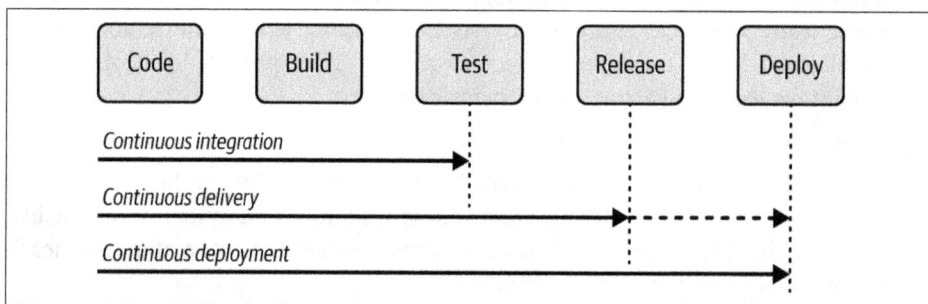

Figure 1-9. CI/CD pipelines explained

---

19 Continuous delivery makes the build artifact ready for release and requires a manual release approval. Continuous deployment automatically releases the build artifact after it's tested in an automated way.

Let's check out the roles of each pipeline type:

- Continuous integration—This pipeline builds the artifact. CI steps involve performing the following:
  - Lint—Checking if the source code adheres to coding standards
  - Static code analysis— Preventing code from including undesirable, complex, or insecure (e.g., hardcoded secrets or code injection) programming patterns
  - Dependency analysis— Checking the code for potentially outdated or unlicensed libraries
  - Build—Building the artifact
  - Test—Testing the functionality of the built artifact
  - Security scan—Checking the built artifact for vulnerabilities and performing automated penetration testing

    The CI pipeline results in an artifact—for example, a container image, a native binary, or a platform-specific package. The artifact then is delivered to the target repository, such as Docker Hub (*https://hub.docker.com*), GitHub Packages (*https://oreil.ly/80QID*), JFrog Artifactory (*https://oreil.ly/iejv0*), or an old-style File Transport Protocol (FTP) server.

- Continuous delivery—This pipeline is triggered after the CI pipeline. It deploys the artifact built by CI to the desired environment after a manual approval. The *deployment strategy* (*https://oreil.ly/4hw1Y*) depends on many factors, such as the API's complexity, organizational requirements, and infrastructure capabilities. Popular deployment strategies include blue-green and canary deployments.

- Continuous deployment—This pipeline automatically deploys artifacts to the desired environment and doesn't require human interaction. Automatic tests associated with this stage are end-to-end tests, smoke tests (to verify the most important functionality), and load and stress tests, to name a few.

Besides technical aspects, the DevOps movement tries to break the "wall" between the development and operations teams by establishing a close collaboration, as well as shared responsibility and accountability for the product lifecycle. DevOps teams also try to address security challenges by following a *shift-left* approach, which moves the security focus early into the product lifecycle rather than to the end (*shift right*). This approach is called *DevSecOps*.

An anonymous internet quote notices that "Shift left increases friction, shift right increases correctness." Placing an increased burden on developers reduces the capacity to develop new software features. When facing frequently failing security checks, teams may disable the checks, making the shift-left approach ineffective.

The DevOps movement is based on automation, and an increased shift down (*https://oreil.ly/153p3*) of the operational tasks, by including security checks into the underlying platform, is believed to reduce developer burden. However, the existence of separate DevOps or DevSecOps teams suggests that some ideas promoted by the DevOps movement may be infeasible, because of the limited capacity of a single developer to handle multiple, distinct tasks.

Once you have the built API artifact, the next question is where to deploy it. This is the traditional buy-versus-build dilemma. Depending on your needs, an API artifact could be deployed to a proprietary cloud-vendor platform, a self-hosted cloud native environment, or on-premises machines. If you choose the build path, will you incur the higher labor cost of setting up and maintaining a platform like Kubernetes (*https://kubernetes.io*), which supports highly available deployment and scaling of containerized applications? Or will you opt for the lower initial labor cost needed by a simpler tool like Kamal (*https://kamal-deploy.org*), knowing it may lead to higher labor costs later due to manual capacity management?

The buy-versus-build dilemma affects not only the deployment target but also other services that support the API operations. You'll need to decide whether it's more cost-effective to use an integrated, proprietary cloud-vendor system that provides proxying, logging, secrets, and security management, or to roll out your own, more controllable solution, composed of open source or built-in-house components.[20]

Another question is in how many environments to deploy your API. The production environment is where the API lives, but testing in production may be disallowed for compliance reasons, and deploying changes directly to production without testing them in a live environment is risky. Deploying the API to a staging (or testing) environment allows running tests before deploying the API artifact to the production environment. Moreover, you may also need one or more dedicated development (or feature) environments, to perform potentially destructive experiments without suffering the consequences of making the shared staging environment unavailable.

---

[20] A choice also needs to be made for the CI/CD system. Will you spend labor costs on debugging deployment failures in a remote-only, YAML-based CI/CD system, or instead invest in the development of a local, code-based CI/CD environment? For a perspective on YAML, see "I'm Sorry About the YAML" (*https://oreil.ly/q0J3t*) by Joe Beda.

When maintaining multiple environments, you'll also need to decide how your version-control branching strategy maps to the various environments.[21]

Be aware that adding additional environments requires maintenance effort, and each might exhibit behavior that isn't reproducible in production.[22]

Staging is not production. It will never be production.

—Charity Majors, 2019

As you can see, deploying an API requires considering many factors, such as hosting infrastructure, environments, source-code branching, packaging, testing, security, scalability, logging, and monitoring. The deployment strategy depends on your API's scale, complexity, and expected usage.

Maintenance

Maintenance is the ongoing phase in the API lifecycle, and it's known to incur significant costs. In this phase, the software is patched, updated, documented, improved, and monitored for performance, security threats, and user activities. The goal of maintenance is to keep the API relevant and up-to-date as long as it is operational.

Figure 1-10 shows the traditional ISO/IEC/IEEE 14764 classification (*https://oreil.ly/8V2mi*) of maintenance types resulting from a modification request. A modification request can be due to either a software correction or an enhancement. The corrective request addresses software defects, whereas enhancement modifies existing features or adds new ones.

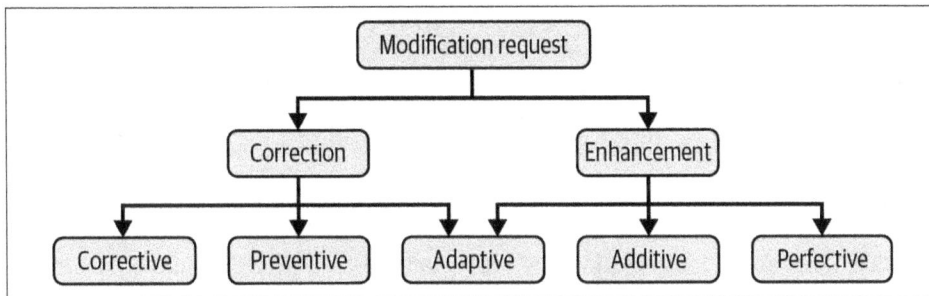

Figure 1-10. ISO/IEC/IEEE 14764 maintenance type classification

---

21 "An environment branch is an appealing approach…. It is, however, the classic example of an Anti Pattern—something that looks appealing when you start, but soon leads to a world of misery, dragons, and coronaviruses." By Martin Fowler in "Patterns for Managing Source Code Branches" (*https://oreil.ly/SpuOp*).

22 See the "I Test in Production" talk (*https://oreil.ly/3kuby*) by Charity Majors.

Let's explore the five maintenance types that result from a modification request:

Corrective

Addresses software malfunctions, usually caused by bugs or errors that require a fix. Corrective maintenance is expensive and might take a long time. A form of corrective maintenance is *emergency maintenance*, which requires an unscheduled modification to keep a system operational.

Preventive

Focuses on anticipating and preventing software faults. An accompanying technique is *software rejuvenation*, which focuses on removing accumulated error conditions and freeing up system resources.

Adaptive

Provides corrections or enhancements to the environment in which the software operates. The maintenance is driven by the nonstatic environment in which software operates.

Additive

Is driven by the need to add new functionality or enhance existing ones. This is usually the most common type of maintenance.

Perfective

Introduces enhancements to software to improve its qualities, such as performance, maintainability, and user experience. Performance maintenance might apply software tuning to address performance bottlenecks and refactoring to address maintainability.

Observability and analytics are part of the maintenance phase. *Observability* is about monitoring effects of requests and responses generated by the API—for instance, successful and unsuccessful responses, the volume of traffic coming in, who sends the traffic, where it's coming from, and when the API was last used. The collected telemetry is then visualized via metrics dashboards. In the maintenance phase, maintainers also set up alerting tools to help them respond to urgent situations.

So far, we have covered activities that lead to API creation: planning, design, testing, implementation, deployment, and maintenance. The following section discusses tactics that focus on API deprecation and retirement.

Retirement

APIs don't last forever, and *retirement* is the last stage of the API lifecycle. Typical circumstances that lead to an API being retired by the organization are as follows: the API doesn't fulfill the organization's objectives, the API is a threat to security, new functionality cannot be added to an existing API, API costs exceed revenues, or the organization changes monetization strategy from a free API to a paid API.

Organizations that don't have a retirement plan for APIs will more likely end up with a security threat like *zombie APIs*, which are abandoned APIs and no longer maintained but exist within the organization. Zombie APIs exist in a hibernated state, meaning they're forgotten but active, and they can be accessed and interacted with. On the other hand, if API retirement is done incorrectly, it can harm the API team and the organization's reputation.[23]

In the retirement phase, a migration plan may be used to support multiple API versions (old and new) running in parallel. Moreover, the phase should have an end-of-life plan that states how to deprecate the API without affecting operations and how to communicate API retirement to API users.

Deprecation means that the API is operational but will be scheduled for removal or replacement later. The decision to deprecate an API depends on your API release cadence. For instance, when managing an API, you might have a policy that will support a maximum of two API releases, which means that with the third release of the API, you'll remove the first release. For example, let's say you've released two API versions, *v1* and *v2*, and now you are about to make a third release, *v3*. This means that when releasing *v3*, you'll delete *v1*, keeping only *v2* and *v3*.

Deprecation and retirement have dates associated with them. The deprecation date indicates the time from which the API will have limited support for updates and bug fixes. On the other hand, the retirement date indicates a point in time from which the API will no longer be accessible.

If you choose to deprecate an API, you'll need to notify the API users about your intent. For instance, Kubernetes (*https://kubernetes.io*), when creating a deprecated artifact via a CLI, will print a warning message, as illustrated in Figure 1-11.

```
Warning: networking.k8s.io/v1beta1 Ingress is deprecated in v1.19+,
unavailable in v1.22+; use networking.k8s.io/v1 Ingress
ingress.networking.k8s.io/echomap
```

Figure 1-11. Deprecated Kubernetes API

Another way to inform users about API deprecation is to display a deprecation banner on the API documentation website. Figure 1-12 shows a deprecation warning for Google's PaLM API.

---

23 Read "Twitter Only Gave Meerkat 2 Hours Notice before Cutting Access to the Social Graph" (*https://oreil.ly/ATBvS*) by Sarah Kessler.

Warning: The PaLM API is **decommissioned**. The Vertex AI PaLM API is scheduled to be decommissioned in October 2024. Please upgrade to the Gemini API. Learn more about this in the PaLM API deprecation guide.

Figure 1-12. Banner informing users about an API deprecation

Yet another option is to add headers about API deprecation to the API response. This approach is shown in Example 1-4.[24]

Example 1-4. HTTP deprecation and sunset headers

```
Sunset: Wed, 11 Nov 2026 11:11:11 GMT
Deprecation: @1688169599
Link: <https://developer.example.com/deprecation>; rel="deprecation"
```

The timestamp in the `Deprecation` header may point toward a past or a future date. A date in the past means the API is already deprecated. However, the date in the `Sunset` header will always point to the future, indicating when the API will be retired. The API sunset for a public API usually stretches for months.

The `Link` header may provide additional information about the API deprecation, including a documentation link. The retirement date isn't the only significant piece of information to share. You could enrich the deprecation message with contact information, a migration guide, and, if any, the schedule of the next version's release. The information about the deprecation and retirement of the API may need to be preserved for the purpose of compliance audits or historical references.

API Governance, Management, and Platform

If you are a small company that uses a single team to manage APIs, then that team makes all decisions about the API, at each phase of its lifecycle. However, if you are an organization with multiple teams that build APIs, you need to have a plan for managing and governing them. Unmanaged APIs can become a potential security risk, leading to unauthorized access, data breaches, or API abuse. API management helps you create a plan to address these risks.

Governance is the set of written and unwritten rules and processes by which an organization is directed and controlled. Governance utilizes the organization's power structure to enforce these rules.

---

24 For details about the sunset headers and deprecation headers, see RFC 8594 (*https://oreil.ly/09ryX*) and "The Deprecation HTTP Header Field" (*https://oreil.ly/Z35cR*).

To govern APIs means to create practices, standards, and policies; propagate them to API teams; and implement them in the API. To ensure that policies are met, governance requires monitoring of APIs and teams to adhere to the processes.

The absence of governance leads not only to inconsistent APIs but also to the emergence of *shadow APIs*, which are actively used but unmanaged, undocumented, and deployed without the official supervision of the organization. On the other hand, governance contributes to APIs being secure, stable, reusable, and compliant with regulatory policies.

The goal of API management is to standardize the process surrounding API development in each phase of the API lifecycle. For example, in the planning and design phase, you'd like to follow standards and best practices for API design. In the implementation and deployment phase, you'd like to have tools to build, test, and deploy APIs. In the maintenance phase, you'd like to monitor the API and gather feedback from the API users.

An *API platform* is software that helps catalog, govern, and manage APIs and engage with API users. Its suite of tools allows API teams to develop, publish, manage, and consume APIs. The API platform integrates with external tools such as CI/CD pipelines, cloud infrastructure, monitoring tools, and security and compliance tools. Common API platforms include Amazon API Gateway (*https://oreil.ly/t87B6*), Azure API Management (*https://oreil.ly/LBZhB*), Google Cloud Apigee (*https://oreil.ly/FXFVz*), Kong (*https://konghq.com*), and MuleSoft Anypoint Platform (*https://oreil.ly/4JbwO*).

> API Landscape (*https://apilandscape.apiscene.io*) is a website showing various tools to help you design, develop, and manage your APIs. Don't be overwhelmed by its look. Many tools are listed more than once.

Future of APIs

With the basics and history of APIs covered, let's discuss their future.

According to Statista (*https://www.statista.com*), the estimated number of connected IoT devices reached 18 billion in 2024 (*https://oreil.ly/UbZaO*), including 7.2 billion smartphone subscriptions (*https://oreil.ly/zJmTN*) connecting about 67.1% of the world population (*https://oreil.ly/IEqOP*). The number of IoT devices is expected to increase in the next few years. These devices require network-based APIs for many of their features.

Cloudflare, a content delivery network (CDN) provider, states in its 2024 API Security Report (*https://oreil.ly/Q0QLD*) that 60% of dynamic (noncacheable) traffic is API-based. APIs are also the fastest-growing Cloudflare traffic category.[25]

Another aspect that will create demand for APIs is the development of artificial intelligence (AI) and LLMs. Training of LLMs requires consuming data, such as text, images, audio, and video, that largely come from APIs. As companies create their own LLM-based services, existing and new API styles will enable their growth, acting as funnels through which data will enter and leave.

AI can also help with tasks related to each phase of the API lifecycle, such as design, documentation, implementation, and security. Therefore, AI will contribute to the increased number of available APIs. Even today, when you provide a few examples of requests/responses, AI can attempt to roughly program an API.[26]

With the growth of AI and IoT devices, security will become an even more important aspect of APIs. Gartner predicted in 2021 (*https://oreil.ly/52qic*) that API attacks will become the most frequent attack vector on enterprise web applications. Kong's 2023 API Impact Report (*https://oreil.ly/Xoayu*) forecasts that the number of API attacks will more than double globally by 2027.

New protocols will contribute to the formation and security of new API styles. HTTP is evolving and reached its third release (HTTP/3) in June 2022 (*https://oreil.ly/3CK30*). The WebTransport protocol (*https://oreil.ly/GSqqu*) aims to address shortcomings of the WebSocket protocol. Model Context Protocol (MCP) (*https://oreil.ly/5uKl4*) aims to facilitate resource discovery and use by LLMs and agentic AI.

If these forecasts are to be believed, we see no indication that API growth would slow down or reverse.

---

25 See Cloudflare's "Landscape of API Traffic" (*https://oreil.ly/PTWww*) by Daniele Molteni.

26 One may hope that one day, APIs will be composed of "programs that know how to figure out how to talk to each other" (Bret Victor's "The Future of Programming" (*https://oreil.ly/qOIjv*)).

Summary

This chapter introduced you to the concept of APIs, focusing on network-based APIs, which are the main topic of this book. You learned the vocabulary needed for understanding network-based APIs, such as *message, synchronous and asynchronous communication*, and *network protocol*. You looked at the history of APIs and considered future predictions, which suggest that API usage will continue to grow.

You got an overview of the set of APIs covered in the book, organized by their defining characteristics, or style. A large part of the chapter covered the API lifecycle, which is the process of creating and managing APIs.

The following chapter will present common design patterns for APIs.

## CHAPTER 2

API Design Patterns

This chapter is a practical guide for the design phase of the API lifecycle. It aims to raise awareness of common API topics such as API design patterns, API security patterns, and API best practices.

A software design pattern is a blueprint for solving a particular, commonly occurring problem when creating software. Designing an API is a multidimensional process, but certain challenges are common regardless of the API style. Design patterns can guide the development of solutions to these challenges.

This chapter presents these patterns individually, in a cookbook-like format, to help you select them and integrate them into your design process. To see how API design patterns are applied in practice, you'll implement some of these patterns in Chapter 5 when building an example REST API.

Examples of API Design Patterns

No matter what API style you work with, you need to answer questions such as: what natural language to use for API documentation, how to version the API, how to name interfaces, what encoding to use, and how to serve data. This section explores the patterns commonly used to address these questions.

To study API design patterns further, we recommend *API Design Patterns* by JJ Geewax (Manning, 2021), or additional sources such as these:

- Google's API design guide (*https://google.aip.dev/1*)
- Microsoft's REST API design guidance (*https://oreil.ly/q7A9o*)
- The REST API Tutorial (*https://restfulapi.net*) and Learn REST API Design (*https://www.restapitutorial.com*) overviews of REST APIs

Most of the time, you'll develop APIs without access to their target users, who would otherwise provide you with feedback. In this situation, try to ask LLMs for feedback on your API design or the patterns you are using. Note that LLMs are tools whose objective is to generate text, not to help you design an API. Therefore, use LLMs but verify the correctness of the information they generate.

API Language

Let's consider which natural language should be used when building APIs. This language is still English: it has become the language of information technology due to the leading role the United States and the United Kingdom played in the development of computing. Although spoken English comes in many flavors, the two main spellings are American and British. American English is recommended because of its prevalence, unless you have specific requirements for your API's target audience.

API Naming

One of the most challenging parts of creating an API is naming its interfaces, schemas, fields, parameters, etc. As a developer building an API, ask users for feedback before committing to an interface name because once it's used in production, changing it may be difficult due to the need to update all the existing clients.[1]

Whether you are naming an endpoint/route/interface, function/method/procedure/subroutine, property, query parameter, etc., the chosen name needs to be expressive, intuitive, and pronounceable; match its context; and express the intent. A good name conveys the meaning in a way that doesn't create doubts that could lead to misinterpretation. Names should be consistent and follow chosen guidelines (e.g., pluralization, verb-noun patterns, ensuring scalar fields contain units, and more) and naming conventions (e.g., *hungarianNotation*, *CamelCaseNotation*, or *snake_notation*).

Remember that names used in APIs don't exist in isolation. There is always a context surrounding the APIs. For example, the word *channel* in the context of communication, broadcasting, or civil engineering can mean different things.

> Despite your attempts to create a sound name, there is a chance that it could be misinterpreted. Therefore, provide auxiliary documentation that API developers can use in the case of doubt.

Making a resource name singular or plural depends on the API style in which they appear. In a REST API, the norm is to use resource-oriented names and plurals—for

---

1 For the definition of *client* and *server*, see "Socket API" on page 78.

example, */orders/123*. On the other hand, GraphQL, gRPC, and broker-based APIs typically follow the intent-oriented approach, offering more flexibility in resource naming, allowing for both singular and plural names of actions.

Resource-Oriented Versus Intent-Oriented APIs

APIs can be divided into two categories: resource-oriented and intent-oriented. The concept of a resource is described in more detail in "HTTP, Resource, and URI" on page 151, but for this discussion, think that a resource represents data.

Resource-oriented APIs focus on data. In these APIs, it's common to use nouns to name the resources, such as *bookings*, *orders*, and *users*. Resource-oriented APIs originate from the REST architectural style (see Chapter 5) and use HTTP verbs, such as POST, GET, PUT, PATCH, DELETE, and others to manipulate resources. The limited number of standard HTTP verbs is a drawback of the resource-oriented approach, but also its strength. Specific operations that focus on custom actions, such as *archive user* or *backup server*, don't have corresponding HTTP verbs. As a workaround, a resource-oriented approach usually implements custom actions using action-related fields within the resource, or departs from resource orientation and uses custom verbs instead of nouns to name specific endpoints. The limited number of standard HTTP verbs is also the strength of the resource-oriented APIs, since sharing the same HTTP verbs across all APIs introduces an element of predictability.

In contrast, *intent-oriented APIs* focus on the goal of the operation performed on data. Interface names used by the intent-oriented APIs typically include verbs—for example, *createUser*, *archiveUser*, and *backupServer*. Stripe's Payment Intents (*https://oreil.ly/HRU7q*) is an example of an intent-oriented REST API. Intent-oriented APIs allow for more flexibility in naming compared to the resource-oriented APIs, at the risk of larger variability and the creation of many endpoints, where each endpoint represents a specific action.

To further understand the distinction, resource-oriented APIs can be described as declarative APIs, whereas intent-oriented APIs can be described as imperative APIs.

Declarative APIs focus on the final state of a resource rather than the specific steps needed to achieve that state. The standard HTTP verbs, such as GET or POST, abstract away the specific implementation details of how the operations are performed. Therefore, REST APIs can be considered declarative.

On the other hand, imperative APIs are action-oriented, and their names emphasize how a desired outcome should be achieved. gRPC APIs can be thought of as imperative because they focus on focus on actions/procedures. See Chapter 8 for more details. GraphQL APIs are a mix of declarative and imperative APIs with declarative queries and imperative mutations. More on GraphQL in Chapter 6.

Table 2-1, Table 2-2, Table 2-3, and Table 2-4 show examples of interface names for REST, gRPC, GraphQL, and RabbitMQ APIs, respectively. Note that the order of operations in the tables follows *CRUD* (Create, Read, Update, and Delete). See "CRUD" on page 167 for more information.

Table 2-1. Resource-oriented REST API

Operation	HTTP method	Endpoint
Create a new order	POST	/api/orders
Retrieve all orders	GET	/api/orders
Retrieve a single order	GET	/api/orders/{orderID}
Update an order	PUT	/api/orders/{orderID}
Delete an order	DELETE	/api/orders/{orderID}

Table 2-2. Intent-oriented gRPC API

Operation	RPC method
Create a new order	CreateOrder()
Retrieve all orders	ListOrders()
Retrieve a single order	GetOrder()
Update an order	UpdateOrder()
Delete an order	DeleteOrder()

Table 2-3. Mixed intent-oriented and resource-oriented GraphQL API

Action	GraphQL operation	Field/operation
Create a new order	Mutation	createOrder
Retrieve all orders	Query	orders
Retrieve a single order	Query	order
Update an order	Mutation	updateOrder
Delete an order	Mutation	deleteOrder

Table 2-4. Intent-oriented broker-based RabbitMQ API

Operation	Message type	Routing key
Create a new order	Command	orders.create
Retrieve all orders	Query	orders.list
Retrieve a single order	Query	orders.get
Update an order	Command	orders.update
Delete an order	Command	orders.delete

Let's look at the pluralization of nouns. In English, pluralizing regular nouns happens by adding *s* or *es*. However, there are exceptions, such as nouns like *die*, *person*, and *louse*, whose plurals are *dice*, *people*, and *lice*, respectively. In doubtful situations like these, the advice is to follow English grammar or look for substitute words.

Often your API response fields contain scalar values such as temperature, speed, altitude, pressure, size, duration, length, and weight. Most APIs lack information about which unit system is being used by the API—for example, whether a metric system (International System of Units [SI] (*https://oreil.ly/sxYjG*) or imperial units (*https://oreil.ly/ocDC6*)) is used. In a situation like this, developers may assume units that are convenient for them, which might lead to crashes (*https://oreil.ly/IrAJR*), like the Tokyo Disneyland roller-coaster derailment (*https://oreil.ly/U1MIk*) or the NASA Mars Climate Orbiter failure (*https://oreil.ly/JtOLy*). To reduce risks of unit errors, the name of the scalar could include the unit—for example, *durationSeconds*, *lengthMeters*, *temperatureCelsius*, *weightGrams*, or *widthPixels*.

Evolving APIs

APIs will change and evolve. Because of that, you need to think about versioning, which will allow the API to serve all its users as change happens.

In an API, a change can be either additive or subtractive, and it can appear at two levels: the interface (an endpoint, a procedure, query, or mutation) and the resource (message). In additive change, new features are added to the API, whereas in a subtractive change, features are removed from the API. A modification of existing functionality can be viewed as a subtractive change followed by an additive change. The effect of a change on the API system can be breaking or nonbreaking.[2]

Instead of trying to describe the effects of a change in general, the examples in Table 2-5 show breaking and nonbreaking effects on clients of a REST API. Although the examples use a REST API as the context, the idea of a breaking/nonbreaking change can be extended to other API styles. All examples in Table 2-5 assume that we are performing an HTTP GET request to a fictitious *https://api.example.com/v1/die/roll* endpoint, and we expect the response to be JSON-encoded, as shown in Example 2-1.

---

2 See a discussion about breaking changes and versioning of software in the "Speculation Keynote" talk (*https://oreil.ly/azu75*) by Rich Hickey.

Example 2-1. API response payload encoded as JSON (JavaScript Object Notation)

```
{
  "data": {
    "message": "Rolling 5",
    "outcome": 5
  }
}
```

Let's look at Table 2-5, which lists potential changes that could happen to the API and the effects of these changes.

Table 2-5. API changes and their effects

Change	Effect	Example
Renaming the endpoint	Breaking	Renaming */v1/roll/die* to */v1/roll-die*
Removing the API version	Breaking	Removing *v1*
Changing or not supporting the content type	Breaking	Asking for `application/xml` instead of `application/json` or changing `application/xml` to `application/json`
Removing a field	Breaking	Deleting the `outcome` field
Renaming a field	Breaking	Renaming the `outcome` field to the `roll` field
Changing the data type of a field	Breaking	Changing `int` (5) to `string` ("5")
Adding new field(s), endpoint(s)	Nonbreaking	Adding the `sides` field to data
Adding a query parameter with the default value	Nonbreaking	Adding the `sides` query parameter (e.g., */v1/roll-die?sides=6*)
Adding a new content type	Nonbreaking	Adding the `application/xml` content type
Adding optional custom headers	Nonbreaking	Adding a custom header (e.g., *Example-Service-ID*)

Note that renaming, removing, or reordering representations of data in a REST API will result in a breaking change of the API clients that use the features affected by the change.[3]

Breaking changes may also arise from client behavior modifications without the corresponding change to the API. This can happen when a client makes assumptions about the API's behavior or structure that aren't guaranteed. For example, if a client starts expecting a status field to return `enabled` instead of the API's actual value `active`, it'll break the client logic even if the API response remains consistent.

---

3 If a client expects data to appear in a certain order, reordering the data will affect the client.

API Backward and Forward Compatibility

The terms *backward compatibility* and *forward compatibility* are often used in the context of APIs. When we say that an API is backward compatible, we mean that the changes introduced to the new API don't break the old consumers of the API. On the other hand, a forward-compatible API means that new consumers are compatible with older API versions.

Backward compatibility is more of a concern for APIs operating in a client-server architecture. Additive changes to the API are preferred since they tend to be backward compatible with the old clients (which may ignore the new functionality). However, there will be moments after the API has been deployed when it won't be possible to make a backward-compatible change—for example, a change of data type in the payload, fixing a field typo, or removing an endpoint. These types of changes may require redeploying a new API and sunsetting the old consumers (clients).

Forward compatibility is a greater concern in messaging-based APIs (like event-driven systems, queues, or pub/sub systems), because they often support multiple versions of independently evolving message producers and consumers within the same system. As a result, messages of different versions may be in transit or processed simultaneously. The need to consider forward compatibility in addition to backward compatibility is a trade-off for decoupling components in messaging-based systems.

API Versioning

Commonly, an API is referred to as a *contract*, meaning it's an agreement between the API client and the API provider. The API contract describes the API's data shape, form, and behavior. The API contract acts as a specification whereby the client and server have a shared understanding. The specification tells what the API offers on the one hand, and what the client can do with the API on the other. The reality is that the contracts are often amended, and so are the APIs. Versioning in the API indicates the changes in the contract and allows the old clients to continue using the old API, and the new clients to use the latest version of the API.

Table 2-6 shows several approaches to how an API can be versioned.

Table 2-6. API versioning approaches

Versioning approach	Example
Path-based versioning	• *https://example.com/v1/orders* • *https://api.v1.example.com/orders*
Query parameter versioning	• *https://example.com/orders?api-version=v1* • *https://example.com/v1/orders?resource-version=2.1.3*
Header-based versioning	• *Api-Version: v1* • *Accept: application/vnd.example+json;api-version=1* • *Accept: application/vnd.example+json;resource-version=2* • *Accept: application/vnd.example+json;api-version=1;resource-version=2.1.3*

Message payload versioning	`{`
	    `"version": "v1",`
	    `"data": {...}`
	`}`

The list below describes common API versioning strategies:

Path-based versioning

The API version is explicitly listed as part of the path (e.g., */api/v1/resource* or */api/v2/resource*). This approach clearly signals version changes to clients and is well-suited for APIs with breaking changes or independently evolving resources. Because the version applies to the entire API, this method operates at a coarse-grained level. Unlike strategies like header-based versioning, path-based versioning doesn't allow fine-grained control over individual endpoints. Without proper refactoring (e.g., shared libraries for common logic), maintaining multiple API versions may result in redundant code and increased maintenance effort.

Query parameter versioning

The API version is provided in the URL as a query parameter. The advantage of query parameter versioning is that the scope of change is limited to a resource. This results in the URL being constant across all clients, meaning that the base URL doesn't need to change unless endpoints are renamed or removed. This versioning approach is more granular because versioning is applied at the request level rather than tied to the resource identifier.

Query parameter versioning can become challenging in request routing because routing isn't determined by the URL path (as it is in path-based versioning), but is processed within the function that receives the request. This can expand the codebase, requiring supplementary logic to route requests to the correct handler (class/function) for the specific API version. Additionally, every resource needs to be documented at the query level.

Header-based versioning

This versioning approach stores the API version in a request header, such as *Accept-Version: v1*, allowing clients to use the same URL regardless of API evolution. This approach is less transparent than URL-based or path-based versioning because the version information isn't immediately visible. Reduced visibility complicates debugging and logging because developers and testers must inspect request headers to determine the API version.

Although header-based versioning follows RESTful content negotiation principles, it can introduce ambiguity and make version management more challenging. Additionally, some intermediary systems, such as proxies, may strip or block custom headers.

Message payload versioning

Versioning can also be performed at the level of the message payload, typically as a field in the message schema. This strategy is common for event-driven architecture (EDA) and broker-based APIs, where a message can be long-lived or stored for later processing. The advantage is that you can deploy multiple messages to the system, each with a separate version. The disadvantage is that the receiver of the messages now has to handle each versioned message separately, making it more challenging for the consumer to manage.

It's possible to combine various API versioning strategies. For example, path-based versioning mixed with query parameter versioning would result in an endpoint that would look like this: */api/v1/orders/123?version=1.2.3*. We don't recommend this approach because it complicates the application, makes resource identification and precedence determination challenging, and interferes with caching.

For intent-oriented APIs, such as GraphQL, the version is expressed by renaming the field name (e.g., `updateOrderV2`). gRPC, on the other hand, prefers to version the package and service name. Appending a version suffix to gRPC method names (`UpdateOrderV2`) is possible but less common. Another approach is to avoid the versioning of APIs entirely.[4]

---

4 Roy Fielding's recommendation, given at the 2013 Evolve conference (*https://oreil.ly/9xlZU*), is to avoid introducing breaking changes: "DON'T—versioning an interface is a polite way to kill deployed applications."

An additional question to consider is, what type of format should you use to version your API? Several approaches, and combinations of them, exist:

Semantic versioning (https://semver.org)
> Label versions in the format of `MAJOR.MINOR.PATCH` (e.g., `1.3.5`), where the `MAJOR` number indicates a breaking change, `MINOR` a backward-compatible change, and `PATCH` a backward-compatible bugfix

Calendar versioning (https://calver.org)
> Uses calendar dates to label versions (e.g., `2024-11-01` or `2024.47`)

Hash versioning (https://oreil.ly/4j6UK)
> Uses a hash—for example, a version-control commit hash, as a version label (e.g., `237a2b4f`)

The challenge with versioning is conveying a potentially large set of API changes into a single version label. Therefore, in addition to explaining the meaning of the version label in the chosen approach, the ability to inform users about new features and breaking changes of the API, as well as provide the time to adapt to the changes, is needed. For that, you could use communication channels like a changelog on the API's documentation website, Atom feeds, or even a dedicated metadata section in your API response describing the upcoming changes.

> JSON Schema (*https://json-schema.org*) can help you describe and validate the shape of your JSON-encoded data. You can use this tool to figure out whether an introduced change will break the API.
>
> Remember to work only with online tools that are verified and those that you can trust. Otherwise, you are risking sharing sensitive information with third parties.

Encoding

When data grows, the overhead of data transfers among systems increases. This might not be noticeable at the megabyte scale, but as data expands to gigabytes and beyond, the time and cost associated with moving data among systems can become an issue. For example, a high volume of incoming API data can overwhelm the receiving system, leading to performance issues. Conversely, excessive data output from an API can strain system resources and be costly due to the cloud provider's pricing model. In both cases, this may impact the user experience for those interacting with the affected parts of the system. To address some of these problems, you can use compression, which is a type of encoding.

Encoding is the process of converting data from one format to another. *Decoding* is the reverse process, which converts the encoded format back into the original format.

In the context of APIs, the encoding/decoding cycle involves taking data from the sending system, encoding it to a specific format, and sending it to the receiving system. The receiving system decodes the received data, uses it, and creates a response that is then encoded and sent back to the sender.

Encoding is not compression. While every compression is encoding, not all encoding compresses (reduces the size of) data.

Compression is a type of encoding that addresses the problem of reducing data size, but at the cost of increased CPU usage. Therefore, when using compression, balance data size and performance by selecting the right compression algorithm and level.

The concept of encryption also relates to encoding, but the goal of encryption is to secure the data. Encryption normally increases the size of the data.

Transmitted or stored data can be encoded into text or binary formats.[5] The text-encoded format is both machine- and human-readable, making it convenient for developers in the context of logging or debugging. However, human readability comes with the penalty of text-encoded data being larger and slower to parse by machines. Popular text-encoding formats include ASCII (*https://oreil.ly/DsP8w*), UTF-8 (*https://oreil.ly/WP71s*), XML (*https://oreil.ly/OIkpM*), JSON (*https://www.json.org*), and YAML (*https://yaml.org*).

Example 2-2 shows the encoding and representation of Latin alphabet text.

Example 2-2. ASCII, hexadecimal, and binary encoding

```
# Echo text to file ❶
echo -n "Hello" > message

# Determine the type of the file ❷
file --brief message
ASCII text, with no line terminators

# Print file's binary content ❸
```

---

5 Some application layer protocols allow the compression of text-encoded data at the message level. For example, HTTP allows the use of algorithms such as gzip or Brotli.

```
xxd -groupsize 1 -bits message
00000000: 01001000 01100101 01101100 01101100 01101111  Hello

# Print file's content as hexadecimal and ASCII text ❹
xxd -groupsize 1 message
00000000  48 65 6c 6c 6f  Hello

# Convert hexadecimal to ASCII text ❺
echo -n "48 65 6c 6c 6f" | xxd -plain -revert
Hello
```

❶ The echo command writes "Hello" text into the *message* file. The --n option modifies the default echo behavior so that it doesn't output the trailing newline.

❷ The file command checks the file's content and briefly describes its type. This provides information on whether the file is a text file or binary.

❸ The xxd command prints the file content. The first column contains the position (displayed as a hexadecimal value) of the first byte of each line in the file relative to the start of the file. The subsequent columns contain the values of each byte in the file. In this case, we see a binary representation of five 8-bit words. The last column shows the ASCII representation of the contents of the file.

❹ The xxd command prints the file content as hexadecimal and ASCII values.

❺ The echo command writes five hexadecimal numbers and pipes them to the xxd program to convert these numbers into ASCII text.

Binary encoding, as the name indicates, represents data as a sequence of binary 0s and 1s. The advantages of binary encoding are a smaller encoded data size and faster parsing, because it's faster for machines to operate on numbers than to parse text. For example, the number 12345 takes 5 bytes as ASCII text but can be represented by just 14 bits (almost 2 bytes) in binary: 11000000111001. Furthermore, binary formats often omit unnecessary metadata, further reducing the amount of data. Some popular binary encoding protocols/formats include Amazon Ion (*https://oreil.ly/MG5Bt*), Apache Avro (*https://avro.apache.org*), MessagePack (*https://msgpack.org*), Protocol Buffers (*https://protobuf.dev*), and Apache Thrift (*https://thrift.apache.org*).

Encoding Versus Serialization

While encoding is a general process of changing the format of data, *serialization* focuses on converting a programming language data structure into a byte stream (sequence of bytes), which can be stored or transmitted. *Deserialization* is the reverse process, converting the byte stream back into the original data structure. Figure 2-1 illustrates the process of serialization and deserialization.

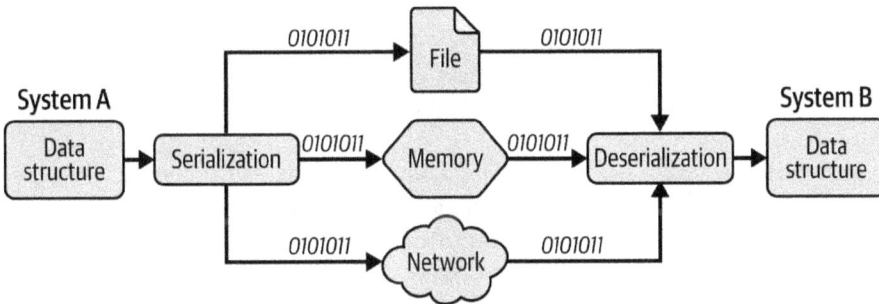

Figure 2-1. Serialization and deserialization of data

Example 2-3 shows encoding and decoding of data using the Avro serialization format, and Example 2-4 shows inspection of the binary-encoded Avro file using `file` and xxd tools.

> The printed code presented in this book is optimized for readability. Because of that, the code in the book doesn't always mirror the source code included in the book's code repository. Truncated code is indicated by "..." (three dots).

Example 2-3. Apache Avro serialization in Python

```
import avro.schema
from avro.datafile import DataFileReader, DataFileWriter
from avro.io import DatumReader, DatumWriter

user_avsc = '''{  ❶
 "type": "record",
 "name": "User",
 "fields": [
    {"name": "email", "type": "string"},
    {"name": "active", "type": "boolean", "default": false},
    {"name": "access_level", "type": "int", "default": 0}
 ]
}'''
```

```
schema = avro.schema.parse(user_avsc)  ❷

with DataFileWriter(open("users.avro", "wb"), DatumWriter(), schema) as writer:  ❸
    writer.append({"email": "ld@example.com", "active": False, "access_level": 0})
    writer.append({"email": "md@example.com", "active": True, "access_level": 3})

with DataFileReader(open("users.avro", "rb"), DatumReader()) as reader:  ❹
    for user in reader:
        print(user)

# Program output:
# {'email': 'ld@example.com', 'active': False, 'access_level': 0}
# {'email': 'md@example.com', 'active': True, 'access_level': 3}
```

❶ The multiline string holds the JSON definition of the Avro schema. The schema defines an Avro record representing a user, and the record type must contain type, name, and fields keys. The fields key defines an array of JSON objects with properties used to serialize/deserialize records: name, type, and default.

❷ The JSON string is converted into an Avro schema.

❸ The purpose of the writer object is to append two records to the *users.avro* binary file. Both the Avro schema and data are written into the file.

❹ The reader object opens the *users.avro* file, deserializes it, and prints every record present in this file. The program output shows a deserialized record.

Example 2-4. Apache Avro file inspection

```
file --brief users.avro  ❶
Apache Avro version 1

xxd -groupsize 1 users.avro  ❷
00000000: 4f 62 6a 01 04 14 61 76 72 6f 2e 63 6f 64 65 63  Obj...avro.codec
00000010: 08 6e 75 6c 6c 16 61 76 72 6f 2e 73 63 68 65 6d  .null.avro.schem
00000020: 61 86 03 7b 22 74 79 70 65 22 3a 20 22 72 65 63  a..{"type": "rec
00000030: 6f 72 64 22 2c 20 22 6e 61 6d 65 22 3a 20 22 55  ord", "name": "U
00000040: 73 65 72 22 2c 20 22 66 69 65 6c 64 73 22 3a 20  ser", "fields":
00000050: 5b 7b 22 74 79 70 65 22 3a 20 22 73 74 72 69 6e  [{"type": "strin
00000060: 67 22 2c 20 22 6e 61 6d 65 22 3a 20 22 65 6d 61  g", "name": "ema
00000070: 69 6c 22 7d 2c 20 7b 22 74 79 70 65 22 3a 20 22  il"}, {"type": "
00000080: 62 6f 6f 6c 65 61 6e 22 2c 20 22 6e 61 6d 65 22  boolean", "name"
00000090: 3a 20 22 61 63 74 69 76 65 22 2c 20 22 64 65 66  : "active", "def
000000a0: 61 75 6c 74 22 3a 20 66 61 6c 73 65 7d 2c 20 7b  ault": false}, {
000000b0: 22 74 79 70 65 22 3a 20 22 69 6e 74 22 2c 20 22  "type": "int", "
000000c0: 6e 61 6d 65 22 3a 20 22 61 63 63 65 73 73 5f 6c  name": "access_l
000000d0: 65 76 65 6c 22 2c 20 22 64 65 66 61 75 6c 74 22  evel", "default"
```

```
000000e0: 3a 20 30 7d 5d 7d 00 4b e1 68 72 66 79 5c 50 ac   : 0}]}.K.hrfy\P.
000000f0: a2 1e 91 95 bb 11 f9 04 44 1c 6c 64 40 65 78 61   ........D.ld@exa
00000100: 6d 70 6c 65 2e 63 6f 6d 00 00 1c 6d 64 40 65 78   mple.com...md@ex
00000110: 61 6d 70 6c 65 2e 63 6f 6d 01 06 4b e1 68 72 66   ample.com..K.hrf
00000120: 79 5c 50 ac a2 1e 91 95 bb 11 f9                  y\P........
```

❶ The `file` command shows that the *users.avro* file type is Apache Avro version 1.

❷ The xxd command shows the hexadecimal and ASCII representation of every byte in the *users.avro* file.

When transferring data among systems, be aware of serialization and deserialization nuances, which may occur due to different treatment of data types by different programming languages. Let's take as an example a language-independent data format like JSON, which supports only the following JavaScript data types: *object, array, string, number, boolean,* and *null.*

Example 2-5 shows some unexpected output when serializing and deserializing JSON in Python and JavaScript.

Example 2-5. Serialization and deserialization of JSON

```
# Parse JSON string to Python dictionary ❶
python -c "import json; print(json.loads('{\"a\": null, \"b\": true}'))"
{'a': None, 'b': True}

# Convert JavaScript object to JSON string ❷
node --eval "console.log(JSON.stringify({number: 9007199254740999}))"
{"number": 9007199254741000}

# Parse JSON string and read a value ❸
node --eval "o = JSON.parse('{\"a\": 0.3}'); console.log(o.b)"
undefined
```

❶ When a string containing JSON is deserialized in Python, the JavaScript `null` and `true` values are interpreted as None and True.

❷ Trying to represent a number outside of the data type of a programming language results in a numerical precision loss. As a result, the number 9007199254740999 is rounded to 9007199254741000. Serialization doesn't help with this problem.

❸ Accessing a missing value from a deserialized JSON string results in an unde fined JavaScript value instead of an error.

> Representing numbers as strings can improve portability when working across systems with varying numeric support, particularly for large integers or when precision must be preserved exactly. However, this approach involves a trade-off in terms of performance and storage, and might lead to unexpected results such as loss of precision when converting to native numbers.

Handling API data types requires consistent decisions within your system. For example, decide whether to treat `null` as `""` (empty string), `undefined`, or a `null` type (like Python's `None`). Likewise, establish a rule for handling missing fields. Some serialization formats, like Protocol Buffers, use a default value if the message's field is absent. For example, for `int32`, the default value is `0`; for string, the default value is `""` (empty string); and for `bool` the default value is `false`.

When handling Boolean values (true or false), they should be represented using standard encoding conventions for the given format (e.g., true/false in JSON). Deviations from these standard representations are to be avoided to ensure consistency and interoperability. Therefore, refrain from representing Booleans as numbers—`0` (false) and `1` (true)—or strings—`no` and `yes`, or `on` and `off`.[6] When naming a Boolean representing state, favor the Boolean's positive aspect over the negative—for example, `allowed` over `disallowed`, and `enabled` over `disabled`. Double negations are hard for humans to process; compare, for example, `!enabled` (not enabled) and `!disabled` (not disabled). If possible, use the default value for each Boolean, and avoid using prefixes; for example, use `activated`, not `isActive`.[7]

Consider also the bounds of data types assigned to API fields.[8] You might think that a length of 255 characters for a surname might be insufficient, but what about 1024? The second bound is big enough to fit the longest name in the world, which counts 747 characters.[9] Setting the field's data minimum length can be tricky too. How short can a name be? It could be four characters, or two, or what about one?

> Value bounds and default values are among the subjects of *Humans vs Computers* (*https://oreil.ly/V7uDc*) by Gojko Adzic (Neuri Consulting, 2017). If you don't have time to read the whole book, have a look at his "People That Make Computers Go Crazy" talk (*https://oreil.ly/Bm3Dm*).

---

6 Be aware of the Norway problem in YAML 1.1 (*https://oreil.ly/Iesmx*).

7 See the Google API documentation on Booleans (*https://oreil.ly/DM6X9*).

8 A common strategy employed when validating input fields is to use regular expression (regex) checks.

9 See the Guinness World Record for the longest personal name (*https://oreil.ly/C3nOu*).

Many programming languages support *enumerators* (*enums*), which are data structures that aggregate a group of constants into one type. Binary serialization formats such as Avro or Protocol Buffers support enums natively, but text-encoded serializers like JSON don't. When dealing with serialized formats that don't support enums, you could use strings to represent the enum values. Representing an enum by a string requires extra effort on the application because additional logic needs to be implemented to check that the received string value is one of the values defined to represent the enum.

Filtering

Filtering allows you to retrieve specific data from a larger dataset based on selection conditions. In REST APIs, filtering is most commonly implemented by adding criteria as query parameters to the URI (e.g., *https://example.com/api/v1/books?order_by=published_date&language=en*). There are two approaches to transferring filtering criteria to the API, and both use query parameters.

The first approach uses a *filter string*, which is passed to the API in the query parameter. The format of the filter string depends on the underlying storage technology. For instance, if you use a Structured Query Language (SQL) database, you could create a filter string that contains a portion of a SQL query that the backend sanitizes, controls, and interprets. For example, `country='Denmark' AND snowfall >= 0.5 AND rain >= 0.1`. Don't pass the whole SQL queries (`SELECT * FROM weather WHERE country='Denmark' AND snowfall >= 0.5 AND rain >= 0.1`). Otherwise, you'll risk an *SQL injection* attack, in which a malicious SQL statement is interpolated into the context of the executable query, such as injecting a `DROP` statement.

The advantage of using the filter string approach is that it's easier to respond to changes related to data format without modifying the API. Since the API is responsible for parsing, sanitizing, and validating any changes to the underlying data model, the client needs only to update the query parameter filter string. That's because the API takes care of any necessary changes or interpretations, thereby reducing the need for changes when the underlying data model evolves. As an example, imagine that the underlying model renamed the database column from `snowfall` to `snowfall_amount`. This change requires the client to update the filter string, but it doesn't necessarily force the API to treat the query string differently than before the column was renamed. This means that the API could use the new schema (`snowfall_amount >= 0.5`) without modifying its codebase. The downside of using a filter string in a query parameter is that the client must know how to construct this string to match the dataset's schema. Additionally, this method requires a custom parser that understands the filter string.

The second approach, called *field-based filtering*, uses filtering data supplied to the API as query parameters (e.g., `country=Denmark&snowfall>=0.5&rain>=0.1`). This approach is more controlled but less flexible because the API defines and manages the filtering logic and structure. The field-based filtering approach has several advantages: reduced risk of SQL injection due to input serialization and validation, easier integration with API's backend frameworks, and more-precise error messages because you know exactly which field is being validated. But the downside is that this method requires work to keep the API functional due to less flexibility in adapting to new changes. This is the most common approach.

Which filtering approach to follow is up to you. If you work with a framework, follow its recommendations.

Additionally, filtering can be used to shape the response data. For instance, GraphQL allows the client to request specific data on a granular level (as specified in the query). REST APIs are capable of filtering out unwanted data, but they require more implementation on the API side. For example, by using the `exclude_fields` query parameter, a client can control the shape of the returned data.

Counting and Sorting

Counting and sorting records is a common functionality desired by frontend applications. *Counting* determines the number of total records matching a query and is often used in pagination (see "Pagination" on page 59). *Sorting* is ordering sortable data in ascending or descending order, using properties such as time, name, or numbers. However, this functionality may negatively impact performance.

In small-scale systems, counting and sorting tend to perform well, creating the impression that the system is optimized. However, as data volume grows, performance issues may emerge due to missing database indexes, or the $1 + n$ problem (*https://oreil.ly/CaKMC*) (also called $n + 1$). The $1 + n$ problem is a performance issue that occurs when related data is fetched with many queries instead of one. In relational databases, this is usually caused by not using SQL JOINs.

Distributed systems introduce further complexity. When data is partitioned across multiple nodes, operations like counting and sorting can require coordination, leading to slower response times. This can negatively affect API responsiveness unless the underlying database is explicitly optimized for such aggregate operations.

Implementing counting and sorting is typically feasible and recommended if your backend relies on a nondistributed database. However, in distributed systems, these operations require features to support distributed data processing. In some cases, it may be best to limit or disable counting and sorting for large datasets, or to explore alternatives such as approximate counts, cached metadata, or deferred processing.

Pagination

Pagination, or *paging*, is a design pattern that addresses the problem of loading a large dataset in pages (chunks). Each page contains a subset of the data, determined by the page size (number of items), and acts as a window into the dataset, providing only a portion of the entire dataset at any given time. Users or systems can navigate the entire dataset by moving through these pages, sliding back and forth, allowing them to move to the next or previous page, or jumping to a specific page.

There are several approaches to implementing pagination, but the most common are offset-based and cursor-based pagination, which are described next.

Offset-based pagination

The *offset-based pagination* method is commonly used and comes in several flavors. The first offset-based pagination style uses the page number in the request query parameter, as shown in Example 2-6. Notice that the page value in the next and pre vious fields is increased and decreased by one, respectively, and the count field indicates the number of objects in the dataset.

Example 2-6. Offset-based pagination with the page query parameter

```
curl https://example.com/api/v1/orders?page=2&page_size=100
{
  "count": 1478,
  "next": "https://example.com/api/v1/orders?page=3&page_size=100",
  "previous": "https://example.com/api/v1/orders?page=1&page_size=100",
  "results": [...]
}
```

The second approach to offset-based pagination is to use limit and offset query parameters, as shown in Example 2-7. The limit controls the total number of items returned, and the offset indicates where the results should start relative to the complete, unpaginated set of items.

Example 2-7. Offset-based pagination with the limit and offset query parameters

```
curl https://example.com/api/v1/orders?limit=100&offset=400
{
  "count": 1478,
  "next": "https://example.com/api/v1/orders?limit=100&offset=500",
  "previous": "https://example.com/api/v1/orders?limit=100&offset=300",
  "results": [...]
}
```

The advantage of offset-based pagination is that it allows the clients to estimate the total number of pages (based on the number of records and page size), and to jump to a specific page. The disadvantage is that pagination may become inefficient with vast datasets, leading to slow response times. This is because the database needs to scan or skip over many records to reach the desired offset before returning the results for that page. For example, if you're requesting page 1000 in a dataset, the database has to skip through the records of the previous 999 pages.

Another disadvantage of offset-based pagination appears when combined with item deletion or insertion. For example, when you delete an item from the previous page, the subsequent items shift backward by one position, which may result in skipping some items that should have appeared on the next page. Conversely, when you insert an item into a previous page, the subsequent items shift forward by one position, potentially leading to duplication as items are pushed into positions that overlap with the current or previous page.

Table 2-7 shows the effect of deletion or insertion on pagination. Notice that after deletion, the last page contains one fewer item, and after insertion, the pages shift forward, causing one item to move to the next page.

Table 2-7. Effect of deleting and inserting items on pagination

Page no.	Initial pagination	After deleting "B"	After inserting "Z"
1	A, B, C	A, C, D	A, Z, B
2	D, E, F	E, F, G	C, D, E
3	G, H, I	H, I	F, G, H

Offset-based pagination relies on skipping a fixed number of items (offset). If items are deleted or inserted before the current offset while a client is paginating, the dataset shifts. This can cause the client to either skip items (on deletion) or see duplicate items (on insertion) on subsequent page requests.

Cursor-based pagination

Cursor-based pagination uses a cursor (pointer) to indicate the position in the dataset. A cursor needs to be a unique and sequential value to be sortable, such as a database primary key. The cursor is encoded and appears as a token not understood by the client, but understood by the API. The API knows how to decode the cursor and use it to maneuver through the database.

A commonly used technique for generating a cursor involves combining the base cursor value with a *nonce* (a number used only once, whose purpose is to ensure randomness) and encoding the result using Base64 encoding. Example 2-8 shows responses for the API that uses cursor-based pagination.

Example 2-8. Cursor pagination

```
# The first response from the cursor-based paginated REST API ❶
curl https://example.com/api/v1/orders?limit=100
{
 "next": "123abc",
 "results": [...]
}

# The second response from the cursor-based paginated REST API ❷
curl https://example.com/api/v1/orders?limit=100&next=123abc
{
 "next": "456cde",
 "results": [...]
}
```

❶ In the first request, the client uses the limit parameter to control the size of the paginated data. The API response contains the next cursor, which indicates how to retrieve the next page of results. The client uses the next value to continue fetching data. An empty value of next would indicate there are no more results.

❷ In the second request, the curl client uses next to paginate to the next page of results. The API provides the new cursor pointing to the next page of results.

> One implementation of cursor pagination, described in the Slack API documentation (*https://oreil.ly/QZvu0*), uses different field names. The API response includes next_cursor, and the client requests include cursor.

Cursor-based pagination performs well with large datasets because the cursor identifies a specific item in the dataset, enabling the system to efficiently retrieve the next set of results. It is especially suitable for dynamic environments, such as live feeds, where data changes frequently. Unlike offset-based pagination, which can lead to skipped or duplicated records when items are deleted or inserted, cursor-based pagination behaves more consistently. This is because the cursor represents a position relative to a known item, allowing for a stable continuation of pagination regardless of changes in surrounding data.

The disadvantage of cursor-based pagination is the complexity of implementing logic for jumping to a specific page or navigating among pages arbitrarily.

Long-Running Tasks

API requests can be used to trigger tasks such as processing a video file, generating a financial report, or training a machine learning model. A client communicating with APIs in a response-request model for every sent request expects to receive a response, and if the request is sent with a REST API, then the response is expected to be timely. Typically, clients and API servers use predefined timeouts to avoid indefinite waiting periods. However, this timeout mechanism is effective only for tasks with relatively short processing duration, and fails in scenarios where the task computation time exceeds the timeout, such as churning through a large amount of data or performing video transformations. This is where the *long-running task* pattern (aka *long-running operations*) can help.

In a long-running task approach, a client sends a request to the API that triggers task processing (the task is usually processed on a machine other than the one serving the API). Instead of returning a result of processing to the client, the API returns a unique identifier of the started task, which the client uses to look up the task status (progress). When the REST API accepts the task, the response status code should be 202 (Accepted). One way to expose a task through an API is to define a task resource at the top level of the API—for example, *https://example.com/api/v1/tasks*.

The long-running task approach requires the API to persist and track the task's meta-data, such as status, progress, start and completion timestamps, and errors. Some tasks may return results such as metadata; others may include the location where the results are stored—for example, the location of a file.

The task can be described using a state machine, which captures the behavior of the task for every possible state transition. Some long-running tasks support state management by allowing the task to be paused, resumed, or canceled. However, in the case of fire-and-forget tasks (tasks for which the client doesn't receive updates once the task is initiated), client state management is absent. For tasks that aren't binary, meaning they have more states than just success or failure (e.g., cancelable, pausable, resumable), you'll need to address these states by implementing custom actions in your API to manage them. That would lead you to create an interface that might look like this: *https://example.com/api/v1/tasks/1?action=resume*.

> Notice that the custom action is constructed using the query parameter */resource/ID?action* instead of */resource/ID/action*. The problem with the latter pattern is that *action* could be interpreted as a resource (the *action* resource).

A question arises: how does a client who initiated the long-running task know when the task is completed? A client can use polling (see Chapter 10) to periodically ask the API for the task status. The downside of polling is the excess of requests that the client creates.

An alternative method to polling is to establish a long-lived connection to the API. In this case, the API keeps the connection open and closes it after completing the task and sending the message to the client. The trade-off of keeping the connection open is that the API must manage the underlying connections, which can increase resource usage on the API server.

Request Deduplication

Request duplication occurs when the same request is sent more than once. It could be caused by rapid clicks on a UI element, or by faulty application logic. Duplicated, nonidempotent requests are undesirable, especially in financial contexts, when repeated requests could lead to a customer's credit card being charged twice for the same product. However, in some cases repeating a request is necessary—for example, when a server, network, or validation error occurs, and the original request needs to be retried. These cases are described in "Request Retry" next.

To prevent the undesirable effects of request duplication, a client can generate a unique request ID and include it in the request. When the API receives a request with the same request ID for the second time, it handles the duplication appropriately— for example, by returning the previous successful response or an error.

The request ID generated by a single client needs to be unique. Universally unique identifiers (UUIDs) are designed to minimize (but not eliminate) the risk of identifier collisions.

Request Retry

Another aspect that you need to tackle as an API designer is when to retry a failed request. A request can fail because it's invalid or due to a network failure, server-side error, or incorrect application logic. If the failure is due to a problem with the request itself (e.g., invalid data or formatting), the request should be corrected and sent again. However, if the failure is on the API side, the original request should be retried later, after the issue is likely resolved.

A *thundering herd* problem occurs when many clients simultaneously attempt to access a resource, causing spikes in load and resource contention. A related issue is a *retry storm* that happens when many clients repeatedly retry their failed requests, overwhelming the API and potentially prolonging downtime.

The reason for sending retries is an assumption that a retry will soon succeed. However, when a retry is unlikely to succeed, retries should be paused for a certain amount of time. Instead of helping, a retry storm can prolong the outage. To temporarily pause retries, you can use a maximum retry (cutoff method) to limit the maximum number of retries, combined with a cutoff expiration timer. Alternatively, you can use a more advanced circuit-breaker pattern (*https://oreil.ly/e1mZS*) that takes into account the number of successful and failed requests.

The frequency of retry requests can be controlled by a retry interval, a time after which the client sends another request. The retry interval can be modified using *timing jitter*, which adds a random delay to each retry interval to spread the retries. Furthermore, client requests should use a *request timeout*, a time window within which the client expects to receive a response. This way, a client can send a retry request after receiving an unsuccessful response or after a request timeout.

Another method is to dynamically adjust the retry interval by using the *exponential back-off* method, which increases the retry interval with every retry. For example, if the initial retry interval is 2 seconds, the following retries will happen after 4, 8, 16 seconds, and so on. Figure 2-2 illustrates retries that use an *exponential back-off* method with a cutoff. Notice that the time between retries doubles. After the fourth failed retry, the cutoff pauses the retries until the cutoff timeout (not shown in the diagram) expires.

A server may also participate in the retry control, by including an HTTP `Retry-After` header in the response, indicating when clients should attempt to retry.

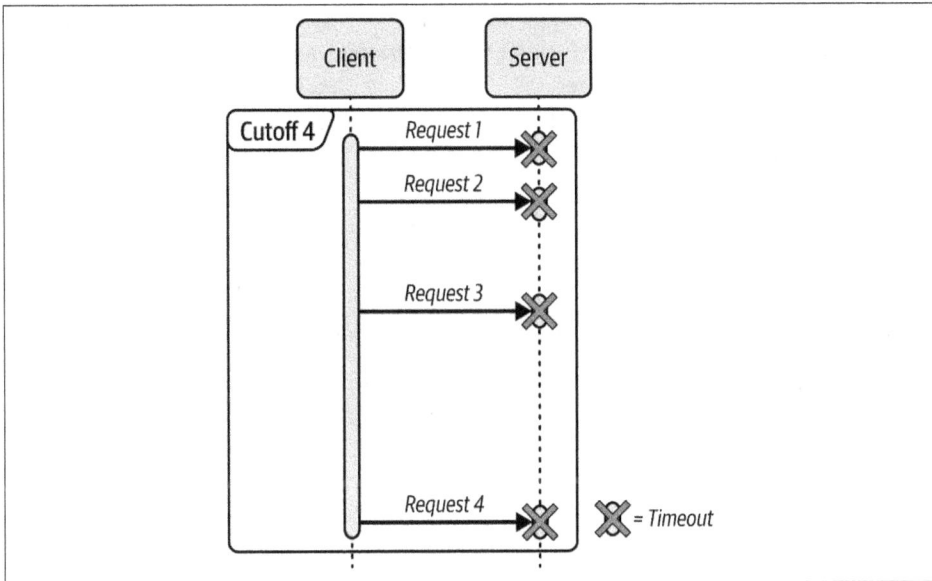

Figure 2-2. Exponential back-off method with a cutoff

Rate Limiting

Rate limiting, also known as *throttling*, can be used to protect the API from an influx of legitimate or malicious requests. Throttling limits the number of requests that can be made by a single client to the same endpoint in a given time interval. This assumes that a client can be identified. For example, by performing throttling based on the client IP address, the API avoids using resources for request processing. Throttling should ideally happen as early as possible on the network path of the request.

Throttling can be used to reduce the impact of traditional brute force or denial-of-service (DoS) attacks. Imagine you built an API that exposes a reset-password functionality. This functionality is needed by users who forget passwords. A user provides an email associated with the account for which the password reset is needed, a request is sent to the API, and, a few seconds later, the user receives an email in their inbox (or spam) folder with password reset instructions.

However, this scenario assumes that the person who goes through the reset procedure is the email owner and performs a single or small number of reset requests. An attacker who wants to harm the API can use this functionality to perform a DoS attack. Example 2-9 shows an infinite loop that sends an HTTP POST request to the forgot_password endpoint. One attacker's client is unlikely to overwhelm the service, but many clients might, leading to a distributed denial-of-service attack (DDoS). Every client participating in a DDoS may perform only a few requests, making throttling alone insufficient to mitigate this type of attack.

Example 2-9. A DoS attack attempt using an infinite while-loop

```
while true; do
  curl 'https://example.com/api/v1/forgot_password' \
    --header 'Content-Type: application/json' \
    --data '{"email": "user@example.com"}' \
    --request POST
done
```

Caching

Caching is a technique that optimizes the request-response cycle by reducing the need for clients to refetch resources from the server. Caching improves client responsiveness and reduces server load. Caching can be implemented on both the client side and server side of communication.

In *client-side caching*, a client requests resources from the server and saves them locally. An example is a web browser that can cache HTML, CSS, and JavaScript, and static assets of other resources, to speed up the page load on subsequent visits. Client-side caching reduces network traffic and improves client responsiveness, since it's faster to load resources from disk than over the network. The downside of client-side caching is that it may use stale content and require manual cache invalidation. To ensure response freshness and automatic cache invalidation, the servers can assist clients with mechanisms such as cache expiration (e.g., time-to-live, or TTL) or validation headers (ETag, Last-Modified), which help clients automatically determine whether cached content is still valid.

In *server-side caching*, the server checks whether a requested response is already stored in the cache. If not, the server generates the response, stores it in cache storage (usually local server memory for better performance, but distributed caches can also be used), and then sends the response to the client. Server-side caching offers more control over cached resources, as it doesn't depend on individual clients' caching behavior. While it may not reduce network traffic to the same extent as client-side caching, it reduces load on backend systems and improves overall response time.

Deletion

The discussion of deletion in this section is REST-oriented. Deleting resources in REST APIs is implemented in two ways: soft-delete or hard-delete. *Soft-delete* preserves the resource but marks it as deleted, whereas *hard-delete* deletes the resource from the system.

> Soft-delete doesn't fully address the data-erasure requirements mandated by various data protection regulations, such as the General Data Protection Regulation (GDPR) in the European Union or the California Consumer Privacy Act (CCPA).

Soft-delete requires some kind of labeling of the resource—for example, using a `soft_delete` flag, together with the timestamp of the transition, to indicate if and when the resource is soft-deleted. Alternatively, you could use multiple states to describe the resource deletion status: `active`, `pending_deletion`, or `soft_deleted`. The issue with using more than two states is that in order to track the progression of the resource's deletion status, a history of transitions needs to be maintained.

When performing a soft-delete in REST APIs, return a resource representation with an updated state and 200 (OK) status code. A subsequent soft-delete request on an already soft-deleted resource should return a 412 (Precondition Failed).[10]

Implementing hard-delete together with soft-delete requires adding an erase (wipe or prune) action to the API resource—for example, HTTP `DELETE /api/orders/123?action=erase`. When performing a hard-delete, the response should return either a 200 (OK) status code along with the deleted resource, or a 204 (No Content) status code with no content. A subsequent hard-delete request on an already deleted resource should return a 404 (Not Found) status code.

> Remember to document any nonstandard behavior of HTTP methods to avoid potential confusion.

---

10 More details about soft-delete can be found in Chapter 25, "Soft Deletion," in *API Design Patterns* by JJ Geewax.

In versioned APIs, adding soft-delete can be a breaking change. Before introducing it, consider how it might affect the data returned by the API and whether it changes what users expect. If soft-delete could cause existing clients to behave unexpectedly (such as missing data they used to see), release the soft-delete under a new version of the API.

Depending on whether you are implementing soft-delete or hard-delete, the way the API returns resources changes. For example, to retrieve the resource after it has been soft-deleted, the method should return the resource, not the HTTP 404 (Not Found) status code as it would for hard-delete. Moreover, when requesting multiple resources, the response should return only requests with the `soft_delete` flag set to `false`. The API interface should have a flag `include_deleted` that allows the client to see (receive) soft-deleted resources. Without the `include_deleted` flag, the API response needs to filter out these soft-deleted resources so that the client won't receive them in the response.

Your API also needs an action to undelete (restore) soft-deleted resources. For that, you can implement a custom action on the resource—for example, *https:// example.com/api/v1/order/1?restore*. In case you are restoring an already restored object, your API should return the HTTP 412 (Precondition Failed) status code. Furthermore, you could add `expiration_date` on a resource to periodically remove soft-deleted resources from the database.

API Security

Nowadays, organizations are increasingly adopting the software-as-a-service (SaaS) model, which allows them to migrate to off-the-shelf online software. This shift requires attackers to focus not only on technological weaknesses, hoping, for example, that the solution is misconfigured, but also on exploiting human behavior.

Social engineering, also called *human hacking*, involves psychological manipulation to gain unauthorized access to IT systems. Common methods are as follows:

Phishing
 The attacker deceives the target into providing sensitive information.

Pretexting
 The attacker creates a false scenario as a pretext to obtain data.

Baiting
 The attacker leaves a malicious item, hoping that the victim will use it. For example, an attacker leaves a USB stick containing malicious software in a parking lot.

OWASP Top 10 API Security

The Open Web Application Security Project (OWASP) (*https://owasp.org*) is an online community that creates articles, methodologies, documentation, tools, and technologies in web application security. OWASP aims to improve software security through open source initiatives and community education.

OWASP has several projects (*https://oreil.ly/qape2*), including the Top 10 project (*https://oreil.ly/XOHc6*). The OWASP Top 10 project has become the reference standard for web application security risks.

Moreover, OWASP has the API Security Top 10 project (*https://oreil.ly/rU9sQ*) dedicated to API security. This project serves as a reference for understanding API security risks and methods of mitigation. The OWASP API Top 10 risks may be grouped into three main categories:

Authentication and authorization
> When implemented incorrectly, authentication or authorization (these terms are defined in "Encryption, Authentication, and Authorization" on page 70) may allow attackers to assume other users' identities, or to gain unauthorized access to protected data. The attacks in the authentication category are possible due to compromised authentication tokens, incorrect implementations of authentication flows, or brute-force attacks on weak passwords.
>
> Authorization attacks exploit access control policies that are incorrectly set up, or a lack of separation of duties between administrative and regular user roles. An example attack in this category is a *privilege escalation attack*, where an attacker exploits authentication or authorization weaknesses to gain privileged access.

Inventory management
> Misconfiguration or insecure programming practices of the API and its supporting services may facilitate attacks. Examples of misconfiguration include misconfiguration of a firewall, missing software security patches,[11] leaking secrets in API logs, missing Transport Layer Security (TLS), or using weak encryption standards. Example attacks in this category include the following:

---

11 Cloud providers and SaaS companies are currently not required to disclose vulnerabilities of their services, even if user actions are required to mitigate these vulnerabilities. See "Security Industry Call-to-Action: We Need a Cloud Vulnerability Database" (*https://oreil.ly/L3jVB*) by Shir Tamari and Alon Schindel and the Open Cloud Vulnerability and Security Issue Database (*https://www.cloudvulndb.org*).

- *Man-in-the-middle* (MITM)—The attacker intercepts communication between the client and the server.

- *Code injection attack*—The attacker compromises the system by injecting malicious code via various pathways such as SQL injection (*https://oreil.ly/a0hwv*).

- OS command injection (*https://oreil.ly/pUxMy*) or cross-site scripting (*https://oreil.ly/TAc44*).

Resource management

When the usage of APIs isn't monitored, unconstrained calls may result in unexpected costs. If the API functionality integrates with external systems that provide services such as SMS, email, or phone calls, and they are paid per request, then the attackers can increase the operational costs of the service. An example attack in this category is DoS, in which the attacker overwhelms the API with a flood of requests.

Examples of API Security Patterns

APIs are susceptible to technological security risks. The OWASP project aims to provide a classification of these risks and tracks their historical evolution. This section describes selected patterns to reduce these risks.

Encryption, Authentication, and Authorization

Encryption is the most common way of protecting API traffic by ensuring the confidentiality, integrity, and authenticity of the data in transit. Encryption is the process of converting data from its original format, plaintext, into ciphertext by using an encryption algorithm and an encryption key. Ciphertext isn't readable without the decryption key.

> For more details about encryption, visit the *src/network/README.md* file in the book's code repository.

API traffic encryption typically relies on TLS. Additionally, TLS allows the client to authenticate (confirm the identity of) the server using a digital certificate issued by a trusted certificate authority (CA). In some cases, mutual TLS authentication (mTLS) is used, where the client and server authenticate each other. Finally, TLS ensures data integrity by verifying that the data hasn't been altered during transit. This is achieved through message authentication codes (MACs), which help detect data tampering.

Authentication is the process of verifying an entity's identity. *Authorization* ensures that the entity has access to the requested resources. When returning data to API clients, apply the principle of *least privilege*, which states that users should be granted only the minimum permissions necessary to perform their tasks.

> In later chapters, encryption, authentication, and authorization will be described in more detail when implementing various API styles. For example, see "Security" on page 182.

Sanitization and Validation

Sanitization and validation aim to protect APIs from attacks that exploit input or manipulate output data, such as injection attacks or data leaks.

Sanitization is the first step to ensure that the data is in a safe format for processing. Sanitizing data means removing unwanted input, such as unexpected characters, or stripping whitespaces at both ends of the input string. Validation, on the other hand, seeks to ensure that the input obeys validation constraints and policies. For example, validated data is expected to be in the correct range, and strings are expected to be correctly formatted (e.g., correct zip code).

API input and output data should be sanitized and validated. As a developer who writes secure code, never trust the input data. Trusting input data allows attackers to write malicious code into a request field. Without validation, this can lead to security risks such as data breaches or unauthorized access. When validating input data, be sensitive not only to data values but also to data types.

When working with input data, use serializers. Serializers are a common part of many frameworks and programming languages. Often serializers include data validation features. Additionally, most frameworks include built-in validators that support validation at the model level (object-relational mappers [ORMs]).

The API's output data also needs to be inspected because insecure APIs often expose excessive data, sometimes even sensitive information. For example, when building an API for a car rental service, you'd like to track vehicle locations. Implementing this feature requires adding a location field as an array containing a history of the vehicle locations. This field shouldn't be exposed to unprivileged API clients. When returning data to clients, think of the principle of least privilege (*https://oreil.ly/SuSn3*). Enforcing the least privilege principle on APIs helps control data access, preventing unnecessary exposure of sensitive information.

Another aspect of validating the input and output is the concept of a "dry run." In a dry run, the goal isn't to execute the application logic but to observe the effects of request validation. One way to achieve this is to add a `validate_only` flag to the request interface. When testing requests with `validate_only`, the process should be both idempotent and safe.[12]

An additional consideration about APIs is protecting the data. Suppose an attacker aims to extract data from the system rather than modify its behavior. In that case, the attacker could use a technique called *data scraping* (also called *excessive data gathering*), which extracts data from APIs or web pages. Data is then used for various purposes, some of which may be unauthorized or malicious. The next section covers data scraping mitigation.

Scraping Mitigation

Data scraping allows a program to extract data from another program. The most widespread form of scraping is *web scraping*, which extracts data from websites. Other forms may involve extracting data from APIs, desktop applications, or databases. Companies use scrapers to consume other companies' data for further processing and analysis. Scraping competitors' websites may be used to give an unfair competitive advantage. This can raise legal and ethical concerns.

To protect your website from popular, well-behaved web crawlers like search engine crawlers, expose *robots.txt* at the root of your API server (e.g., *https://example.com/robots.txt*). Note that *robots.txt* is a voluntary standard, and not all bots respect it. This method won't protect your organization's data from malicious web crawlers.[13]

Another pattern used to protect public API endpoints is to avoid using predictable sequences for resource identifiers. If integers are user resource identifiers, such as *1* in *https://example.com/api/v1/books/1*, then scrapers can grab the resources one by one by incrementing the identifier. If, instead of integers, you use UUIDv4 identifiers of the form, say, *9f287bb6-7a74-44dc-b95f-2046116c5a78*, guessing such identifiers would take too much time for the scrapers due to the vast space of UUIDv4. A UUIDv4 is a 128-bit identifier, with 6 predetermined bits and 122 bits randomly generated, which gives a total possible space of approximately 5.32×10^{36} (5.32 undecillion) unique IDs.

---

12 See "HTTP Idempotency, Safety, and Caching" on page 168. While POST requests are normally nonidempotent and unsafe, the `validate_only` flag creates an exception to this rule. When this flag is present, the endpoint treats the request as a special case, making it both idempotent and safe. This allows clients to test an operation's validity without actually performing it.

13 Malicious bots that don't respect *robots.txt* may instead need to be trapped in honeypots, described in the Cloudflare blog post "Trapping Misbehaving Bots in an AI Labyrinth" (*https://oreil.ly/eXGvV*) by Reid Tatoris et al.

API Design Best Practices

The "How to Design a Good API and Why It Matters" article by Joshua J. Bloch contains a set of maxims about API design.[14] Although these maxims were stated from the perspective of a software library, they are applicable to a wide range of APIs, including network-based APIs. Therefore, before introducing a set of high-level best practices for network-based API design, we'll present selected maxims. You are invited to explore the full set on your own.

We'll start by answering the question of why good API design matters:

> APIs can be among your greatest assets or liabilities. Good APIs create long-term customers; bad ones create long-term support nightmares.
>
> Public APIs, like diamonds, are forever. You have one chance to get it right so give it your best.
>
> All programmers are API designers. Good programs are modular, and intermodular boundaries define APIs. Good modules get reused.
>
> —Joshua J. Bloch, 2006

Let's interpret the author's thoughts in the space of network-based APIs. Two decades ago, Bloch noticed that an API is a customer-facing asset; today, we treat an API as a product that, if designed well, can be cost-effective. API design matters because once the API is in production, we have limited capabilities to change it, and maintaining a poorly designed API is a nightmare. An API is built from modules (endpoints, procedures, fields, etc.), and each module provides reusable functionality and is designed to last as long as the API exists.

Bloch's set of maxims ends with the following one, which states that design maxims or patterns are meant to be a guidance, not a rule:

> API design is an art, not a science. Strive for beauty, and trust your gut. Do not adhere slavishly to the above heuristics, but violate them only infrequently and with good reason.
>
> —Joshua J. Bloch, 2006

---

14 Joshua Bloch, "How to Design a Good API and Why It Matters" (*https://oreil.ly/RZxP3*), in *Companion to the 21st ACM SIGPLAN Symposium on Object-Oriented Programming Systems, Languages, and Applications* (2006): 506–507.

Here is a high-level selection of best practices for the design of network-based APIs:

Tailored to the audience

API is designed to match its client's needs. A client can be a web browser, mobile device, smartwatch, IoT device, AI agent, etc. Some API styles have more flexibility than others to adjust to the client's needs. For example, GraphQL allows clients to request data in their preferred format.

Intuitive

An intuitive API can be navigated even without documentation. A REST API with HATEOAS is an example of this, as a response contains links to related resources and admissible actions.

Maintainable

A maintainable API evolves without disrupting clients, either by making backward-compatible changes or by indicating breaking changes through versioning.

Documented

An API comes with documentation. The existence of documentation affects the usability and adoption of an API, and a lack of documentation can hinder its use.

Hard to misuse

The API follows the principle of least surprise, meaning that simple tasks should be straightforward, complex tasks achievable, and errors difficult to make. This principle helps create an API that delivers a predictable experience for developers by using standard design practices, error messages, and data validation.

Testable

API developers or users should have the means to test the API that they build or use. If API testing isn't possible due to its setup, an appropriate mock API should be used to substitute the real API.

Secure

API is a gateway to your system. The input needs to be validated to reduce the risk of exploiting API vulnerabilities. The output of the APIs shouldn't expose sensitive information. Libraries and external services that the API uses should be updated with the latest security patches. A secure API handles duplicate requests and can suppress an undesirable excess of incoming requests.

Efficient

An API attempts to minimize the utilization of the system resources. By allowing clients to customize responses, the API can reduce data transfers and optimize resource usage. This can be achieved through techniques like field filtering (e.g., sparse fieldsets in REST APIs) or query-oriented APIs such as GraphQL.

Communicates errors

An API communicates its state through standard error codes appropriate to the API style. For instance, REST APIs use HTTP status codes, while gRPC APIs use gRPC status codes. In addition to standard error codes, the API provides human-readable error messages that offer context and guidance for resolving issues. This combination of standard error codes and descriptive messages helps developers understand and address operational problems.

General Tips to Improve API Performance

Here are some tips to improve API performance:[15]

1. Compression— Choosing an appropriate data compression algorithm, such as gzip or Brotli, reduces the size of API responses, enabling faster data transfer over the network. Smaller payloads improve performance, especially under bandwidth-constrained conditions. However, compression increases CPU usage, so API designers need to balance computation and bandwidth costs.

2. Encoding— The encoding format impacts API performance. Binary formats, such as Protocol Buffers (*https://protobuf.dev*) and Avro (*https://avro.apache.org*), typically outperform text-based formats like JSON (*https://www.json.org*) and XML (*https://www.w3.org/XML*) in terms of size and processing speed. However, text-based formats may be preferable for debugging or human readability.

3. Caching—By putting a cache in front of your API, you will reduce the utilization of resources that the API relies on, such as databases or storage. Caching can be done on the client or server side. The side effect of caching is increased memory usage. If not synchronized with the source of data, cached data might be stale or lost. Furthermore, caching involves increased development and operational costs.

4. Hardware—Vertical scaling (scaling up), which consists of replacing or upgrading the hardware instance with another one that provides more CPU, memory, or storage resources, may improve system performance. However, this method may hide the underlying causes of the performance problems. Furthermore, hardware scaling has its limits; beyond that point, horizontal scaling (scaling out by adding more hardware) becomes necessary.

5. API rate limits—Limiting the number of API requests per client within the given time interval reduces abuse and protects backend resources.

---

15 For more performance tips, see "Evergreen Performance Best Practices" in *High Performance Browser Networking* (*https://oreil.ly/gUTTa*) by Ilya Grigorik (O'Reilly, 2013).

Summary

This chapter introduced you to common design patterns used in network-based APIs. The API design patterns described in this chapter focus on REST APIs, but they may also be applied to other API styles. The discussed patterns included API naming, versioning, filtering and pagination, handling long-running tasks, request deduplication and retry, throttling, caching, and deleting API resources. The explored API security patterns, such as encryption, authentication and authorization, and data validation, are also common across various API styles.

The chapter ended with a set of best practices for designing network-based APIs, including performance tips. However, the takeaway from this chapter is that while many design patterns exist for you as the API designer to choose from, they are meant to be a guidance, not a rule.

In Chapter 3 and Chapter 4, you'll explore the low-level functionalities of the Transmission Control Protocol (TCP) and HTTP protocols that underlie many APIs. Then, in Chapter 5, you'll apply some of the API design patterns when building an example REST API.

Network

In Chapter 1, we explored the common concepts of data exchange over computer networks, such as transmission modes and synchronicity. This chapter introduces you to network protocols. It explains why network protocols and their programmatic APIs are needed and how they are used. These concepts are demonstrated in practice by implementing a Transmission Control Protocol (TCP) ECHO server and clients. Throughout the chapter, you'll become familiar with software tools like `netcat`, `scapy`, `openssl`, `tcpdump`, and `tshark`, and use them to explore the basics of the TCP and Transport Layer Security (TLS) protocols. This will help you understand how various APIs discussed in this book communicate over the network.

Network Protocols

Have you wondered what happens on the network level when a browser opens a website? The goal of this chapter, and the following Chapter 4, is to examine some of the details of how this network communication is performed.

The purpose of networking is to enable communication by facilitating data exchange. Since today's computers are binary, networking is about getting the 0s and 1s from one side of the communication to another.

> The communication channel used to exchange binary data doesn't need to be binary itself. For example, a homing pigeon (*https:// oreil.ly/pw0G3*) can help transfer chunks of binary data.

As an example, let's take a copper cable used in computer networks. How do we identify the data being transmitted between the sender and receiver? First, how is the binary data represented? One approach is to use a low/high voltage to directly repre-sent a 0/1. Second, how do you identify where the message starts? To solve this prob-lem, a pattern of 0s and 1s is declared to identify the beginning of the message so that both the sender and receiver can synchronize.

These rules are somewhat arbitrary within their physical limitations. The practical challenge of networking is making the data flow while being subject to these rules. Establishing and codifying these rules ensures that both sides of the communication understand each other. This is the purpose of a network protocol.

> A *network protocol* defines a set of rules for communication between network devices.

Some network protocols are implemented in the operating system. This reduces the burden placed on the network users, who would otherwise need to understand and program the details of these protocols into their applications. The functions exposed by the operating system (system calls) also provide the advantage of a standardized API.[1] Generally, networking applications interact with the operating system, and the operating system interacts with hardware.[2]

Socket API

An example of a suite of network protocols implemented in the operating system is TCP/IP. TCP stands for Transmission Control Protocol, and IP for Internet Protocol. TCP/IP is called a suite of protocols, because it includes more protocols than the main two that compose its name. The adoption of TCP/IP was enforced by the US Advanced Research Projects Agency Network (ARPANET) on its systems in early 1983. ARPANET was the first wide-area packet-switched computer network. It con-nected the United States, the United Kingdom, and Norway.

The existence of multiple interoperable implementations of a given protocol is a required characteristic of an internet standard.[3] There were several versions and

---

1 The standardization may go even further, down to the ABI level, which deals with interfacing low-level, binary machine code between programs, as opposed to API, which deals with a high-level source code.

2 Note exceptions like network stack kernel-bypass, where applications talk directly to the network card (hard-ware). An example of this is Remote Direct Memory Access (RDMA), used for high-performance applica-tions, where two remote computers access each other's memory, reducing the latency and CPU usage.

3 "Internet standard...requires multiple interoperable implementations." By Scott Brander from "IETF New-comers Presentation: IETF Documents" (*https://oreil.ly/6tBJT*).

---

implementations of TCP/IP at that time. Work on implementing TCP/IP into the Berkeley Unix operating system was ongoing, funded by the Defense Advanced Research Projects Agency (DARPA). The implementation was officially released in mid-1983, and its interface is known today as the socket API (*https://oreil.ly/E31mf*).

The *socket API*, a set of operating system calls,[4] is the main mechanism for applications to interact with the operating system network stack. The application invokes the socket API, which provides operations such as opening network connections, sending and receiving messages, and closing connections.

> The *client* is defined as the side that initiates the connection, and the *server* is the side that is awaiting connections from a client.

Let's discuss a typical example of TCP socket API usage.[5] Figure 3-1 shows a client making a single request to the server, receiving a response, and then closing the connection. The solid arrows denote the order of the socket API system calls. Note the loop between `send` and `recv` system calls. It indicates that both the client and the server could exchange multiple messages. Notice also that the server, after calling `close`, can perform an `accept` call and wait for new clients' connections. The vertical dotted lines are included in the diagram to relate the system calls to the exchanged messages.

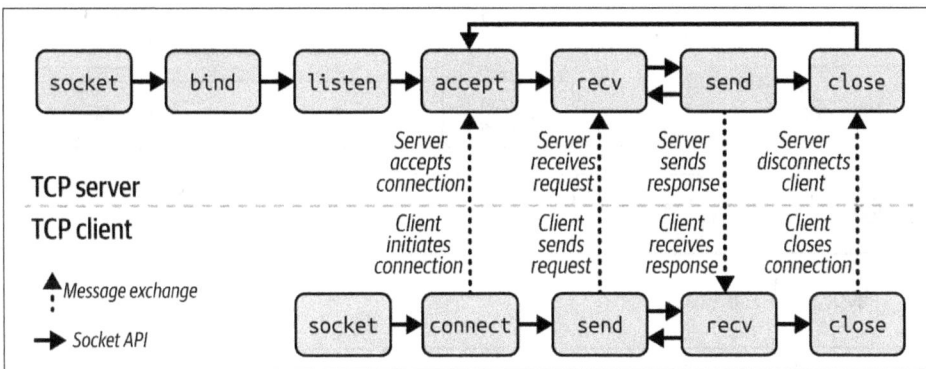

Figure 3-1. Sequence of client and server TCP socket API system calls

---

4 Commonly referred to as *system calls*—including in this book—these are actually user-space wrapper functions that invoke the underlying kernel system calls.

5 See Douglas E. Comer and David L. Stevens, *Internetworking with TCP/IP*, Vol. III: *Client-Server Programming and Applications, Linux/Posix Sockets Version* (Prentice Hall, 2000). This book provides an introduction to Linux network programming in C.

TCP/IP and the OSI Model

Today, TCP/IP is responsible for handling the majority of internet traffic. TCP/IP is usually discussed in relation to the OSI model (see Figure 3-2). The OSI model was published in 1984 (as the ISO/IEC 7498 standard) and is commonly used when teaching networking concepts. The OSI model introduced a strictly layered approach that continues to shape the way we categorize networking devices. For instance, under the OSI model, a network switch operates at layer 2 (*Data link*), while a router functions at layer 3 (*Network*). Nowadays, the OSI model has mostly a conceptual value.[6]

> Layers provide specialized names for some of their protocol data units: Ethernet *frame*, IP *packet*, TCP *segment*, UDP *datagram*, and *message* or *data* for higher layers or generic protocols. The purpose of these names was to clarify which layer is being discussed.

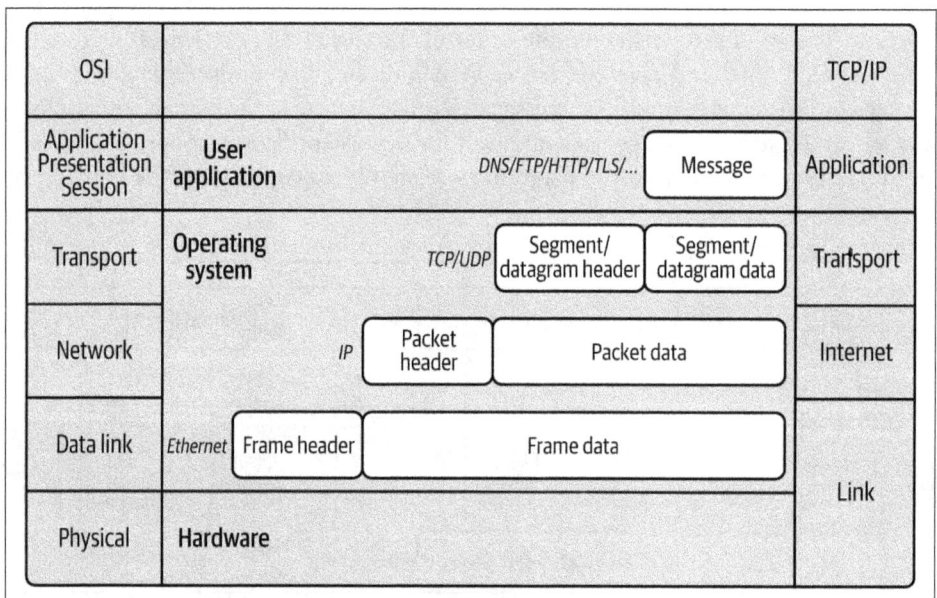

OSI				TCP/IP
Application Presentation Session	**User application**	DNS/FTP/HTTP/TLS/...	Message	Application
Transport	**Operating system**	TCP/UDP	Segment/ datagram header Segment/ datagram data	Transport
Network		IP	Packet header Packet data	Internet
Data link	Ethernet Frame header		Frame data	Link
Physical	**Hardware**			

Figure 3-2. Overview of the OSI and TCP/IP (RFC 1122) models

---

6 See "OSI: The Internet That Wasn't" (*https://oreil.ly/S4h32*) by Andrew L. Russell and Vint Cerf's "Keynote: The Evolution of the Interplanetary Internet" (*https://oreil.ly/GnJTh*), in which he says, "OSI doesn't exist, OSI is the fantasy."

A description of the OSI model layers present in Figure 3-2 is given next. It's difficult to grasp this level of abstraction without playing with some protocols in practice, so the list is included here only as an overview:

1. *Physical*—Transmits signals over physical media and defines related specifications like connector types, current voltages, or radio frequencies.

2. *Data link*—Provides device addressing on a local network and performs error detection.

3. *Network*—Assigns configurable addresses to devices and routes data among different networks.

4. *Transport*—Provides additional transmission mechanisms to maintain data order, perform retransmissions in case of errors, or react to network congestion.

5. 6. 7. *Session/Presentation/Application*—These are three different layers within the OSI model, present in the TCP/IP model as a single *Application* layer. Their purpose is to support application functionalities, like encryption (on the *Presentation* layer), or web data exchange protocols like HTTP (on the *Application* layer).

The layered approach to network protocols can be compared to Matryoshka dolls (*https://oreil.ly/pLQlA*), which are a set of wooden dolls, with each smaller doll nesting within the larger one.

Let's take IP packet data as an example. It includes the header of its immediate higher protocol (such as a TCP segment header), as well as the data of the higher protocol beyond that (TCP segment data). In other words, a higher-layer protocol's header and data (TCP in this case) are embedded inside the data of a lower-layer protocol (IP). Additionally, the header of the lower layer (IP) contains a field that identifies the higher-level protocol. This allows the operating system (or application, in the case of user-space networking) to invoke the appropriate procedures to handle the next-higher layer.

> The details of protocol specifications, including the structure of the headers, are beyond the scope of this book. Modern tools like tshark can identify and present the layers without the user having to read through binary data. If you are interested in such details, consult other resources.[7]

Continuing with the Matryoshka analogy, a physical signal arriving at a network card can be thought of as the biggest doll. Just like disassembling the doll by removing its

---

7 See Douglas E. Comer, *Internetworking with TCP/IP*, Vol. I (Pearson, 2013). This book provides an introduction to network protocols from a system/network administrator perspective, including header specifications.

outer layers, the operating system or software *decapsulates* the data by peeling off the header, and passes the remaining data for handling to the next (higher) protocol layer. The top application layer message (data) is like the smallest doll. When an application sends a message, the process follows the reverse path. The data is *encapsulated* by adding the header, and then passed down to the next (lower) protocol layer, with data becoming bigger and bigger. This process continues until the physical layer (the biggest doll) is reached, and the signal is sent out through the network card.

Despite its conceptual appeal, the strict layering of the OSI model turned out to be double-edged,[8] and criticized in "Layering Considered Harmful" (*https://oreil.ly/ 17VY3*) for preventing cross-layer optimizations. Therefore, the separation between layers is sometimes not strictly followed, and certain protocols combine the functionalities traditionally associated with different OSI layers. For example, Internet Protocol Security (IPsec) (*https://oreil.ly/ey730*) adds encryption, which is traditionally associated with the OSI *Presentation* layer, to the IP protocol associated with the *Network* layer. Similarly, QUIC (*https://oreil.ly/9FLk3*) combines encryption with the *Transport* layer UDP (User Datagram Protocol).

Before we demonstrate the socket API in a hands-on lab environment, you may find it helpful to review the basics of TCP/IP. If you enjoy instructional videos, consult the suggested resource.[9] Here, instead of a low-level analysis of the bits that compose network packets, as is usually done in network administration books, a high-level functioning of TCP/IP is illustrated using an office analogy.[10]

An Office Analogy for TCP/IP

Imagine you (a client) work for a company that has an open-plan office on every floor. You are a happy part of a local network of colleagues on your floor, where you are identified by the IP address 1.1.1.1 on the *Network* layer. Your desk is identified by the clientMAC address, which corresponds to the Ethernet Media Access Control (MAC) address on the *Data link* layer.

Now, you want to communicate with a colleague (a server), identified by the IP address 2.2.2.2. Your colleague works on another floor, which represents a remote network. You'll search the company's online directory to find your colleague's floor. The process of finding a path to a remote network is called *routing*. In this case, a

---

8 "Layering wasn't a strategy to modularize the implementation, it was the strategy to modularize the design committees." By David Clark from "The Network and the OS" (*https://oreil.ly/QcMNu*).

9 See Ben Eater's "Networking Tutorial" (*https://oreil.ly/Z1NUV*). This series of videos covers the basic concepts of networking in two hours.

10 For an alternative example that uses a letter sent by airmail, have a glance at pages 114 to 115 of Charles Kozierok's *TCP/IP Guide* (No Starch Press, 2005).

---

single elevator (the router itself), with a routerMAC address on the *Data link* layer, will take you to the floor. Note that if your colleague works on your floor, you'd go straight to the desk, since you know who sits where.

After reaching the right floor, you interrupt people's work by loudly announcing, "Who has 2:2:2:2?" while looking for your colleague's desk location. This is called *broadcasting*, and in this context, it's used by the Ethernet ARP (Address Resolution Protocol) on the *Data link* layer. For the analogy to more closely match the network protocols, the elevator routerMAC should broadcast this question, and your server colleague's desk serverMAC should respond, but offices aren't that automated yet.

Broadcasting may seem disruptive, but open spaces are designed to allow for this type of communication. Your colleague will respond, and you'll start by shaking hands, introducing yourself, and confirming you met to talk— this is the *three-way hand-shake* of the TCP protocol on the *Transport* layer.

Then you say "Hello" and immediately disappear back to your office. Your colleague will now perform the reverse procedure to reach you in your office and respond with "Hello" to you. Then you proceed to end the conversation. What a strange encounter! What has just happened is an example of a *TCP ECHO service*, routed between two networks. This example is further analyzed and implemented in the chapter.

In this analogy, you may also wonder which protocol uses the names of your client and your colleague's server (as opposed to their IP addresses). This is the DNS (Domain Name System) protocol, which provides a mapping from a name to the IP address. This protocol is needed because people are better at remembering names than sequences of numbers.

Implementing TCP ECHO Service

In this section, you'll implement the TCP ECHO service, using the Python Socket API (*https://oreil.ly/YbOzp*) module for the server, and using three approaches for the client: an existing command-line tool (which requires no code implementation from your side), a low-level implementation in Python, and a high-level implementation using the Python Socket API. The reason for using these three client implementations is to focus on the TCP ECHO service usage, the TCP protocol itself, and the features of the socket API, respectively.

> The TCP ECHO service consists of a server that waits for an incoming connection from a client, reads data from the connection, and writes the data back over the connection until the client terminates it.

Network Lab Setup

To set up the lab, you'll need to run shell scripts in a terminal. From the root of the book's code repository (see Figure P-2), run the scripts as shown in Example 3-1.

Example 3-1. Network lab setup

```
cd src/network ❶
bash scripts/setup_containers.sh  ❷
bash scripts/setup_network.sh  ❸
```

❶ Navigate to the *src/network* directory. All commands in this chapter are to be issued from this directory.

❷ Create three containers: client, router, and server.

❸ Set up the necessary networks and routing between the client and server containers through the router, as illustrated in Figure 3-3.[11]

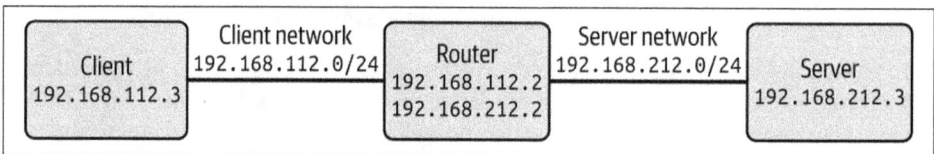

Figure 3-3. Network topology of the lab

At this point, it's helpful to look more closely at routing (briefly mentioned in the open-plan office analogy). Routing is needed to pass network packets across networks. The original Ethernet network protocol was designed to connect peer devices on the same wire, and didn't include connecting multiple networks or preventing loops caused by incorrectly connected cables.[12] Routing requires devices in a network to store a table of directions on how to reach other networks. When a device sends network traffic, it either sends it to its local (e.g., Ethernet) network or, if the traffic is destined to a remote network, sends it to the most specific route that matches the destination IP address of the traffic.

In our example, the routing table on the client will look like Example 3-2. Execute this command in the terminal used to set up the lab.

---

11 The chosen network ranges in this lab aim to avoid conflicts with your 192.168.X.0/24 home network.

12 For a historical perspective on Ethernet, see, for example, Radia Perlman's keynote address "Network Protocol: Myths, Missteps, and Mysteries" (*https://oreil.ly/vSBLW*) from the 2023 SharkFest Wireshark Developer and User Conference; or Bob Metcalfe's Turing Lecture at the 2023 Association for Computing Machinery (ACM) Web Conference (*https://oreil.ly/hesYZ*).

Example 3-2. Client routing table (requires setup from Example 3-1)

```
docker compose exec client bash -c "ip route" ❶

default via 192.168.112.1 dev eth0              ❷
192.168.212.0/24 via 192.168.112.2 dev eth0     ❸
192.168.112.0/24 dev eth0 proto kernel scope link src 192.168.112.3 ❹
```

❶ The `ip route` command displays the routes available on the client container.

❷ This output line indicates that the default route is taken via the gateway with the IP address `192.168.112.1`, through the eth0 network interface. The default route is taken if no other route in the routing table matches the destination IP address of the packet. A network interface is a software representation of a network card, managed by the operating system. The terms *gateway* and *router* are often used interchangeably; however, *gateway* is a more general term, as opposed to *router*; the latter operates on the OSI network layer. Note that this route and the gateway are automatically configured by Docker.

❸ This line shows that the network packets destined for the `192.168.212.0/24` remote network (server network) are sent via the router with IP address `192.168.112.2`, through the client's eth0 network interface. This route and the router are created explicitly during the lab setup.

❹ This line represents a route for the local `192.168.112.0/24` network. The locality is indicated by the *scope link*, which refers to the OSI link layer, reachable directly on the eth0 interface. There is no via gateway specified, and the `src` is the client IP address. This line indicates that packets destined for the local network can be delivered directly and don't require routing through an intermediary. This routing line is configured by Docker.

For routing to be possible, the router must be able to reach (to have a leg in) each network through which it's routing. Therefore, the router has an IP address in both the client and the server network, and these addresses are `192.168.112.2` for the client and `192.168.212.2` for the server. Additionally, the server needs a routing table analogous to the one present on the client. You can explore it using the `ip route` command.

Example 3-3. Server routing table (requires setup from Example 3-1)

```
docker compose exec server bash -c "ip route"

default via 192.168.212.1 dev eth0
192.168.112.0/24 via 192.168.212.2 dev eth0
192.168.212.0/24 dev eth0 proto kernel scope link src 192.168.212.3
```

TCP ECHO Service

This section explains the protocol-level details of the messages exchanged during the TCP ECHO client-server communication. In Example 3-4, the packet capture of the TCP ECHO service connection is read by tshark (*https://www.wireshark.org*), a command-line network protocol analyzer. The currently uninteresting information is trimmed away from the output.

Example 3-4. TCP ECHO client packet capture read with tshark *(requires setup from Example 3-1)*

```
CLIENT=netcat
docker compose exec client bash -c \
      "tshark --read-file tests/tcp_echo_client_${CLIENT}_reference.pcap | \
      bash scripts/trim_client_pcap.sh"
```

The output displays the sequence of Ethernet frames, as in Example 3-5. The sequence is annotated with explanations of the message exchanges at the TCP protocol level, including the TCP three-way handshake (lines 3 to 5), the exchange of the "Hello" messages (lines 6 to 9), and the TCP connection termination (lines 10 to 12).

> The explanations of Example 3-5 are long, and detailed enough to give you the material to support your further studies of TCP.
>
> To be better prepared for the discussion that follows, consider watching one of the following videos: 10-minute "TCP Connection Walkthrough" by Ben Eater (*https://oreil.ly/g9ukF*), "How TCP Works—The Handshake" by Chris Greer (*https://oreil.ly/vEXrV*), or an over-two-hour, two-part, live demonstration of TCP Fundamentals by Chris Greer (*https://oreil.ly/Cv5gn*).

Example 3-5. TCP ECHO client packet sequence

```
clientMAC → Broadcast ARP Who has router? Tell client                            ❶
routerMAC → clientMAC ARP router is at routerMAC                                 ❷
client → server    TCP [SYN]      Seq=0=c0                          Len=0 ❸
server → client    TCP [SYN, ACK] Seq=0=s0         Ack=1=c0+1       Len=0 ❹
client → server    TCP [ACK]      Seq=1=c0+1       Ack=1=s0+1       Len=0 ❺
client → server    TCP [PSH, ACK] Seq=1=c0+1       Ack=1=s0+1       Len=5 ❻
server → client    TCP [ACK]      Seq=1=s0+1       Ack=6=c0+1+5     Len=0 ❼
server → client    TCP [PSH, ACK] Seq=1=s0+1       Ack=6=c0+1+5     Len=5 ❽
client → server    TCP [ACK]      Seq=6=c0+1+5     Ack=6=s0+1+5     Len=0 ❾
client → server    TCP [FIN, ACK] Seq=6=c0+1+5     Ack=6=s0+1+5     Len=0 ❿
server → client    TCP [FIN, ACK] Seq=6=s0+1+5     Ack=7=c0+1+5+1 Len=0 ⓫
client → server    TCP [ACK]      Seq=7=c0+1+5+1 Ack=7=s0+1+5+1 Len=0 ⓬
```

❶ The client consults the routing table to obtain the router's IP address. It then broadcasts an Ethernet ARP request to discover the router's MAC address (routerMAC). The purpose of ARP is to provide a mapping from the IP address to the MAC address on the local network.

❷ The routerMAC responds to the client over Ethernet, confirming that the router's IP address corresponds to the routerMAC MAC address.

❸ The TCP three-way handshake starts. The client initiates a TCP connection by sending a segment with zero payload size (Len=0), and the SYN flag set, marking the segment with its own sequence number (Seq=0). Both the client's initial sequence number (c0) and the server's initial sequence number (s0) are generated according to an algorithm and are usually nonzero. However, for the purpose of human readability, each is taken by tshark as the relative zero reference (Seq=0) for the client and server.

❹ The server responds to the client with a segment of zero payload size, setting its own sequence number (Seq=s0), and acknowledging receipt of the client's phantom byte (*https://oreil.ly/7tAbl*) (also called *ghost byte*) by adding 1 byte to the client's sequence number (Ack=c0+1). As mentioned prior, tshark will present this as Ack=1 (instead of Ack=c0+1, which may be a large number). This acknowledgment may seem unexpected, as the payload length is zero, but 1 byte is acknowledged. This is because segments with SYN or FIN flags set are counted as having an additional 1-byte length, known as a *phantom byte*. The sent segment has both SYN and ACK flags set.

❺ The client advances its sequence number by 1 byte (Seq=c0+1) due to having sent a phantom byte, and acknowledges receipt of the server's phantom byte by adding 1 byte to the server's initial sequence number (Ack=s0+1). The client sends this segment with the ACK flag set. At this point, the TCP three-way handshake is complete, and the client is ready to send messages.

❻ The client sends the 5-byte message "Hello" (Len=5) to the server. The PSH flag is set, indicating that the TCP stack on the server should immediately deliver the segment to the application without buffering.

❼ The server acknowledges receipt of the 5-byte segment from the client (Ack=c0+1+5).

❽ The server echoes to the client the same 5-byte "Hello" message of Len=5.

⑨ The client advances its sequence number by the length (5) of the "Hello" message it sent (Seq=c0+1+5) and sends an ACK segment.

⑩ The client sends a FIN segment to indicate its desire to terminate the connection. This is when the client has no more messages to send.

⑪ The server advances its sequence number by the length of the "Hello" message it echoed to the client, acknowledges receipt of 7 bytes in total (Ack=c0+1+5+1) from the client (including two phantom bytes), and confirms the end of the connection by setting the FIN flag.

⑫ The client advances its acknowledgment number by the phantom byte received from the server, and confirms the connection termination with the ACK flag.

TCP Connection Versus TCP Stream

A *TCP stream* is a sequence of *TCP segments* transmitted over a *TCP connection*. Segments are composed of *bytes*, which are units of data consisting of 8 bits each.

Sometimes, instead of *TCP connection*, the term *TCP session* is used, but it's absent from the TCP RFCs. *Session* is a term that appears in higher layer protocols.

The TCP stream described in Example 3-5 exercises only a fraction of the TCP state machine (*https://oreil.ly/ZIDus*). Our example is limited to the TCP three-way handshake, followed by the client sending a "Hello" message to the server, the server responding with the same message to the client, and the client initiating the TCP connection termination. For simplicity, intentionally, there are no network errors happening during the connection; it can be considered a TCP "happy path."

The full TCP is capable of dealing with various network errors, like lost, duplicated, or delivered out-of-order packets. TCP handles retransmissions, adjusts the amount of data sent using flow control, and detects and minimizes network congestion. TCP requires a connection to be established and maintained at two communicating ends: client and server.

> *User Datagram Protocol* (*UDP*) is a connectionless network transport protocol, as opposed to TCP (which is connection-oriented). Both protocols are part of the TCP/IP suite. UDP is simpler than TCP, and it doesn't perform the initial connection handshake, nor does it provide the reliability features of TCP, like retransmissions, guaranteed delivery order, or network congestion control. This allows UDP to transfer data faster, and has applications in gaming or media streaming, which can tolerate occasional data loss.

TCP ECHO Server

In Example 3-5, we exchanged a "Hello" message between the client and the server. Example 3-6 shows the full Python code for the TCP ECHO server that produces our example TCP connection. The code uses the TCP server socket API system calls illustrated in Figure 3-1: socket, bind, listen, accept, recv, send, and close.

Note that it's not a complete or robust implementation of a TCP server. In particular, it doesn't support simultaneous client connections, or cover terminating the connection when the client or server crashes or shuts down.[13]

Example 3-6. TCP ECHO server

```
# src/network/src/tcp_echo/server.py

import socket


BUFSIZE_BYTES = 8   ❶
CLOSE_WAIT = 8   ❶

with socket.socket(socket.AF_INET, socket.SOCK_STREAM) as server_socket:   ❷
    server_socket.bind(("", 8080))   ❸
    server_socket.listen()   ❹
    while True:   ❺
        print("Waiting for a new connection from client ...")
        conn_socket, client_address = server_socket.accept()   ❻
        while True:   ❼
            data = conn_socket.recv(BUFSIZE_BYTES)   ❽
            if data:
                data_decoded = data.decode()   ❾
                print(f"Received {data_decoded} from client {client_address}")
                conn_socket.send(data)   ❿
                print(f"Sent {data_decoded} to client {client_address}")
            conn_state = conn_socket.getsockopt(socket.SOL_TCP, socket.TCP_INFO)
            if conn_state == CLOSE_WAIT:   ⓫
                print(f"Client {client_address} closed connection")
                conn_socket.close()
                break
```

❶ This block defines parameters used by the socket API.

❷ The program creates a server's TCP socket for the IP version 4 (AF_INET). The server_socket is created using the with context manager. The purpose of the

---

13 See W. Richard Stevens, *Unix Network Programming. The Sockets Networking API*, Vol. I (Pearson Education, 2004).

context manager is to close the socket when the code within the with block is finished, even if errors occur.

❸ The bind() method (system call) binds the server socket to any network interface on the server host and 8080 port.

❹ The server starts listening on the socket for a new client connection.

❺ The infinite outer loop is used to await a new client connection.

❻ When a client connection appears, it is accepted by the accept() method (system call). This method creates and returns the server connection socket for the connected client, along with the connected client tuple (IP address, port).

❼ This infinite inner loop waits for the client to either send data or close the connection.

❽ The server's connection socket receives data (encoded as bytes) from the client. The buffer is of BUFSIZE_BYTES size, and this size must be a power of two.

❾ The decode() method converts the data from bytes to a string, in order for the data to be printed.

❿ The server sends the encoded data back to the client, on the existing connection socket.

⓫ This condition monitors the state of the TCP connection established with the client. If the connection is in CLOSE_WAIT state, the connection socket is closed, and the server's TCP socket returns to waiting for a new client connection.

TCP ECHO Client with Netcat

This section uses a high-level netcat command-line client to demonstrate the TCP ECHO service usage. Netcat (*https://nc110.sourceforge.io*) is a Unix command-line utility for exchanging data using TCP or UDP. The tool eliminates the need to write any client network code, helping you to focus on the data flow instead. In the following exercise, you'll use netcat as a client to send a "Hello" message to the server.

Figure 3-4 shows a screenshot of the sequence of commands for this exercise.

```
$ docker compose exec server bash -c "sudo python src/tcp_echo/server.py"
Waiting for a new connection from client ...
Received Hello from client ('192.168.112.3', 8080)
Sent Hello to client ('192.168.112.3', 8080)
Client ('192.168.112.3', 8080) closed connection
Waiting for a new connection from client ...


$ CLIENT=netcat
$ PCAP_FILE=/tmp/tcp_echo_client_${CLIENT}.pcap
$ docker compose exec client bash -c \
>         "sudo rm -f ${PCAP_FILE} && \
>         sudo tcpdump -c 12 -w ${PCAP_FILE} 'not icmp and not icmp6' && \
>         cp ${PCAP_FILE} tests"
tcpdump: listening on eth0, link-type EN10MB (Ethernet), snapshot length 262144 bytes
12 packets captured
12 packets received by filter
0 packets dropped by kernel
$


$ docker compose exec client bash -c "sudo ip neigh flush all"
$ docker compose exec client bash -c \
>         "(echo -n Hello | netcat -p 8080 -i 1 -q 1 server 8080) && echo"
Hello
$
```

Figure 3-4. TCP ECHO service usage with netcat *(requires setup from Example 3-1)*

If you're working hands-on, perform the steps shown in Example 3-7. You'll need a three-pane window. Consider using tmux for this purpose. See Example P-2 for an introduction to tmux.

Example 3-7. TCP ECHO service usage with netcat *(requires setup from Example 3-1)*

```
# In a terminal run ❶
tmux new-session \; split-window -v \; split-window -v \;

# In the top pane run ❷
docker compose exec server bash -c "sudo python src/tcp_echo/server.py"

# In the middle pane run ❸
CLIENT=netcat
PCAP_FILE=/tmp/tcp_echo_client_${CLIENT}.pcap
docker compose exec client bash -c \
      "sudo rm --force ${PCAP_FILE} && \
      sudo tcpdump -c 12 -w ${PCAP_FILE} 'not icmp and not icmp6' && \
      cp ${PCAP_FILE} tests"

# In the bottom pane run ❹
docker compose exec client bash -c "sudo ip neigh flush all"
docker compose exec client bash -c \
      "(echo -n Hello | netcat -p 8080 -i 1 -q 1 server 8080) && echo"
```

❶ Create three panes with tmux.

❷ Start the TCP ECHO server.

❸ Start tcpdump to capture packets. For now, tcpdump will be waiting, but after the TCP ECHO service message exchange is complete, the tcpdump program will exit, capturing the expected number of 12 packets. It will save the *tcp_echo_client_netcat.pcap* file into the *tests* directory. You'll also find there all reference *.pcap* files from this chapter, available as **_reference.pcap*.

❹ Before invoking the client, in the third pane, clear the ARP cache on the client. The ARP cache stores the IP address to MAC address mappings, and it needs to be cleared here so it can be demonstrated that the client performs an ARP request, instead of using the cache. Then invoke the TCP ECHO client by using netcat. The client is expected to print the "Hello" message received back from the server and then exit.

> If you receive OSError: [Errno 98] Address already in use when starting the server, wait a couple of minutes for TCP to automatically remove leftover connections from your previous attempts. If the number of captured packets differs from the expected number, make sure no old TCP socket connections are present on the server. Old TCP socket connections can be listed with the ss (socket statistics) command:
>
> ```
> docker compose exec server ss --all --numeric --tcp
> ```
>
> If the command prints any socket connections in the state TIME-WAIT, then again, wait a couple of minutes, and they'll clean up themselves. In the case of other problems—for example, if additional ARP requests or TCP Previous segment not captured appear in the packet capture—performing the steps given in "Network Lab Teardown" on page 102, followed by Example 3-1, may be necessary to restore the lab setup to its original state. If you are on Linux, you may also need to stop the *avahi* service (e.g., **sudo systemctl stop avahi-daemon** on Debian/Ubuntu) to prevent its traffic from appearing in the packet capture.

After both the client and tcpdump exit, you can stop the server by pressing Ctrl+C. The captured packet sequence is expected to match the one in Example 3-5.

TCP ECHO Client with Scapy

"TCP ECHO Client with Netcat" on page 90 demonstrated how to send messages using `netcat` as a TCP client, and explained how data is exchanged between the client and the server using TCP. This section discusses a low-level implementation of a TCP ECHO service client in Python, to reveal more details about TCP itself.

Scapy (*https://scapy.net*) is a Python library for manipulating network packets. It operates on layers, such as IP, TCP, and more, which are exposed as Python classes. Using these layers, a TCP connection can be managed on a lower level than using a client like `netcat`, or even a client that uses the socket API, but still without going too deep into the byte-level structure of the protocols. With this tool, you can explicitly calculate TCP sequence and acknowledgment numbers, add phantom bytes, or set TCP flags. This can help to better understand the TCP state machine.

In Example 3-8, let's focus only on the TCP three-way handshake, as it demonstrates the main capabilities of `scapy` when working with TCP.

Example 3-8. TCP ECHO client with scapy

```
# src/network/src/tcp_echo/client_scapy.py

from scapy.all import IP, RandInt, TCP, send, sr

F = {  ❶
    "ACK": "A",
    "FIN-ACK": "FA",
    "PSH-ACK": "PA",
    "SYN": "S",
    "SYN-ACK": "SA",
}

ip = IP(src="client", dst="server")  ❷

sport = dport = 8080  ❸
c0 = int(RandInt())  ❹

tcp = TCP(sport=sport, dport=dport, flags=F["SYN"], seq=c0)  ❺
packet = ip / tcp  ❻
ans, unans = sr(packet, verbose=0)  ❼

s0 = ans[0][1][TCP].fields["seq"]  ❽

tcp = TCP(sport=sport, dport=dport, flags=F["ACK"], seq=c0 + 1, ack=s0 + 1)  ❾
packet = ip / tcp
send(packet, verbose=0)  ❿
```

❶ This dictionary holds verbose names of TCP flags as keys, to make them more understandable compared to their corresponding short names used by scapy.

❷ scapy's IP layer defines the source (client) and the destination (server) addresses. Note that the client and the server names are internally resolved to their IP addresses.

❸ The client's (sport) and the server's (dport) TCP port numbers are defined. Both the client and the server use the same port number, each on its own machine.

❹ The TCP initial sequence number for the client (c0) is set to a random integer value. The value of c0 is set, so that it can be used for manual calculations of the client's sequence numbers. Note, however, that a secure selection of the initial sequence number is more complex.[14]

❺ scapy's TCP layer defines the SYN TCP segment to be sent by the client to the server.

❻ This line defines the IP packet, composed of IP and TCP layers. The / operator in scapy denotes a composition between two layers.

❼ The TCP three-way handshake starts. scapy's sr() function is used to send and receive packets. The function returns a couple (a tuple composed of two elements) of two lists. The first element, ans, is a list of couples (packet sent, response), and the second element, unans, is a list of packets for which no response was received. Verbose printing of the packet-exchange progress is disabled by setting verbose=0.

❽ This line extracts the server's initial sequence number (s0) from the server response. Our code controls the client's initial sequence number (c0), but the server controls its own.

❾ This line defines the TCP layer for the ACK TCP segment, to be sent by the client to the server.

❿ The TCP three-way handshake finishes with the client sending the ACK segment to the server.

---

14 See RFC 1948, "Defending Against Sequence Number Attacks" (*https://oreil.ly/Exp1y*).

To try the code in practice, proceed analogously with the `netcat` client, as outlined in "TCP ECHO Client with Netcat" on page 90. The commands in Example 3-9 are similar to the preceding `netcat` example, except for the `CLIENT=scapy` environment variable (which is used to save the *.pcap* file with the desired name) and the use of the *client_scapy.py* script, instead of `netcat` as the TCP client.

Example 3-9. TCP ECHO service usage with scapy (requires setup from Example 3-1)

```
# In a terminal run
tmux new-session \; split-window -v \; split-window -v \;

# In the top pane run
docker compose exec server bash -c "sudo python src/tcp_echo/server.py"

# In the middle pane run
CLIENT=scapy
PCAP_FILE=/tmp/tcp_echo_client_${CLIENT}.pcap
docker compose exec client bash -c \
    "sudo rm --force ${PCAP_FILE} && \
    sudo tcpdump -c 12 -w ${PCAP_FILE} 'not icmp and not icmp6' && \
    cp ${PCAP_FILE} tests"

# In the bottom pane run
docker compose exec client bash -c "sudo ip neigh flush all"
docker compose exec client bash -c \
    "sudo python src/tcp_echo/client_scapy.py && echo"
```

The `scapy` client is expected to produce the same sequence of packets as `netcat`, shown in Example 3-5.

Security

Security considerations of network protocols date back to their early days, despite these protocols initially evolving within trusted communities of researcher institutions. For instance, TCP connections were discovered in the 1980s to be prone to hijacking attacks, due to initial sequence number guessing, and defense methods against them were proposed in "Defending Against Sequence Number Attacks" (RFC 1948) (*https://oreil.ly/ObzPA*).

Encryption is a common way to enhance the security of network communication today. However, standardized encryption wasn't feasible at the time, due to the so-called Crypto Wars (*https://oreil.ly/ltIKL*) (not to be confused with the more recent cryptocurrency wars), where the United States and its allies limited the public's and other nations' access to cryptography. Restrictions on foreign access to encryption technology were lifted in the 1990s, leading to the development of web encryption protocols such as SSL/TLS (Secure Sockets Layer/Transport Layer Security).

As you can see in Figure 3-5, TLS uses three domains of cryptography: *asymmetric ciphers*, *symmetric ciphers*, and *hash functions*. Cryptography is a branch of *cryptology*, the field of science that explores methods of secure communication. Cryptology comprises *cryptography*, which deals with securing the communication, and *cryptanalysis*, which attempts to break the security.[15] Cryptography aims to achieve its security goals, including confidentiality, integrity, authenticity, and nonrepudiation, using cryptographic primitives.[16]

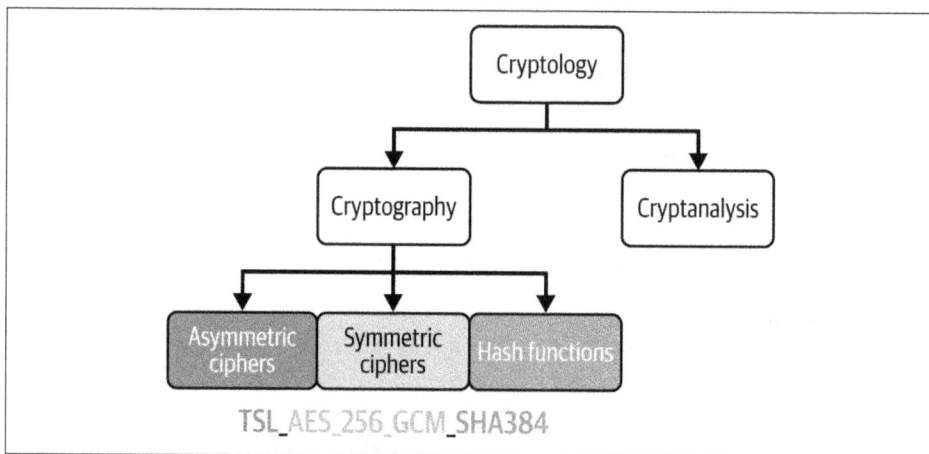

Figure 3-5. Cryptography domains used by a TLS version 1.3 cipher suite

Before discussing TLS, you have the opportunity to review the basics of cryptography and refresh your familiarity with the TLS certificates. The introductory, hands-on text is located in the book's code repository, in *src/network/README.md*. If you are already familiar with cryptography and X.509 public key infrastructure certificates, or prefer to start with the discussion of TLS, proceed to the next section.

TCP ECHO Client with OpenSSL

Using an X.509 certificate chain required to authenticate the server, the TCP ECHO service can be secured with TLS. Most operating systems don't implement TLS in the kernel space by default. Instead, the implementation is provided by third-party

---

15 For a theoretical, mathematically oriented introduction to cryptography, consult *Understanding Cryptography* by Christof Paar et al. (Springer, 2024) and the associated set of freely available lectures by Paar (*https:// oreil.ly/sQM71*). For a programmer's perspective on cryptography, including implementations of the main algorithms, see the freely available set of courses by Cyrill Gössi on YouTube (*https://oreil.ly/8uC11*), or *Practical Cryptography in Python* by Seth James Nielson and Christopher K. Monson (Apress, 2019).

16 See the "Cryptography with Python 2: Cryptography and Its Classic Security Goals" lecture by Cyrill Gössi (*https://oreil.ly/3SOYZ*).

libraries in the user space. It's feasible to implement the TCP ECHO client over TLS using Python's standard SSL library API (*https://oreil.ly/nbFNU*). However, in this section, to reduce the amount of code, you'll use the `openssl` command-line tool as the ECHO service client secured with TLS. The resulting packet capture in Example 3-12 is explained to highlight the protocol-level features of TLS.

X.509 Public-Key Infrastructure Certificates

The *X.509 standard* attempts to reduce the likelihood of MITM attacks by introducing certificates. An X.509 certificate binds the public key to additional identity information, such as a server name, and signs this information using a digital signature algorithm.

Since certificates make use of digital signature algorithms, which are based on public-key cryptography, the certificates themselves are susceptible to MITM attacks. As a consequence, X.509 certificates (also called *SSL* or *TLS* certificates) don't rely exclusively on technology to prevent MITM attacks, but also require an external source of trust. Certificate authorities (CAs), which are real-world institutions operated by people, are used as trust anchors. This trust is developed and maintained using certificates. However, the initial trust in the CA is established through a separate communication channel, such as the distribution of trusted certificates by operating system vendors.

To follow along, proceed as in Example 3-10, after ensuring that the lab environment is set up as described in Example 3-1.

Example 3-10. TCP ECHO service secured with TLS (requires setup from Example 3-1)

```
# In a terminal run ❶
tmux new-session \; split-window -v \; split-window -v \;

# In the top pane run ❷
docker compose exec server bash -c "sudo python src/tcp_echo/server.py"

# In the middle pane run ❸
CLIENT=openssl
PCAP_FILE=/tmp/tcp_echo_client_${CLIENT}.pcap
docker compose exec client bash -c \
      "sudo rm --force ${PCAP_FILE} && \
      sudo tcpdump -c 18 -w ${PCAP_FILE} 'port 443' && \
      cp ${PCAP_FILE} tests"

# In the bottom pane run ❹
docker compose exec client bash -c \
      'export SSLKEYLOGFILE=tests/SSLKEYLOGFILE.client && \
      (echo -n Hello && sleep 1 && echo -n) | \
```

```
            openssl s_client -brief -connect server:443 \
            -CAfile ca.crt -verify_return_error \
            -keylogfile ${SSLKEYLOGFILE} -servername server -tls1_3'
```

❶ Create three panes with `tmux`.

❷ Start the server. The difference here is that, in addition to the server, the `stunnel` program (not shown explicitly here) was started in the background. It is listening on port 443, and acting as a TLS wrapper over the TCP ECHO server.[17]

❸ Start `tcpdump`, this time capturing traffic on TLS port 443. For simplicity, the ARP traffic is excluded from the capture.

❹ Invoke the `openssl` client. As with all demonstrations in this chapter, the client prints the "Hello" received from the server and exits. The presence of the root CA certificate (`ca.crt`) among the command-line options is worth noticing. This emphasizes that the decision to trust the given CA is made on the client side.

Operating systems, or larger programs like web browsers, come with their own trust store, which contains the certificates of the CAs they have decided to trust. However, a client can choose to place any certificate in the trust store, or trust a CA in a one-off manner, as in this case.

Another element worth mentioning is the *SSLKEYLOGFILE* file (called `SSLKEY LOGFILE.client` in this case). Many programs that implement TLS, like `openssl` or web browsers, support the creation of an *SSLKEYLOGFILE* file, which stores various types of secrets needed to decrypt the data exchanged during the TLS session. Avoid creating this file, or keep it private when working on real systems!

Example 3-11 shows how the generated packet capture is decrypted using the secrets read from *SSLKEYLOGFILE*, and stored in a *.pcapng* (PCAP Next Generation Dump File Format) file.

Example 3-11. TLS packet capture decryption with `editcap` (requires setup from Example 3-10)

```
CLIENT=openssl
docker compose exec client bash -c \
        "cd tests && \
        editcap --inject-secrets tls,SSLKEYLOGFILE.client \
        tcp_echo_client_${CLIENT}.pcap tcp_echo_client_${CLIENT}.pcapng"
```

---

17 For configuration details of `stunnel`, see *src/network/scripts/setup_containers.sh*.

The decrypted packet sequence, when read with **tshark --read-file tests/tcp_echo_client_openssl.pcapng**, will look as in Example 3-12.

The following discussion is long, but it still covers only the main features of TLS. For example, the preshared key, session tickets, and some types of derived secrets aren't mentioned.[18] You are invited to compare our sequence with a more complete, reference example of a TLS version 1.3 session (*https://tls13.xargs.org*).

Example 3-12. Decrypted OpenSSL ECHO client packet sequence

```
client → server TCP     [SYN]      Seq=0                   Len=0        ❶
server → client TCP     [SYN, ACK] Seq=0      Ack=1        Len=0        ❶
client → server TCP     [ACK]      Seq=1      Ack=1        Len=0        ❶
client → server TLSv1.3 Client Hello (SNI=server)                      ❷
server → client TCP     [ACK]      Seq=1      Ack=254 Len=0            ❸
server → client TLSv1.3 Server Hello, Change Cipher Spec,              ❹
                        Encrypted Extensions, Certificate, Certificate Verify, ❺
                        Finished                                       ❻
client → server TCP     [ACK]      Seq=254    Ack=1569 Len=0
client → server TLSv1.3 Change Cipher Spec, Finished                   ❼
client → server TLSv1.3                                                ❽
server → client TCP     [ACK]      Seq=1569   Ack=361   Len=0
server → client TLSv1.3                                                ❾
client → server TCP     [ACK]      Seq=361    Ack=1596  Len=0
client → server TLSv1.3 Alert (Level: Warning, Description: Close Notify)  ❿
client → server TCP     [FIN, ACK] Seq=385    Ack=1596  Len=0          ⓫
server → client TLSv1.3 Alert (Level: Warning, Description: Close Notify)  ❿
client → server TCP     [ACK]      Seq=386    Ack=1620  Len=0
server → client TCP     [FIN, ACK] Seq=1620   Ack=386   Len=0          ⓫
client → server TCP     [ACK]      Seq=386    Ack=1621  Len=0          ⓫
```

❶ A TCP three-way handshake is established from the client to the server.

❷ The client starts the TLS handshake by sending the Client Hello. The Client Hello is a type of message defined by the TLS protocol, distinct from the "Hello" message example contained in the TCP segment. In particular, Client Hello contains the list of supported cipher suites, with TLS_AES_256_GCM_SHA384 often listed first (see Figure 3-5) as the client's preference.

The Client Hello also includes various additional information such as TLS extensions. The extensions include the server name as Server Name Indication (SNI), the supported certificate signature algorithms, the version of TLS desired by the client, and the client's public-key share to be used for key establishment.

---

18 For an overview of these topics, see the "TLS Essentials 29: TLS 1.3 Master Secret, PSK, Encryption Keys and HKDF" lecture by Cyrill Gössi (*https://oreil.ly/GepH8*).

For example, the client may select the X25519 elliptic curve for key establishment. All this information is sent unencrypted over the network.

As an exercise, try to identify this information in the Client Hello by opening the packet capture with the Wireshark GUI.

❸ The server acknowledges reception of the TCP segment containing the TLS Client Hello request from the client. The overhead of the TLS handshake is already noticeable from the few hundred bytes value of the ACK. The details of the TCP session, including the sequence and acknowledgment numbers, aren't discussed here. Instead, consult the explanation of TCP in Example 3-5 for comparison.

❹ The server continues the TLS handshake by sending several TLS records inside a single TCP segment. Note that Server Hello is a type of message defined by the TLS protocol, not a server's "Hello" response contained in the TCP segment. The Server Hello confirms the cipher suite used. Inside the TLS extensions, the server confirms the TLS version used, and sends its public-key share calculated using the key establishment algorithm selected by the client. The legacy Change Cipher Spec record follows, which is no longer used actively in TLS version 1.3.

From this point, the subsequent TLS records until the TLS session termination are encrypted. If *SSLKEYLOGFILE* wasn't used to decrypt the traffic, all TLS records would appear as encrypted Application Data. The encryption until the end of the TLS handshake happens using the handshake secret derived from the shared secret, and the SHA384 hash of the Client Hello and Server Hello, using HMAC (hash-based message authentication code)–based Extract-and-Expand Key Derivation Function (HKDF).[19] However, the client hasn't yet seen the server certificate, and therefore the server hasn't been authenticated yet.

❺ The server sends its certificate chain in one or more TLS records, depending on the size of the certificates. Then the server follows with a Certificate Verify record. This record contains the digital signature of the hash of the TLS handshake messages, signed using the server's private key associated with the server's certificate. The purpose of this is to prove to the client that the server owns the certificate presented to the client during this TLS session. This signature ties the server's ephemeral public key generated during this TLS session (and present in Server Hello), with the server's private key associated with the server's certificate. The client uses the server's public key from the certificate to verify this signature.

---

19 See RFC 5869, "HMAC-Based Extract-and-Expand Key Derivation Function" (*https://oreil.ly/L7uxz*).

6 The server follows with a `Finished` record, which contains the `SHA384` hash of all the TLS handshake records up to this point (`Client Hello` to server `Certifi cate Verify`), encrypted using the handshake secret. The purpose of this hash is to agree on it with the client, to guarantee the handshake integrity. The server now has all the information needed to derive the final application secrets.

7 The client verifies the signature of the certificate sent by the server and sends a legacy `Change Cipher Spec` and its own `Finished` record, based on all handshake records (`Client Hello` to server `Finished`). This finishes the TLS handshake. Both the client and the server have now derived the client and server application secrets. The client application secret derived by the client matches the client application secret derived by the server. Similarly, the server application secret derived by the client matches the server application secret derived by the server.

8 The client sends the "Hello" message to the server, encrypted with `AES_256_GCM` using the client application secret.

9 The server responds with the "Hello" message, encrypted with `AES_256_GCM` using the server application secret.

10 The client, which has no more data to send, indicates to the server the TLS connection termination using a TLS `Alert` record. The server confirms it with its own TLS `Alert` record.

11 The client initiates TCP connection termination, and the connection is eventually terminated.

To end this chapter, you'll be presented with a summary of the purpose of the various cipher suite components included in the TLS version 1.3 cipher suite `TLS_AES_256_GCM_SHA384`,[20] used in the examples discussed in this section.

The TLS component of `TLS_AES_256_GCM_SHA384` represents the key establishment algorithm, negotiated during the TLS handshake, which could be either Diffie-Hellman Ephemeral (DHE), Elliptic Curve Diffie-Hellman Ephemeral (ECDHE), or a preshared key. The `AES_256_GCM` component provides confidentiality, integrity, and authenticity to the application data exchanged over TLS, by means of symmetric encryption. The final `SHA384` component is the hash function used by HKDF to derive various secrets, based on the shared secret calculated using the key

---

20 See the video "TLS Essentials 10: TLS Cipher Suites Explained" (*https://oreil.ly/aR3vM*) on the same topic by Cyrill Gössi.

establishment algorithm. The X.509 certificates are used to authenticate the parties during the TLS version 1.3 handshake. The public-key cryptography algorithms used for certificates are specified by the certificates themselves and aren't listed as part of the TLS cipher suite.

Exercises

1. Following the example of the TCP ECHO service connection included earlier in this chapter, extend the provided TCP three-way handshake scapy code to send and receive the "Hello" message. Implement also the TCP connection termination. Save the code as *src/network/src/tcp_echo/client_scapy.py*, relative to the root of the book's code repository. Note that the full exercise solution code is already available at this location. Use F["PSH-ACK"] for the client segment TCP flags, and ans, unans = sr(packet, multi=True, timeout=0.1, verbose=0) for the client send-receive, since two TCP segments are expected as the server response: ACK followed by PSH-ACK. Remember to use the phantom byte during the TCP connection termination.

2. Write a client for the ECHO server, using the Python socket API. Save the code as *src/network/src/tcp_echo/client.py*. An example implementation is available in the book's code repository.

The implementations of both exercises can be tested by setting up the lab (Example 3-1), starting the server, starting tcpdump with the CLIENT=scapy and CLIENT=python environment variables, respectively, then clearing the client ARP cache, and starting the desired client, for example:

```
docker compose exec client bash -c \
        "sudo python src/tcp_echo/client.py && echo"
```

The implementations can also be tested using the included script. Running these unattended tests, without the need to manually open panes in windows, requires GNU Screen (*https://oreil.ly/50BkG*) to be installed:

```
CLIENT=python
bash tests/tcp_echo_client.sh $CLIENT
```

If you don't have Screen, examine the created *.pcap* file with tshark, as shown in Example 3-5. Your packet capture is again expected to contain the same sequence.

> **Network Lab Teardown**
>
> Once the network lab from this chapter is no longer needed, you can stop the containers by executing the following command:
>
> ```
> bash scripts/teardown_containers.sh
> ```

Summary

This chapter introduced you to network protocols using the examples of TCP and TLS. The implementation of a TCP ECHO server and clients, which exchanged text messages over TCP, brought you closer to understanding the subject of the next chapter: HTTP, which serves as the foundation of the web. In simplified terms, HTTP consists of a set of rules for exchanging text messages over TCP.

In addition to HTTP, Chapter 4 also covers other aspects of network protocols relevant to the web, including performance, reliability, and security.

Web Protocols

In the previous chapter, you used TCP/IP to send and receive a sequence of bytes representing a text. This idea is the base of the Hypertext Transfer Protocol (HTTP), the most widely used protocol on the web today.

This chapter describes HTTP and its purpose and evolution. You'll programmatically explore the protocol variations, using network analysis tools like `netcat`, `tcpdump`, `iperf`, `curl`, `nghttp2`, `tshark`, or Wireshark. We believe that the chronological introduction of the HTTP versions allows for a more gentle explanation of HTTP features, which otherwise could be overwhelming. Demonstrations of HTTP and the related QUIC protocol at the network packet level will prepare you for the higher-level topics of network-based APIs, with a focus on APIs that use HTTP. The discussion in this chapter focuses on the features of HTTP from the perspective of web API clients, including web browsers.

What Is Hypertext?

The term *hypertext* was introduced by Ted Holm Nelson in 1965:[1]

> Let me introduce the word *hypertext* to mean a body of written or pictorial material interconnected in such a complex way that it could not conveniently be presented or represented on paper.
>
> —Ted Holm Nelson, 1965

---

[1] Ted Holm Nelson, "Complex Information Processing: A File Structure for the Complex, the Changing and the Indeterminate" (*https://oreil.ly/wAO7I*), in *ACM '65: Proceedings of the 1965 20th National Conference* (1965): 84–100.

However, this isn't the only meaning of hypertext.[2] Today's web focuses more on the information-linking aspect of hypertext than on the information representation.[3]

Hypermedia is a term similar to *hypertext*, indicating it isn't limited to text only.

To understand hypertext, let's explore its origins and purpose. Hypertext is about facilitating connections among various pieces of information. This idea has appeared in various forms throughout the history of human thought, and the following overview will include only a few events.

Already in the first century of the Common Era, a Roman philosopher, Seneca, recommended note-taking and combining the notes.[4] The *Codex Atlanticus* (*https://oreil.ly/Ux8Oj*), a set of drawings and writings by Leonardo da Vinci from the 15th and 16th centuries, represents this tradition. Although it lacks connections among the notes, it has marginal notes and comments. In other works, like in *Species Plantarum* (*https://oreil.ly/GNGnC*) by Carl von Linné, written in the 18th century, the connections among concepts are present as references to the work and page number.

In the 1930s, Vannevar Bush, inspired by microfilm technology (also investigated by other inventors),[5] envisioned that a mechanical device[6] could help with navigating indexed references. This device, which has never been built, inspired Ted Nelson's hypertext, and some of the functionality of modern browsers. Bush described the device as follows:[7]

---

2 Agreeing on concepts and their relationships is difficult, as the Tower of Babel story shows. The Semantic Web (*https://oreil.ly/J6swr*) is an approach for establishing the meaning of the information present on the web. Quoting Berners-Lee et al. from 2001, "The Semantic Web is an extension of the current web in which information is given well-defined meaning, better enabling computers and people to work in cooperation."

3 Berners-Lee, in his 1989 "Information Management: A Proposal" (*https://oreil.ly/2jYCQ*), defined *hypertext* as "Human-readable information linked together in an unconstrained way."

4 Seneca, "Moral Letters to Lucilius, Letter 84: On Gathering Ideas" (*https://oreil.ly/THUti*).

5 See *The Internet Before the Internet: Paul Otlet's Mundaneum* (*https://oreil.ly/WV5yj*) by Sidney Perkowitz.

6 Vannevar Bush, "As We May Think" (*https://oreil.ly/zLxqU*), *Atlantic Monthly*, 1945.

7 As early as 1968, Doug Engelbart's "Mother of All Demos" featured clickable links.

If the user wishes to consult a certain book, he taps its code on the keyboard, and the title page of the book promptly appears before him, projected onto one of his viewing positions.... A special button transfers him immediately to the first page of the index. Any given book of his library can thus be called up and consulted with far greater facility than if it were taken from a shelf. As he has several projection positions, he can leave one item in position while he calls up another. He can add marginal notes and comments.

—Vannevar Bush, 1945

The adoption of hypertext increased after the implementation of the proposals by Tim Berners-Lee from 1989 and 1990 at the European Organization for Nuclear Research (CERN), and the subsequent release of the source code of his WorldWide-Web program (the browser) on a royalty-free basis in 1993.[8] A dedicated application layer network protocol, HTTP, was developed to support the implementation.[9] This was the beginning of the web as we know it today.

HTTP Lab Setup

Before exploring HTTP, let's configure the lab environment that will be used to investigate the protocol details. From the root of the book's code repository (see Figure P-2), execute the commands listed in Example 4-1.

Example 4-1. HTTP lab setup

```
cd src/http ❶
bash scripts/setup_containers.sh  ❷
```

❶ All commands in this chapter are to be issued from the *src/http* directory. Therefore, this command navigates to it.

❷ This script creates three Docker containers: `client`, `http-server`, and `https-server`.

Having set up the lab, let's discuss the first version of HTTP. This version differs from the HTTP we know today, as it lacked features such as headers and status codes, and was limited to the `GET` method. Throughout this chapter, you'll explore the history and purpose of these and other HTTP features.

---

8 See "A Short History of the Web" on the CERN website (*https://oreil.ly/cVT0a*).

9 For a condensed, 20-page overview of HTTP, up to and including HTTP/2, see "HTTP Protocols" by Ilya Grigorik, or the freely available *High Performance Browser Networking* (*https://hpbn.co*) (O'Reilly, 2014) by the same author.

HTTP/0.9

The original HTTP, as defined in 1991, is known as HTTP/0.9. The protocol was designed to run on top of any connection-oriented transport protocol—in particular, TCP.[10] The reliance on an in-order, reliable[11] delivery of data provided by TCP allowed the HTTP specification to focus on the actual functionality of a search-and-retrieve of text information, such that the protocol[12] can be summarized in the following few sentences.

After the client establishes a TCP connection with the server (listening by default on port 80), it sends to the server a request consisting of a line of ASCII characters (*https://oreil.ly/epG2A*) terminated by a <CR><LF> (<CR> = carriage return = \r, <LF> = line feed = \n) pair or <LF> itself. The request sent consists of the word GET, a space, and the document address. The document address consists of a single word, with no spaces; however, it omits the http:, host, and port, unless the request is destined at a gateway. The server response is in Hypertext Markup Language (HTML) format and uses ASCII characters. The lines in the response are delimited by an optional <CR> followed by a mandatory <LF>. The server closes the TCP connection when the whole response document has been transferred.

> The data sent in the TCP segment is a sequence of bytes, even if it represents ASCII characters. It is the task of the sender to encode the text as bytes before passing it to TCP, and of the receiver to decode the bytes into text. For example, the word "Hello" is encoded using the ASCII character-encoding scheme as the sequence of the bytes [72, 101, 108, 108, 111] in decimal notation.
>
> ASCII encoding uses 7-bit binary numbers, and in order to align them with 8-bit bytes, the most significant bit is set to 0.

HTTP was created on top of TCP to facilitate the exchange of data over the network, HTML was created based on the existing Standard Generalized Markup Language (SGML) to provide the structure of the hypertext to support links among documents, and HTTP document addressing (*https://oreil.ly/uimzH*) was created to allow for addressing of the documents.

---

10 See "How DNS Affects Browser Connections" on page 117 for an example of an application layer protocol that doesn't require a connection-oriented transport.

11 TCP reliability is defined in RFC 9293 (*https://oreil.ly/VhS6f*) as consisting of detecting packet losses (via sequence numbers) and errors (via per-segment checksums), as well as correction via retransmission. Of course, TCP provides only reliability mechanisms; it doesn't provide an absolute guarantee of delivery.

12 See "The Original HTTP as Defined in 1991" at the World Wide Web Consortium (W3C) website (*https://oreil.ly/3BbSI*).

HTTP and HTML in Action

The early HTML specification (*https://oreil.ly/CkZBG*) doesn't include any mandatory HTML tags, so a response from the HTTP server can in principle be any ASCII text. This is the case of the example of HTTP/0.9, presented to you in this section, where the client sends a `GET /Hello.html` request to the server, in order to retrieve the contents of *Hello.html* (an HTML document that contains the word "Hello"). This let's you compare the network packets exchanged using HTTP in Example 4-4, with the packets exchanged using TCP in Example 3-5 from Chapter 3. By comparing the two, you'll see that HTTP/0.9 is a set of rules for exchanging text documents over TCP/IP.

In our example, */Hello.html* in the client request is the document address. Other examples of document addresses could include "/" or *https://www.w3.org/Addressing/HTTPAddressing.html*. An example of a search document address is *https://www.oreilly.com/search/?q=learning+api+styles*, which searches for the keywords `learning`, `api`, and `styles` in the index located at *https://www.oreilly.com/search*. Recall that in most cases, the `http` scheme, `":"`, `host`, and `port` are omitted from the HTTP `GET` request line and are used only to establish a TCP connection with the server.

Figure 4-1 shows the expected execution flow of the exercise, demonstrating the HTTP/0.9 client request.

```
$ CLIENT=http0.9
$ PCAP_FILE=/tmp/client_${CLIENT}.pcap
$ docker compose exec client bash -c \
>       "sudo rm -f ${PCAP_FILE} && \
>       sudo tcpdump -w ${PCAP_FILE} 'port 80' && \
>       cp ${PCAP_FILE} tests"
tcpdump: listening on eth0, link-type EN10MB (Ethernet), snapshot length 262144 bytes
^C10 packets captured
10 packets received by filter
0 packets dropped by kernel
$

$ docker compose exec client bash -c \
>       "echo -en 'GET /Hello.html\r\n\r\n' | netcat -p 8080 http-server 80"
Hello
$
```

Figure 4-1. HTTP/0.9 request with netcat

Typical Execution Flow of Examples in This Chapter

Most hands-on examples in this chapter will have a similar execution flow. You'll open a two-pane window and execute commands in the panes: in the top pane, capture the network traffic with tcpdump, and in the bottom one, invoke a client request to generate the traffic, then stop the tcpdump capture and read it with tshark.

In such common cases, only the executed commands and their output will be provided, but no screenshots. You may come back here for a visual overview of this type of exercise. Screenshots will be provided if the execution flow differs.

Note that the tcpdump, tshark, and netcat tools used in this chapter were introduced in Chapter 3. The reference *.pcap* files from this chapter are available as **_reference.pcap* files in the *tests* directory.

Example 4-2 contains the executed commands, annotated with explanations. To follow hands-on, you'll need a two-pane window. You can open the panes with the help of tmux. For an introduction to tmux usage, see Example P-2.

Example 4-2. HTTP/0.9 demo execution flow (requires setup from Example 4-1)

```
# In a terminal run ❶
tmux new-session \; split-window -v \;

# In the top pane run ❷
CLIENT=http0.9
PCAP_FILE=/tmp/client_${CLIENT}.pcap
docker compose exec client bash -c \
      "sudo rm --force ${PCAP_FILE} && \
      sudo tcpdump -w ${PCAP_FILE} 'port 80' && \
      cp ${PCAP_FILE} tests"

# In the bottom pane run ❸
docker compose exec client bash -c \
      "echo -en 'GET /Hello.html\r\n\r\n' | netcat -p 8080 http-server 80"
```

❶ Create two panes with tmux.

❷ Start a fresh packet capture by using tcpdump on the client. The captured traffic will be saved into the *client_http0.9.pcap* file located in the *tests* directory.

❸ Invoke the GET /Hello.html HTTP request from the client using netcat. The client is expected to print the HTML (in our case the "Hello" text) received back from the http-server and exit.

Stop tcpdump by pressing Ctrl+C, and read the saved packet capture with tshark, as shown in Example 4-3.

*Example 4-3. Packet capture file read with **tshark** (requires setup from Example 4-2)*

```
CLIENT=http0.9
docker compose exec client bash -c \
    "tshark --read-file tests/client_${CLIENT}.pcap"
```

You will see a sequence like that in Example 4-4. Note that in this chapter, some packets present in the captures, like ACK or FIN TCP segments, aren't explained since it is assumed that you are already familiar with TCP, covered in Chapter 3.

Example 4-4. HTTP/0.9 client packet sequence

```
client → server TCP  8080 → 80   [SYN]       Seq=0             Len=0 ❶
server → client TCP    80 → 8080 [SYN, ACK] Seq=0  Ack=1  Len=0 ❶
client → server TCP  8080 → 80   [ACK]       Seq=1  Ack=1  Len=0 ❶
client → server HTTP             GET /Hello.html\r\n\r\n       ❷
server → client TCP    80 → 8080 [ACK]       Seq=1  Ack=20 Len=0 ❸
server → client HTTP             Continuation                  ❹
client → server TCP  8080 → 80   [ACK]       Seq=20 Ack=8  Len=0 ❺
server → client TCP    80 → 8080 [FIN, ACK] Seq=8  Ack=20 Len=0 ❻
client → server TCP  8080 → 80   [FIN, ACK] Seq=20 Ack=9  Len=0 ❻
server → client TCP    80 → 8080 [ACK]       Seq=9  Ack=21 Len=0 ❻
```

❶ A TCP three-way handshake is established from the client on port 8080 to the server on port 80. Normally, the client port is random, but it's fixed here to 8080 for clarity.

❷ The client makes the HTTP request to retrieve the */Hello.html* document from the server. Note the line ending with \r\n\r\n (<CR><LF> <CR><LF>) instead of \r\n (<CR><LF>) as an artifact of the implementation of HTTP/0.9 on this particular server, which assumes that HTTP headers are present after the first <CR><LF> pair. However, HTTP 0.9 doesn't use any headers. The length of this TCP segment data is 19 bytes.

❸ The server acknowledges (Ack=20=1+19) the reception of the HTTP request from the client.

❹ Continuation means that the HTTP response doesn't contain any headers, but it is still recognized as HTTP since its TCP data ends with <CR><LF>. That is, the TCP segment data returned by the server is Hello\r\n, with 7 bytes in length.

❺ The client acknowledges the reception of the HTTP response from the server.

❻ After sending the whole HTML document to the client, the server initiates TCP connection termination, and the connection is terminated.

The packet sequence given here demonstrates the main features of HTTP/0.9. The underlying transport protocol is TCP, which HTTP uses to exchange ASCII-encoded messages. Moreover, the example shows that the server closes the TCP connection. The connection is terminated after the server has fully sent its message in response to a single request by the client.

HTTP/1.0

In the 1990s, the internet kept evolving, with the number of websites reaching 10 thousand in 1994, 75 thousand in 1995, 600 thousand in 1996, and 9 million in 1999.[13] Modifications to the original HTTP protocol started appearing, and in 1996, an informational Request for Comments (RFC) document[14] was published.[15] It described the common usage of HTTP at that time, referred to as HTTP/1.0.

HTTP/1.0 defined HTTP as "an application-level protocol with the lightness and speed necessary for distributed, collaborative, hypermedia information systems."

The document codified several already existing features of HTTP, such as these:

- The protocol version and the version compatibility rules to be obeyed by clients and servers
- A split into message headers and message body, to provide a mechanism to transfer metadata (information about the data) in HTTP requests and responses
- Content codings to support message body compression in `x-gzip` and `x-compress` formats specified in the `Content-Encoding` header
- Message modifiers based on Multipurpose Internet Mail Extensions (MIME) types (now more commonly referred to as *media types*), to specify with the `Content-Type` header a desired representation of the HTTP body

---

13 See the Netcraft Web Server Survey (*https://oreil.ly/4U08P*). Note that the number of active websites plateaued between 2010 and 2024 at around 200 million, and the number of all websites is currently in decline from a 1.8-billion peak in 2017.

14 An informational RFC isn't an internet standard.

15 See RFC 1945, "Hypertext Transfer Protocol—HTTP/1.0" (*https://oreil.ly/HOlgK*).

- Additional request methods apart from GET: HEAD, POST, and further PUT, DELETE, LINK, and UNLINK, to allow for changing the state on servers as a result of HTTP client requests[16]
- A requirement for a POST request to contain the Content-Length header
- Status codes: 1xx (Informational), 2xx (Success), 3xx (Redirection), 4xx (Client Error), 5xx (Server Error)
- Basic authentication scheme, as well as the specification for additional authentication schemes and encryption mechanisms

HTTP Message Headers and Body

Comparing a GET request in HTTP/0.9 and HTTP/1.0 will show several of the 1.0 protocol features: the protocol version, the response status code, and the separation of the message into headers and body. The execution flow of commands for this exercise is given in Example 4-5.

> An HTTP/1.0 or HTTP/1.1 message consists of a start-line followed by <CR><LF> and a sequence of header lines, an empty line indicating the end of the headers, and an optional message body.[17]

This time, let's use a valid HTML document instead of the "Hello" text. The minimal HTML document that includes "Hello" is <!DOCTYPE html><title>Hello</title>, as indicated by the HTML5 spec (*https://oreil.ly/ocJ6G*).

For this example, you'll need a two-pane window. This demonstration is an example of the typical execution flow, described in "Typical Execution Flow of Examples in This Chapter" on page 110.

Example 4-5. HTTP/1.0 demo execution flow (requires setup from Example 4-1)

```
# In a terminal run ❶
tmux new-session \; split-window -v \;

# In the top pane run ❷
CLIENT=http1.0
PCAP_FILE=/tmp/client_${CLIENT}.pcap
```

---

16 LINK and UNLINK were later removed from the HTTP/1.1 specification due to their lack of adoption; see "HTTP/1.1" on page 128. This illustrates that HTTP has been, and continues to be, evolving based on its usage.

17 See the HTTP/1.1 internet standard RFC (*https://oreil.ly/BASAg*) from 2022.

```
docker compose exec client bash -c \
      "sudo rm --force ${PCAP_FILE} && \
      sudo tcpdump -w ${PCAP_FILE} 'port 80' && \
      cp ${PCAP_FILE} tests"

# In the bottom pane run ❸
docker compose exec client bash -c \
      "echo -en 'GET /HelloValid.html HTTP/1.0\r\n\r\n' | \
      netcat -p 8080 http-server 80"
```

❶ Create two panes with tmux.

❷ Start a fresh packet capture using tcpdump on the client. The .pcap file will be saved in the *client_http1.0.pcap* file located in the *tests* directory.

❸ Invoke the GET /HelloValid.html HTTP request from the client using netcat. Note that HTTP/1.0 doesn't require any headers to be included in a GET request. The client will print the HTML received from the http-server and exit.

As you can see in Example 4-6, in addition to the HTML content, more text information is printed in the server response—namely, the response's 200 (OK) status code and various HTTP headers.

Example 4-6. HTTP/1.0 server response

```
HTTP/1.0 200 OK\r\n                                  ❶
Date: Wed, 17 Jul 2024 17:48:40 GMT\r\n              ❷
Server: Apache/2.4.61 (Unix)\r\n                     ❸
Last-Modified: Wed, 17 Jul 2024 17:48:35 GMT\r\n     ❹
Content-Length: 37\r\n                               ❺
Connection: close\r\n                                ❻
Content-Type: text/html\r\n                          ❼
\r\n
<!DOCTYPE html><title>Hello</title>\r\n
```

❶ The HTTP status code (200 OK) indicates that the server successfully processed the client's request. The <CR><LF> sequence isn't visible in the printed output, but it is explicitly included in this snippet, to remind us about its existence.

❷ The Date header contains the timestamp of the response at the server (origin).

❸ The Server header indicates the server's software. This header normally would be removed to avoid exposing the server version information to attackers.

❹ The `Last-Modified` header contains the timestamp of the last modification of the HTML document—in other words, the modification timestamp of the */HelloValid.html* file on the server.

❺ The `Content-Length` header contains the length in bytes of the HTTP body.

❻ The `Connection` header appears first in HTTP/1.1. The appearance of this header here is an HTTP/1.0 implementation artifact in this particular server software.[18]

❼ The server sends the `text/html` media type, shown by the `Content-Type` header.

Stop `tcpdump` by pressing Ctrl+C, and read the saved packet capture with `tshark`, as shown in Example 4-7.

Example 4-7. Packet capture file read with `tshark` (requires setup from Example 4-5)

```
CLIENT=http1.0
docker compose exec client bash -c \
      "tshark --read-file tests/client_${CLIENT}.pcap"
```

You will see a sequence like in Example 4-8. It doesn't differ significantly from Example 4-4, except for `tshark` now recognizing both the request and response as HTTP.

Example 4-8. HTTP/1.0 client packet sequence

```
client → server TCP  [SYN]      Seq=0              Len=0    ❶
server → client TCP  [SYN, ACK] Seq=0    Ack=1     Len=0    ❶
client → server TCP  [ACK]      Seq=1    Ack=1     Len=0    ❶
client → server HTTP GET /HelloValid.html HTTP/1.0\r\n\r\n  ❷
server → client TCP  [ACK]      Seq=1    Ack=34    Len=0    ❸
server → client HTTP HTTP/1.0 200 OK  (text/html)          ❹
client → server TCP  [ACK]      Seq=34   Ack=234 Len=0     ❺
server → client TCP  [FIN, ACK] Seq=234 Ack=34    Len=0    ❻
client → server TCP  [FIN, ACK] Seq=34   Ack=235 Len=0     ❻
server → client TCP  [ACK]      Seq=235 Ack=35    Len=0    ❻
```

❶ A TCP three-way handshake is established from the client to the server.

❷ The client makes the HTTP request with a total length of 33 bytes.

---

18 Some implementations of HTTP/1.0 support an explicitly negotiated persistent TCP connection by using the `Connection: Keep-Alive` header and value from "Changes from HTTP/1.0" in RFC 9112 (*https://oreil.ly/sBhxp*).

❸ The server acknowledges (Ack=34=1+33) the HTTP request from the client.

❹ The server responds successfully with an HTML message of the text/html media type.

❺ The client acknowledges reception of 233 (234 − 1) bytes since the last server response. This consists of 196 bytes of HTTP status code and headers, and 37 bytes of the HTTP body message.

❻ The client initiates TCP connection termination, and the connection is terminated.

The introduction of headers and standardized status codes in HTTP/1.0 provides a way to pass and obtain additional (meta) information about the message. On the other hand, this creates overhead, since the headers are included in every request and response. HTTP/1.0 allows the message body to be compressed, but not the message headers. The compression of headers became part of the HTTP/2 specification, described in "HTTP/2" on page 133.

HTTP in a Browser

Until now, we've looked at HTTP from the perspective of a client making a single request. This use case reflects how the web initially started (it was about fetching one complete document). However, today's websites consist of multiple resources, like Cascading Style Sheets (CSS) (*https://oreil.ly/b2CWw*); images; or JavaScript. According to the State of the Web report (*https://oreil.ly/pbjxd*), the median website size in 2024 was over 2 megabytes (MB), comprising 70 resources, and requiring 10 TCP connections per page. The size and number of resources affect the website's loading time. The loading time of small resources is limited by the latency of fetching them over the network, and the loading time of large resources is limited by the network bandwidth. Dependencies among objects in the HTML Document Object Model (DOM), the CSS Object Model (CSSOM), and JavaScript affect the order in which these resources are loaded, and this also affects the website loading time.[19]

At the same time, human perception of acceptable response times remains approximately unchanged: up to 0.1 seconds for a feeling of instantaneous response, and order of several seconds for starting to lose attention.[20]

---

19 See "Primer on Web Performance" (*https://oreil.ly/utgiA*) by Ilya Grigorik, or the more recent "HTTP/3 Prioritization Demystified" (*https://oreil.ly/SmtMt*) by Robin Marx.

20 See "Response Times: The 3 Important Limits" (*https://oreil.ly/jJLwD*) by Jakob Nielsen.

Latency Versus Bandwidth

Latency is the time measured from the moment the source sends a message until the destination receives it. A related concept is round-trip time (RTT), which is the time taken for a message to travel from the source to the destination and back. In general, the latency isn't equal to half of the RTT, since the latencies of two trips may differ. Note that the values reported by network tools like `ping` or `traceroute`, though often colloquially referred to as latency, represent RTT.

Connection Health Check (*https://oreil.ly/DTAa1*) provides an online measurement of RTT from your machine to various Amazon Web Services (AWS) regions. In 2024, the maximum RTT to some locations reached or exceeded one second. Note that there are typically multiple intermediaries on the route from source to destination, and every device adds some latency.

Bandwidth is a measure of the maximum amount of data transferred in a unit of time. The typical unit of bandwidth today is Mbit/s (Megabit per second = 1,000,000 bits per second, also abbreviated as *Mbps*).

Using an analogy of a garden hose, the latency is determined by the length of the hose, and the bandwidth by its diameter.

Using the garden hose analogy, a way to improve the loading time of an individual website resource at the network level is to shorten the hose (reduce RTT), make the water fill the hose faster, and either use multiple hoses (multiple TCP connections) or send different resources through the hose simultaneously (multiplex them).[21] The first three ideas are included in HTTP/1.1, and the last one in HTTP/2 (see "HTTP/2" on page 133) and HTTP/3 (see "HTTP/3" on page 139).

How DNS Affects Browser Connections

The IP that underlies the TCP/IP suite operates on IP addresses. However, when a browser or other client makes an HTTP request to a website, such as *http://example.com*, it typically targets the name (*example.com*) of the HTTP server. This is because clients are operated by humans, who are better at remembering names than numerical addresses. A fixed name also offers a more stable reference compared to the potentially changing IP address. The DNS protocol operates on the application layer and provides the required mapping from a human-readable server domain name to an IP address.

---

21 The word *multiplex* originates from Latin, and means "many interwoven parts." In the context of network communication, multiplexing means that multiple signals are transmitted over a single connection.

Traditionally, DNS uses UDP,[22] another transport protocol belonging to the TCP/IP suite. DNS over UDP uses a four-tuple (source IP address, source port, destination IP address, destination port), where the source is the client, and the destination is a DNS server, to request from the DNS server the IP address of the HTTP server. Only one active instance of the given four-tuple can be on the machine at a given time.

The IP address of the HTTP server needs to be known by the client before a TCP (or QUIC) connection can be established. The mapping from the server domain name to the IP address doesn't change often, and it's cached by the browser (typically for a minute) and the operating system. Nevertheless, when an HTTP request is made to a server that hasn't been accessed before, the latency due to the DNS RTT needs to be considered in the overall analysis of the HTTP client performance.

An isolated DNS request/response can be performed using a `docker compose exec client bash -c "dig +short example.com"` command. Example 4-9 shows the corresponding packet sequence read with `tshark`. `192.168.114.2` is the client IP address, `1.1.1.1` is the DNS server IP address (it may differ for you), and `93.184.215.14` is the IP address of the *example.com* HTTP server.

Example 4-9. DNS request/response

```
192.168.114.2 → 1.1.1.1      DNS query example.com
      1.1.1.1 → 192.168.114.2 DNS query response example.com 93.184.215.14
```

This request-response sequence has only two DNS messages, each encapsulated within its UDP datagram. This reflects the transaction-oriented character of the underlying UDP transport protocol,[23] as opposed to TCP (which is connection-oriented). The connection-oriented TCP establishes a connection and keeps track of its state, analogously to a subscription to an online service, which results in obligations on both sides until termination. On the other hand, transaction-oriented UDP means that programs exchange data in individual request-response units, similarly to one-off financial transactions (without establishing a long-term contract). From this perspective, UDP is also described as connectionless, where every datagram is treated as an independent entity, and the sender and receiver don't keep track of previously sent or received datagrams.

---

22 In DNS over UDP, the server name and the client IP address are sent unencrypted. Over time, other DNS protocols, like DNS over TLS (DoT) or DNS over HTTPS (DoH), appeared, which hide the server name from third-party observers, or even hide the client IP address, as in the case of Oblivious DNS over HTTPS (ODoH). These protocols add additional RTTs compared to UDP-based DNS, due to TCP and TLS.

23 See RFC 768, "User Datagram Protocol" (*https://oreil.ly/w0uSX*). It's one of the shortest internet standards.

The UDP client makes a request to the server, which is the receiver of the request. This transaction can be unidirectional, like making a donation to charity. Other examples of such protocols are Simple Network Management Protocol (SNMP) and Network Time Protocol (NTP), which don't expect a response from the server. The transaction can also involve an exchange, like paying cash at a flea market. DNS uses UDP in this way; the client sends a DNS query and expects a DNS response from the server. However, as in real life, the request may arrive damaged (if the UDP checksum doesn't match, the datagram will be discarded), or the response may be lost.

Without the reliability features at the transport layer, it's the responsibility of the application layer protocol, such as DNS, to handle such issues. For example, when a DNS client doesn't receive a response within a timeout (one second on Windows and five seconds on Unix-like systems), it will retry the request. Or, when the DNS response arrives truncated due to the data size exceeding 512 bytes (when Extension Mechanisms for DNS [EDNS] isn't used), the DNS client will switch from UDP to TCP and make a new request, in an attempt to reliably obtain the full, ordered DNS message in several TCP segments.

UDP doesn't offer the reliability features of TCP, but most of the time they are unnecessary, since the DNS response usually fits within a single UDP datagram. This is the case even if the response contains several IP addresses, like when the HTTP server is behind a load balancer. The advantage is that by avoiding the TCP three-way handshake, UDP delivers the DNS response to the client within a single RTT.[24]

Parallel TCP Connections in a Browser

You can analyze the performance of a browser loading a website by using dedicated tools like Web Vitals (*https://oreil.ly/7QOt4*). Here, we'll look instead at the protocol-level network traffic generated by a web browser loading a website using HTTP/1.1. Figure 4-2 shows the website as rendered by a web browser, and Example 4-10 shows the website's HTML source code. It's a basic website that contains CSS and JavaScript.

---

24 The lack of a mechanism similar to the TCP three-way handshake exposes UDP-based DNS to UDP-based amplification attacks (*https://oreil.ly/BinS7*).

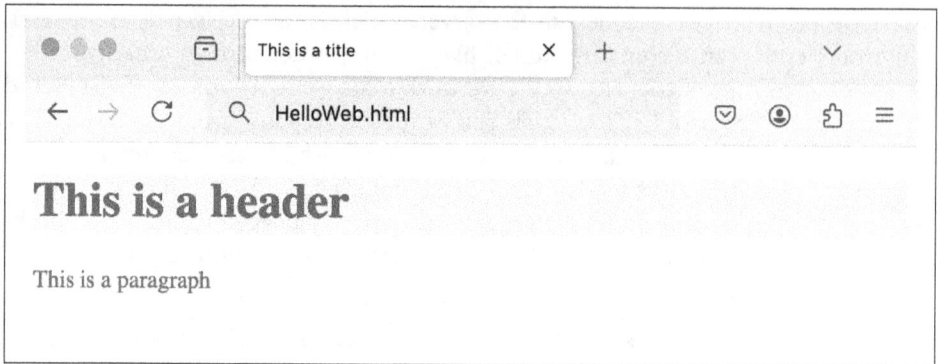

Figure 4-2. Website in Firefox

Example 4-10. HelloWeb.html *source code*

```
<!DOCTYPE html>
<html>
<head>
    <title>This is a title</title>
    <link rel="stylesheet" href="background.css">
    <link rel="stylesheet" href="heading.css">
    <link rel="stylesheet" href="paragraph.css">
    <script src="script1.js"></script>
</head>
<body>
    <h1>This is a header</h1>
    <p>This is a paragraph</p>
    <script src="script2.js"></script>
</body>
</html>
```

To capture the traffic generated by Firefox loading this site, follow Example 4-11.

Example 4-11. Firefox demo execution flow (requires setup from Example 4-1)

```
# In a terminal run ❶
tmux new-session \; split-window -v \;

# In the top pane run ❷
CLIENT=firefox
PCAP_FILE=/tmp/client_${CLIENT}.pcap
docker compose exec client bash -c \
    "sudo rm --force ${PCAP_FILE} && \
    sudo tcpdump -w ${PCAP_FILE} 'port 80' && \
    cp ${PCAP_FILE} tests"

# In the bottom pane run ❸
docker compose exec client bash -c \
```

```
"rm -rf ~/.cache/mozilla/firefox/* && \
rm -rf ~/.mozilla/firefox/*.profile && \
firefox --headless --screenshot /tmp/website-in-firefox.png \
http://http-server/HelloWeb.html && \
cp /tmp/website-in-firefox.png tests"
```

❶ Create two panes with tmux.

❷ Start a fresh packet capture by using tcpdump on the client. The captured traffic will be saved into the *client_firefox.pcap* file located in the *tests* directory.

❸ Load the website with a headless firefox. Firefox will save the screenshot of the website and exit.

Stop tcpdump by pressing Ctrl+C. There are many packets in the capture, and therefore it's more readable to present them by opening the capture in Wireshark (*https://www.wireshark.org*). Your packet capture will differ, but the main message is that there are several (in our case, three, highlighted on the screenshot) TCP SYN segments, showing that the browser opens multiple TCP connections to the server, in order to fetch the resources in parallel.

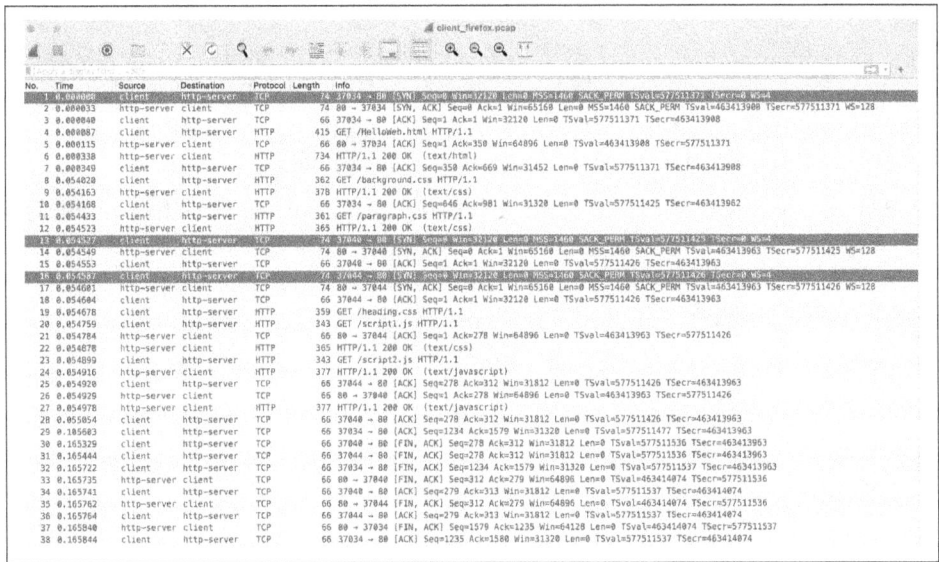

Figure 4-3. Network traffic generated by Firefox accessing a website

You can explore the TCP stream (see "TCP Connection Versus TCP Stream" on page 88 for the definition of a stream) in Wireshark, by selecting a SYN segment, right-clicking, and choosing Follow → TCP Stream. You'll see that the first TCP stream fetched the HTML and all CSS files, and the remaining two TCP streams fetched one JavaScript file each.

Limitations of TCP

The original HTTP/0.9 protocol was chosen to operate on top of TCP (see "HTTP/0.9" on page 108). Because of that, HTTP benefits from TCP features, such as reliability and in-order delivery, but is also affected by TCP limitations.

Two TCP characteristics that negatively affect the performance behavior of HTTP are worth mentioning: TCP head-of-line blocking and TCP slow start and congestion avoidance. Modern versions of HTTP, such as HTTP/2 ("HTTP/2" on page 133) and HTTP/3 ("HTTP/3" on page 139), introduce optimizations to mitigate these issues.

TCP Head-of-Line Blocking

The reliability and in-order delivery features of TCP can potentially increase the communication latency since the lost segments need to be retransmitted.[25]

This issue is commonly referred to as *head-of-line (HOL) blocking*. The term *head* comes from queuing theory, indicating the first segment (*head*). In TCP HOL blocking, when a TCP segment is lost, the subsequent segments are buffered and can be reassembled in the correct order only after the lost segment is retransmitted.[26]

TCP HOL blocking is discussed often, however, usually only with the help of illustrative diagrams. Therefore, let's see an example of TCP HOL blocking, to better understand at what point blocking occurs and how it may affect latency. Figure 4-4 shows a screenshot of the expected execution flow.

---

25 "If low levels of the communication system try to accomplish bit-perfect communication, they will probably introduce uncontrolled delays in packet delivery, for example, by requesting retransmission of damaged packets and holding up delivery of later packets until earlier ones have been correctly retransmitted." From "End-To-End Arguments in System Design" (*https://oreil.ly/rfr4h*) by J. H. Saltzer, D. P. Reed, and D. D. Clark, in *ACM Transactions on Computer Systems (TOCS)* 2, no. 4 (1984): 277–288.

26 See "Head-of-Line Blocking" in *High Performance Browser Networking* (*https://oreil.ly/ocWbl*) by Ilya Grigorik.

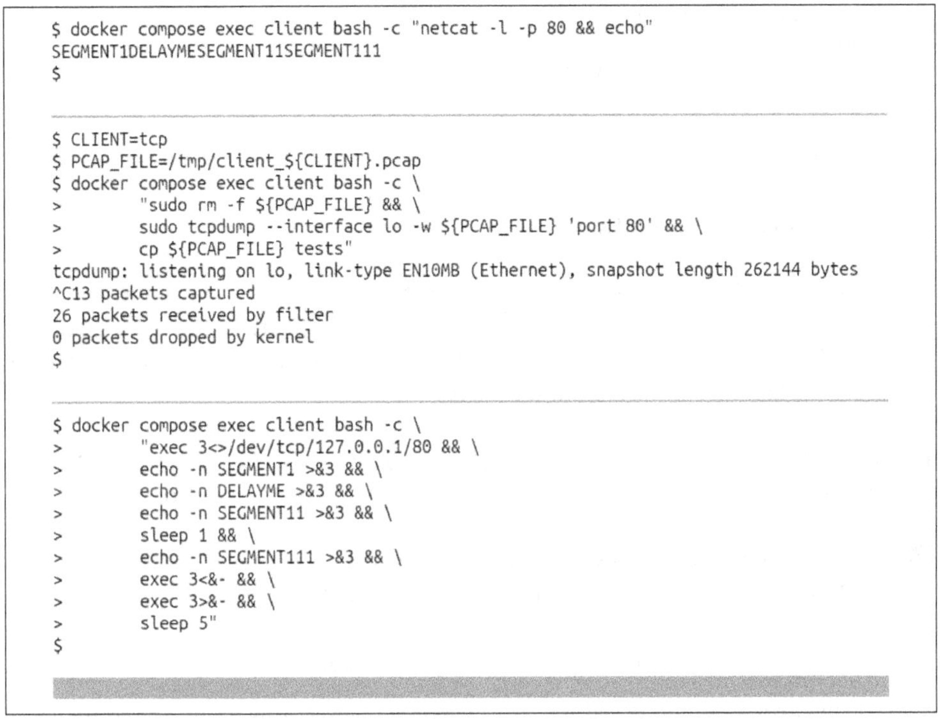

```
$ docker compose exec client bash -c "netcat -l -p 80 && echo"
SEGMENT1DELAYMESEGMENT11SEGMENT111
$
```

```
$ CLIENT=tcp
$ PCAP_FILE=/tmp/client_${CLIENT}.pcap
$ docker compose exec client bash -c \
>       "sudo rm -f ${PCAP_FILE} && \
>       sudo tcpdump --interface lo -w ${PCAP_FILE} 'port 80' && \
>       cp ${PCAP_FILE} tests"
tcpdump: listening on lo, link-type EN10MB (Ethernet), snapshot length 262144 bytes
^C13 packets captured
26 packets received by filter
0 packets dropped by kernel
$
```

```
$ docker compose exec client bash -c \
>       "exec 3<>/dev/tcp/127.0.0.1/80 && \
>       echo -n SEGMENT1 >&3 && \
>       echo -n DELAYME >&3 && \
>       echo -n SEGMENT11 >&3 && \
>       sleep 1 && \
>       echo -n SEGMENT111 >&3 && \
>       exec 3<&- && \
>       exec 3>&- && \
>       sleep 5"
$
```

Figure 4-4. TCP head-of-line blocking demo

This time, to obtain the packet capture, you'll need a three-pane window.

Example 4-12. TCP HOL demo execution flow (requires setup from Example 4-1)

```
# In a terminal run ❶
tmux new-session \; split-window -v \; split-window -v \;

# In the top pane run ❷
docker compose exec client bash -c "netcat -l -p 80 && echo"

# In the middle pane run ❸
CLIENT=tcp
PCAP_FILE=/tmp/client_${CLIENT}.pcap
docker compose exec client bash -c \
      "sudo rm --force ${PCAP_FILE} && \
      sudo tcpdump --interface lo -w ${PCAP_FILE} 'port 80' && \
      cp ${PCAP_FILE} tests"

# In the bottom pane run ❹
docker compose exec client bash -c \
      "exec 3<>/dev/tcp/127.0.0.1/80 && \
      echo -n SEGMENT1 >&3 && \
      echo -n DELAYME >&3 && \
```

```
echo -n SEGMENT11 >&3 && \
sleep 1 && \
echo -n SEGMENT111 >&3 && \
exec 3<&- && \
exec 3>&- && \
sleep 5"
```

❶ Create three panes with `tmux`.

❷ Start the TCP server using `netcat`. Note that the server is started in the *client* container, and both the client and the server communicate over the *loopback* network interface to simplify the setup. The server will block and exit after receiving the complete TCP stream from the client.

❸ Start a fresh packet capture by using `tcpdump` on the client. The captured traffic will be saved into the *client_tcp.pcap* file located in the *tests* directory.

❹ Use the functionality of *bash* to open a TCP socket, and send data over it. Four TCP segments are sent: `SEGMENT1`, `DELAYME`, `SEGMENT11`, and `SEGMENT111` with an explicit delay of one second before the last segment. The segments are named so their length in bytes is identifiable in the packet capture.

The `DELAYME` segment is artificially delayed by five seconds to induce HOL blocking, using `iptables` and `tc` tools. The method of achieving this behavior is omitted from this section, but in order to follow the examples hands-on, you need to perform this configuration. Please consult *tests/client.sh* for details, where you will find the relevant commands. The corresponding five-second-delay is added after the client sends all its TCP segments, so TCP can recover from the HOL blocking introduced by delaying the `DELAYME` segment.

Wait until the server exits after receiving the complete TCP stream from the client, stop `tcpdump` by pressing Ctrl+C, and read the saved packet capture with `tshark`, as shown in Example 4-13.

Example 4-13. Packet capture file read with `tshark` (requires setup from Example 4-12)

```
CLIENT=tcp
docker compose exec client bash -c \
        "tshark --read-file tests/client_${CLIENT}.pcap"
```

You will see a sequence like that in Example 4-14. The discussion of this sequence goes more into detail about TCP, so you may want to review Example 3-5 in Chapter 3 before proceeding.

The SEGMENT1, DELAYME, SEGMENT11, and SEGMENT111 strings are present in the TCP segment data. They can be found by using Wireshark to explore the packet capture; however, the segment data isn't shown in the basic summary of the sequence, where only the data length (Len) is reported.

Example 4-14. TCP HOL blocking packet sequence

```
0.0000 client → server                       [SYN]            Seq=0          Len=0 ❶
0.0000 server → client                       [SYN, ACK]       Seq=0  Ack=1   Len=0 ❶
0.0000 client → server                       [ACK]            Seq=1  Ack=1   Len=0 ❶
0.0002 client → server                       [PSH, ACK]       Seq=1  Ack=1   Len=8 ❷
0.0002 server → client                       [ACK]            Seq=1  Ack=9   Len=0 ❸
0.2173 client → server [TCP Previous ...]    [PSH, ACK]       Seq=16 Ack=1   Len=9 ❹
0.2174 server → client [TCP Dup ACK 5#1]     [ACK]            Seq=1  Ack=9   Len=0 ❺
1.0054 client → server                       [FIN, PSH, ACK]  Seq=25 Ack=10  Len=8 ❻
1.0054 server → client [TCP Dup ACK 5#2]     [ACK]            Seq=1  Ack=9   Len=0 ❼
5.0029 client → server [TCP Retransmission]  [PSH, ACK]       Seq=9  Ack=1   Len=7 ❽
5.0032 server → client                       [ACK]            Seq=1  Ack=36  Len=0 ❾
5.0089 server → client                       [FIN, ACK]       Seq=1  Ack=36  Len=0
5.0090 client → server                       [ACK]            Seq=36 Ack=2   Len=0 ❿
```

❶ The TCP three-way handshake is established from the client to the server. Note that in the actual packet capture, both client and server use *loopback* IP addresses of 127.0.0.1, and they can be identified instead by their ports. Note also that since the traffic is exchanged over *loopback*, the latency is submilliseconds.

❷ The client sends SEGMENT1 (Len=8) to the server.

❸ The server acknowledges the reception of SEGMENT1.

❹ The client sends SEGMENT11 (Len=9) to the server, after having sent SEGMENT1 (Len=8) and DELAYME (Len=7) segments, as indicated by Seq=1+8+7=16. [TCP Pre vious segment not captured] isn't part of the TCP segment, but a label added by tshark.

❺ After seeing Seq=16 in the segment sent by the client, the server notices it is missing a segment, and acknowledges again the last fully received SEGMENT1, to indicate the loss problem to the client. This problem is labeled by tshark as [TCP Dup ACK 5#1], a duplicate ACK. This ACK also contains a SACK (selective acknowledgment) range 16–25 (not shown here), which indicates that the server also received SEGMENT11. TCP SACK is a mechanism to deal with packet loss, for the receiver to inform the sender about all segments that have arrived successfully, so the sender retransmits only the segments missing on the receiver.[27]

❻ The client is at Seq=1+8+7+9, meaning it sent SEGMENT1, DELAYME, and SEGMENT11 segments. The client continues by sending SEGMENT111 (Len=10) to the server, and since this is its last segment, the client indicates TCP connection termination with the FIN TCP flag. Note also that the one-second delay is present on the client side as expected.

❼ The server insists that SEGMENT1 is the last received segment before a loss. This problem is labeled by tshark as [TCP Dup ACK 5#2]. This ACK also contains SACK range 16–36 (again not shown here), which indicates that the server also received SEGMENT111 and the FIN segment.

❽ After the artificially introduced delay of five seconds expires, the client retransmits the DELAYME segment of Len=7, at Seq=1+8=9 (after sending SEGMENT1). This event is labeled by tshark as [TCP Retransmission].

❾ The server acknowledges the reception of all segments by sending Ack=1+8+7+9+10+1=36. The final +1 is due to the phantom byte (see Example 3-5 in Chapter 3).

❿ The TCP connection is terminated.

In summary, HOL blocking is triggered in this example by introducing a delay within a TCP stream. The server (receiver) sees this delay as a packet loss but keeps accepting subsequent segments from the client (sender), by buffering them and reminding the client about the loss. Only after receiving the retransmitted segment can the server assemble all segments and the TCP connection terminate. On a submillisecond-latency *loopback* network, the expected latency of the whole sequence is about one second, as a result of the explicit one-second delay on the client (application) side. However, due to a packet loss (delay), the actual latency is about five seconds.

---

27 See a live demo of this behavior in "How TCP Works—Selective Acknowledgment (SACK)" (*https://oreil.ly/dX768*) by Chris Greer.

TCP Slow Start and Congestion Avoidance

TCP implemented congestion control in order to achieve the maximum bandwidth possible under the given network conditions, and also to provide a mechanism to implement fairness in the network usage among the machines sharing the network. The main congestion control mechanisms include TCP slow start and congestion avoidance.[28]

> To explore TCP slow start and congestion avoidance in practice, consult the example in the *src/http/README.md* file in the book's code repository.

The *TCP slow start* consists of the sender probing the network by sending an increasing number of segments within a single RTT, if all segments are acknowledged by the receiver. This increase is typically multiplicative, meaning that the sender may start from, for example, two segments, and after receiving their ACKs, send four segments, and so on.[29] The sender will back off (reduce the number of segments) if a packet loss is detected. Note that both sides of the TCP connection independently perform congestion control.

The outcome of this approach is that TCP quickly increases the amount of data sent in a unit of time. Subsequently, after reaching a *slow start threshold* (*ssthresh*), the congestion control algorithm switches to a *congestion avoidance* phase, which is less greedy. The TCP slow start phase, despite its name, is faster at increasing bandwidth than the congestion avoidance phase. It is also clear that the congestion control takes time, and the consequence of this is that it performs poorly for short-lived TCP connections, like those when a browser fetches a small-sized resource.

---

28 For more information, see "Congestion Avoidance and Control" (*https://oreil.ly/6fooP*) by Ilya Grigorik.

29 The "Increasing TCP's Initial Window" RFC draft from 2013 (*https://oreil.ly/l9BeZ*) recommended increasing the initial number of segments from between 2 and 4 to 10.

HTTP/1.1

HTTP continued to evolve, and in 1997, less than a year after HTTP/1.0, the protocol reached version HTTP/1.1.[30] It was followed by an RFC draft standard in 1999.[31]

The 1997/1999 HTTP/1.1 specification, while staying within the boundaries provided by the TCP transport, tried to improve the speed of loading hypertext resources.[32] The specification also tried to address other concerns that arose in the 1990s, like the IPv4 address pool exhaustion.[33]

Here are some of the features introduced in HTTP/1.1:

Chunked transfer coding
> The server can use a single TCP connection to send the response body divided into chunks generated on the fly. This is useful if the client can accept partial results, arriving in a streamed fashion.

Persistent TCP connections used by default
> The server is no longer required to close the TCP connection after sending the whole document to the client. This feature improves the latency of fetching subsequent resources, saving one RTT by performing the TCP three-way handshake only once, instead of once per resource fetch. Using the garden hose analogy, this is like watering your garden multiple times without putting away the garden hose between each event.
>
> Persistent connection also improves bandwidth, since long-lived TCP connections have a better chance to utilize TCP congestion control algorithms to optimize data transfer under given network conditions. Following the analogy, this is like increasing the rate of water flow.

Pipelining the HTTP requests
> Sending multiple requests without waiting for the server's answer. The server must send responses in the same order as the requests. This feature didn't gain popularity, due to the HOL blocking, as well as lack of interoperable implementations of pipelining in clients, servers, and intermediaries.

---

30 See RFC 2068, "Hypertext Transfer Protocol—HTTP/1.1" (*https://oreil.ly/LQANn*).

31 "Hypertext Transfer Protocol—HTTP/1.1" (*https://oreil.ly/KIZId*), and several other RFCs appeared afterward. But the first internet standard of HTTP/1.1 (*https://oreil.ly/UGtuU*) was published in only 2022.

32 For a broader discussion about the performance of HTTP versions 1 and 2 in browsers, see *HTTP/2 in Action* by Barry Pollard (O'Reilly, 2019). The book also includes performance analysis of loading real websites using WebPageTest (*https://www.webpagetest.org*).

33 See "IPv4 Address Exhaustion" on Wikipedia (*https://oreil.ly/vodvR*).

Addition and removal of HTTP methods

The new `OPTIONS`, `TRACE`, and `CONNECT` request methods were added. Those that didn't gain implementation traction, like `PATCH`, `LINK`, and `UNLINK`, were removed.[34]

Addition of more HTTP status codes

More HTTP status codes were added, including `101 Switching Protocols` still used today for the WebSocket protocol (see Chapter 10).

Content negotiation

Indicates to the server what the client's preferences are with the help of request headers like `Accept` or `User-Agent`.

Specification of HTTP caching

Caching reduces the number of sent requests and responses.[35]

Requirement to include the `HOST` header in client requests

It was introduced to support HTTP server virtual hosting.[36] Virtual hosting is a feature of serving HTTP content from multiple domains (e.g., *server1.example.com* and *server2.example.org*) using a single IP address. The client chooses the virtual server by sending the desired domain in the request header—*Host: server1.example.com*. This feature reduced the usage of IP addresses.

A recommendation for clients to use multiple TCP connections to the server

The recommendation in RFC was to use at most two connections, but browsers settled for about six connections per domain. Using the garden hose analogy, this corresponds to using multiple narrower hoses instead of a single wide one, with an equal total cross-sectional area. The total bandwidth is the same,[37] but multiple TCP streams may result in a faster fetch completion of some resources.

---

34 A separate RFC exists to restore the `PATCH` method for HTTP (*https://oreil.ly/QZm9f*).

35 "An interesting observation about network-based applications is that the best application performance is obtained by not using the network." By Roy Thomas Fielding (*https://oreil.ly/sSySy*).

36 "One of the worst mistakes in the early HTTP design was the decision not to send the complete URI that is the target of a request message, but rather send only those portions that weren't used in setting up the connection. The assumption was that a server would know its own naming authority based on the IP address and TCP port of the connection. However, this failed to anticipate that multiple naming authorities might exist on a single server, which became a critical problem as the Web grew at an exponential rate and new domain names (the basis for naming authority within the http URL namespace) far exceeded the availability of new IP addresses." By Roy Thomas Fielding from his dissertation (*https://oreil.ly/CiIDl*).

37 Remember that traffic from all connections goes through the (usually) single network card on the device.

HTTP Connection Persistence

The most important addition in HTTP/1.1 is arguably the persistence of the TCP connection. Let's explore it in practice in Example 4-15, and demonstrate HTTP pipelining at the same time, since it depends on the connection persistence. While doing so, you'll see other interesting features of HTTP/1.1 in the headers. To obtain the packet capture, you'll need only a two-pane window.

Example 4-15. HTTP/1.1 demo execution flow (requires setup from Example 4-1)

```
# In a terminal run ❶
tmux new-session \; split-window -v \;

# In the top pane run ❷
CLIENT=http1.1
PCAP_FILE=/tmp/client_${CLIENT}.pcap
docker compose exec client bash -c \
      "sudo rm --force ${PCAP_FILE} && \
      sudo tcpdump -w ${PCAP_FILE} 'port 80' && \
      cp ${PCAP_FILE} tests"

# In the bottom pane run ❸
docker compose exec client bash -c \
      'GET="GET / HTTP/1.1\r\nHost:host\r\n" && echo -en \
      "${GET}Connection:keep-alive\r\n\r\n${GET}Connection:close\r\n\r\n" | \
      netcat -p 8080 http-server 80'
```

❶ Create two panes with `tmux`.

❷ Start a fresh packet capture by using `tcpdump` on the client. The captured traffic will be saved into the *client_http1.1.pcap* file located in the *tests* directory.

❸ Send two consecutive, pipelined `GET /` requests to the server using `netcat`. The first request uses `Connection:keep-alive` explicitly, despite it being an implicit HTTP/1.1 default (verify this by removing the header). The second request uses `Connection:close`, so the server closes the connection after sending the whole document, which is the default behavior for HTTP versions earlier than 1.1. The value of `host` in `Host:host` used in this example is arbitrary, since the server has a default virtual host configured, but this header must be present in an HTTP/1.1 request. Try to verify whether the server conforms to the specification, by removing the header!

The client is expected to print twice the default `http-server` response, containing the "It works!" HTML document, and exit. You see this output in Example 4-16.

Example 4-16. HTTP/1.1 server response

```
HTTP/1.1 200 OK                              ❶
Date: Tue, 23 Jul 2024 16:47:14 GMT
Server: Apache/2.4.61 (Unix)
Last-Modified: Mon, 11 Jun 2007 18:53:14 GMT
ETag: "2d-432a5e4a73a80"                     ❷
Accept-Ranges: bytes                         ❸
Content-Length: 45
Keep-Alive: timeout=5, max=100               ❹
Connection: Keep-Alive                       ❺
Content-Type: text/html

<html><body><h1>It works!</h1></body></html>
HTTP/1.1 200 OK
Date: Tue, 23 Jul 2024 16:47:15 GMT
Server: Apache/2.4.61 (Unix)
Last-Modified: Mon, 11 Jun 2007 18:53:14 GMT
ETag: "2d-432a5e4a73a80"                      ❻
Accept-Ranges: bytes
Content-Length: 45
Connection: close                            ❼
Content-Type: text/html

<html><body><h1>It works!</h1></body></html>
```

❶ The HTTP 200 (OK) status code in the server response indicates that the client's request has succeeded. Remember that every response line ends with an invisible <CR><LF> sequence.

❷ The ETag header is named after *entity tag*. *Entity* refers to the document resource—in this case, the default *index.html* file from 2007 (this Apache serves old content!), served by the server. ETag depends on various resource information, like the size of the HTML file or its modification date, and is used to support caching.

❸ The Accept-Ranges header indicates that the server supports partial content requests, which provides the client with functionalities such as requesting a part of the file or retrying the file download.

❹ The Keep-Alive header notifies the client about the server's persistent connection limits. In this case, the server will wait five seconds for the next request from the client on the same connection, and accept a maximum of 100 requests on a single connection.

❺ The Keep-Alive value of the Connection header informs the server to keep the connection open after the server sends the whole document to the client.

❻ The value of the `ETag` header is unchanged, indicating that the *index.html* file hasn't been modified since the previous client requests.

❼ The `close` value of the `Connection` header informs the server to close the connection after it sends the whole document to the client; in other words, it behaves as in HTTP before version 1.1.

Stop `tcpdump` by pressing Ctrl+C, and read the saved packet capture with `tshark`, as shown in Example 4-17, to identify the persistence of the TCP connection.

Example 4-17. Packet capture file read with `tshark` (requires setup from Example 4-15)

```
CLIENT=http1.1
docker compose exec client bash -c \
      "tshark --read-file tests/client_${CLIENT}.pcap"
```

You will see a sequence like that in Example 4-18.

Example 4-18. HTTP/1.1 client packet sequence

```
client → server TCP  [SYN]       Seq=0               Len=0 ❶
server → client TCP  [SYN, ACK] Seq=0    Ack=1      Len=0 ❶
client → server TCP  [ACK]       Seq=1    Ack=1      Len=0 ❶
client → server HTTP GET / HTTP/1.1 GET / HTTP/1.1    ❷
server → client TCP  [ACK]       Seq=1    Ack=100 Len=0 ❸
server → client HTTP HTTP/1.1 200 OK  (text/html)      ❹
client → server TCP  [ACK]       Seq=100 Ack=327 Len=0
server → client HTTP HTTP/1.1 200 OK  (text/html)      ❺
client → server TCP  [ACK]       Seq=100 Ack=616 Len=0
server → client TCP  [FIN, ACK] Seq=616 Ack=100 Len=0 ❻
client → server TCP  [FIN, ACK] Seq=100 Ack=617 Len=0 ❻
server → client TCP  [ACK]       Seq=617 Ack=101 Len=0 ❻
```

❶ A TCP three-way handshake is established from the client to the server.

❷ The client makes two pipelined HTTP requests to retrieve the default "/" document from the server.

❸ The server acknowledges reception of the HTTP requests from the client.

❹ The server sends the first HTTP response to the client. The server keeps the TCP connection open.

❺ The server sends the second HTTP response to the client.

❻ The server, having sent the whole HTML document to the client, initiates TCP connection termination, and the connection is terminated.

The preceding packet sequence confirms that in HTTP/1.1 the persistence of the TCP connection avoids the three-way handshake RTT in the case of a subsequent HTTP request, reducing its latency.

HTTP/2

The increase in the HTTP major version number from 1 to 2 indicates that the format of a message within the protocol has changed.[38] Work on a protocol called SPDY was revealed by Google in 2009,[39] which later became HTTP/2.[40] The main motivation for HTTP/2 was to further improve the loading speed of websites, compared to HTTP/1.1. The approach taken by Google was to design and evolve the protocol based on experimental results from real web traffic.[41] This was possible thanks to Google's control over both its clients (the Chrome browser was released in 2008) and the server infrastructure. The main features of the HTTP/2 protocol can be summarized as follows:[42]

- HTTP/2 separates HTTP messages into binary encoded frames, with each frame type having a purpose in the protocol—for example, DATA (HTTP message body), HEADERS (HTTP message headers), SETTINGS (various HTTP/2-related settings), or GOAWAY (intent to not start any new streams, or to signal serious errors). Thanks to the inclusion of the message length in the frame format,[43] the HTTP/2 frames are easier to read by machines than HTTP/1. In HTTP/2, the length and type of the frame are read from the beginning of the frame, then the data is read and interpreted according to the frame type. In HTTP/1, the message boundaries are marked by <CR><LF>, and the message body length is determined by the Content-Length header.[44]

---

38 See RFC 2145, "Use and Interpretation of HTTP Version Numbers" (*https://oreil.ly/pr01D*).

39 See "A 2x Faster Web" announcement from the Chromium blog in 2009 (*https://oreil.ly/CEF6z*).

40 See RFC 7540, "Hypertext Transfer Protocol Version 2 (HTTP/2)" (*https://oreil.ly/36n4d*) from 2015.

41 Despite HTTP/2 and HTTP/3 being deployed on the internet, they don't necessarily make every website load faster. In the same way as websites got optimized for HTTP/1, they may need to be adjusted to newer HTTP protocols, to take advantage of their features.

42 Some less often used features of HTTP/2, like resource prioritization or server push (which was already removed from Chrome), aren't covered here. For an extensive description of HTTP/2, see *HTTP/2 in Action* by Barry Pollard (Manning, 2019).

43 See "Frame format" at HTTP/2 (*https://oreil.ly/axiwI*).

44 See the "The HTTP/2 Protocol" chapter in *Learning HTTP/2*.

- HTTP message headers are compressed in HTTP/2. Due to the stateless nature of HTTP (let's ignore the existence of cookies here), headers are sent repeatedly with every HTTP request/response. While HTTP/1.0 already allows for HTTP message body compression, HTTP/2 compresses the headers in a custom HPACK compression format.[45] For HTTP requests, this leads to a reduction in the proportion of the size of the HTTP message headers compared to the message body, and also results in gains for HTTP responses.[46]

- HTTP/2 multiplexes different HTTP messages, as illustrated in Figure 4-6. HTTP/2 still uses TCP as the transport protocol, and a TCP segment's data may contain several HTTP/2 frames.

HTTP/2 introduces the concept of a stream (which is different from a TCP stream, see "TCP Connection Versus TCP Stream" on page 88), defined as "an independent, bidirectional sequence of frames exchanged between the client and server within an HTTP/2 connection." This means that a single TCP segment can contain HTTP/2 frames belonging to different HTTP document resource streams (e.g., different CSS files).

A TCP segment may also carry a single HTTP/2 DATA frame belonging to the given stream, and such TCP segments may be present in the TCP stream in a round-robin fashion. A client can also dynamically request a change to the priority of these streams, by sending a PRIORITY frame. These features of HTTP/2 effectively allow for multiplexing.

It should be noted that despite multiplexing, HTTP/2 doesn't solve the HOL blocking problem (see "TCP Head-of-Line Blocking" on page 122), since it uses a single TCP connection.[47] Multiplexing at the application layer as implemented in HTTP/2 allows for lower latency fetching of multiple HTTP resources in networks without packet loss. When a loss occurs, a TCP segment that carries one HTTP/2 stream will block the reassembly of the remaining segments in the TCP stream, also blocking other HTTP/2 streams.[48]

---

45 The "HPACK: Header Compression for HTTP/2" format (*https://oreil.ly/K9ija*) was designed to reduce vulnerability of compression to CRIME-like (Compression Ratio Info-leak Made Easy) security attacks.

46 See the Cloudflare blog "HPACK: The Silent Killer (Feature) of HTTP/2" (*https://oreil.ly/6qZaR*) by Vlad Krasnov.

47 For more details and examples of HOL blocking in HTTP/2, see the section "HOL blocking in HTTP/2 over TCP" (*https://oreil.ly/Jghqj*) in Robin Marx's post.

48 Since HTTP/2 doesn't solve the TCP HOL blocking problem, it was questioned whether speeding up HTTP with minimal protocol changes (*https://oreil.ly/jx5J9*) was possible by adding additional headers to HTTP/1.1.

While the message delivered over HTTP/2 is similar in format to HTTP, the binary framing makes HTTP/2 look unusual at the network packet level. This has consequences for the possibilities to deploy such a novel protocol over the internet, due to the existence of middleboxes,[49] which, together with the end-user devices, restrict the evolution of network protocols, resulting in so-called *protocol ossification*.

Some middleboxes may block unrecognized traffic or modify the metadata information (e.g., HTTP or TCP headers), breaking the new protocol version. It may take years for middleboxes and operating systems to adopt a new protocol version. A solution to this problem is to hide the packet structure from middleboxes' eyes by using encryption, and implement the protocols outside of the operating system kernel space, in the user space (see "HTTP/3" on page 139). The HTTP/2 specification doesn't require encryption, but web browsers support only the HTTP/2 encrypted version, called h2. Other client types also support the cleartext version, called h2c.

HTTP/2 Frames and Streams

The main features of HTTP/2 that make it different from HTTP/1.1 include binary-encoded frames, header compression, and multiplexing using streams. When becoming familiar with HTTP/2, you may find it helpful to use the nghttp2 client (*https:// oreil.ly/vhHNM*), which understands the protocol and presents an overview of the exchanged messages in a human-readable way. Example 4-19 shows an example of performing an HTTP/2 request using nghttp2.

Example 4-19. HTTP/2 demo execution flow (requires setup from Example 4-1)

```
# In a terminal run ❶
tmux new-session \; split-window -v \;

# In the top pane run ❷
CLIENT=h2c
PCAP_FILE=/tmp/client_${CLIENT}.pcap
docker compose exec client bash -c \
      "sudo rm --force ${PCAP_FILE} && \
      sudo tcpdump -w ${PCAP_FILE} 'port 80' && \
      cp ${PCAP_FILE} tests"

# In the bottom pane run ❸
docker compose exec client bash -c \
      "nghttp --verbose --timeout 3 --no-dep --hexdump \
      http://https-server:80"
```

---

49 A *middlebox* is defined as any intermediary device performing functions other than the functions of an IP router; see RFC 3234, "Middleboxes: Taxonomy and Issues" (*https://oreil.ly/umnRJ*). Examples of middleboxes include NAT, firewalls, load balancers, intrusion detection and prevention systems, and CDN caches.

❶ Create two panes with `tmux`.

❷ Start a fresh packet capture by using `tcpdump` on the client. The captured traffic will be saved into the *client_h2c.pcap* file located in the *tests* directory.

❸ Send an HTTP/2 request to the server using the `nghttp2` client. The client will exit after successfully receiving the response from the server. Note that the destination server is called `https-server`, but in addition to serving h2 on the default port 443 (default HTTPS port), it is configured to support cleartext h2c on port 80. To simplify the discussion, the `--no-dep` argument of `nghttp2` is used, to avoid the client sending resource prioritization information to the server.

When working hands-on, you'll get output like that in Example 4-20, but colored.

Example 4-20. h2c server response to the `nghttp2` request

```
[  0.001] Connected
[  0.001] send SETTINGS frame <length=12, flags=0x00, stream_id=0>        ❶
          (niv=2)
          [SETTINGS_MAX_CONCURRENT_STREAMS(0x03):100]
          [SETTINGS_INITIAL_WINDOW_SIZE(0x04):65535]
[  0.001] send HEADERS frame <length=32, flags=0x05, stream_id=1>         ❷
          ; END_STREAM | END_HEADERS
          (padlen=0)
          ; Open new stream
          :method: GET
          :path: /
          :scheme: http
          :authority: https-server
          accept: */*
          accept-encoding: gzip, deflate
          user-agent: nghttp2/1.62.1
[  0.005] recv SETTINGS frame <length=18, flags=0x00, stream_id=0>        ❸
          (niv=3)
          [SETTINGS_MAX_CONCURRENT_STREAMS(0x03):128]
          [SETTINGS_INITIAL_WINDOW_SIZE(0x04):65536]
          [SETTINGS_MAX_FRAME_SIZE(0x05):16777215]
[  0.005] recv WINDOW_UPDATE frame <length=4, flags=0x00, stream_id=0>
          (window_size_increment=2147418112)
[  0.005] recv SETTINGS frame <length=0, flags=0x01, stream_id=0>
          ; ACK
          (niv=0)
[  0.005] recv (stream_id=1) :status: 200                                 ❹
[  0.005] recv (stream_id=1) server: nginx/1.27.0
[  0.005] recv (stream_id=1) date: Sat, 27 Jul 2024 19:21:01 GMT
[  0.005] recv (stream_id=1) content-type: text/html
[  0.005] recv (stream_id=1) content-length: 55
[  0.005] recv (stream_id=1) last-modified: Sat, 27 Jul 2024 19:17:56 GMT
```

```
[  0.005] recv (stream_id=1) etag: "66a547e4-37"
[  0.005] recv (stream_id=1) accept-ranges: bytes
[  0.005] recv HEADERS frame <length=106, flags=0x04, stream_id=1>
          ; END_HEADERS
          (padlen=0)
          ; First response header
[  0.005] send SETTINGS frame <length=0, flags=0x01, stream_id=0>
          ; ACK
          (niv=0)
<!DOCTYPE html><title>Welcome to nginx!</title></html>                    ❺
[  0.008] recv DATA frame <length=55, flags=0x01, stream_id=1>
          ; END_STREAM
[  0.008] send GOAWAY frame <length=8, flags=0x00, stream_id=0>            ❻
          (last_stream_id=0, error_code=NO_ERROR(0x00), opaque_data(0)=[])
```

❶ After connecting to the server, the client sends its HTTP/2 protocol settings in a
SETTINGS frame—the number of concurrent streams and the initial window size,
which controls how much data is initially sent in a stream. The settings are
always exchanged over stream 0.

❷ The client sends a HEADERS frame, which contains HTTP headers, in stream 1.

❸ The server sends several SETTINGS and WINDOW_UPDATE frames.

❹ The server sends the HTTP message headers. Note that due to the implementation details (*https://oreil.ly/FCJM1*) of nghttp2, the actual values of the headers
show up in the output before the HEADERS frame, which appears a few lines
below.

❺ The server sends the HTTP message body. The DATA frame containing the data
also appears in the output after the actual data.

❻ The client indicates the intention not to start any new streams, by sending a
GOAWAY frame to the server.

Stop the tcpdump by pressing Ctrl+C, and read the saved packet capture with tshark,
as shown in Example 4-21.

*Example 4-21. Packet capture file read with tshark (requires setup from
Example 4-19)*

```
CLIENT=h2c
docker compose exec client bash -c \
       "tshark --read-file tests/client_${CLIENT}.pcap"
```

You will see a sequence like that in Example 4-22. The sequence shows the relation of HTTP/2 to TCP, including the functionality of several HTTP/2 frames being carried by a single TCP segment.

Example 4-22. h2c client packet sequence

```
client → server TCP   [SYN]      Seq=0             Len=0    ❶
server → client TCP   [SYN, ACK] Seq=0    Ack=1    Len=0    ❶
client → server TCP   [ACK]      Seq=1    Ack=1    Len=0    ❶
client → server HTTP2 Magic, SETTINGS[0], HEADERS[1]: GET / ❷
server → client TCP   [ACK]      Seq=1    Ack=87   Len=0
server → client HTTP2 SETTINGS[0], ..., HEADERS[1]: 200 OK  ❸
client → server TCP   [ACK]      Seq=87   Ack=165  Len=0
client → server HTTP2 SETTINGS[0]
server → client HTTP2 DATA[1] (text/html)                   ❹
client → server HTTP2 GOAWAY[0]                             ❺
client → server TCP   [FIN, ACK] Seq=113 Ack=229 Len=0     ❻
server → client TCP   [FIN, ACK] Seq=229 Ack=114 Len=0     ❻
client → server TCP   [ACK]      Seq=114 Ack=230 Len=0     ❻
```

❶ A TCP three-way handshake is established from the client to the server. Recall that, in this case, the server accepts the cleartext h2c traffic.

❷ The client sends a so-called "magic" message, indicating the HTTP/2 protocol,[50] followed by SETTINGS and HEADERS frames.

❸ The server responds with its own SETTINGS and several other frames, including its HEADERS.

❹ The server sends the HTTP body message to the client in a DATA frame, over stream number 1.

❺ The client indicates the intention not to start any new streams, by sending a GOAWAY frame to the server.

❻ The client initiates TCP connection termination, and the connection is terminated.

---

50 The magic message is PRI * HTTP/2.0\r\n\r\nSM\r\n\r\n, possibly in relation to the secret PRISM program (*https://oreil.ly/cENO7*) revealed by Edward Snowden in 2013.

HTTP/3

From the early 2010s, with the rise of mobile devices like smartphones (iPhone was announced in 2007) or tablets, with their less performant networks, reducing the latency of fetching web resources continued to be the first priority for HTTP. Additionally, the concept of multihoming (a device using multiple network interfaces or IP addresses) and connection migration became important. When mobile devices move between home WiFi and cellular network like 5G, or travel longer distances on a cellular network, like during a fast-speed train trip, they change their IP addresses. This leads to TCP connection termination and reestablishment.[51]

Around that time, several protocols already existed to address some of the limitations of TCP: T/TCP (Transaction TCP RFC from 1994) (*https://oreil.ly/6elYM*), STCP (Stream TCP RFC from 2000) (*https://oreil.ly/mCzYq*), MPTCP (Multipath TCP draft RFC from 2012) (*https://oreil.ly/Ueg8S*), or TCP Fast Open (draft RFC from 2012) (*https://oreil.ly/55Gva*). However, they were incomplete solutions, had security problems, or lacked adoption due to the ossification of TCP deployed on the internet.

In 2013 Google announced work[52] on a transport protocol called QUIC,[53] which was inspired by ideas from protocols like Stream TCP and TCP Fast Open, and became the basis of HTTP/3 (*https://oreil.ly/I7U34*). As with HTTP/2, QUIC used the idea of hiding the protocol details from middleboxes by using encryption. The use of mandatory encryption in QUIC coincided with the increasing TLS adoption on the internet (e.g., Let's Encrypt was formed in 2014). Other factors to facilitate the adoption of QUIC included creation of a protocol that operates in application (user space), instead of the operating system (kernel space), and basing the protocol on UDP instead of creating a new protocol, which could have taken years to be deployed on the internet.

Figure 4-5 depicts selected protocol-level features of HTTP/3 and QUIC, in comparison with the HTTP/1.1 and HTTP/2 versions.

---

51 "When we split IP from TCP, I thought it was very clever to use the IP address as part of the end-point connection identifier...Turns out to have been a bad mistake. It screwed up multi-homing, it screwed up mobility where IP addresses were changing." By Vint Cerf from "Reimagining the Internet" (*https://oreil.ly/xagef*) in 2010.

52 See Google's 2013 announcement of QUIC (*https://oreil.ly/WDECL*). For a more recent overview of the factors that led to the creation of QUIC, see the YouTube video "AWS re:Invent 2022—Deliver Great Experiences with QUIC on Amazon CloudFront" (*https://oreil.ly/h8bmt*) by Jim Roskind, the architect of QUIC at Google.

53 For a comparison of TCP and QUIC, see the YouTube video "Explaining QUIC: The Protocol That Is Both Very Similar to and Very Different from TCP" (*https://oreil.ly/GnWF0*) by Peter Doornbosch.

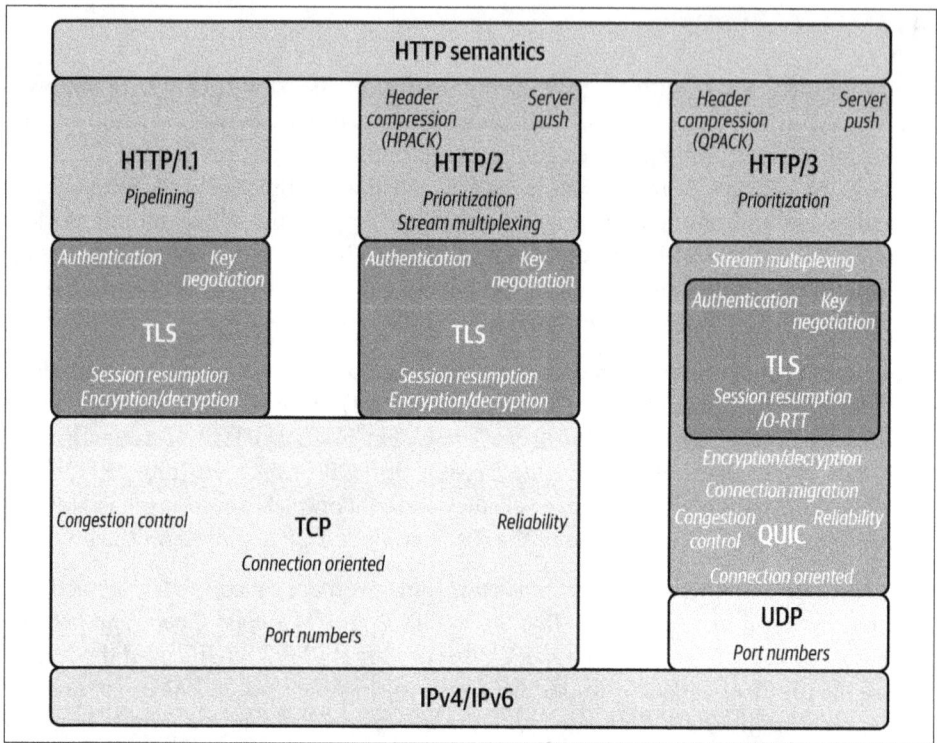

Figure 4-5. Evolutionary comparison of HTTP versions (after Robin Marx)[54]

Here is a list of the main features of QUIC:[55]

Mandatory encryption[56] and tight integration with TLS
QUIC doesn't use TLS in a traditional OSI model layer sense. Instead, QUIC uses some TLS APIs to obtain cryptographic information. QUIC encrypts every packet individually, while TLS operates on records of a maximum of 16 KB size, meaning a TLS record will spread across multiple TCP segments. TLS needs the whole record to decrypt the data, and this results in potential TLS HOL blocking, which QUIC eliminates.

---

54 See the section "HTTP/3 Protocol Stack Diagrams" (*https://oreil.ly/128mT*) in Robin Marx's post.

55 For a detailed overview of QUIC and HTTP/3, see the series of posts by Robin Marx at "HTTP/3 From A To Z: Core Concepts" (*https://oreil.ly/0BmQb*).

56 One of the last unencrypted pieces is Server Name Indication (SNI) sent in ClientHello, which reveals the target domain. See "Encrypted Client Hello—The Last Puzzle Piece to Privacy" (*https://oreil.ly/ziZNH*) by Achiel van der Mandele et al.

Reduction of the number of RTTs before the client sends HTTP messages

QUIC achieves this by using an optimistic handshake. In the QUIC handshake, the client sends its guess about the server's TLS parameters, and this allows for a reduction in the initial connection to one RTT. Moreover, similarly to TCP Fast Open, QUIC supports 0-RTT (a feature of TLS 1.3) reconnection, in the case of a returning client and using a safe HTTP method (*https://oreil.ly/0agNj*). With 0-RTT, the client can send an HTTP message immediately. This is possible thanks to optimistically assuming that the TLS information didn't change since the last client connection. An additional mechanism consisting of a validation token and a fallback to using more RTTs exists to prevent reflection attacks, in case the client isn't legitimate. The reduction of the number of RTTs in QUIC will more noticeably benefit high-latency (e.g., mobile) networks.

Support for connection migration

Instead of the four-tuple used by TCP for connection identification (source IP address, source port, destination IP address, destination port), QUIC uses a set of encrypted *connection IDs* that are generated and exchanged during the handshake. During the connection migration, the client, for privacy reasons,[57] uses one of these connection IDs, and this allows the server to migrate the connection without a disruption. This feature may have a noticeable impact on web applications that require continuous interaction with users.

Reduction of the HOL blocking problem compared to TCP

QUIC uses independent streams, as illustrated in Figure 4-6, and therefore the HOL blocking problem is limited to the streams affected by the loss of the given packet carrying them. QUIC can multiplex streams within a single packet and among packets. However, packet loss on the internet is often bursty, meaning QUIC packets carrying multiple streams may be lost within the given time interval. Therefore, the gains thanks to HOL blocking reduction are unclear in such cases. A consequence of the QUIC HOL blocking on the stream level is that while QUIC streams are ordered internally, they aren't necessarily ordered across different streams. A dedicated QPACK header compression algorithm was developed due to this behavior, as HPACK compression used by HTTP/2 required an ordered delivery of streams.

---

57 The connection ID is present in plaintext in the packet, and would allow tracking of the client.

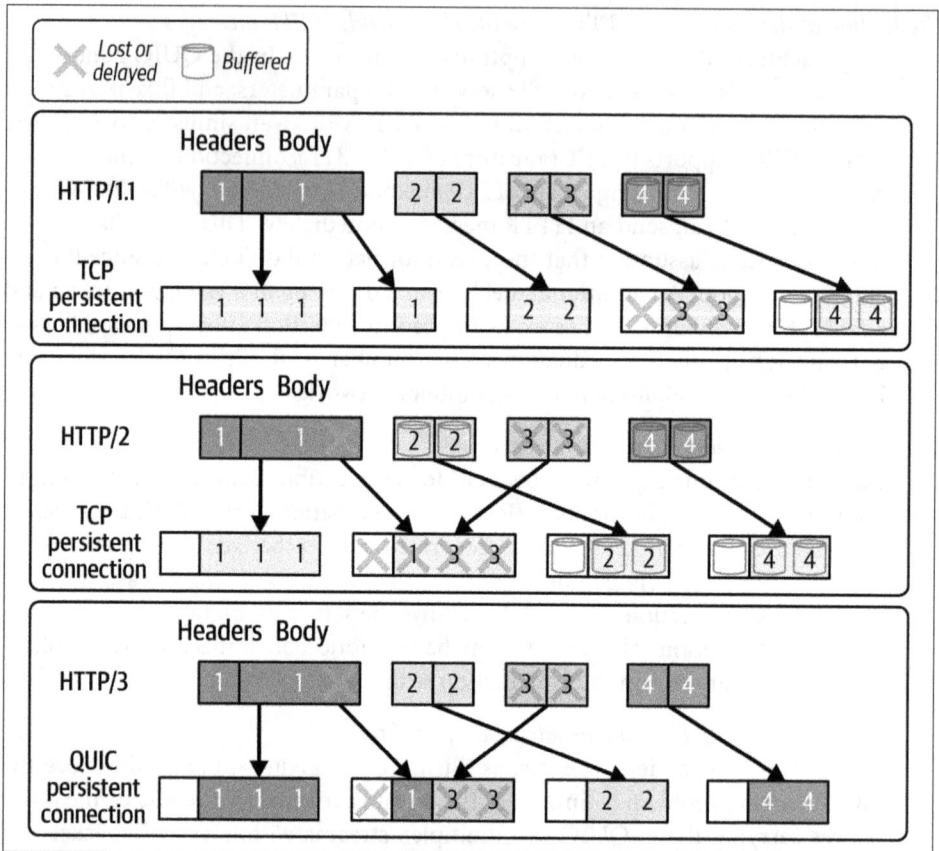

Figure 4-6. Overview of multiplexing and head-of-line blocking in HTTP

In HTTP/1.1, when a TCP segment (labeled 3 on the diagram) is lost or delayed, the subsequent segments are sent by the sender, but buffered at the receiver. As a consequence, the HTTP messages (3 and 4) cannot be delivered to the receiver application, until the missing segments are retransmitted, and TCP reassembles the stream. This is because TCP persistent connection operates on the whole stream, indicated by the uniform, light gray color—where each TCP segment must be delivered in order.

HTTP/2 allows for multiplexing of HTTP/2 frames that belong to different HTTP messages in a single TCP segment, as well as multiplexing of different HTTP messages among TCP segments. In the case shown in the diagram, this results in HTTP messages 2 and 4 being buffered, since the lost/delayed second TCP segment contains both the parts of HTTP 1 and 3 messages.

In the case of HTTP/3, the problem of HOL blocking is reduced, since each QUIC stream is independent, as indicated by different shades. When the QUIC packet carrying the frames that belong to HTTP messages 1 and 3 is lost or delayed, the HOL blocks only the streams that contain these frames.

QUIC 1-RTT Connection Establishment

Figure 4-7 visualizes the differences in the number of RTTs needed during the initialization of the connection with the server, before the client can send the first HTTP request. Both HTTP/2 and HTTP/1 require two RTTs, and HTTP/3 requires one. The diagram also shows the reconnection (the mobile client on WiFi disconnects from the server and connects again) and connection migration (the client moves from WiFi to a 5G network), which under ideal conditions can operate as 0-RTT, meaning that the HTTP request can be sent by the client within the first RTT.

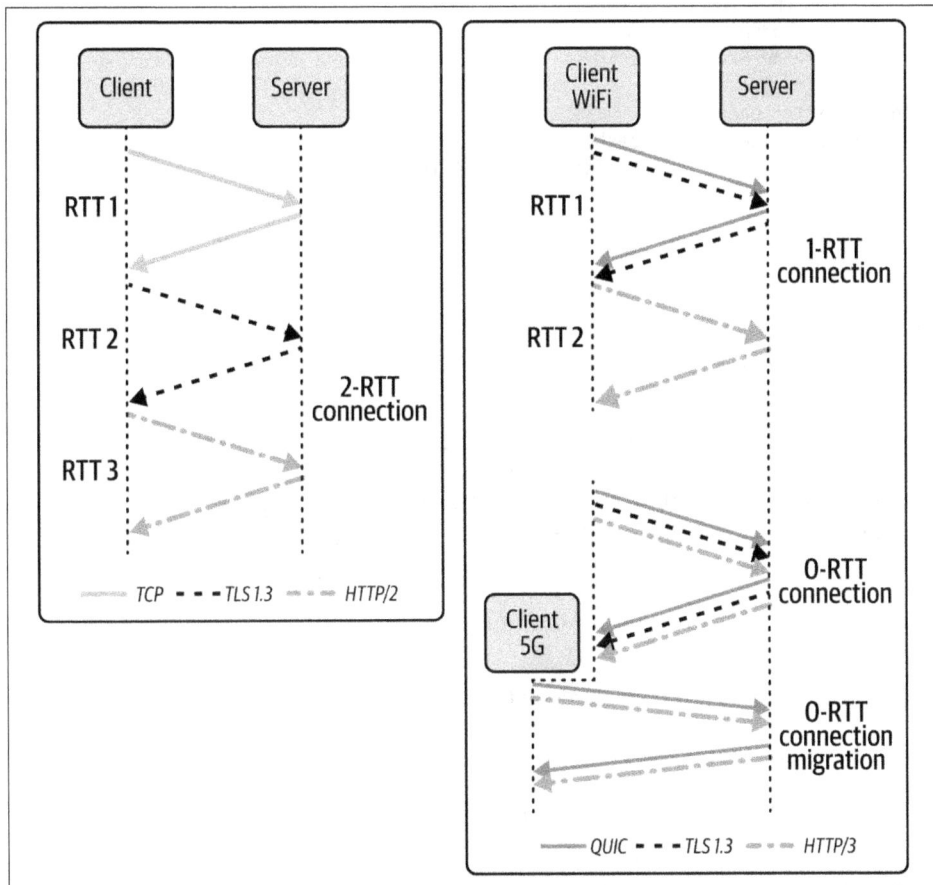

Figure 4-7. RTTs and connection migration in HTTP/3

Using Example 4-23, let's examine a packet sequence for a QUIC 1-RTT connection establishment in HTTP/3, to see how it differs from TLS. For this, we'll need a two-pane window.

Example 4-23. HTTP/3 demo execution flow (requires setup from Example 4-1)

```
# In a terminal run ❶
tmux new-session \; split-window -v \;

# In the top pane run ❷
CLIENT=http3
PCAP_FILE=/tmp/client_${CLIENT}.pcap
docker compose exec client bash -c \
      "sudo rm --force ${PCAP_FILE} && \
      sudo tcpdump -w ${PCAP_FILE} 'port 80 or port 443' && \
      cp ${PCAP_FILE} tests"

# In the bottom pane run ❸
docker compose exec client bash -c \
      "export SSLKEYLOGFILE=tests/SSLKEYLOGFILE.client && \
      curl --http3 --insecure --verbose https://https-server"
```

❶ Create two panes with `tmux`.

❷ Start a fresh packet capture by using `tcpdump` on the client. The captured traffic will be saved into the *client_http3.pcap* file located in the *tests* directory.

❸ Send an HTTP/3 request to the server using the `curl` command-line tool (*https://curl.se*). In `curl`, *c* stands for *client*, and the tool supports many web network protocols. The client will exit after successfully receiving the response from the server. The `--insecure` option is needed in our case, since it allows the client to accept the self-signed TLS certificate from the server.

Example 4-24 shows the expected `curl` output.

Example 4-24. HTTP/3 server response to the curl request

```
* Host https-server:443 was resolved.
* using HTTP/3
* [HTTP/3] [0] OPENED stream for https://https-server/  ❶
* [HTTP/3] [0] [:method: GET]
* [HTTP/3] [0] [:scheme: https]
* [HTTP/3] [0] [:authority: https-server]
* [HTTP/3] [0] [:path: /]
* [HTTP/3] [0] [user-agent: curl/8.8.0]
* [HTTP/3] [0] [accept: */*]
> GET / HTTP/3
```

```
> Host: https-server
> User-Agent: curl/8.8.0
> Accept: */*
>
* Request completely sent off
< HTTP/3 200                                    ❷
< server: nginx/1.27.0
< date: Wed, 31 Jul 2024 19:16:10 GMT
< content-type: text/html
< content-length: 55
< last-modified: Sat, 27 Jul 2024 19:17:56 GMT
< etag: "66a547e4-37"
< alt-svc: h3=":443"; ma=86400                  ❸
< accept-ranges: bytes
<
<!DOCTYPE html><title>Welcome to nginx!</title></html>  ❹
```

❶ After connecting to the server, the client sends an HTTP GET / request over QUIC stream 0.

❷ The client receives HTTP message headers from the server.

❸ The server using the alt-svc header indicates that it supports HTTP/3 for the next 24 hours.

❹ The HTTP message body follows the headers in the server response.

Stop tcpdump by pressing Ctrl+C. Example 4-25 shows how the generated packet capture is decrypted using the secrets read from *SSLKEYLOGFILE* and is stored in a *.pcapng* file.

Example 4-25. HTTP/3 packet capture decryption with editcap (requires setup from Example 4-23)

```
CLIENT=http3
docker compose exec client bash -c \
    "cd tests && \
    editcap --inject-secrets tls,SSLKEYLOGFILE.client \
    client_${CLIENT}.pcap client_${CLIENT}.pcapng"
```

The *.pcapng* file can be read now with `tshark`, shown in Example 4-26, or loaded into Wireshark for more detailed explorations.

Example 4-26. Packet capture file read with `tshark` (requires setup from Example 4-25)

```
CLIENT=http3
docker compose exec client bash -c \
    "tshark --read-file tests/client_${CLIENT}.pcapng"
```

You will see a sequence like in Example 4-27. This packet capture provides more details about the QUIC protocol than the client-side view from `curl`. Expect that when new versions of QUIC are implemented, some details of this sequence may change. Therefore, only the most prominent features of HTTP/3 are annotated.

Example 4-27. HTTP/3 client packet sequence

```
0.000 client → server QUIC    Initial, DCID=a, SCID=b, PKN: 0, CRYPTO, PADDING    ❶
0.003 server → client QUIC Handshake, DCID=b, SCID=c, PKN: 0, CRYPTO, CRYPTO      ❷
0.003 server → client QUIC Handshake, DCID=b, SCID=c, PKN: 1, CRYPTO, CRYPTO      ❸
0.006 client → server QUIC Handshake, DCID=c, SCID=b, PKN: 0, ACK, CRYPTO         ❹
0.006 client → server QUIC  PP (KP0), DCID=c, PKN: 1, PING, PADDING               ❺
0.007 client → server HTTP3 PP (KP0), DCID=c, PKN: 2, STREAM(0), HEADERS: GET /   ❻
0.007 server → client HTTP3 PP (KP0), DCID=b, PKN: 0, ACK, CRYPTO, DONE, NCI, ...
0.008 client → server QUIC  PP (KP0), DCID=c, PKN: 3, ACK
0.010 server → client HTTP3 PP (KP0), DCID=b, PKN: 1, STREAM(0),
                                                      HEADERS: 200 OK, DATA       ❼
0.011 client → server QUIC  PP (KP0), DCID=c, PKN: 4, PING, PADDING
0.011 client → server QUIC  PP (KP0), DCID=c, PKN: 5, CC                          ❽
```

❶ The client sends the `Initial` QUIC packet to the server. The `CRYPTO` frame contains the TLS 1.3 `Client Hello`, and various TLS extensions, including the Application-Layer Protocol Negotiation (ALPN), in which the client indicates to the server that it supports h3 (HTTP/3). The SNI, which contains the domain name of the server, is also present. Additionally, various QUIC transport parameters are present in the `CRYPTO` frame. The `PADDING` frame is added to artificially increase the packet size, in an attempt to prevent website fingerprinting attacks (guessing the visited website based on the analysis of the packet sizes). The client sets `DCID` (destination connection ID) to a value it chooses, which will be overwritten by the actual value provided by the server, by its `SCID` (source connection ID) in the next QUIC packet. The `PKN` (package number) is increasing within each packet type (`Initial`, `Handshake`, and `1-RTT` types), and there is a separate sequence for sent and received packets. The `PKN` is similar in role to the TCP sequence number. Note that this QUIC packet is unencrypted.

❷ The server responds with the `Handshake` packet, which contains `CRYPTO` frames. It contains the TLS 1.3 `Server Hello` and the server certificate fragment. The information, like the certificate or ALPN, is encrypted. The timestamp of this packet provides an estimate of the RTT of about 0.003 seconds.

❸ The server finishes transferring the encrypted certificate.

❹ The QUIC (and TLS) handshake is finished.

❺ This packet starts the `1-RTT` packet type sequence. `PP` is an abbreviation for *Protected Payload*, indicating that the QUIC packets are protected using 1-RTT traffic secrets. The `PING` frame is a liveness indication from the client.

❻ The client sends an HTTP request in stream 0. Note that this happens during the second RTT, as expected.

❼ The server sends the HTTP message headers and body.

❽ The client sends the `CC` (`CONNECTION_CLOSE`) frame.

In 2024, all three HTTP versions (HTTP/1.1, HTTP/2, and HTTP/3) are in active use on the web. How much traffic each one carries depends on the kind of client (e.g., desktop browsers, mobile apps, or automated bots) and the kind of server they talk to.[58] About 60% of websites (accessed using a browser) support HTTP/2, and this fraction has been stable over the past few years, showing a slight decrease. On the other hand, about 30% of websites support HTTP/3, and this support is still growing.[59] However, in terms of the HTTP version used for APIs, HTTP/1.1 still dominates with about 50% of requests, but it's also showing a slight decrease. Despite this, some search or social media bots use HTTP/1.1 almost exclusively.

What are the consequences of HTTP/3 for web APIs? The performance gains from the reduced number of RTTs may be noticeable on high-latency networks, in regions with less performant network infrastructure. However, a client may decide first to use HTTP/1.1 or HTTP/2, and only after the confirmation of HTTP/3 support from the server, in the form of an `alt-svc: h3=":443"; ma=86400` header, the client will switch to HTTP/3. This will result in additional RTTs and negate the initial

---

58 For details, see the "Examining HTTP/3 Usage One Year On" Cloudflare blog post (*https://oreil.ly/FQaYA*) by David Belson and Lucas Pardue and the State of the Web report (*https://oreil.ly/UrAHU*).

59 HTTP/3 support has been available in major browsers since mid-2024, according to the Can I Use website (*https://oreil.ly/AVr1J*). This is also the case for the `curl` program on Debian Linux, used for demonstrations in this chapter; see "Debian's curl Now Supports HTTP/3" (*https://oreil.ly/GE9lY*) by Samuel Henrique.

connection latency reduction benefits of QUIC. However, an advantage of HTTP/3 is header compression, which helps reduce internet traffic size.

On the other hand, QUIC currently incurs processing costs on the devices since UDP isn't as optimized as TCP, and TLS operations per packet are relatively more frequent compared to operations per record. HTTP/3 isn't supported natively on some cloud application hosting platforms, like Google App Engine, Azure App Service, or AWS Elastic Beanstalk, which require the use of a proxy, such as a CDN, gateway, or load balancer service to support HTTP/3 traffic. Enterprises may rely on older middle-boxes, which don't support TLS 1.3, and even if they do, they may block QUIC (and UDP) traffic. Instead, middleboxes, which are in an MITM attack position,[60] prefer the older TLS 1.2 protocol so that they can use static keys to more easily decrypt and inspect the traffic.

The main immediate advantage of HTTP/3 could be its use as a vehicle for the deployment of QUIC on the internet.[61] This opened possibilities to develop other protocols on top of QUIC and HTTP/3, like Apple's iCloud Private Relay over QUIC, Microsoft's Server Message Block (SMB) over QUIC, Secure Shell (SSH) over HTTP/3, or WebTransport over HTTP/3.

Exercises

1. The `http-server` implements an HTTP POST using a Common Gateway Interface (CGI) script, located in the *src/http/httpd/post.sh* file. CGI is a feature of a web server to execute a program following an HTTP request. The following `curl` request returns a 400 HTTP status error code. Consult the HTTP/1.0 and HTTP/1.1 RFCs to verify if the implementation of the script conforms to the expected POST behavior, and find out how to make a successful POST request against this server. Hint: what headers are required from an HTTP/1.1 POST request?

   ```
   docker compose exec client bash -c \
           "curl --data 'test' --http1.1 \
           --header 'Content-Length:' \
           --verbose http://http-server/cgi-bin/post.sh"
   ```

2. The `http-server` also implements chunked transfer coding using CGI. Try it out and understand its CGI implementation, located in *src/http/httpd/chunked.sh*:

---

60 Middleboxes are commonly used in enterprises. For an explanation, see the Cloudflare blog "Understanding the Prevalence of Web Traffic Interception" (*https://oreil.ly/ESMLv*) by Ellie Bursztein.

61 See "A Sleight of Hand!" by Jana Iyengar, part of the YouTube video "IETF 115 Technology Deep Dive: QUIC Part 1" (*https://oreil.ly/PCzOI*).

```
docker compose exec client bash -c \
      "curl --http1.1 \
      --verbose http://http-server/cgi-bin/chunked.sh"
```

3. Modify Example 4-11 to export the `SSLKEYLOGFILE` environment variable before starting Firefox, and access an HTTP/3-enabled website: *https://www.google.com* or *https://cloudflare-quic.com*. Save the decrypted packet capture as *.pcapng*, as in Example 4-25, load this file into Wireshark, and try to answer questions like these: Does the browser use HTTP/3? Does it use HTTP/3 immediately, or does it perform a connection upgrade by using the `alt-svc` header? How many connections does it open per domain?

Summary

This chapter guided you through the transport and application layer protocols used on the web today. You learned about modern features of HTTP by comparing them to those of the initial HTTP/0.9 protocol, which allowed only fetching ASCII-encoded, unencrypted text over TCP. You got to know the latest version, HTTP/3, which exchanges text and other file formats over a binary-encoded, encrypted, UDP-based QUIC transport protocol.

While the main goal of optimizing HTTP has been to improve browser speed for fetching websites, understanding HTTP features is useful when working with HTTP-based APIs. Throughout the chapter, you looked at how various characteristics of the network protocols affect HTTP security (like default encryption in QUIC), performance (such as the impact of DNS and the TCP three-way handshake on latency), and reliability (like the ability of TCP and QUIC to recover from packet losses and network errors). Familiarity with HTTP also creates a conceptual base for working with lesser-known APIs like gRPC or WebSocket, described in further chapters.

This concludes the introduction to the protocol aspects of network-based APIs discussed in this book. In the remaining part of the book, you'll explore various API styles, starting with REST in Chapter 5.

REST

Representational State Transfer (REST) is the most popular network-based API.[1] The REST architectural style[2] was formulated in 2000 by Roy Fielding in his Ph.D. dissertation "Architectural Styles and the Design of Network-Based Software Architectures" (*https://oreil.ly/YJo5o*), as an approach to create internet-scale network-based applications.

This chapter goes through the origins, implementation, testing, security, documentation, and trade-offs of REST APIs. You'll implement a REST API by using the Django REST Framework (DRF) (*https://www.django-rest-framework.org*), for the Weather Forecast Service (WFS), introduced in "Weather Forecast Service" on page xv.

HTTP, Resource, and URI

In practice, the architectural goals of REST translate into three main components: HTTP, a resource, and a URI.

HTTP is the blood vessel of the internet, and the majority of API styles described in this book use HTTP to exchange messages. It's supported by clients such as web browsers, command-line tools like curl (*https://curl.se*), and libraries for various programming languages. HTTP is an application layer protocol that can be text-based or binary.[3] You can find more details about HTTP in Chapter 4.

---

1 Postman's "State of the API Report" (*https://oreil.ly/3LG67*) places REST as the most popular API technology.

2 Roy Fielding defines an *architectural style* in "Architectural Styles and the Design of Network-Based Software Architectures" (*https://oreil.ly/GuS8w*) as "a coordinated set of architectural constraints that restricts the roles/features of architectural elements and the allowed relationships among those elements."

3 HTTP protocols until the HTTP/1.1 version are text-based, and from version HTTP/2 are binary.

In REST, any information that can be named can be a resource—for example, a document, an image, a numerical value of zero, or even a person (a human being, a non-virtual named entity not accessible via the internet).[4] A resource is anything that can be a target of a hypertext reference.[5]

A resource can be static or dynamic. A *static resource* is immutable, like an image served from a file by a web server. As long as the static resource exists, the same content is served to every client. If the resource is changed, it's treated as a new resource. On the other hand, a *dynamic resource* is tailored to individual clients. For example, the */user/profile* endpoint returns content specific to the logged-in user.

Both static and dynamic resources are identified by their media types (formerly known as MIME types, a term that is still commonly used). A *media type* describes the file format or content type of a resource, helping clients understand how to process it. For example, a static resource like an image might have a media type of *image/png*, an HTML web page will have *text/html*, and dynamic JSON data will use *application/json*. There exist over 1,600 official media types (*https://oreil.ly/aijMf*), and over 3,000 known media types for various kinds of data (*https://oreil.ly/Jcg78*).

The internet contains approximately 1.1 billion websites (*https://oreil.ly/W4jFt*), composed of multiple resources, such as files, images, videos,[6] blogs, tutorials, news, journals, and many others. The purpose of a Uniform Resource Identifier (URI) (*https://oreil.ly/fiIDU*) is to provide an identifier to distinguish the given resource from other resources. A URI distinguishes but doesn't guarantee an identity of a resource, since the underlying resource can be changed.[7]

A *URI* is a string of characters that identifies a resource. Uniformity allows different types of resource identifiers to follow a common structure, making them interoperable. URI is a broad term that encapsulates two additional terms: *Uniform Resource Locator* (URL) and *Uniform Resource Name* (URN) (*https://oreil.ly/nhBF6*).

The URL specifies both how to access the resource (protocol), and the location of the resource. For example, *https://example.com/rfc3986.txt* contains the resource access mechanism (*https*), the name of the server hosting it (*example.com*), the location("/"), and the resource name (*rfc3986.txt*).

---

4 See "Resources and Resource Identifiers" in Chapter 5, "Representational State Transfer (REST)" of Fielding's dissertation (*https://oreil.ly/te5si*).

5 The concept of hypertext dates back to Ted Holm Nelson in 1965 and was later described by Tim Berners-Lee in 1989 as human-readable information linked together in an unconstrained way. See "What Is Hypertext?" on page 105 for the origins and meaning of hypertext and hypermedia.

6 There were approximately 4.3 billion YouTube videos in 2024 (*https://oreil.ly/geY8l*).

7 Identity is difficult to define in general, as the myth of Ship of Theseus (*https://oreil.ly/GhC43*) shows.

On the other hand, the URN serves as a location-independent persistent resource identifier. In other words, a URN is a URI that identifies a resource without describing how or where to access it. For example, *urn:ietf:rfc:3986* identifies the RFC number 3986 published by the Internet Engineering Task Force (IETF). The *urn:* prefix is a way to indicate that the given string is a URN.

In summary, a URI can either be a URL, which includes both an access mechanism and a location of a resource, or a URN, which identifies a resource without describing how or where to access it.[8]

Table 5-1 shows various examples of URI types (URL and URN) to highlight differences between them.

Table 5-1. Examples of URIs

URI type	Example
URL	*https://www.example.com*
URL	*https://www.example.com/rfc3986.txt*
URL	*ftp://example.com/rfc3986.txt*
URL	*mailto:John.Doe@example.com*
URL	*tel:+1-816-555-1212*
URN	*urn:ietf:rfc:3986*
URN	*urn:isbn:978-1-098-15399-1*

Figure 5-1 shows the anatomy of an HTTP URL, and Table 5-2 explains its elements. Note that elements like the port could be omitted. If so, the omitted value is replaced by a default value associated with the scheme.

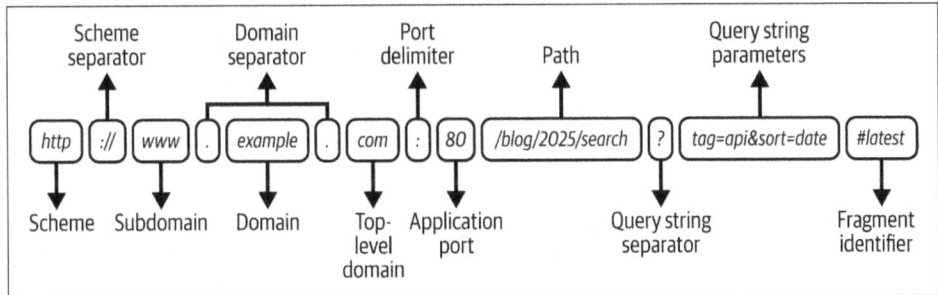

Figure 5-1. Anatomy of an HTTP URL

---

8 For more details about the relations among URI, URL, and URN, consult RFC 3986 (*https://oreil.ly/E6h4e*).

Table 5-2. Explanation of HTTP URL parts

URL value	URL term	Explanation
http	Scheme	The application layer protocol used to access the resource
://	Scheme separator	Separates the scheme from the rest of the URL
www	Subdomain	Identifies a subdivision of the domain
example	Domain	The main domain name identifying the server
.	Domain separator	Separates parts of the domain name
com	Top-level domain (TLD)	Represents the highest level of the domain hierarchy
:	Port delimiter	Separates the domain name from the application port number
80	Application port	The port number on which the application handles requests
/blog/2025/search	Path	The location of the resource on the server
?	Query string separator	Separates the path from the query string
tag=api&sort=date	Query string parameters	Key-value pairs used to pass additional data to the server
#	Fragment identifier	Marks the beginning of a fragment identifier within the resource
latest	Fragment	The section or element within the resource

Client-Server Communication

Concepts of computer networking and HTTP were described, respectively, in Chapter 3 and Chapter 4. This section provides you with an overview of these topics, focusing on HTTP-based communication.

HTTP uses a *client-server* architecture. "Socket API" on page 78 defined *client* and *server*: a client initiates the connection, and the server waits for the connection from the client. Figure 5-2 shows a client (a web browser) requesting content from a server (a web server) identified by the *example.com* domain. The client requests the *index.html* page from the web server by sending the HTTP GET request, and the server provides the requested resource. Using the HTTP 200 (OK) status code, the server indicates that it successfully processed the client request.

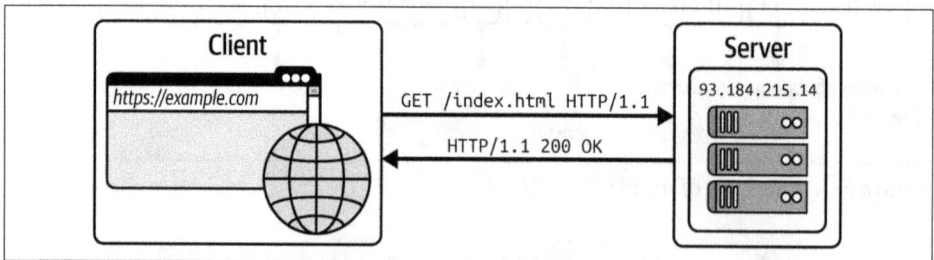

Figure 5-2. Web browser and server interaction in HTTP

Request and response are terms that indicate the direction of the data flow between the client and the server. The client sends a request to the server, which receives it, processes it, and returns a response. The *request-response model* (including HTTP) can be implemented synchronously or asynchronously (see "Synchronous and Asynchronous Communication Types" on page 9).

HTTP resides in the top layer of the OSI model (layer 7), called the application layer. But what does it mean for a protocol to be an application layer protocol? Application protocols define rules for structuring, exchanging, and interpreting messages that enable communication among software applications (see "Message" on page 6 for an explanation of messages). As long as software applications understand and follow the protocol's rules, regardless of differences in programming languages, frameworks, runtime environments, architectures, or operating systems, applications can communicate and exchange data. A web browser and a web server, or a `curl` client and various HTTP server libraries, are examples of different software technologies that use the same application layer protocol, HTTP.

The *HTTP message* is line-oriented text (a sequence of characters), where each line ends with a carriage return (<CR>) followed by a line feed (<LF>) character (<CR><LF>). The HTTP message contains the following:

1. *Request line* for the HTTP request message
2. *Status line* for the HTTP response message
3. *Headers*
4. An *empty line* (<CR><LF>) that separates the headers from the body
5. The *body* containing the data (depending on the HTTP method, body is optional)

Figure 5-3 shows HTTP request and response messages obtained from visiting *http://example.com/index.html*. For readability, the response headers were reduced to a few common headers.

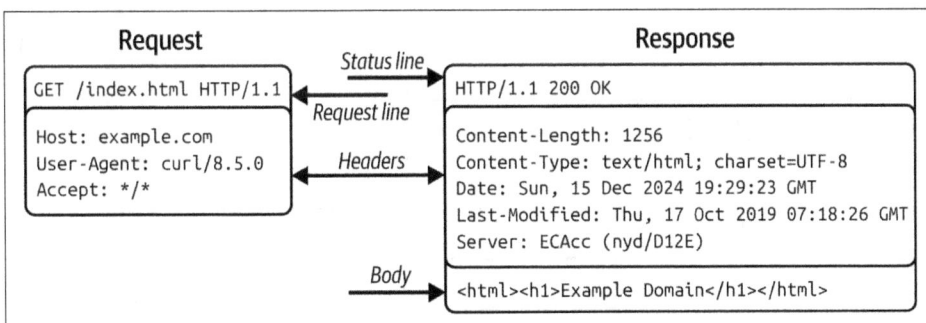

Figure 5-3. HTTP request and response messages

HTTP is layered over TCP, which then is layered over IP. By encapsulating HTTP messages within TCP segments, HTTP inherits the reliable, ordered, and error-checked transport of messages provided by TCP. Because HTTP is layered over TCP, the HTTP messages are sent as a data payload inside the TCP segment (the payload can be either text or binary).

To help you understand how these various elements play together, have a look at Figure 5-4, which is a sequence diagram of client-server communication over the internet, showing the information flow between a client and a server. The diagram combines all the aforementioned patterns and protocols discussed in this section. Nowadays, HTTP traffic is encrypted with TLS. However, the diagram presents plaintext HTTP to reduce the amount of details. For more information about TLS see "Security" on page 95.

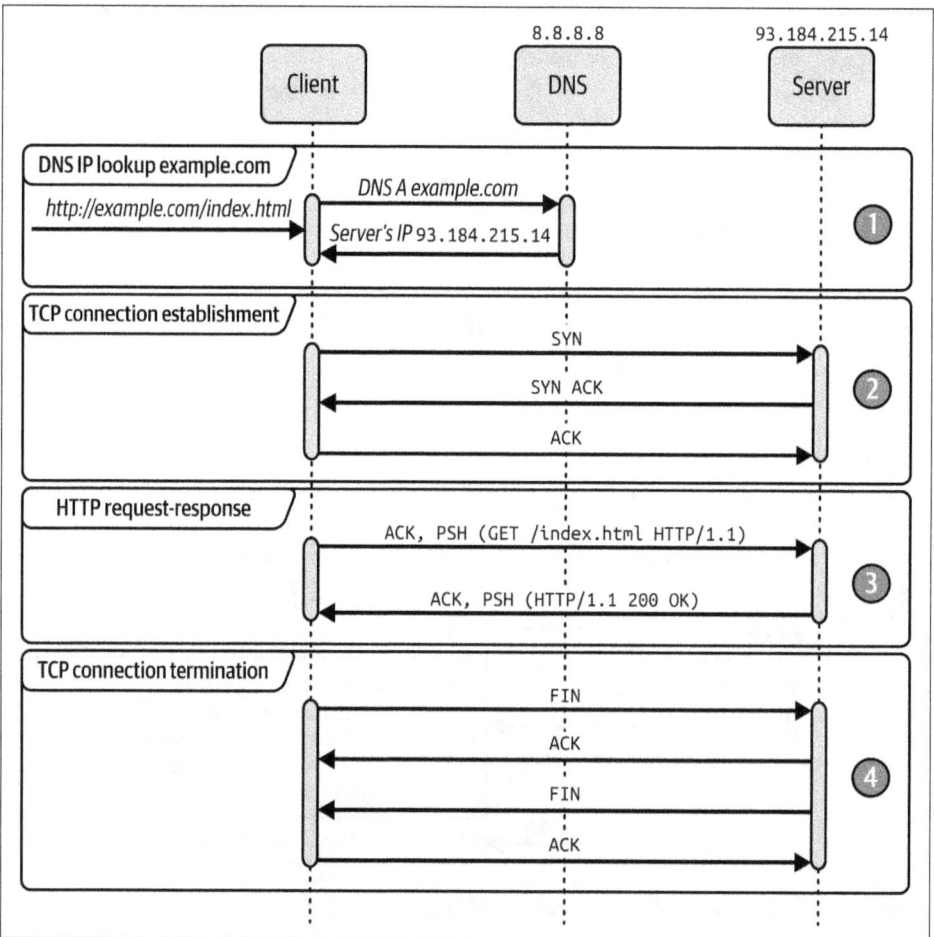

Figure 5-4. HTTP communication lifecycle

Let's explain the sequence flow:

1. The client attempts to view *http://example.com/index.html*. The URL scheme sets the protocol to `http`. The domain name *example.com* identifies the web server. Since a port number is not explicitly specified, the value 80 is used (the default HTTP port for unencrypted communication). The resource *index.html* is located at the "/" (root) of the web server.

   First, using the DNS protocol,[9] the client sends an "A"[10] record query to the DNS server IP address of `8.8.8.8`, which resolves the domain name *example.com* into the web server's IP address, `93.184.215.14`.[11]

2. The server's IP address and port number 80 are used to establish a TCP connection over the internet between the client and the server (let's ignore routing here). The connection is established by following the TCP three-way handshake (see Example 3-5). The client's IP address and a random port are omitted from the diagram.

3. Once the TCP connection is established, the client sends an HTTP `GET` request, requesting the server to provide the contents of the *index.html* resource located at the root ("/") of the server. The server fulfills the client's request and responds with the contents, together with the HTTP 200 (OK) status code, by which the server indicates that it successfully processed the client request. HTTP is layered over TCP; therefore, HTTP messages are text (or binary data) sent as a data payload inside the TCP segment, along with TCP flags such as `ACK` or `PSH`.

4. After receiving the HTTP response, the client terminates the TCP connection with the server.

Origins of REST

The REST architectural style came from Fielding's interest (*https://oreil.ly/D17wG*) in understanding and designing network-based applications for the internet scale.

For an overview of REST from a web development perspective, read "REST—Explained For Beginners" (*https://oreil.ly/Y5Vh0*) by Carson Gross.

---

9 For more information about DNS, see "How DNS Affects Browser Connections" on page 117.

10 The "A" record query applies to IP version 4 (IPv4). An "AAAA" record query is used for IPv6.

11 DNS responses are cached based on the DNS time-to-live (TTL) value, so the client doesn't perform the DNS query on every request.

Fielding aimed to address challenges such as consistency when trying to connect hypermedia-based systems across the internet, independent deployment of software components, *anarchic scalability* (a system's ability to maintain function despite being exposed to unanticipated load), and support for intermediary components such as proxies, or caches to improve scalability (a system's ability to handle a growing amount of work). These challenges led to the formulation of the REST constraints:[12]

1. Client-server architecture—Separates responsibilities between the client and the server, where the client makes the request, and the server produces the response. This constraint leads to improved portability across platforms because clients and servers can evolve independently.

2. Stateless interaction—Each client request contains all the information needed to understand and complete the request by the server (independently of any previous requests). The server doesn't store any session state; if the application requires state persistence, that state is maintained on the client.

3. Cacheable resources—Responses should explicitly indicate whether they are cacheable. Caching improves network efficiency, reduces latency, and provides better user-perceived performance by allowing clients and intermediaries to reuse responses when appropriate.

4. Uniform interface—System components are described by uniform interfaces, which improves the visibility of interactions. A standardized interface simplifies and decouples component interactions. This constraint is divided into the following:

   a. Identification of resources—Each resource is uniquely identified, typically through the URI.

   b. Manipulation of resources through representations—Resources can be represented in various formats (e.g., HTML, JSON, XML) to meet client needs.

   c. Self-descriptive messages—Each message includes all the information necessary for understanding and processing it. For example, HTTP message information is contained in the message body and headers.

   d. Hypermedia As The Engine of Application State (HATEOAS)—Clients should be able to navigate through REST APIs using hyperlinks included in the API's response. Ideally, clients need to know only the initial entry point and can then explore available interactions through hypertext/hypermedia links.

---

12 See Chapter 5, "Representational State Transfer (REST)" (*https://oreil.ly/TCYQK*) of Fielding's dissertation.

5. Layered system—Component behavior can be encapsulated within a hierarchy of layers, where the interaction of the layer is limited to the layers with which it's interacting. As a result of this constraint, content can move, for example, through gateways, proxies, and reverse proxies, with each acting as a layer.[13]

6. Code-on-demand (optional)—Client functionality can be extended by allowing the client to download and execute scripts from the server. This enables new behaviors within the client without requiring redeployment.

API Maturity Models

Maturity models are used to measure and evaluate the maturity of processes or technologies. In software, maturity models assess how well the software is designed and implemented. There are two commonly used maturity models for HTTP-based APIs: Classification of HTTP-based APIs (CohA) (*https://oreil.ly/PoJtO*) and *Richardson Maturity Model* (RMM) (*https://oreil.ly/WB0ys*). We'll focus on the latter.

In 2008, Leonard Richardson proposed a framework for describing the maturity of web services (web APIs) by their adherence to the design principles of the REST architecture style. The RMM revolves around three constraints: methods of HTTP, the use of URI, and hypermedia controls (known as HATEOAS).

> Hypertext and hypermedia are explained in "What Is Hypertext?" on page 105.

RMM is divided into four levels, starting from the least (level 0) and ending at the most mature (level 3):

Level 0
An API at this level uses a single URI and single HTTP method. An example is the SOAP API, which typically uses one URI (endpoint) and the HTTP POST method to transfer a SOAP-based payload.

Level 1
An API at this level uses separate URIs to identify system resources and a single HTTP method (typically POST).

---

13 Layered systems can negatively impact user experience by introducing overhead and latency.

Level 2

An API at this level uses separate URIs to identify system resources and uses several HTTP methods on each resource, allowing it to perform Create, Read, Update, and Delete (CRUD) operations.

Level 3

An API at this level inherits all properties from level 2, but it's enriched by hypermedia controls. The controls consist of self-descriptive links that provide information about possible actions in the given state of the API resource. HATEOAS allows API consumers to navigate through APIs, and promises to reduce developers' reliance on API documentation.

Knowing how to classify APIs allows you to evaluate and improve them according to each level of the RMM.

RESTful, RESTless, or REST

By saying that an API is RESTless, we mean that it doesn't reach level 3 of the RMM. Most developers call their API RESTful, but the reality is that it's more likely *RESTless*. In this book, we'll focus on REST APIs (RESTless according to our definition), and we reserve the "ful" suffix in RESTful only for REST APIs that use HATEOAS.

> Due to the prevalence of RESTless APIs, we'll focus on them in the remaining part of the text and call them *REST APIs*.

If you want to be a purist and call your REST API RESTful, then it needs to use HATEOAS. Let's explain what it means for the API to use HATEOAS by looking at Example 5-1. In particular, focus on the _links field.

Example 5-1. HATEOAS request and response

```
# HTTP request message
POST /order/123 HTTP/1.1
Host: example.com
Content-Type: application/json
Authorization: Bearer jwt_token

# HTTP response message
HTTP/1.1 200 OK
Content-Type: application/json
Date: Tue, 19 Mar 2025 10:00:00 GMT
Content-Length: 830
```

```
{
  "data": {  ❶
    "id": 123,
    "status": "processing",
    "item": "Laptop",
    "quantity": 1
  },
  "_links": {  ❷
    "self": {
      "href": "/order/123",
      "method": "GET",
      "description": "Get this order details."
    },
    "cancel": {
      "href": "/order/123/cancel",
      "method": "POST",
      "description": "Cancel this order.",
      "body": null
    },
    "notification": {  ❸
      "href": "/order/123/notification",
      "method": "POST",
      "description": "Subscribe to this order notifications.",
      "content_type": "application/json",
      "body": {
        "parameters": {
          "channels": {
            "type": "array",
            "items": {
              "type": "string",
              "enum": ["sms", "email", "in-app"]
            },
            "description": "Preferred notification channels.",
            "required": true
          }
        }
      }
    }
  }
}
```

❶ The data field contains details about a specific order.

❷ The field _links indicates that it comes from Hypertext Application Language (HAL) (*https://oreil.ly/WoVx8*), a specification for building APIs that allow clients to navigate around the resources by following links. The _links field contains three actions that can be performed on the object: self, cancel, and notification. Each action contains the href field, a hypermedia link pointing toward a resource location. The method describes the HTTP method used when interacting with the resource, and `description` is used to document the action. An HTTP `POST` method has a body field, set to `null` if the body is empty.

❸ The `notification` field describes the `POST` method, and its type is identified by the `content_type` field (indicating a JSON payload). In this example, the payload has a required `channels` field, which is a JSON array containing preferred notification channels.

> To further investigate what a response in the RESTful (HATEOAS) API looks like, visit Adobe's Experience Platform (*https://oreil.ly/KvZqY*) or Experience Manager (*https://oreil.ly/FyzPd*), and look through API responses. Focus on the `links` or `actions` fields. We are pointing you toward these resources because they were described as RESTful (HATEOAS) by Roy Fielding himself.[14]

Is Being RESTless Good Enough?

The question arises: should your APIs be RESTful? The answer depends on the context, but more likely, it's no; you don't need your API to be RESTful. Being REST (RESTless) is fine, but calling your API RESTful when it's not is not OK.[15]

Let's look at APIs designed by several well-known companies. For example, Google APIs Explorer (*https://oreil.ly/4Z2hU*) allows you to find and interact with various Google APIs. Take any API from the list, make a request to it, and investigate its responses. You'll see that it most likely doesn't implement HATEOAS, which means it's RESTless, not RESTful. You'll arrive at the same conclusion after investigating Meta's Graph API (*https://oreil.ly/Qehtq*).

Even though HATEOAS offers API discoverability (responses are self-documented) and decoupling (references to hypermedia are controlled by the server), the question is, why, despite these benefits, companies like Google, Meta, and others don't build RESTful APIs? There are several technical and nontechnical reasons:[16]

Server complexity
Maintaining HATEOAS APIs is challenging as new requirements come in, such as adding new resources and maintaining relationships among them. The server needs to dynamically generate responses with hypermedia links, considering the application state and user permissions.

---

14 See slide 25 in Roy Fielding's "REST in AEM" presentation (*https://oreil.ly/xThub*).

15 See Roy Fielding's post "REST APIs Must Be Hypertext-Driven" (*https://oreil.ly/gBsWR*).

16 See common challenges and limitations of HATEOAS (*https://oreil.ly/8UGC4*).

Additionally, the message size and processing time increase as the API generates more links (bigger payload), and testing the correctness of API responses requires more validation.

Furthermore, fragmentation among hypermedia formats, such as HAL (*https:// oreil.ly/w0YpX*), Hydra (*https://oreil.ly/iNqaC*), JSON-LD (*https://json-ld.org*), JSON Hyper-Schema (*https://oreil.ly/FD5Iq*), and Siren (*https://oreil.ly/ar50N*), affects interoperability. In terms of security challenges, a RESTful API needs to be designed such that its hypermedia won't expose sensitive endpoints, which should remain hidden or restricted.

Last but not least, versioning and backward compatibility of RESTful APIs are difficult to achieve, due to the presence of a larger number of links compared to RESTless APIs. In the case of RESTless APIs, the burden of versioning is pushed more toward the API clients, programmed manually by developers.

Client complexity

A HATEOAS API client needs to be capable of managing and navigating the application state, interpreting hypermedia links, and making decisions based on the links provided by the server. Relying on hypermedia links can increase network usage because the client dynamically discovers actions at runtime. For instance, if multiple sequential calls are needed to navigate resources, this can potentially degrade application performance and user experience.

Additionally, debugging and testing HATEOAS clients is more difficult due to the need to simulate various server states and hypermedia responses. Since the client follows links provided by the server, any server-side error in link generation or structure can disrupt client functionality.

Updating API versions also impacts HATEOAS clients, as they adapt to new, changed, or deprecated actions. As the number of resources grows, the client architecture becomes more sophisticated to handle dynamic interactions and maintain performance.

Pragmatism

Building and consuming a HATEOAS API can increase development effort, especially for applications that don't leverage supportive frameworks. This approach requires more up-front design to manage the challenges of embedding and interpreting navigational links. Reaching level 3 of the RMM is possible for organizations with the necessary commitment, discipline, and expertise from both backend and frontend developers. REST APIs at level 2 don't follow HATEOAS-driven design, and use multiple URIs and HTTP verbs, resulting in reduced overhead compared to APIs at level 3. Therefore, level 2 of the RMM is often sufficient for most needs.

Documentation

HATEOAS allows an API server to guide clients through available actions by embedding hypermedia links within resources (see Example 5-1). This approach makes the API more discoverable, as clients can follow these links to interact with related resources instead of hardcoding specific URLs. By relying on hypermedia links provided by the server, clients become decoupled from the exact URL structure, reducing the risk of breaking changes if the API evolves. This decoupling enables flexible integrations, allowing clients to adapt to different interactions or resource paths based on server-provided links and metadata.

However, links in a HATEOAS API indicate only part of the API usage. While these links help with navigation, a developer still needs to get familiar with API documentation to understand the set of available endpoints, endpoint functionality, usage examples, error handling, validation rules, and other details.

Consider implementing RESTful APIs in scenarios where there is a frequent change to application logic that needs to be discoverable by clients, and when there is a need for a self-documenting API.

Knowing the origins of REST APIs, HATEOAS, and that level 2 of RMM is good enough for the majority of REST use cases, we'll move to the implementation of REST APIs.

Implementation

This section demonstrates how to implement a REST API using DRF (*https://www.django-rest-framework.org*). The implementation follows the API design patterns described in Chapter 2. To execute the code examples included in this chapter, first set up the lab environment, as shown in Example 5-2.

Example 5-2. REST lab setup

```
cd src/django ❶
docker compose build --build-arg UID=$(id -u) --build-arg GID=$(id -g) ❷
docker compose up --detach --wait ❸
```

❶ Navigate to the lab's directory.

❷ Build Docker images.

❸ Start Docker containers.

API Endpoints

The API design patterns described in Chapter 2 started with two concepts: API language ("API Language" on page 42) and naming ("API Naming" on page 42). The language we choose to describe APIs is American English, and we will stick to its spelling. To explain naming, let's look at the REST API endpoints for our WFS.

The WFS's REST API endpoints/routes/interfaces are shown in Example 5-3. The presented code shows the application's endpoints and their respective handlers (classes). In this chapter, you'll implement the `CityView` and `CityListView` classes.

Example 5-3. WFS REST API endpoints

```
# src/django/app/config/urls.py

from core.api.rest.v1.views import CityListView
from core.api.rest.v1.views import CityView
from core.api.rest.v1.views import GeocodingView
from core.api.rest.v1.views import WeatherForecastListView
from core.api.rest.v1.views import WeatherHistoryListView
from core.api.rest.v1.views import WeatherSeedView
...

urlpatterns = [
    ...
    path("api/cities", CityListView.as_view()),                        ❶
    path("api/cities/<uuid:uuid>", CityView.as_view()),                ❷
    path("api/forecasts", WeatherForecastListView.as_view()),          ❸
    path("api/geocoding", GeocodingView.as_view()),                    ❹
    path("api/history", WeatherHistoryListView.as_view()),             ❺
    path("api/seed", WeatherSeedView.as_view())],                      ❻
    ...
]
```

❶ The */api/cities* endpoint is responsible for listing all cities for which a weather forecast can be obtained.

❷ The */api/cities/<uuid:uuid>* endpoint returns a city resource identified by uuid.

❸ The */api/forecasts* endpoint provides weather forecasts for a given city.

❹ The */api/geocoding* endpoint converts city names into geographic coordinates, and vice versa.

❺ The */api/history* endpoint provides the city's historical weather data.

❻ The */api/seed* endpoint is used to seed the content of the WFS database with weather data.

Our API revolves around the *cities* resource, which is spelled in plural. A *uuid* identifies the city resource within its parent collection *cities/uuid* (this endpoint manages the individual city object). Notice that the word *history* is both countable and uncountable, and its plural is *histories* (*https://oreil.ly/CG5Ui*). We choose a singular form to indicate the weather history of an individual city. If we instead chose to name the endpoint *histories*, it could imply several different weather histories for a given city, which contradicts common sense.

Another particular naming choice is the name of the resource responsible for forecasting weather data. American English more commonly uses the *weather forecast* phrase (e.g., "Have you checked the weather forecast for tomorrow?"). However, going with the singular form of the word *forecast* would indicate that API provides a forecast for only one day. Therefore, going against the common usage of the phrase, we choose plural *forecasts*, indicating that a forecast can be obtained for several days in the future.

Furthermore, you might ask, why not make *forecast* and *history* endpoints part of the *cities* endpoint (*cities/uuid/forecast* and *cities/uuid/history*)? The problem with this solution could be that the forecast would be returned only for a given city, and wouldn't anticipate a scenario in which one could fetch forecasts for multiple cities. Another reason against placing *forecast* and *history* endpoints under the *cities* endpoint is that weather forecast and history serve different purposes. Additionally, keeping endpoints flat (avoiding nesting) leads to consistency, ease of use, and caching since they are less likely to change.

> Consult Jeff Schnitzer's blog post, "How to (and How Not to) Design REST APIs" (*https://oreil.ly/6wqnt*), which contains more advice on organizing resources in REST.

API Versioning

In "API Versioning" on page 47, we talked about several approaches that might be used to version APIs.

Looking at the REST endpoints of the WFS listed in Example 5-3, you might think that our API doesn't expose any API version. This is because we use query parameter versioning (e.g., */api/cities?version=v1*). If not specified, our API assumes you are communicating with the API at v1 (the default API version set by us).

Example 5-4 shows DRF's API versioning configuration and how to use it in the API view class.

Example 5-4. API versioning implementation

```
# src/django/app/config/base.py

REST_FRAMEWORK = {  ❶
    ...
    "DEFAULT_VERSIONING_CLASS": "rest_framework.versioning.QueryParameterVersioning",
    "DEFAULT_VERSION": "v1",
    "ALLOWED_VERSIONS": ("v1", "v2"),
    "VERSION_PARAM": "version",
    ...
}

# src/django/app/core/api/rest/v1/views/city_views.py

class CityListView(GenericAPIView):
    ...
    def get_serializer_class(self):  ❷
        if self.request.version == REST_FRAMEWORK["DEFAULT_VERSION"]:
            return CitySerializer
        return super().get_serializer_class()
    ...
  ...
```

❶ This block configures the DRF's settings to enable query parameter versioning using `QueryParameterVersioning` (*https://oreil.ly/8c3Cw*). DEFAULT_VERSION sets the default API version to v1, and ALLOWED_VERSIONS defines a tuple of strings representing the API versions that the server supports. VERSION_PARAM specifies the name of the query parameter used for versioning.

❷ The `get_serializer_class()` method customizes the serializer based on the API version specified in the incoming request. If the request's version matches the default version (v1), the method returns `CitySerializer` as the serializer class. Otherwise, it falls back to the parent class's implementation.

CRUD

Dating back to 1983, the term *CRUD* appears in the context of persistent storage, and four operations (Create, Read, Update, and Delete) that can be performed on it.[17] Since then, it's been adopted from databases to APIs and UIs, as shown in Table 5-3.

---

17 The term appears in James Martin's *Managing the Data Base Environment* (*https://oreil.ly/xS79e*) (Prentice Hall, 1983) on page 381.

After defining the endpoints, the next step is to implement request handlers (in Django, they are called *views*). In this section, you'll implement the `CityListView` and `CityView` classes. These classes hold CRUD operations for the city resource.

> We intentionally omitted the implementation details for the Update operation. The Update operation is similar to Create, but it's lengthy; therefore, we didn't include it in this section. Instead, the details of implementing Update (and other operations) from CRUD are described in the book's code repository.

Table 5-3. CRUD operation across databases, applications, and user interfaces

CRUD operation	SQL	HTTP	UI
Create	INSERT	POST	Add
Read	SELECT	GET	View, Retrieve, or Search
Update	UPDATE	PATCH, PUT	Edit
Delete	DELETE	DELETE	Remove

HTTP Idempotency, Safety, and Caching

HTTP methods can be classified according to three properties: idempotency (*https://oreil.ly/MIu2d*), safety (*https://oreil.ly/BVAwC*), and caching (*https://oreil.ly/VdFAj*).

An *idempotent* HTTP method has the same effect on the server when called once or multiple times. For example, no matter how many times you retrieve a resource with the `GET` method, it'll return the same data. The same applies to the `DELETE` method. When performing an initial `DELETE` request, the server will respond with an HTTP 200 (OK) status code, and any consecutive `DELETE` request to the same resource will return an HTTP 404 (Not Found) status code. This is because idempotency considers only the state of the server.

An operation is "safe" if it doesn't modify the server's state. For example, the `POST` method is not safe because it will create a new resource. But a safe method doesn't necessarily have to be read-only. Reading a resource may still cause side effects on the server, such as logging or rate-limiting of the requests. The method is considered safe as long as the client does not initiate those side effects.

Idempotency and safety in HTTP are defined in terms of the intended effect of a client's request. This means that even safe (e.g., `GET`) and idempotent (e.g., `PUT`) methods can trigger side effects on the server, as long as the end result for the client remains as intended. This ambiguity in the definitions arises because the HTTP specification doesn't distinguish between an operation's primary effect and its side effects.

The term *caching* describes conditions in which an existing response can be used to satisfy subsequent requests. Caching is used to reduce the response time and network bandwidth consumption. Caching happens through the use of a *cache* (local or remote store) that controls the response storage, retrieval, and deletion.[18]

Table 5-4 shows standard HTTP methods classified based on idempotency, safety, and cacheability characteristics.[19]

Table 5-4. HTTP methods: idempotency, safety, and cacheability

HTTP method	Idempotent	Safe	Cacheable[a]
GET (*https://oreil.ly/ob3a5*)	Yes	Yes	Yes
HEAD (*https://oreil.ly/ebspK*)	Yes	Yes	Yes
POST (*https://oreil.ly/EmlNu*)	No	No	No
PUT (*https://oreil.ly/4oiLs*)	Yes	No	No
DELETE (*https://oreil.ly/ZhqKK*)	Yes	No	No
CONNECT (*https://oreil.ly/5vfnE*)	No	No	No
OPTIONS (*https://oreil.ly/26Fsx*)	Yes	Yes	No
TRACE (*https://oreil.ly/3vVWB*)	Yes	Yes	No
PATCH (*https://oreil.ly/Kn7az*)	No	No	No

[a] Note that caching commonly applies to reading operations, and it can seldom be applied to writes for state-change operations. For example, POST can be cacheable only if the server explicitly provides cache control headers in the response.

Create

Example 5-5 shows how to implement CRUD's Create operation. The Create operation uses the HTTP POST method.

Example 5-5. Create operation implementation

```
# src/django/app/core/api/rest/v1/views/city_views.py

from core.helpers import error_response
from core.helpers import InputDataHandler
from core.helpers import InputDataValidator
from core.helpers import IsSuperuser
from core.helpers import success_response
from core.helpers.serializers import CitySerializer
```

---

18 See "HTTP Caching" (*https://oreil.ly/TdtTO*).

19 If not enforced by the API developer, the idempotency, safety, and cacheability aren't guaranteed.

```
from core.helpers.utils import get_serializer_errors
from rest_framework.generics import GenericAPIView
from rest_framework.permissions import IsAuthenticated
...

class CityListView(GenericAPIView):           ❶
    allowed_methods = ["GET", "POST"]          ❷
    input_handler = InputDataHandler(InputDataValidator)     ❸
    permission_classes = [IsAuthenticated & IsSuperuser]     ❹
    serializer_class = CitySerializer          ❺

    def get_serializer_class(self):            ❻
        if self.request.version == "v1":
            return CitySerializer

        return super().get_serializer_class()

    def get_permissions(self):                 ❼
        if self.request.method == "GET":
            return []

        return super().get_permissions()

    def post(self, request):                   ❽
        serializer = self.get_serializer(data=request.data)     ❾

        if not serializer.is_valid():          ❿
            errors = get_serializer_errors(serializer)
            return error_response(errors, 400)

        try:
            serializer.save()      ⓫
        except Exception:
            return error_response(["Failed to create City object."], 500)

        return success_response(serializer.data, 201)     ⓬
    ...
```

❶ The definition of the `CityListView` class is bound to the */api/cities* endpoint
(Example 5-3). The `CityListView` class inherits from DRF's `GenericAPIView` (a
class-based (*https://oreil.ly/j1nux*) view, which provides common functionality
for API views).

❷ The `allowed_methods` specifies a list of methods the resource allows. For this
view, `GET` retrieves a list of cities, and `POST` is used to create a city resource. The
DRF's class-based views (*https://oreil.ly/GNarL*) require all HTTP methods on
the given endpoint in a single class. The details of this functionality are described
on the Django REST framework site (*https://oreil.ly/iQnUl*).

❸ The `input_handler` is a custom class implemented by you to validate data provided in the request's body or query parameter.

❹ The `permission_classes` field sets the permissions required to access the view. An API user must be authenticated and have superuser status to manipulate the city resource.

❺ The `serializer_class` binds the view with `CitySerializer`, which handles the serialization and deserialization of `City` model objects. Serializer (*https://oreil.ly/ snCmV*) is used to convert Django's models (*https://oreil.ly/P3ZzX*) and Query-Sets (*https://oreil.ly/GuEfn*) to Python data types that can be encoded to JSON (*https://www.json.org*) and XML (*https://www.w3.org/TR/xml*).

❻ The `get_serializer_class()` method overrides the default serializer to the `City Serializer` for API version `v1`. For different API versions, it takes a serializer from the parent class (default serializer).

❼ The `get_permissions()` method exempts HTTP `GET` requests from permission checks while enforcing permissions (`permission_classes`) for other methods.

❽ The `post()` method responds to the HTTP `POST` request, allowing it to handle resource creation.

❾ The `serializer` instance contains client request data used to create a new city.

❿ This block of code validates the request data content. If the content is invalid, the HTTP response with a 400 (Bad Request) status code is returned. Application errors such as 400 (Bad Request) aren't logged by default. This is because DRF generates logs only for responses generated by raised exceptions.[20]

⓫ The `serializer` attempts to save the city object to the database. If the save fails, the HTTP response with a 500 (Internal Server Error) status code is returned.

⓬ If the save succeeds, the HTTP response with a 201 (Created) status code is returned. The response contains the data about a newly created resource.

---

20 Learn more about Django's custom exception handling (*https://oreil.ly/SPlNJ*).

Defensive Programming

Notice the order of stages that each code block in the `CityView` and the `CityListView` class represents. The flow starts with validation of the request, goes through resource manipulation, and ends with retrieving the resource. Along all these stages, the program handles the errors according to each stage.

This approach is called *defensive programming*, which anticipates that the provided input can be invalid or malicious (which might cause software to misbehave). By preparing for these scenarios, defensive programming ensures that the program can handle invalid input and that the software works correctly.

The method of validating the input usually will have several layers of validations, including sanitization, input validation, authentication, and authorization.

By using a defensive programming approach, developers can reduce the risk of unexpected behavior caused by invalid input, increase security, and improve system reliability. However, the downside of this approach is that it may increase complexity.

Example 5-6 shows the `curl` client making the `POST` request to create a new city resource via the */api/cities* endpoint. The example assumes that the `$ACCESS_TOKEN` is already available as the environment variable, extracted as shown in Example 5-18. We are using the `jq` program (*https://jqlang.org*) to display the response JSON payload in a human-readable way.

> Note that the instructions for extracting the `ACCESS_TOKEN` are shown in Example 5-18, and that the UUID(s) presented in this book will be different from yours.

Example 5-6. City resource created via HTTP POST (requires setup from Example 5-2)

```
CREATE_CITY_PAYLOAD='{"name":"Copenhagen",
  "country":"Denmark",
  "region":"Europe",
  "timezone":"Europe/Copenhagen",
  "latitude":55.676100,
  "longitude":12.568300}'

docker compose exec app bash -c \
        "curl \
        --data '$CREATE_CITY_PAYLOAD' \
        --header 'Authorization: Bearer $ACCESS_TOKEN' \
        --header 'Content-Type: application/json' \
        --request 'POST' \
        --silent \
```

```
  'http://localhost:8000/api/cities' | \
  jq"

{
  "results": [
    {
      "uuid": "2a39b5ba-1dc5-4bd9-bba4-95c465067785",
      "name": "Copenhagen",
      "country": "Denmark",
      "region": "Europe",
      "timezone": "Europe/Copenhagen",
      "latitude": "55.676100",
      "longitude": "12.568300"
    }
  ]
}
```

Read

In this section, you'll implement the Read operation from CRUD. The operation will apply to the */api/cities* endpoint, meaning it expects to return multiple cities. Example 5-7 shows implementation details of how to retrieve multiple resources.

In addition to the Read operation, you'll implement the endpoint in a way that it'll allow you to filter, search, and sort resources. The end goal of this implementation is to allow the API to return a partial response. A partial response returns only a subset of the resource, not the whole resource.[21]

Example 5-7. City resource list Read implementation

```
# src/django/app/core/api/rest/v1/views/city_views.py

from config import to_boolean
from core.helpers import InputDataHandler
from core.helpers import InputDataValidator
...

class CityListView(GenericAPIView):  ❶
    def get(self, request):
        fields = self.serializer_class.Meta.fields  ❷
        fields, fields_errors = self.input_handler.handle_fields(request, fields)
        search, search_errors = self.input_handler.handle_search(request, fields)
        sort, sort_errors = self.input_handler.handle_sort(request, fields)
        include_deleted = request.query_params.get("include_deleted", False)
        include_deleted = to_boolean(include_deleted)

        errors = get_errors(fields_errors + sort_errors + search_errors)  ❸
```

---

21 A partial response is the most distinct feature of GraphQL.

```
    if errors:
        return error_response(errors, 400)

    try:  ❹
        cities = CityRepository.get_all().order_by(sort).filter(**search)
        if not include_deleted:
            cities = cities.filter(deleted=False)
    except Exception:
        return error_response(["Failed to read from City database."], 500)

    return success_response_paginated(  ❺
      self.serializer_class, request, cities, fields
    )
...
```

❶ The `CityListView` class defines a `get()` method that handles the HTTP `GET` requests to retrieve a list of cities.

❷ This code block validates `fields`, `search`, and `sort` query parameters using `handle_fields()`, `handle_search()`, and `handle_sort()` methods, respectively. The respective method returns a Python list containing a validation error message (if data is invalid), and the query parameter value extracted from the field name suffixed to the `handle_()` method.

❸ This function concatenates lists of errors. If validation errors are found, the HTTP response with a 400 (Bad Request) status code is returned.

❹ This code block handles sorting and field-based filtering on Django's QuerySet (*https://oreil.ly/uH38c*) describing all cities. The `include_deleted` variable, read from the request's query parameter, is set to `False`, and it controls whether the soft-deleted resources should be included in the response. The `order_by()` method performs sorting, and field-based filtering is done by `filter()`.

❺ The `fields` query parameter carried by a variable with the same name controls what fields to include in the response. The `success_response_paginated()` function passes the `fields` variable as a keyword argument down to `serializer(…, fields=fields)`, described in Example 5-12. This way, the API returns a partial response limited to data described in the fields query parameter.[22]

---

22 This is what GraphQL allows by design, which we'll discuss in Chapter 6.

> The DRF comes with filtering (*https://oreil.ly/bo7NQ*) classes that you can use when working with GenericAPIView and ListAPIView (*https://oreil.ly/2IuZJ*).

Filtering, searching, sorting, and partial response are common features provided by API servers (see "Filtering" on page 57). Filtering in APIs allows clients to limit data to their needs. Searching is a form of filtering that allows clients to find data based on specific matches. Sorting, on the other hand, allows clients to reorder the returned data. The usual approach for REST APIs is to add query parameters that express the filtering intent. For example, `fields` is used to limit returned data, `search` is used to search specific data, and `sort` is used to reorder the data.

Example 5-8 shows an example use of these capabilities on the */api/cities* endpoint, and Example 5-7 looks into the implementation details. The API's query parameters are `fields`, `search_` suffixed with City model fields such as `uuid`, `name`, `country`, `region`, `timezone`, `latitude`, `longitude` (e.g., `search_region`), and `sort`.

Example 5-8. City resource read using field-based filtering (requires setup from Example 5-2)

```
QUERY_PARAMS="fields=name&search_region=Africa&sort=-name"
docker compose exec app bash -c \
    "curl --silent \
    'http://localhost:8000/api/cities?$QUERY_PARAMS' | \
    jq '.results'"

[
  {
    "name": "Cairo",
  }
]
```

Note that the API response returns only the `name`. This example demonstrates that REST API responses can be partial.

Delete

The API pattern of resource deletion was described in "Deletion" on page 67. This section shows how to implement a soft-delete pattern.

Example 5-9 shows how to delete a single city resource. This example requires the `ACCESS_TOKEN` to be obtained using instructions described in Example 5-18.

Example 5-9. City resource deleted via HTTP DELETE (requires setup from Example 5-2)

```
CITY_UUID=$(docker compose exec app bash -c \
  "curl --silent 'http://localhost:8000/api/cities?search_name=Mexico' | \
  jq --raw-output '.results[0].uuid'") ❶

docker compose exec app bash -c \
      "curl \
      --header 'Authorization: Bearer $ACCESS_TOKEN' \
      --request 'DELETE' \
      --silent 'http://localhost:8000/api/cities/$CITY_UUID?soft_delete=true' | \
      jq" ❷

{
  "results": [
    {
      "uuid": "c1dc3ff5-5579-438b-bd8d-0aa0610cdb12",
      "name": "Mexico City",
      "country": "Mexico",
      "region": "North America",
      "timezone": "America/Mexico_City",
      "latitude": "19.432600",
      "longitude": "-99.133200",
      "deleted": true
    }
  ]
}
```

❶ This command extracts the UUID for Mexico City and assigns it to the CITY_UUID environment variable.

❷ This command calls the authenticated */api/cities/uuid* endpoint using the HTTP DELETE method. The query parameter soft_delete controls whether the resource is soft-deleted (hidden) or hard-deleted (removed).

Example 5-10 shows the implementation behind resource deletion.

Example 5-10. City resource delete implementation

```
# src/django/app/core/api/rest/v1/views/city_views.py

from config import to_boolean


class CityView(GenericAPIView):  ❶
    permission_classes = [IsAuthenticated & IsSuperuser]  ❷

    def delete(self, request, uuid):  ❸
        soft_delete = to_boolean(request.query_params.get("soft_delete", True))
```

```
    try:
        city = CityRepository.get_by_id(uuid)  ❹
    except Exception:
        return error_response(["Failed to read from City database."], 500)

    if not city:  ❺
        return error_response(["Referenced City not found."], 404)

    double_soft_delete = (city and city.deleted and soft_delete)
    if double_soft_delete:  ❻
        return error_response(["Referenced City is already soft deleted."], 412)

    city = CityRepository.delete(uuid, soft_delete)  ❼
    if not city:
        return error_response(["Failed to delete City object."], 500)

    serializer = self.get_serializer(city)

    return success_response(serializer.data)  ❽
```

❶ The definition of the `CityView` class extends DRF's `GenericAPIView`.

❷ The `permission_classes` attribute is set to ensure that only authenticated users with superuser status can perform the `DELETE` operation.

❸ The `delete()` method handles HTTP `DELETE` requests to delete a resource identified by its `uuid`.

❹ If a database read fails while retrieving the record (resource) from the database, the HTTP response with a 500 (Internal Server Error) status code is returned.

❺ If the resource doesn't exist, the HTTP response with a 404 (Not Found) status code is returned.

❻ If a resource has already been soft-deleted, the program returns a response with an HTTP 412 (Precondition Failed) status code.

❼ The `soft_delete` variable read from the query parameter controls the resource deletion type. If the deletion fails, the HTTP response with a 500 (Internal Server Error) status code is returned.

❽ If deletion is successful, the HTTP response containing the created resource with a 200 (OK) status code is returned.

Pagination

Approaches to pagination were described in "Pagination" on page 59. In this section, we'll implement a pagination design pattern by using the offset-based approach.

Pagination allows the API server to limit the number of items returned at once to the API client. Pagination is needed for larger datasets. The split of the dataset into smaller chunks leads to better API performance and a lower memory footprint (on the client and server). However, pagination requires that API clients understand, parse, and handle the paginated data, which increases the risk of data inconsistencies among paginated requests.

The WFS REST API */api/cities* endpoint returns the paginated data response. To test our implementation of pagination, call the WFS API by executing the command shown in Example 5-11, and compare responses for different values of `page` and `page_size` query parameters. Example 5-11 shows the second page of offset-paginated data (Example 5-12) that contains only one data record.

Example 5-11. REST API pagination usage (requires setup from Example 5-2)

```
docker compose exec app bash -c \
        "curl --silent 'http://localhost:8000/api/cities?page=2&page_size=1' | \
        jq"
{
  "count": 6, ❶
  "next": "http://localhost:8000/api/cities?page=3&page_size=1", ❷
  "previous": "http://localhost:8000/api/cities?page_size=1", ❷
  "results": [ ❸
    {
      "uuid": "89ee4c08-f483-4b73-a145-abb69892d39f",
      "name": "Istanbul",
      "country": "Turkey",
      "region": "Asia",
      "timezone": "Europe/Istanbul",
      "latitude": "41.008200",
      "longitude": "28.978400"
    }
  ]
}
```

❶ The count field indicates the total number of city records available, which is six in this example. It allows clients to know the size of the data set.

❷ The next and previous fields hold a URL pointing to the next and previous results page. The next URL directs to the third page, and the previous URL points back to the first page. The page_size controls the number of items returned per page.

❸ The `results` array contains the actual data items returned by the API. Each object within the array represents a city.

Example 5-12 shows the necessary configuration for DRF and the implementation of `success_response_paginated()`, first mentioned in Example 5-7.

Example 5-12. Response pagination implementation

```
# src/django/app/config/base.py

REST_FRAMEWORK = {  ❶
    ...
    "DEFAULT_PAGINATION_CLASS": "rest_framework.pagination.PageNumberPagination",
    "PAGE_SIZE": 3,
    ...
}

# src/django/app/core/helpers/handlers/response_handler.py

from rest_framework.pagination import PageNumberPagination
...

def success_response_paginated(
    serializer, request, queryset, fields=None, status_code=200
  ):
    paginator = PageNumberPagination()  ❷
    paginator.page_size = int(request.query_params.get("page_size", 3))  ❸
    paginated_queryset = paginator.paginate_queryset(queryset, request)  ❹

    paginated_serializer = serializer(  ❺
      paginated_queryset, many=True, fields=fields
    )

    return paginator.get_paginated_response(paginated_serializer.data)  ❻
```

❶ The `REST_FRAMEWORK` dictionary holds the DRF configuration. `DEFAULT_PAGINA TION_CLASS` specifies that the API will use page number pagination, allowing clients to request specific pages of data by providing a page number in their requests. The `PAGE_SIZE` key determines the number of items displayed per page.

❷ `PageNumberPagination` is a DRF paginator providing paginated responses.

❸ The `page_size` option controls the size of the paginated page. By default, the page size is set to hold three items, and it can be controlled by the request's query parameters with the same name.

❹ The paginator obtains initial data from the `queryset` parameter, which is controlled by `request`.

❺ The result, `paginated_serializer`, is a Python data structure that is used to generate a JSON representation of the paginated data, ready to be sent as an API response. This line limits the initial query set and reduces data to that controlled by the `fields` (query parameter).

❻ The paginated response is returned by calling `get_paginated_response()` on the `paginator` object.

Rate Limiting

In "Rate Limiting" on page 65, we described rate limiting, a technique that protects APIs from being overwhelmed by excessive requests, preventing abuse, and ensuring fair API usage. Rate limits are often used to nudge unpaid users to upgrade to paid plans. A common strategy that companies offer is to expose the full capacity of their public APIs, but limit the number of requests per unit of time, like second, minute, hour, or day. One of the goals of this rate limiting is to encourage users to upgrade to paid subscriptions, which typically offer higher usage limits.

The DRF provides API rate-limiting tools under the alternative name *throttling*. Example 5-13 shows how to implement throttling on the */api/cities* endpoint.

Example 5-13. Throttling implementation

```
# src/django/app/config/base.py

REST_FRAMEWORK = {
    ...
    "DEFAULT_THROTTLE_CLASSES": ("rest_framework.throttling.AnonRateThrottle",),  ❶
    "DEFAULT_THROTTLE_RATES": {"anon": "1000/minute"},  ❷
    ...
}

# src/django/app/core/api/rest/v1/views/city_views.py

from rest_framework.throttling import AnonRateThrottle
from rest_framework.decorators import throttle_classes
...

class CityListView(GenericAPIView):
    ...
    @throttle_classes([AnonRateThrottle])  ❸
    def get(self, request):
        ...
```

❶ The `DEFAULT_THROTTLE_CLASSES` setting includes the `AnonRateThrottle` class, which limits requests from anonymous clients.

❷ `DEFAULT_THROTTLE_RATES` setting defines the throttle rate for anonymous (`anon`) clients, allowing them to make 1,000 requests per minute. A client is uniquely identified by an IP address.[23]

❸ The `throttle_classes` decorator applies the `AnonRateThrottle` class, which guards the `get()` method that exposes the */api/cities* endpoint.

Caching

API caching was described in "Caching" on page 66. In this section, you'll implement server-side caching for the */api/cities* endpoint that exposes its data using the idempotent and safe HTTP `GET` method. Caching improves the responsiveness of APIs by saving consecutive API requests to a cache storage (usually in-memory storage). The initial client request propagates via the system layers cache, backend, and database, generating a response. The following responses to the same request are served from the cache instead of propagating again through the system. The disadvantage of caching is that data is stale for some time, which might not guarantee data freshness.

Example 5-14 shows how to implement server-side caching with the DRF, using an in-memory Redis database (*https://redis.io*).

Example 5-14. Caching implementation

```
# src/django/app/config/base.py

CACHES = {  ❶
    "default": {
        "BACKEND": "django.core.cache.backends.redis.RedisCache",
        "LOCATION": f"{REDIS_PROTOCOL_SCHEMA}://{REDIS_HOST}:{REDIS_PORT}",
        "TIMEOUT": 300,
        "OPTIONS": {
            "db": 1
        }
    }
}

# src/django/app/core/api/rest/v1/views/city_views.py
```

---

23 Proxies or load balancers can hide the client's IP address. In such cases, you could use persistent or session cookies to store the server-generated client's UUID in the browser. When the client makes subsequent requests, the cookie is sent back to the server, which recognizes the client regardless of the IP address.

```
from django.utils.decorators import method_decorator
from django.views.decorators.cache import cache_page
...

class CityListView(GenericAPIView):
    ...
    @method_decorator(cache_page(30))  ❷
    def get(self, request):
        ...
```

❶ Defines the cache settings for the Django application. BACKEND specifies that Redis will be used as the cache backend. The other options specify the Redis service location and database number (db option).

❷ The generic method decorator @method_decorator(), which applies a specialized @cache_page() decorator to the get() method that handles the /api/cities endpoint to cache the response for 30 seconds.

Security

In 2024, Cloudflare released its Application Security Report (*https://oreil.ly/fWdsO*), which says that "60% of dynamic (noncacheable) traffic is API-related." This growth is led by the adoption of API as the primary communication channel among applications, databases, IoT, and other systems.

However, APIs may enter production without adequate cataloging, authentication, or auditing, exposing them to potential security risks. This can still happen despite the *API-first approach*, where API specification is created before implementation, and shift-left practices (see "Deployment" on page 30). In the *shift-left* approach, development practices, such as testing, security measures, and QA, are integrated early in the SDLC or the API lifecycle.

Beyond TLS, REST APIs are commonly protected by industry-standard authentication and authorization. One such method that supports authentication and authorization is JSON Web Token (JWT) (*https://oreil.ly/UGaui*), which allows for the representation of claims to be transferred between two parties. Another method is OAuth 2.0 (*https://oreil.ly/9IfVx*) (and OAuth 2.1 (*https://oreil.ly/CgFlF*)), which is an authorization-only protocol. OAuth 2.0 provides specific authorization flows for web, desktop, and mobile applications. OpenID Connect (OIDC) (*https://oreil.ly/DaOnL*) is another authentication protocol based on the OAuth 2.0 framework that adds an identity layer by including user information and identity verification. OIDC is often used for single sign-on applications.

For improved API security, organizations employ tools like OpenAPI for documentation, API management platforms for centralized control (see "API Governance, Management, and Platform" on page 36), and auditing practices.

JSON Web Token

Before we proceed with implementing JWT, let's explain what it is. JWT (*https://oreil.ly/vEOZD*) is a concatenation of three sections (each being a Base64url-encoded (*https://oreil.ly/4MT8i*) string): header, payload, and signature, separated by periods ("."). Example 5-15 shows an encoded version of JWT.

> Be aware that sending tokens in query parameters can expose them in the browser's history or server logs.

Example 5-15. JWT example

```
eyJhbGciOiJIUzI1NiIsInR5cCI6IkpXVCJ9.
eyJzdWIiOiIxMjM0NTY3ODkwIiwibmFtZSI6IkpvaG4gRG9lIiwiaWF0IjoxNTE2MjM5MDIyfQ.
cThIIoDvwdueQB468K5xDc5633seEFoqwxjF_xSJyQQ
```

> Visit the jwt.io website (*https://jwt.io*) to decode JWT. Be vigilant when pasting private information into the internet, and use only the tools that you trust and that are verified. Otherwise, you are risking sensitive information exposure to unauthorized third parties.

The header and the payload section of JWT contain a Base64url-encoded JSON object that contains claims (pieces of information about the token) and data. The last section is a signature HMAC that uses the Secure Hash Algorithm (SHA) function with a 256-bit length from a string that contains a Base64url-encoded header and payload, which are concatenated with a period ("."), and a secret. Table 5-5 shows the decoded JWT taken from Example 5-15.

Table 5-5. JWT anatomy

Header	Payload	Signature

{
  "alg": "HS256",
  "typ": "JWT"
}
	{
	  "sub": "1234567890",
	  "name": "John Doe",
	  "iat": 1516239022
	}
		HMAC_SHA256(secret, base64url(header) + "." +
		base64url(payload))

JWT has several advantages:

Secure

To ensure the integrity and authenticity of JWTs, cryptographic algorithms are used to generate a signature. These algorithms can be symmetric, such as HMAC (*https://oreil.ly/sPSk5*), or asymmetric, like RSA (*https://oreil.ly/es87d*) / ECDSA (*https://oreil.ly/soU1X*), which use a private-public key pair. JWTs also include claims, such as the *"exp"* (expiration) claim, which specifies the time after which the token is no longer valid. Once the expiration time is reached, the token cannot be used for access unless the issuing system explicitly renews it.

Stateless

The JWT doesn't rely on session stores to keep users' data. This characteristic makes the JWT a suitable choice for authentication in distributed systems that use APIs in cross-domain communication. Note that statelessness is limited only to the JWT authentication use case. Storage employment cannot be avoided when implementing functionality such as token access control by creating allow and deny lists or token revocation.

Self-contained

A JWT contains claims such as user ID, roles, and permissions, allowing the server to treat a valid token as proof of authentication and reducing the need for frequent database lookups.

Portable

The JWT encoding is URL-safe and compatible with text-based protocols such as HTTP.[24] JWT can be sent within an HTTP request query parameter, body, or header.

Customizable

JWT contains claims (e.g., user role, token expiration time) that can be customized to the application's needs.

Knowing what JWT is, let's protect WFS REST APIs with JWT.

We chose to use the DRF (*https://www.django-rest-framework.org*) to implement the REST API. We also found a compatible Python package, *djangorestframework-simplejwt* (*Simple JWT*) (*https://oreil.ly/OV8G3*), that implements the JWT. Otherwise, we would need to implement the JWT functionality from scratch. Integrating Simple JWT into the DRF requires setting the default authentication class in the DRF config, as shown in Example 5-16.

---

24 There exist "unreserved characters" (*https://oreil.ly/IFUjl*), which are safe to use in URLs.

Example 5-16. JWT configuration

```
# src/django/app/config/base.py

REST_FRAMEWORK = {  ❶
    ...
    "DEFAULT_AUTHENTICATION_CLASSES": (
        "rest_framework_simplejwt.authentication.JWTAuthentication",
    ),
    ...
}

SIMPLE_JWT = {  ❷
    "AUTH_TOKEN_CLASSES": ("rest_framework_simplejwt.tokens.AccessToken",),
    "USER_ID_CLAIM": "id",
}
```

❶ The REST_FRAMEWORK dictionary has settings that customize the behavior of the DRF. Setting the JWTAuthentication class in DEFAULT_AUTHENTICATION_CLASSES forces the DRF to use the JWT class provided by the Simple JWT package to authenticate API requests.

❷ This configuration ensures that the Simple JWT library uses the AccessToken class for handling authentication tokens. The class is responsible for creating, validating, and decoding JWT access tokens. USER_ID_CLAIM overwrites the key name that carries the user's ID in the payload to id.

Having authentication classes set for DRF and Simple JWT, next, we need to register endpoints that manage the JWT token. Example 5-17 shows registered endpoints to manage JWT. These endpoints allow us to obtain, refresh, revoke, and verify JWT.

Example 5-17. JWT routes

```
# src/django/app/config/urls.py

...
urlpatterns = [
    ...
    path("api/jwt/obtain", TokenObtainPairView.as_view()),
    path("api/jwt/refresh", TokenRefreshView.as_view()),
    path("api/jwt/revoke", TokenRevokeView.as_view()),
    path("api/jwt/verify", TokenVerifyView.as_view()),
    ...
]
...
```

Example 5-18 shows how to obtain JWT. Notice that the response contains both access and refresh tokens. An access token grants access to protected resources, whereas a refresh token obtains a new access token when the current one expires. Once the access token is obtained, you can interact with API endpoints that require its presence. That usually requires constructing the request so that its headers contain an authorization line, which looks like this: `"Authorization": "Bearer ACCESS_TOKEN"` (the `ACCESS_TOKEN` is to be replaced with a real access token).

Example 5-18. JWT retrieval from the REST API using `curl` *(requires setup from Example 5-2)*

```
CREDENTIALS_PAYLOAD='{"username":"admin","password":"admin"}' ❶
ACCESS_TOKEN=$(docker compose exec app bash -c \
  "curl \
  --data '$CREDENTIALS_PAYLOAD' \
  --header 'Content-Type: application/json' \
  --request 'POST' \
  --silent 'http://localhost:8000/api/jwt/obtain' | \
  jq --raw-output '.access'") ❷
echo $ACCESS_TOKEN ❸
eyJhbGciOiJIUzI1NiIsInR5cCI6IkpXVCJ9.eyJ0b2tlbl90eXBlIjoiYWNjZXNzIiwiZXhwIjoxNzMy...
```

❶ The `CREDENTIALS_PAYLOAD` environment variable contains JSON-encoded credentials.

❷ The `ACCESS_TOKEN` environment variable contains a JWT access token. The token is fetched from the */api/jwt/obtain* endpoint. The command ends with `jq`, which extracts the access token.

❸ The echo command prints the JWT.

In this case, the JWT is used to verify the identity of the user who is interacting with the API. By looking at the token itself, there is no way to distinguish the real user from a hacker that uses the intercepted token. One way to address this problem is to reduce the validity time of the token, making it a *short-lived access token*. This solution improves security at the cost of obtaining (regenerating) a new token.[25] But, even with a short-lived access token, the risk remains.

---

25 See the Auth0 blog "What Are Refresh Tokens and How to Use Them Securely" (*https://oreil.ly/bFs0K*) by Dan Arias and Sam Bellen.

Transport Layer Security

This section describes how to enable TLS to secure the HTTP traffic for the WFS's Django application.

Self-Signed Versus CA-Signed Certificates

TLS presented in this section uses a self-signed certificate (*https://oreil.ly/5wJjQ*). The self-signed certificate comes with the drawback of not being trusted by default web browsers. Visiting a website encrypted with such a certificate is possible only if a user approves the visit (certificate).

As a rule of thumb, self-signed certificates should be avoided. However, they may be suitable for specific scenarios, such as internal testing or development environments where trust among parties is already established. Self-signed certificates aren't recommended for production environments, so when encrypting application traffic with TLS in production, use certificates issued by a verified and trusted CA, commonly referred to as *CA-signed certificates*.

CA-signed certificates are issued by trusted authorities that verify the identity (subject) of the certificate. The verification is classified into four categories of varying checks of the identity of the certificate subject.[26]

To obtain a CA-signed certificate, you can use a free Let's Encrypt service (*https://letsencrypt.org*), which offers automated tools for acquiring and renewing certificates. You could also use cloud providers' managed certificates or purchase a certificate from a verified provider.

> The details on implementing TLS for WFS are described in the book's code repository.

To enable or disable TLS for the WFS, you need to respectively set the environment variable to `TLS_ENABLE=1` or `TLS_ENABLE=0` in *src/django/compose.yaml* file, and restart the WFS with **docker compose up --detach --wait**. Secured traffic can be confirmed by visiting *https://localhost:8000*.[27]

---

26 See "What's the Difference Between DV, OV, IV, and EV Certificates" (*https://oreil.ly/nHsEg*) on the SSL.com website.

27 When working with GitHub Codespaces, you'll use a unique URL containing the Codespace's name instead of the *localhost* URL. The expected URL is bound to port 8000 and can be found in VS Code's PORTS tab.

When visiting *https://localhost:8000* run locally (not in GitHub Codespaces), the browser will display a warning that *your connection is not private*. To allow the connection in the local environment, add the application's SSL certificate to the browser's exception list.

Figure 5-5 shows the WFS's HTTP traffic being encrypted and information about the self-signed certificate used for TLS. Notice the scheme of HTTP is `https://`, not `http://`.

API Style	Endpoint	Methods	Response Content Type
WWW	/	GET	text/html
WWW	/admin	GET	text/html
Atom	/forecast/feed	GET	application/atom+xml
Atom	/forecast/feed_enriched To work, starting the gRPC server manually is required! For details, check the chapter's gRPC implementation.	GET	application/atom+xml
Atom	/forecast/f7dc4f34-08ef-48a2-be3c-98ef79ea9bfb	GET	text/html
GraphQL	/graphql	POST	application/json
GraphiQL	/graphiql	GET, POST	text/html
Webhooks	/webhook/v1/echo	POST	application/json
Webhooks	/webhook/v2/echo	POST	application/json
Webhooks	/webhook/v3/echo	POST	application/json

Figure 5-5. Weather Forecast Service encrypted connection

Documentation

In this section, we'll look at how to document REST API. Regardless of how much effort you put into making your API intuitive, consumers may still misunderstand it. Therefore, API documentation is needed; otherwise, the API may go unused.

The API specification is a contract between the API provider and the API consumer. The API provider uses the specification to describe the API, and the API consumer reads the specification to understand how to work with the API.

OpenAPI Specification

The *OpenAPI Specification (OAS)* (*https://oreil.ly/s7dTX*), formerly known as Swagger, is the most popular tool for documenting HTTP-based APIs. The OAS uses human-readable formats such as YAML (*https://yaml.org*) or JSON (*https://www.json.org*) to define a text document that contains the specification of the API.

The OAS document could be made interactive with tools such as ReDoc (*https://redocly.com*), Postman (*https://www.postman.com*), and Swagger UI (*https://oreil.ly/4v1Yo*). The OAS is popular among developers due to its wide adoption and tooling support. A framework like FastAPI (*https://oreil.ly/Ez21i*) made the OAS its default documentation standard.

> While OAS is a popular choice for describing synchronous APIs, it has limited support for asynchronous APIs. If your APIs operate asynchronously, consider AsyncAPI (*https://www.asyncapi.com*).

Example 5-19 shows a fragment of the WFS APIs documented with the OAS.

Example 5-19. Part of the WFS OpenAPI Specification

```
# src/django/docs/api/rest/api.resource-v1.schema.yaml

openapi: 3.1.0 ❶
info: ❷
  title: Weather Forecast Service - REST API
  version: v1
  description: |
    Documentation of Weather Forecast Service (WFS) REST API.
tags: ❸
  - name: Public
    description: Operations available to all users
paths: ❹
  /api/cities: ❺
    get:
      summary: Obtain all cities
      operationId: api_v1_cities_retrieve
      description: Obtain all cities.
      tags: ❸
        - Public
      parameters: ❻
        - name: version
          in: query
          description: API version
          required: false
          schema:
            type: string
```

```
          default: v1
        style: form
        explode: false
      - name: fields
        in: query
        description: Fields to return
        required: false
        schema:
          type: string
          default: uuid,name,country,region,timezone,latitude,longitude
        style: form
        explode: false
      - name: search_{key}
        in: query
        description: |
          Search parameter with a dynamic key.
          Replace `{key}` with the actual field name, e.g.,
          `uuid`, `name`, `country`, `region`, `timezone`, etc.
        required: false
        schema:
          type: string
    responses: ❼
      200:
        description: OK
      400:
        description: Bad request. Invalid data provided
      500:
        description: Internal server error
```

❶ The openapi field marks the OpenAPI version used by the OAS specification.

❷ The info field has metadata on the API, like title, version, and description.

❸ The tags are used to group operations. The Public tag indicates the public availability of the API. This tag is used further down in the document, for the GET
HTTP method.

❹ The paths field defines the available endpoints and their operations.

❺ This /api/cities path is defined with the HTTP GET method. This endpoint offers
client data containing WFS in all cities.

❻ The parameters field describes available query parameters, including version
(describing the API version), fields, and a search_{key} query parameter,
which is dynamic.

❼ The responses field defines the possible API responses.

OpenAPI provides Swagger Editor that allows developers to design and describe APIs. Swagger Editor is the easiest way to get started with the OAS. The editor is accessible at Swagger Editor (*https://editor-next.swagger.io*). Paste the OAS specification from Example 5-19 into it and explore the editor features. The result should resemble Figure 5-6.

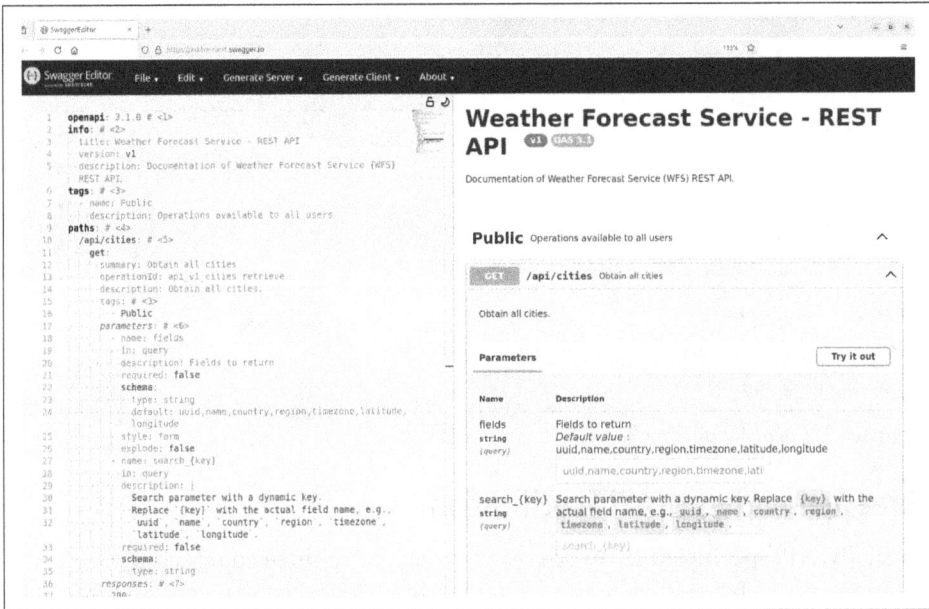

Figure 5-6. Online Swagger Editor

If you prefer to work locally with OAS, you could use the Swagger UI (*https://oreil.ly/qaZQF*) instead of the online editor. Execute instructions from Example 5-20 to see how it works.

Example 5-20. Local Swagger UI started using Docker

```
curl --silent --output schema.yaml http://localhost:8000/api/docs/v1/schema/manual
docker run --env SWAGGER_JSON_URL=schema.yaml \
       --publish 127.0.0.1:8888:8080 \
       --rm \
       --volume ${PWD}/schema.yaml:/usr/share/nginx/html/schema.yaml \
       swaggerapi/swagger-ui
```

The local Swagger UI will display the OAS document as in Figure 5-7.[28]

---

28 When working with GitHub Codespaces, you'll use a unique URL containing the Codespace's name instead of the *localhost* URL. The expected URL is bound to port 8888 and can be found in VS Code's PORTS tab.

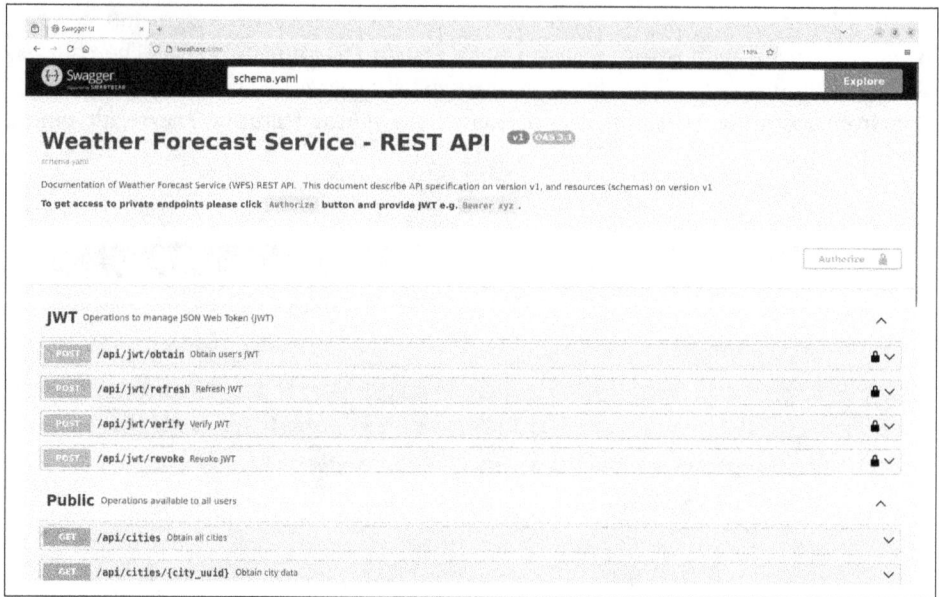

Figure 5-7. Local Swagger UI

Three Approaches to API Specification

Generally, API specification can be created using one of three approaches:

Autogenerated
Specification is autogenerated from the source code. For instance, WFS uses the *drf_spectacular* library (*https://oreil.ly/XNVzo*) designed to work with the DRF. While this approach is appealing for its ease of use, it has some drawbacks. Autogenerated specification provides an incomplete overview of the API, and filling the gaps often requires manually adjusting the source code.

Manual
Specification is created "bottom-up," meaning the API specification is written from scratch. This approach offers complete control and customization but can be time-consuming and prone to inconsistencies with the actual implementation of the API. The preceding section (Example 5-19) used an example of a manually created specification.

Semi-manual
In this hybrid approach, an autogenerated specification provides the initial shape of the API specification, and developers manually fill in missing details. Like the manual approach, this method is also prone to inconsistencies.

The remaining part of this section guides you through the autogenerated and semi-manual methods of documenting REST APIs with OAS.

The first step is to integrate *drf-spectacular* (*https://oreil.ly/b0IRs*) into a Django project as shown in Example 5-21. After installing the *drf-spectacular* Python package, we need to add it to Django's *INSTALLED_APPS*.

Example 5-21. Django drf-spectacular *configuration*

```
# src/django/app/config/base.py

INSTALLED_APPS = [
    ...
    "drf_spectacular",
    ...
]
```

The next step is to register endpoints that will serve OAS. Example 5-22 illustrates the necessary configuration.

Example 5-22. OAS endpoints

```
# src/django/app/config/urls.py

from drf_spectacular.views import SpectacularAPIView
from drf_spectacular.views import SpectacularSwaggerView
from core.www import swagger_rest_schema_view
...

urlpatterns = [
    ...
    path("api/docs/v1", SpectacularSwaggerView.as_view(url_name="oas_manual")),      ❶
    path("api/docs/v1/schema/auto", SpectacularAPIView.as_view(), name="oas_auto"),  ❷
    path("api/docs/v1/schema/manual", swagger_rest_schema_view, name="oas_manual"),  ❸
    ...
]
```

❶ The */docs/api/v1* endpoint exposes Swagger UI (*https://oreil.ly/Rr8OO*) at the *http://localhost:8000/api/docs/v1* location. The rendered documentation is shown in Figure 5-7.

❷ This */docs/api/v1/schema/auto* exposes autogenerated OAS. To see the specification, execute **curl --silent --output wfs.auto.schema.yaml http://local host:8000/api/docs/v1/schema/auto** and open the *wfs.auto.schema.yaml* file.

❸ This */docs/api/v1/schema/manual* exposes semi-manual OAS, but the difference is that the specification was first autogenerated and later manually updated. The code behind the swagger_rest_schema_view() function reads the OAS static file and returns it as the HTTP response (see *src/django/app/core/www/views.py*). To see the specification, run `curl --silent --output wfs.manual.schema.yaml http://localhost:8000/api/docs/v1/schema/manual` and open the *wfs.manual.schema.yaml* file.

> To see the differences between autogenerated and semi-manual OAS, open two tabs in a web browser, and visit Swagger Editor (*https://editor-next.swagger.io*) in each tab. From Example 5-22, copy the contents of *wfs.auto.schema.yaml* to one tab, and *wfs.manual.schema.yaml* to another. Alternatively, you can generate documentation locally using the *swaggerapi/swagger-ui* Docker image (*https://oreil.ly/G5e0b*).

Trade-Offs

Let's review the trade-offs of REST APIs, starting from the advantages:

Scalability
REST was designed to support internet-scale systems. Its stateless nature allows each request to be processed independently, which facilitates horizontal scaling.

Interoperability
REST promotes interoperability by using standardized HTTP. Since HTTP is supported across numerous programming languages, libraries, and platforms, REST APIs can connect systems built using different technologies. Additionally, the stateless nature of REST simplifies integration by allowing components to communicate across different applications and systems.

Debugging and tooling
REST APIs typically use text-based encoding formats like JSON (*https://www.json.org*) or XML (*https://oreil.ly/7WBP2*), which are both human-readable and widely supported. This readability makes it easier to debug issues and track data flows compared to binary alternatives like Protocol Buffers (*https://protobuf.dev*), which require specialized tooling to interpret encoded messages. Furthermore, the REST API style is supported by a vast array of tools, including servers, caching solutions, load balancers, proxies, firewalls, monitoring systems, testing software, debugging utilities, documentation tools, and more.

On the other hand, the disadvantages of REST APIs are as follows:

Limited vocabulary
REST APIs operate on HTTP methods that count only a few verbs (see Table 5-4). These verbs affect the structure of REST APIs and are often insufficient to express operations on resources that fall outside of HTTP vocabulary.

Security challenges

The code-on-demand (an optional feature of RESTful APIs) poses security concerns. The feature allows the server to transfer a code that the client executes. If the code is malicious, then it can lead to authorization exploits and data breaches via methods such as cross-site scripting (XSS) and injection attacks.

Limitations of statelessness

REST APIs are stateless by design, meaning each client request contains all necessary information for processing. The downside of stateless API design is that it leads to larger payloads. It is also not suitable for applications that require state persistence, such as a shopping cart on an e-commerce site, where the order persists across multiple requests. To manage the state in REST APIs, the responsibility often shifts to the client, which can store the state locally (using cookies or local storage).

No standardized versioning

REST wasn't designed with versioning in mind. Clients of REST APIs are sensitive to API changes. For example, Meta's Graph API (*https://oreil.ly/4l1WZ*) (which is a REST API) at the time of this writing is on v22.0, and it has changed 37 times since its initial v1.0 release in 2010. HATEOAS can reduce the likelihood of breaking changes but does not eliminate them. Clients still need to understand the semantics of the actions. You can read more about API versioning in "API Versioning" on page 47.

When to Use REST

REST is suitable for distributed systems, particularly systems with stateless components. It's worth mentioning that distributed systems aren't limited to one API style only. For example, REST could be used to handle *vertical network traffic*, with requests propagating north-south (into and out of the datacenter), and another API style such as gRPC (Chapter 8) or messaging (Chapter 11) could be used to handle *horizontal network traffic* with requests propagating east-west (among individual services of the system).

Because REST is universal and has a wide range of clients, platforms, programming languages, and tooling, it's used for cross-platform integration between internal and external systems, over which you often have no control (including legacy systems), and that require a variety of data formats.

Furthermore, REST uses HTTP as a transport mechanism, making it familiar to backend developers, frontend developers, software architects, and security administrators who have worked with HTTP throughout their careers.

REST APIs support various text-encoding formats that can be compressed, or operate with binary-encoded data. Furthermore, statelessness makes each REST request independent, allowing the system to distribute the requests among multiple servers. Support for caching allows clients to reduce the latency of consecutive server responses. Moreover, REST APIs can use CDNs to cache responses closer to users.

Exercises

1. The documentation section of this chapter describes how to create the OAS using a semi-manual approach, and how to convert it to Swagger UI using a dedicated Python module. In this exercise, your task is to convert the OAS to Swagger UI (*https://oreil.ly/6lLKK*) but without using the *drf-spectacular* library. A rendered Swagger UI is still to be accessible at *localhost:8080*.

   Hint: Use the *swaggerapi/swagger-ui* Docker image (*https://oreil.ly/wn4Li*). The solution to this exercise is available in the *src/django/docs/solutions/rest-exercise.md* file.

2. The OAS is commonly used for documenting APIs. In this exercise, you will try an alternative tool, ReDoc (*https://redoc.ly*). Your task is to convert the OAS to an HTML page using the `redoc` command-line program. The solution to this exercise can be found in *src/django/docs/solutions/rest-exercise.md* file.

Summary

This chapter described the REST API, the most popular web-based API style. You explored the origins of REST, which was designed for internet-scale network-based applications, is based on HTTP, and was expected to make use of HATEOAS. However, most REST API implementations today don't follow the HATEOAS approach.

You implemented a REST API (non-HATEOAS) for the Weather Forecast Service with Django REST Framework, and secured it with TLS and JWT. You also documented the API by using OpenAPI Specification (Swagger).

Besides providing practical REST API implementation skills, this chapter discussed REST trade-offs and prepared you to answer the question of whether REST is appropriate for building your next API. Other API styles discussed in this book, starting from GraphQL in Chapter 6, will refer to and often be compared with REST.

GraphQL

In REST APIs, data retrieval is done by sending a request to a specific endpoint that describes a resource, and in most cases, the returned data comes in a fixed shape. The query-based API style allows you to build APIs in which the data returned by them mirrors the shape of the query. This chapter introduces you to GraphQL, a technology that represents a query-based API style.

While REST is the most popular API technology, GraphQL isn't far behind.[1] It was released by Facebook (now Meta) in 2015 as open source and later moved to the GraphQL Foundation. GraphQL is a *query language* for API, and a *server-side runtime* for executing queries using a *type system* that defines the data.[2] Although GraphQL is agnostic to the transport mechanism, HTTP is the most common choice for data exchange between the GraphQL client and server. GraphQL also supports simultaneous bidirectional data transfers using GraphQL's subscription operation, which often uses the WebSocket protocol (Chapter 10).

This chapter describes GraphQL's origins, specification, security practices, and trade-offs. Next, you'll implement WFS's GraphQL API and compare it to the REST API style from Chapter 5.

---

1 GraphQL is the third most popular API technology according to Postman's "State of the API Report" (*https://oreil.ly/3LG67*).

2 See "Introduction to GraphQL" at the GraphQL website (*https://oreil.ly/BclKH*).

Problems with REST

Despite being the most widely adopted, REST APIs come with shortcomings.

REST APIs are often tightly coupled to the data structures they expose, as their resources typically represent data models revealed by endpoints. This coupling makes it difficult to perform data changes without modifying the API. Modifying how data is exposed through the API may require releasing a new API version and might lead to challenges with maintaining older clients.

Furthermore, REST APIs suffer from the problem of *over-fetching* or *under-fetching* of data. When the API service is over-fetched, it returns more data than the client requires. Inversely, the under-fetched API doesn't provide enough data, resulting in the API client performing additional requests to the API service.

Last but not least, depending on the implementation, a REST API that doesn't use HATEOAS, or embed related data directly in its responses, may struggle to manage relationships between resources. For example, when a client needs data about a user along with their posts and associated comments, multiple API calls are often needed, and their exact format is to be inferred from the API documentation. Alternatively, a custom endpoint that aggregates this data could be implemented, but this approach can increase complexity and couple the client to the server's API structure. Using HATEOAS can simplify navigation between resources because it provides links at which related resources can be found, and embedding data can reduce the number of API calls at the expense of larger payloads.

GraphQL addresses several problems of REST APIs, by enabling clients to fetch only the specific data they need, and by representing relationships between resources with a graph-based model. Like REST, GraphQL can suffer from over-fetching and under-fetching. However, GraphQL's design reduces these risks by allowing clients to specify exact data requirements.

Thinking in Graphs

Learning a new API paradigm like GraphQL requires a mindset shift, especially when transitioning from REST. Let's explain the two main characteristics of GraphQL: *query language* and *static typing*.

> If you are familiar with the basics of JavaScript and are new to GraphQL, have a look at the course "GraphQL for Beginners with JavaScript" (*https://oreil.ly/yDch9*).

A common way to classify programming languages is to divide them into two types: imperative and declarative.

Languages that use *imperative programming* require the developer to provide a step-by-step description of *how* to arrive at the desired outcome. On the other hand, *declarative programming* languages don't require such explicit control flows. Instead, they describe *what* to accomplish and let the execution environment determine the necessary steps. Declarative languages often use queries that abstract away the details of procedural logic. An example of a declarative language is Structured Query Language (SQL), designed for relational database management systems (RDBMSs).

Both SQL and GraphQL are declarative languages that use queries. The difference is that SQL is linked to the relational database layer, enabling you to query specific database systems, whereas GraphQL works at the API layer, allowing you to query different data sources such as databases, filesystems, external APIs, and third-party services.

In GraphQL, the client constructs a query that describes the desired data shape, and the GraphQL service resolves this query, returning the data as described in the query. Every query element in GraphQL has a corresponding type that defines the shape and nature of the data. A type can be one of the predefined GraphQL types or a custom type. The GraphQL type system specifies and enforces types within the GraphQL schema. Like static typing, which allows a type checker to find type-related errors before a program is run, GraphQL delivers similar guarantees. This means that if a GraphQL document passes a static type checker, the document conforms to the schema, reducing the likelihood of runtime errors.

In the context of GraphQL, *server-side runtime* refers to the system (service or environment) that interprets and executes the GraphQL queries by connecting them with the system's underlying data.

The main difference between REST and GraphQL is how the data is requested and structured. The REST API style is centered around the concept of a resource (see "API Maturity Models" on page 159). This way of thinking is reflected in API's interface names, which are named after resources. GraphQL is based on graphs (*https://oreil.ly/d9NT4*), composed of nodes (equivalent of resources) and edges (relationships) connecting them. A GraphQL document defines types where fields represent nodes. If the field is nested within another field, this relationship represents an edge between nodes. The GraphQL service defines the interface, which can interact with any backend (database, legacy system, or external APIs), and the GraphQL client utilizes this interface to interact with the service.

Origins of GraphQL

To understand the roots of GraphQL, you need to look at it from the perspective of the time it was created, and the problems this technology attempted to solve. GraphQL originated in the times when mobile devices were booming. Around 2012, the technological stack of mobile web browsers and HTML5 was insufficient to provide fast rendering and interactivity of web-based applications. GraphQL was born from Facebook's effort to rewrite its iOS and Android applications.[3] This led Facebook (now Meta) to reevaluate the computational demands of REST APIs when retrieving high volumes of graph-like data over the network.

The focus on mobile devices, driven by users shifting content consumption from desktop to mobile, guided the design of GraphQL. Namely, for mobile devices, the two main concerns are network efficiency and energy consumption. These challenges prompted the development of GraphQL as a more efficient way to query data. With GraphQL, the data can be shaped as desired, reducing the amount of data being transferred over the network, and preserving battery life.

An additional factor in the development of GraphQL was the increasing number of client platforms. Supporting a wide variety of clients with a single REST API became a challenge, requiring effort to ensure compatibility and efficiency across all platforms and client versions.

Last but not least, another reason for creating GraphQL was the slow development process of REST APIs contrasting with the expectation of rapid feature development. With REST APIs, the service exposes data in a way that often needs to be modified to account for specific requirements and design changes on the client side. In other words, the service limits the shape of data returned from API endpoints. This hinders iterations and fast development. GraphQL was designed to support faster development for a broader range of applications in which the client determines the shape of data returned from the API.

GraphQL Versus REST

To appreciate the benefits of GraphQL, we first will try to understand how it differs from REST. REST API uses multiple endpoints to expose the data and is resource-oriented. On the other hand, GraphQL API is exposed by a single endpoint.[4] GraphQL is often intent-oriented, meaning its interfaces describe an action executed on a resource.

---

3 See "GraphQL: The Documentary" (*https://oreil.ly/9vrMw*) by Honeypot, and read the "GraphQL: A Data Query Language" post (*https://oreil.ly/oNmNk*) by Lee Byron.

4 While using several endpoints to expose data in GraphQL is possible, this is considered an antipattern.

An analogy of ordering a meal at a restaurant can be used to understand the differences between the REST and GraphQL approaches to APIs. The customer (client) reads the menu and orders the meal (data); the waiter (API) passes the order to the kitchen (server). The kitchen processes the request, prepares the meal, and passes it to the waiter, who delivers it to the customer.

In REST APIs, the restaurant's menu represents fixed API endpoints, where each endpoint delivers a specific meal. If a client wants a specialized meal, it must be added to the menu first, which means updating, printing, and redistributing the menu. This is resource-consuming, especially if frequent updates are required.

In GraphQL, the menu is more flexible than in REST. The GraphQL menu allows the customer to customize the order to their liking. Rather than having fixed menu items, the client can specify the exact ingredients they want. The kitchen then prepares the meal and serves only what the client requested, reducing waste (over-fetching) or the need for additional orders (under-fetching). This flexibility allows GraphQL to handle complex data requirements, all through a single customizable query.

Having described the differences between REST and GraphQL, let's turn to GraphQL's building blocks. The next section describes the anatomy of a GraphQL document.

GraphQL Constructs

This section exposes you to the vocabulary of the GraphQL specification, to help you understand this technology better. The following terminology defines a language that GraphQL developers use when building the GraphQL API. This vocabulary may be too abstract for new GraphQL users. One way for it to stick is to put your hands on this technology, which you will do in this chapter when working with examples in "Implementation" on page 204.

Note that the following list explains only the main terms. For details of GraphQL constructs, consult the latest GraphQL specification (*https://spec.graphql.org*).

Document (https://oreil.ly/PgH6B)
   A GraphQL document can be a request string (or a text file) that describes operations allowed by the schema's type system. GraphQL is statically typed, meaning the document is parsed and validated against types presented in the schema before execution. Parsing ensures that the document follows GraphQL syntax, while validation enforces that the operations are consistent with the types defined in the schema, required arguments, variable usage, and more. The GraphQL document is created by the client.

Type system (https://oreil.ly/6r4aK)

The type system describes the capabilities of the GraphQL API. The type system is also used to validate GraphQL operations, ensuring that the inputs (input objects, arguments, or variables) and outputs (object types or interfaces) conform to the schema's defined types. The separation between how inputs are constrained and how outputs are structured enforces type safety. Validation of the request occurs when the request is received, but before its execution, to ensure that the request conforms to the schema. Types in the type system are categorized into input and output types (*https://oreil.ly/IBpHN*). *Input types* describe the values accepted as a field's arguments or variables. *Output types* describe the values returned by fields.

Schema (https://oreil.ly/tqZe7)

The schema is a collection of types and supported directives. It serves as a root that determines the place in the type system where each kind of GraphQL operation begins. The schema is a server feature.

Operations (https://oreil.ly/LWzbc)

An operation uses a *selection set* (a set of information) (*https://oreil.ly/OKJ4D*) to retrieve or manipulate the data, which allows the client to receive the requested data and nothing more. Three kinds of operations can be performed on data with GraphQL: *Query* to read data; *Mutation* to write data; and *Subscription*, a long-lived operation that fetches data in response to an event in the source system.[5]

Field (https://oreil.ly/cSizW)

A field is a unit of selection in a GraphQL operation that returns a value. The field can optionally have a set of arguments, and it's the main component of the selection set. The field represents a key in the response and is defined in the schema by a name. The field represents a single piece of data that can be requested within a selection set and returns output types (*https://oreil.ly/E7bQ1*).

Resolver (https://oreil.ly/3okpv)

A resolver is responsible for populating a field with data. It's a bridge between the GraphQL schema and the underlying data sources, such as databases or external APIs. Technically, a resolver is a function that contains the logic to retrieve or compute the field value in the schema, when the operation is executed.

---

5 Subscriptions can use the WebSocket protocol (*https://oreil.ly/5dmi9*) but could also be implemented using the HTTP Server-Sent Events (SSE) (*https://oreil.ly/tFb3r*) or long polling (*https://oreil.ly/nEDqD*).

Scalar (https://oreil.ly/BeWK1) and enums (https://oreil.ly/rsJ7K)
> A type that represents a primitive value that can be one of *Int, Float, String, Boolean,* or *ID*. Scalars and enums appear as input or leaf values in the GraphQL operations tree and represent nonnested data. GraphQL also allows you to create custom scalars by defining new custom scalar types (*https://oreil.ly/sQJQ9*).

How GraphQL Works

The base of a GraphQL API is the schema that describes the service's capabilities. A GraphQL schema grows by adding operations such as queries, mutations, and subscriptions, which define how clients can interact with the API. These operations are typically made available to the clients via a single HTTP endpoint.

The schema is built around types, which describe the shape of data. A GraphQL schema contains fields, each representing a piece of information of a given type and every field is backed by a resolver.

A *resolver* is a function that serves as the execution point for the logic required to fetch, modify, or subscribe to the data for a given field. Each field in the schema maps to a specific resolver that handles the logic that retrieves data for that field. Resolvers can be used to interact with databases, internal and external services, or any other data source to fulfill the client's request.

Code-First Versus Schema-First

There are two approaches to building GraphQL APIs: code-first and schema-first. The *code-first* approach starts by creating code that produces GraphQL schema behavior. GraphQL frameworks like Graphene (*https://graphene-python.org*) and Strawberry (*https://strawberry.rocks*) use the code-first approach.

The *schema-first* approach starts by creating a schema file that outlines the GraphQL types that define the GraphQL API's structure. Subsequently, the code is developed to fulfill the requirements specified by the schema. GraphQL frameworks like Ariadne (*https://ariadnegraphql.org*) and Tartiflette (*https://tartiflette.io*) use the schema-first approach.

Let's explore some of the capabilities that GraphQL offers. GraphQL and REST both use HTTP as a transport mechanism, but the main difference is that in REST, you interact with an API by sending a request containing an HTTP verb to one of the API endpoints. HTTP verbs express a limited set of operations to be executed on the resource. For example, GET is used to read; POST, PUT, and PATCH to modify; and DELETE to remove the resource. Furthermore, the query parameters and request body can be used to control the resource properties. In GraphQL, you typically use HTTP POST for all GraphQL operations, and requests are sent to a single endpoint. A possible setup is to use HTTP GET for queries and HTTP POST for mutations.

Implementation

The easiest way to interact with the GraphQL API is via GraphiQL (*https://oreil.ly/ L5WD1*). GraphiQL is an interactive, graphical GraphQL environment accessible in a web browser. It allows interaction with the GraphQL API by constructing and executing documents against the GraphQL service. To access the WFS's GraphQL API, follow the steps shown in Example 6-1.

Example 6-1. GraphQL lab setup

```
cd src/django ❶
docker compose build --build-arg UID=$(id -u) --build-arg GID=$(id -g) ❷
docker compose up --detach --wait ❸
```

❶ Navigate to the lab's directory.

❷ Build Docker images.

❸ Start Docker containers.

GraphiQL

The following example shows different ways of interacting with the GraphQL API. Let's start by obtaining a list of city names along with their UUIDs using GraphiQL. To obtain this list, perform the following steps:

1. Make sure the WFS is running, by following Example 6-1.

2. Visit *http://localhost:8000/graphiql*.[6]

---

6 When working with GitHub Codespaces, you'll use a unique URL containing the Codespace's name instead of the *localhost* URL. The expected URL is bound to port 8000 and can be found in VS Code's PORTS tab.

3. Execute the **query GetCityUUID { cities { uuid name } }** document, as shown in Figure 6-1. In GraphiQL, you can use the "Prettify query" button located below the "Execute query" button to make a query look nicer. The Docs section (not visible on the image) contains the schema root types (query and mutation), and all other schema types exposed by this GraphQL service.

> Notice that our access to the GraphQL API endpoint doesn't require authentication, which is a security risk, especially in a production environment. You can control GraphiQL access by implementing user authentication. For example, to access GitHub's GraphiQL Explorer (*https://oreil.ly/3mTtC*), a GitHub user must first click the "Sign in with GitHub" button.

Figure 6-1. GraphiQL (requires setup from Example 6-1)

The GetCityUUID query demonstrated the fetching capabilities of the GraphQL API.[7] Notice that the GraphQL API returned only the requested data—that is, the uuid and the name of every city. By limiting the number of fields returned in the API response, we reduce the network footprint.

Executing Mutations

The next demonstration shows an example of mutating the WFS data by updating city data through the GraphQL API. In this example, you will use GetJWT and RenameCity operations as shown in Figure 6-1.

Before performing a mutation on the city object, first obtain a UUID of the city that you will want to edit. To do so, execute the following steps:

1. Get a UUID for the city of Tokyo. The UUID (*e6036616-dbae-4b96-956c-06ff7b479322*) was found in the preceding exercise (Figure 6-1), but it will be different in your application.

2. Obtain a JWT that will be used to authenticate the user before performing a RenameCity mutation (see Table 6-1). To get the token, execute the GetJWT mutation as shown in Figure 6-1.

GraphiQL is a convenient tool for testing and exploring GraphQL API, but it's not the only way to interact with it. You can also interact with the GraphQL API using familiar tools like cURL. Example 6-2 shows instructions on how to make a request to the GraphQL API without using GraphiQL.

Example 6-2. JWT retrieval from GraphQL API using curl *(requires setup from Example 6-1)*

```
# Set environment variables ❶
CSRF_TOKEN=$(docker compose exec app openssl rand -hex 16)
MUT='mutation {obtainJwt(username:\"admin\",password:\"admin\"){token{token}}}'

# Get JWT token with curl ❷
docker compose exec app curl --silent \
        --request POST \
        --header "Content-type: application/json" \
        --header "X-csrftoken: $CSRF_TOKEN" \
        --header "Cookie: csrftoken=$CSRF_TOKEN" \
        --data-raw "{\"query\": \"$MUT\"}" \
        "http://localhost:8000/graphql"
```

---

7 Compare this query to Table 6-2.

```
# Output:
{"data": {"obtainJwt": {"token": {"token": "eyJhbGciOiJIU..."}}}}
```

❶ The CSRF_TOKEN variable is for the cross-site request forgery (CSRF) protection
mechanism. The MUT variable holds the GetJWT mutation operation shown in
Figure 6-1, which is used to obtain the JWT access token.

❷ The curl command performs an HTTP request. The destination of the request is
the WFS GraphQL API endpoint exposed at */graphql* (not GraphiQL!). The
request is JSON encoded and has the headers required by the CSRF protection,
that uses CSRF_TOKEN. The JSON object sent to the GraphQL API has only one
key (query, not to be confused with a GraphQL query), containing a GraphQL
document that describes the GraphQL mutation operation. The obtainJwt field
takes user credentials as arguments and returns an access token.

The last step in this example is to rename a city. For that, we'll run the RenameCity
mutation, as described in Table 6-1 and shown in Figure 6-1. This time, the mutation
will be executed using the GraphiQL user interface.

> Independently, whether it's the REST API or GraphQL API, some
> WFS resources are protected by authorization mechanisms that use
> JWT. Therefore, don't forget to add the Authorization header
> when interacting with protected API resources. In GraphiQL, add
> the header to the GraphiQL's Headers section, and remember to
> wrap the header in curly brackets ("{}"), as shown here and in
> Figure 6-1:
>
> ```
> {
>   "Authorization": "Bearer token"
> }
> ```

Table 6-1. GraphQL mutation to rename a city

GraphQL document	API response

``mutation RenameCity(
  $city: UUID = "e6036616-dbae-4b96-956c-06ff7b479322"
) {
  updateCity(data: {uuid: $city, name: "Tokio"}) {
    name
  }
}```
	``{
	  "data": {
	    "updateCity": {
	      "name": "Tokio"
	    }
	  }
	}```

This section showed the frontend developer perspective on how to interact with GraphQL, with and without GraphiQL. The next section looks at the API from a backend developer perspective and explains the implementation details of the WFS GraphQL API.

CRUD

To implement a GraphQL API, we chose the Strawberry library (*https://oreil.ly/5kup5*), available for the Django web framework (*https://www.djangoproject.com*).

You are already familiar with the CRUD implementation of the WFS City model for the REST API introduced in Table 5-3. In this example, you'll implement CRUD for the same model but with GraphQL.

> Before implementing GraphQL APIs in production, consult the "GraphQL Best Practices" document (*https://oreil.ly/r83fM*).

The CRUD in GraphQL differs from the one used in the REST API. GraphQL requests are typically sent via the HTTP POST method.[8] This means you cannot use HTTP DELETE, PUT, or PATCH methods to manipulate resources. Instead, you send a request containing a query or a subscription operation to read the data (R from CRUD). On the other hand, a POST request with a mutation operation will write the data (performing C, U, or D [CUD] from CRUD).

Read

In this example, you'll implement the Read operation on a City model.

Building a GraphQL API starts by defining an endpoint through which it'll receive requests. Contrary to REST API, which exposes multiple HTTP endpoints, the interaction with GraphQL API is typically funneled via a single HTTP endpoint that exposes the GraphQL schema. Example 6-3 shows the definition of the */graphql* endpoint.

---

8 GraphQL could also use the HTTP GET method for queries.

Example 6-3. GraphQL API endpoint configuration

```
# src/django/app/config/urls.py

from django.views.decorators.csrf import csrf_exempt
from strawberry.django.views import AsyncGraphQLView
from core.api.graphql.schema import schema

...
urlpatterns = [
  ...
  path("graphql", AsyncGraphQLView.as_view(  ❶
     schema=schema, graphql_ide=False, allow_queries_via_get=False
  )),
  ...
]
...
if ENVIRONMENT == "development":
   ...
   urlpatterns += [path("graphiql", csrf_exempt(AsyncGraphQLView.as_view(  ❷
      schema=schema, graphql_ide=True, allow_queries_via_get=False
   )))]
...
```

❶ The `path()` function exposes the GraphQL API via the */graphql* endpoint. The `schema` argument points to the variable that contains the GraphQL root schema, which holds GraphQL operations.

❷ This `path()` function makes GraphiQL accessible at the */graphiql* endpoint. GraphiQL is enabled with the `graphql_ide=True` argument in the development environment. The Django framework, by default, expects the CSRF token to be available for all `POST` requests. The `csrf_exempt()` function disables CSRF protection from the GraphiQL view in the development environment, making it easier for developers to work with this technology.

> GraphiQL is useful during testing and development, but in production, it can expose sensitive data or lead to security attacks.

The next step in designing a GraphQL API is to define a schema that will aggregate GraphQL's operations, as shown in Example 6-4.

Example 6-4. GraphQL schema definition

```python
# src/django/app/core/api/graphql/schema.py

from strawberry import Schema
from strawberry_django.optimizer import DjangoOptimizerExtension

from .queries import Query
from .mutations import Mutation


schema = Schema(    ❶
    query=Query,
    mutation=Mutation,
    extensions=[DjangoOptimizerExtension],
)
```

❶ The WFS schema contains queries and mutations available via the `Query` and `Mutation` objects. Additionally, the Strawberry implementation allows for extensions on these operations. In this case, `DjangoOptimizerExtension` (*https://oreil.ly/8rvjq*) is used to address the $1 + n$ problem (*https://oreil.ly/oZm4R*) (also called $n + 1$). The $1 + n$ problem is a performance issue that occurs when related data is fetched with many queries instead of one. The $1 + n$ problem appears in the context of a relational database, where one model uses a foreign key to relate to another. For example, a *WeatherForecast* model has a foreign key to the *City* model, which translates to a one-to-many relation where the city has many weather forecasts. If the problem isn't addressed, the default behavior for an ORM is that for 1 (one) looked-up article, a relational database will perform n additional queries, where n is equal to the number of comments for that article.[9]

After preparing the schema, the next step is to implement the queries and mutations. First, we'll start with the query shown in Example 6-5. The `cities` query returns WFS's cities from the City model.

---

9 A solution of the $1 + n$ problem using dataloaders is described in this blog (*https://oreil.ly/nUxQl*).

Example 6-5. GraphQL query implementation

```
# src/django/app/core/api/graphql/queries.py

import strawberry
from strawberry_django import field

from .filters import CityFilter
from .types import CityType


@strawberry.type
class CityQuery:
    cities: list[CityType] = field(filters=CityFilter, ...)  ❶

...

@strawberry.type
class Query(CityQuery, ...):  ❷
    pass
```

❶ CityQuery is a Python class, promoted to be the GraphQL type by the Strawberry type decorator (@strawberry.type). The field cities is Strawberry's Django (*https://oreil.ly/1Aoew*) field that exposes a query. This field returns a list of cites described by CityType. Additionally, the query allows filtering operations on the query, and CityFilter indicates this. Under the hood, this instruction uses the Strawberry's ORM. Decorating the class with the @strawberry.type creates a resolver on the cities field. Query (*https://oreil.ly/xSnR9*) allows the data to only be read (fetched).

❷ The Query class is a GraphQL type that aggregates all queries in WFS.

Let's investigate the types used in Table 6-2 that describe the city. These types are presented in Example 6-6.

Example 6-6. GraphQL City model types

```python
# src/django/app/core/api/graphql/types.py

import strawberry_django
from typing import Optional
from core.models import City

@strawberry_django.type(City, ...)
class CityType:    ❶
    uuid: UUID
    name: str
    country: str
    ...

# src/django/app/core/api/graphql/filters.py
@strawberry_django.filter(City, lookups=True)
class CityFilter:    ❷
    name: Optional[TextFilterLookup[str]]
    country: Optional[TextFilterLookup[str]]
    ...

# src/django/app/core/api/graphql/inputs.py
@strawberry_django.input(City)
class UUIDInput:    ❸
    uuid: UUID

@strawberry_django.input(City)
class CityInput:    ❸
    name: str
    country: str
    ...

@strawberry_django.partial(City)
class CityInputPartial(UUIDInput):    ❸
    name: Optional[str]
    country: Optional[str]
    ...
```

❶ The `CityType` class represents a GraphQL type created from the strawberry-graphql-django extension (*https://oreil.ly/g4hP4*). The decorator `@strawberry_django.type` binds Django's model `City` with the Strawberry type system, allowing you to expose relevant fields of the `City` model.

❷ The `CityFilter` class allows filtering on a Django model. The filter decorator is bound to the Django `City` model and allows the model to be filtered on specific fields. The `lookups=True` argument allows you to search the `City` model by using *contains*, *endsWith*, *startsWith*, and *regex* capabilities.

❸ This block declares various input classes used for CUD operations (*https:// oreil.ly/53H3T*). Inputs are derived from Django's model and are categorized into two types: partial and input. *Partial* allows you to provide only a portion of input fields, whereas *input* requires all input fields to be provided.

Now, let's test the implementation of the `cities` field. Table 6-2 shows a document containing the `GetAllCities` query operation that retrieves all city names.

Table 6-2. Cities query (requires setup from Example 6-1)

GraphQL document	API response
```query GetAllCities {\n cities {\n name\n }\n}```	```{\n "data": {\n "cities": [\n {"name": "Cairo"},\n {"name": "Istanbul"},\n {"name": "Mexico City"},\n {"name": "Sao Paulo"},\n {"name": "Sydney"},\n {"name": "Tokyo }\n]\n }\n}```

Create, Update, Delete

Having implemented R (read) from CRUD by using a GraphQL query, the next step is to use mutations to implement the remaining CUD operations. This is what Example 6-7 does.

Example 6-7. Create, update, and delete mutations implementation

```
# src/django/app/core/api/graphql/mutations.py

import strawberry
from core.helpers import IsAdmin
from core.helpers import IsAuthenticated
from strawberry_django.mutations import create, update, delete
...

@strawberry.type
class CityMutation:  ❶
    create_city: CityType = create(
        CityInput,
        permission_classes=[IsAuthenticated, IsAdmin]
    )
    update_city: CityType = update(
        CityInputPartial,
```

```
        key_attr="uuid",
        permission_classes=[IsAuthenticated, IsAdmin]
    )
    delete_city: CityType = delete(
        UUIDInput,
        key_attr="uuid",
        permission_classes=[IsAuthenticated, IsAdmin]
    )

...


@strawberry.type
class Mutation(CityMutation, ...):  ❷
    pass
```

❶ CityMutation is a mutation type class with three fields: create_city, update_city, and delete_city, which respectively use create, update, and delete strawberry-graphql-django (*https://oreil.ly/JmSxf*) mutations. Every field uses an input type tailored to it, such as CityInput, CityInputPartial, and UUIDInput. For implementation details, consult Example 6-6. The key_attr argument overrides Strawberry's default model lookup ID (pk) to be uuid.

The permission_classes argument allows mutation to be performed only by permitted users, and it can be used to implement field-level authorization. We use custom-implemented IsAuthenticated and IsAdmin classes that limit endpoint access based on the authenticated user's role, such as admin.

❷ The Mutation class is used to aggregate WFS mutations. The class is exposed to the schema root in Example 6-4.

After implementing all three CUD operations, let's test them. GraphQL allows for the sequential execution of operations containing multiple fields, under the condition that these fields belong to the same operation type. Example 6-8 shows the execution of three mutations.

> Mutations are guarded by permission class, which expects a JWT access token to be present in the request header. Example 6-2 contains instructions on how to obtain a JWT access token.

Example 6-8. Create, update, and delete mutations execution

```
mutation CUDCity($city: UUID = "e6036616-dbae-4b96-956c-06ff7b479322") {
  createCity(
    data: {
      name: "Warsaw", country: "Poland", region: "Europe",
```

```
          timezone: "Europe/Warsaw", latitude: 52.249782, longitude: 21.012176
      }) {
        uuid
        name
        country
        region
        timezone
        latitude
        longitude
  }
  updateCity(data: {uuid: $city, name: "Tokio"}) {
    uuid
    name
  }
  deleteCity(data: {uuid: $city}) {
    uuid
  }
}
```

Example 6-8 shows the mutation named CUDCity, which specifies a $city variable, obtained from the GetAllCities query prior to constructing this document. The city variable is passed to the updateCity and deleteCity fields.

Example 6-9. Responses returned by Example 6-8 mutations

```
{
  "data": {
    "createCity": {
      "uuid": "ed773f3f-84cd-41b3-b067-9961cdb9e912",
      "name": "Warsaw",
      "country": "Poland",
      "region": "Europe",
      "timezone": "Europe/Warsaw",
      "latitude": "52.249782",
      "longitude": "21.012176"
    },
    "updateCity": {
      "uuid": "e6036616-dbae-4b96-956c-06ff7b479322",
      "name": "Tokyo",
    },
    "deleteCity": {
      "uuid": "e6036616-dbae-4b96-956c-06ff7b479322",
    }
  }
}
```

Example 6-9 shows the response returned by the GraphQL API. The shape matches the mutation from Example 6-8. Notice that one request performed three operations (Create, Update, and Delete) on city resources. In a REST API, you'd have to send three requests to achieve this effect. The createCity field creates the Warsaw city. The updateCity field renames Tokyo to Tokio, and deleteCity removes the renamed Tokio city. The last two fields use uuid in the data argument to identify and select the mutated city.

Security

"OWASP Top 10 API Security" on page 69 describes the aspects of API security that cross-intersect various API styles. This section focuses on the attacks specific to GraphQL, as well as how to implement user authentication.

> Check OWASP's GraphQL Cheat Sheet (*https://oreil.ly/kWQes*) for common attacks and their countermeasures.

Attacking GraphQL

In this section, we'll look at common attacks that can be executed against the GraphQL API.

Introspection abuse attack

In the *introspection abuse* attack, an attacker exploits the GraphQL introspection feature to extract the schema. The attack can be carried out with GraphiQL or another tool capable of sending GraphQL queries. To mitigate this risk, introspection can be restricted or turned off.[10]

However, disabling introspection also means losing the ability to autogenerate documentation. To balance security and documentation needs, you can enable introspection in development environments and disable it in production. If introspection is turned off, you'll need to pregenerate and host your documentation externally.

---

10 Be aware that some tools like Clairvoyance (*https://oreil.ly/2vWsF*) that, even if the introspection is disabled, can still extract the GraphQL schema. Read "A Complete Guide to Hacking GraphQL" (*https://oreil.ly/0Fwhg*) by Stefano Lanaro for more details.

> To introspect your GraphQL API, execute a full introspection query (*https://oreil.ly/KyK4G*) against the API endpoint.[11] This query will list all information about your schema.

Undesirable query attack

An *undesirable query* causes a GraphQL service to perform computationally heavy tasks or expose sensitive information. Such queries may include deeply nested queries, queries that request large result sets, or those that perform filtering and sorting.

One way to avoid undesirable queries is to use an allowlist of approved queries. In this approach, the GraphQL server maintains a list of predefined, safe queries. Every incoming client's query is checked against this list. If a query is in the allowlist, the server executes it. If a query is not in the allowlist, it's rejected with an HTTP 403 (Forbidden) response, indicating that the server refuses to handle the request. The media type `application/graphql-response+json` is encouraged to be used when returning 4*xx* and 5*xx* errors from GraphQL.[12]

A common practice in allowlisting is to use *normalized queries*, which are queries where whitespaces are removed and the structure follows alphabetical order. Normalization is handled by the backend, allowing clients to send their queries in any format without worrying about specific normalization rules.

Typically, allowlisting is disabled in development environments to allow developers to test and iterate on new queries freely. Allowlisting ensures that only trusted queries are executed in production, reducing the risk of performance issues and data leaks.

Recursive query attack

In GraphQL, relationships are defined in the schema and described by the client in a document by field nesting. If a model has a circular relationship, you could construct the query that looks like the one in Example 6-10. By all means, this is a legitimate GraphQL query. The problem is that the number of objects that the service returns is multiplicative with the level of nesting, which can be resource-heavy.

Example 6-10. GraphQL recursive query

```
query RecursiveQuery {
  student {
    courses {
```

---

11 The query can be found in GitHub Gist (*https://oreil.ly/nTDCL*).

12 See application/graphql-response+json (*https://oreil.ly/XZ1r3*).

```
    student {
      courses {
        student {
          courses {
            student {
                uuid
                name
            }
          }
        }
      }
    }
  }
}
```

To protect the GraphQL API from recursive nesting, limit the query's nesting depth.

Batch query attack

A *batch query attack* exploits GraphQL's capability to construct a document containing multiple operations. We constructed such a GraphQL document in Example 6-8.

In a batch query attack, an attacker sends numerous queries combined into one GraphQL document. Such a request can overwhelm the GraphQL API service, leading to resource exhaustion or service downtime.

To protect the GraphQL API from this attack, you could limit the number of batch operations allowed for a single query or mutation. For instance, you can set a cap on the batch queries to allow a maximum of three operations per request. Furthermore, you could set time limits to terminate queries that take too long to execute; you could also block clients that send resource-intensive queries.

The batch attack also can take advantage of *GraphQL aliases*, where a field can be given an alias (name). This way, you could run multiple queries by using a single request, as shown in Example 6-11.

Example 6-11. GraphQL alias

```
query AliasQuery {
  Cairo: cities(filters: {name: {exact: "Cairo"}}) {
    uuid
    name
  }
  Sydney: cities(filters: {name: {exact: "Sydney"}}) {
    uuid
    name
  }
}
```

Authentication

In Example 6-7, we briefly mentioned that only authenticated users can perform mutations on city objects. In this section, we explain the authentication flow and its implementation.

The WFS uses strawberry-django-auth (*https://oreil.ly/4WFjL*) for JWT integration. Using this library, you import relevant authentication flow mutations and integrate them into the WFS schema, as shown in Example 6-12.

Example 6-12. JWT mutations implementation

```
# src/django/app/core/api/graphql/mutations.py

import strawberry

from gqlauth.user import arg_mutations
....

@strawberry.type
class JWTMutation:    ❶
    obtain_jwt = arg_mutations.ObtainJSONWebToken.field
    refresh_jwt = arg_mutations.RefreshToken.field
    revoke_jwt = arg_mutations.RevokeToken.field
    verify_jwt = arg_mutations.VerifyToken.field
    ...

@strawberry.type
class Mutation(CityMutation, JWTMutation):    ❷
    pass
```

❶ The JWTMutation aggregates relevant to authentication flow fields to obtain, refresh, revoke, and verify JWT.

❷ The JWTMutation class is added to the Mutation class, which is exposed in the root schema as shown in Example 6-4.

Implementing this code lets you execute the obtainJwt mutation to obtain JWT. The next step is to perform token validation. This is where the IsAuthenticated class comes into play, as shown in Example 6-13.

Example 6-13. GraphQL authentication implementation

```python
# src/django/app/core/helpers/auth/permissions.py

import json
import jwt
...
from django.contrib.auth.models import User
from strawberry.permission import BasePermission as StrawberryBasePermission
from strawberry.types import Info

from config.constants import SECRET_KEY


class IsAuthenticated(StrawberryBasePermission):    ❶
    message = "User is not authenticated"

    async def has_permission(self, source: Any, info: Info, **kwargs) -> bool:    ❷
        authenticated = False

        request = info.context["request"]
        if "Authorization" in request.headers:
            jwt_token = request.headers["Authorization"].split(" ")[-1]    ❸
            if not jwt_token:
              raise Exception("Token is missing.")

            try:
                payload = jwt.decode(jwt_token, SECRET_KEY, algorithms=["HS256"])    ❹

                expiration_dt = datetime.fromtimestamp(int(payload["exp"]))
                token_expired = datetime.now() >= expiration_dt    ❺
                if token_expired:
                    rise Exception("Token has expired.")
                else:
                    authenticated = True

                qs = await sync_to_async(User.objects.filter)(pk=payload["id"])

                info.context.request.user = await sync_to_async(qs.first)()    ❻
            ...
            except Exception as e:
                raise Exception(f"Invalid token. {e}")

        return authenticated    ❼
```

❶ The `IsAuthenticated` class extends functionality from the permission class `StrawberryBasePermission` (`BasePermission`).

❷ The class overwrites the `has_permission()` method that returns a boolean to indicate whether the request is authenticated.

❸ The JWT authentication token is extracted from the HTTP `Authorization` header.

❹ The `jwt.decode()` method performs signature verification and transforms JWT into a payload object. Decoding requires using `SECRET_KEY`, which was used in the JWT encoding step. The code block extracts the token's expiration date `expiration_dt`.

❺ This condition checks whether the token has expired.

❻ At this point, the token is considered valid, and the user is authenticated. The authenticated user is retrieved and inserted into the request context.

❼ If there are no errors during the validation process, the class returns `True`, indicating that the user has the required permissions.

Documentation

Writing documentation is an unavoidable task when delivering an API. Even if the API is well-designed and intuitive, a developer consuming it may still need to make some assumptions about it. The role of the API documentation is to clarify these assumptions.

Another challenge with documenting an API is to keep the documentation in sync with the implementation. Under pressure to deliver the API on time, documentation may become an afterthought, and it is often written after the API is released.

GraphQL addresses the documentation challenge through introspection. Introspection allows browsing GraphQL's schema. Table 6-3 provides an example of an introspection query and a snippet of the query results.

Table 6-3. GraphQL schema types introspection query

GraphQL document	API response
| ```
{
  __schema {
    types {
      name
    }
  }
}
``` | ```
{
  "data": {
    "__schema": {
      "types": [
        {"name": "Query"},
        {"name": "CityType"},
        ...
      ]
    }
  }
}
``` |

GraphiQL includes a built-in *Documentation Explorer* tool that generates documentation using an introspection query. This is done by fetching the schema encoded as JSON from the GraphQL API endpoint that exposes it. Next, the tool transforms those JSON-encoded schema objects into a browsable documentation interface.

Sometimes, due to security considerations, exposing the entire documentation of your GraphQL API via GraphiQL will not be desirable. In this case, rely on tools that translate GraphQL schema into static docs, such as SpectaQL (*https://oreil.ly/UmaoV*) or Voyager (*https://oreil.ly/3KDm8*).

Trade-Offs

Let's discover the trade-offs of GraphQL, and start this section by talking about GraphQL's advantages:

Customizable response data
Data returned from the GraphQL API matches the shape of the operations used to retrieve it. This customizable data format helps clients to avoid over-fetching or under-fetching the data, and that reduces network utilization. Moreover, data customization allows clients to operate on returned data without the need to reshape or normalize it.

Less chatty than REST
In GraphQL, a single API endpoint is used to get data in and out of the API. GraphQL aliases, and the ability to request multiple fields by the GraphQL service, make the GraphQL API less chatty (perform a small number of requests), saving multiple back-and-forth calls.

Schema introspection
GraphQL allows clients to introspect API constructs from its schema. By looking into the schema, you can obtain information about the GraphQL types system such as operations, fields, and scalars. If a type is prefixed with "__" (double underscore), it's an indication of being a part of the introspection system.

Self-documenting
Documentation in GraphQL is available out of the box and is derived from its schema. The schema allows introspecting GraphQL types, providing a view of how different GraphQL components interact. Tools like GraphiQL's Documentation Explorer allow for schema exploration by offering an interactive interface for querying and inspecting the API. Additionally, schema can be translated into static documentation or even code, with tools like GraphQL Codegen (*https://oreil.ly/R6qFT*), making it easier to integrate with other development processes.

Facade for other APIs

GraphQL can serve as a gateway in a *microservice architecture*, consolidating REST, GraphQL, and other APIs of individual microservices into one global GraphQL schema. Each microservice can expose its own endpoint, and the global GraphQL schema allows clients to query data across services.

Popular architectural patterns that apply to GraphQL are backends for frontends (BFF) (*https://oreil.ly/uhCXo*) and federated architecture (*https://oreil.ly/xpaUO*). In the *BFF pattern*, individual frontend clients (web, mobile, others) interact with the GraphQL APIs tailored to their needs. In contrast, *federated* GraphQL services combine data from multiple GraphQL systems into a single queryable graph. This allows for the construction of a query that fetches data from different sources, combines data in a single payload, and returns it in one response.

Versioning

GraphQL emphasizes continuous schema evolution and aims to avoid versioning (*https://oreil.ly/vmCE5*) altogether. Instead of creating new API versions, GraphQL promotes a versionless API because queries are flexible and return customizable data. Expanding the schema with new capabilities is achieved by adding new fields or types, which doesn't introduce breaking changes. This allows clients to request only the data they need, ensuring backward compatibility as the API evolves.[13]

Here are some disadvantages of GraphQL:

Security challenges

Introspection in GraphQL provides clients with documentation by allowing them to query the API schema and see all available types. While this is helpful during development, it also exposes the GraphQL API's types system, which attackers could exploit. Attackers might use this information to discover and access resources not intended to be publicly available.

The difference between GraphQL API and REST API is the surface attack. In REST API, the attacker targets fixed API endpoints, whereas in GraphQL, there is typically only one endpoint. Besides, GraphQL APIs exhibit challenges in the implementation of effective request rate limiting.

GraphQL is prone to over-fetching attacks, where a vast amount of data is retrieved, and under-fetching attacks, where multiple requests are sent to the API. These attacks can be combined too.

---

13 Even though GraphQL avoids versioning, the ultimate decision on versioning is up to the API designers. For example, GitHub's GraphQL API (*https://oreil.ly/14u6c*) occasionally versions its fields.

Heavy queries

Although GraphQL reduces over-fetching, complex queries can still result in performance penalties. For example, queries that request recursive or deeply nested data, fetch numerous fields, or utilize GraphQL's aliasing feature may lead to slower query resolution. To address these issues, API designers should consider the complexity of queries and set limits on their execution.

Caching challenges

Caching in GraphQL is complex due to its dynamic and flexible nature, as all requests are funneled through a single GraphQL API endpoint. This makes it difficult to distinguish between individual queries. GraphQL doesn't have built-in support for HTTP caching headers, so caching must be handled differently. To address GraphQL caching challenges,[14] a standard recommendation is to construct queries that use globally unique identifiers (GUIDs).

No native support for multipart/form-data

The GraphQL specification doesn't support the *multipart/form-data* media type, which is commonly used for file uploads. A file upload functionality might require you to implement a custom REST endpoint, encode the file as a Base64 string (*https://oreil.ly/jx2A9*) at the expense of a larger request, or use the Apollo client library (*https://oreil.ly/50dLY*) for implementing the GraphQL Apollo Upload Client (*https://oreil.ly/86xAu*). Furthermore, enabling multipart/form-data might open a door for security issues, leading to CSRF attacks.[15]

Limited use of HTTP status codes

GraphQL handles errors internally, returning them as part of the response payload instead of relying on HTTP status codes. In GraphQL, the HTTP 200 (OK) status code is used for all responses, regardless of whether the response contains data, errors, or both,[16] which leads to situations where the HTTP 200 (OK) status code may actually be an error response. Status codes such as 4*xx* or 5*xx* may still be returned, but they typically indicate issues external to the GraphQL API.

---

14 See GraphQL Caching (*https://oreil.ly/IE05r*).

15 Read the "Security" section in GraphQL multipart/form-data (*https://oreil.ly/nDpqW*).

16 The draft of the specification from 2024 indicates that GraphQL wants to move away from always using the 200 (OK) status code. See "GraphQL over HTTP" (*https://oreil.ly/CtlW9*).

When to Use GraphQL

GraphQL is designed for applications requiring a low network footprint and low energy usage, such as smartphones, smartwatches, or IoT devices. Moreover, GraphQL is used for combining data from various external sources, such as databases, logging services, legacy systems, or third-party data providers.

Another use case for GraphQL is in applications with nested data structures, which would otherwise require multiple API calls. GraphQL can reduce the number of requests to the server by allowing clients to retrieve desired data in a single request. Additionally, GraphQL may reduce the development time compared to implementing a REST API when rapid prototyping or a proof of concept is needed.

Exercises

1. In Example 6-7, we implemented CUD operations following Strawberry's Create, Update, and Delete (*https://oreil.ly/3ZVRH*) tutorial. However, there is a problem with this approach. If you don't check the source code, you have no understanding of how it's implemented, and although implementation will work for simple cases, it may fall short in more complicated scenarios. In this exercise, you'll refactor the `create_city`, `update_city`, and `delete_city` fields from the *src/django/app/core/api/graphql/mutations.py* file with custom resolvers (*https://oreil.ly/XPmQV*) that will provide adequate functionality to the field. The solution for this exercise is already present in the source code.

2. Implement pagination on every type in *src/django/app/core/api/graphql/types.py* using the Strawberry Django extension. A way to approach the solution is described in offset-based pagination (*https://oreil.ly/rTfP4*) Strawberry Django extension documentation.

Summary

This chapter walked you through the history and concepts of GraphQL, one of the most popular network-based APIs.

You implemented the GraphQL API for WFS, using a code-first approach supported by the Strawberry library. Furthermore, you were exposed to the security challenges of GraphQL, such as authentication, and various unintended performance effects that GraphQL queries are vulnerable to. GraphQL introspection was demonstrated with GraphiQL and a full introspection query.

The chapter ended with a list of GraphQL trade-offs to provide a starting point for evaluating the applicability of GraphQL for your next project.

## CHAPTER 7

Web Feeds

In this chapter, you will be introduced to the concepts of web feeds, with a particular focus on the Atom web feed syndication format. A *web feed*, also known as a *news feed*, is a digital document that typically includes media such as web-page content (HTML) or links to other websites, enabling users to stay updated with new content without constantly checking websites. Web feeds are used for asynchronous information broadcasting. They are utilized in scenarios that require regular information updates, such as news, blog posts, podcasts, or videos.

We'll start this chapter by discussing the evolution of web feeds and why they are important in the context of APIs. You'll be provided with examples of web feeds and instructions on how to implement web feeds following the Atom specification. This chapter also describes common security risks for web feeds and exposes their advantages and disadvantages. To solidify your understanding of the subject, you'll be given a set of exercises that require you to read various web feeds.

Although web feeds flourished in 2000, nowadays this technology is used sparsely, and its users are news media, technology companies, bloggers, or scientists. Web feeds are also useful as an educational exercise due to their historical importance and the use of XML, but they have lost popularity since the content was moved to login-protected social platforms such as Meta or X. Nevertheless, we decided to credit web feeds and write a chapter about this technology.

What Is a Web Feed?

A web feed (*https://oreil.ly/KjuQN*) is a data format that delivers regularly updated content to users by providing a document with lists of related information. While several feed formats exist, including JSON feed (*https://www.jsonfeed.org*) and Media RSS (*https://oreil.ly/PFiyt*), this chapter focuses on the most popular: RSS and Atom.

RSS (https://oreil.ly/G47yw) is a type of web feed that provides updates about website content in a standardized XML format, making it readable by both humans and computers.

Atom (https://oreil.ly/scqYn) is a web standard encompassing the Atom Syndication Format (*https://oreil.ly/03MCd*), an XML-based language designed for web feeds, and the Atom Publishing Protocol (AtomPub) (*https://oreil.ly/2Pb3l*), an HTTP-based application-level protocol for publishing and editing web resources.

Why Web Feeds?

The majority of APIs presented in this book are pull-based APIs, and web feeds belong to this category too. In *pull-based APIs*, the client requests data from the server (the client gets data on demand). In some instances, the client needs to know frequently when new data is available. This is where the web feed becomes useful; it allows for data discovery asynchronously. Let's be clear: the notification about updated feed content is not initiated by the server; it's the client that periodically fetches feeds. The server then returns the document containing the web feed, and the client compares the new content with what it already has and adds any newly published content. The architecture of web feeds is presented in Figure 7-1.

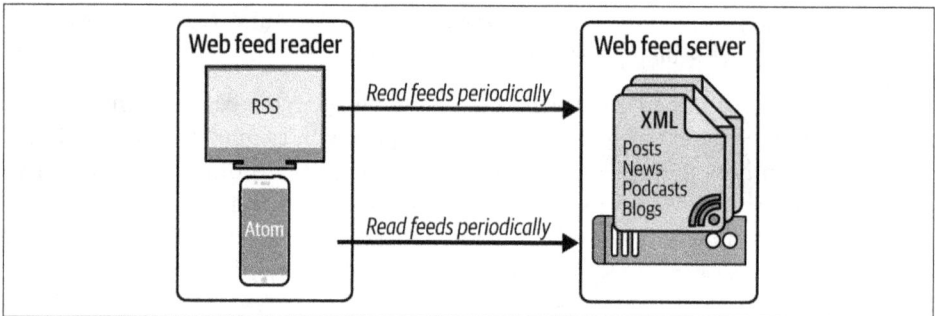

Figure 7-1. The architecture of web feeds

From this chapter's introduction, you know that the web feed allows clients to request the latest data from the server. An example of such a use case is a news website, where the news owner wants to notify the readers about the publication of a new article.

Another use case for web feeds is when working with cloud vendors, who expose their services over APIs and user interfaces. The operations team that utilizes cloud services can follow the vendor's web feed to be notified about any changes to the service, such as new features, deprecations, or outages.

Another example that demonstrates the usefulness of web feeds as a channel for updates is in cybersecurity. Namely, cybersecurity companies can use web feeds to inform about new threats or discovered vulnerabilities. You can follow such a web feed to get the latest updates and respond to these threats.

Table 7-1 lists links to commonly used web feeds and their related websites that track the status of cloud vendors and security advisories.

Table 7-1. Cloud vendors and cybersecurity web feeds

Service	URL	Overview page
AWS	RSS (*https://oreil.ly/9iSH6*)	*https://health.aws.amazon.com*
Azure Cloud	Atom (*https://oreil.ly/FUdeT*)	*https://azure.status.microsoft*
Google Cloud	Atom (*https://oreil.ly/NPnX8*)	*https://status.cloud.google.com*
The Cybersecurity and Infrastructure Security Agency	RSS (*https://oreil.ly/61dNb*)	*https://www.cisa.gov/about/contact-us/ subscribe-updates-cisa*

Evolution of Web Feeds

The *RSS* is an XML 1.0–formatted specification for a web feed published in 1999 by Netscape. An RSS feed contains a summary of the content (a news or a blog) published on a website. The RSS feed follows the RSS specification (*https://oreil.ly/ m19YA*), which describes how to organize a web feed. The content owner maintains a web feed in the form of a text file hosted on a web server or as an HTTP response. A user uses a web feed reader (aggregator) to read the feed, and the reader displays the newly added content. The web feed is identified by a URL. A feed reader can aggregate multiple feeds, making it easier for the user to read the content from various sources in one place rather than visiting each site individually.

Let's look at Example 7-1, which contains an RSS web feed.

Example 7-1. RSS feed specification 2.0

```
<?xml version="1.0" encoding="UTF-8" ?> ❶
<rss version="2.0"> ❷
  <channel> ❸
    <title>News from example.com</title>
    <description>Top stories from example.com</description>
    <link>https://example.com/main.html</link>
    <language>en-us</language>
    <item> ❹
      <title>RSS feed explained.</title>
      <description>Shocking — RSS feed in 15 lines.</description>
      <link>https://example.com/blog/post/1</link>
      <guid>https://example.com/blog/post/1</guid>
      <category>APIs</category>
    </item>
  </channel>
</rss>
```

❶ The feed starts with an XML declaration that indicates the version of the XML specification and encoding used in the document.

❷ The root element of the feed is the `rss` element, which contains the version of the RSS specification used in the feed.

❸ The `channel` element contains metadata about the feed and the elements composing it. According to RSS Specification 2.0 (*https://oreil.ly/VbcnO*), `title`, `description`, and `link` are required elements by channel, whereas `language` is optional.

❹ The `item` element contains the content of the feed. The content can be a newspaper story, blog post, video, content with a link, etc. Nowadays, web feeds typically include a short description and a link to a website. The required item elements are `title`, `description`, and `link`, while the `guid` and `category` elements are optional.[1]

Syndicate and Syndication

In publishing, a *syndicate* is a group of publishers sharing content to broaden their offerings beyond individual capabilities. *Syndication* refers to the act of selling content to other organizations so it can be published or shown in several places. Syndication allows content creators (print, radio, and television) to reach a wider audience.

In the context of web feeds, we're referring to *web syndication*, which is the process of distributing and aggregating content such as blog posts, podcasts, or videos to other websites or platforms.

Nowadays, RSS feeds are considered a legacy technology. The factors that led to the creation of new syndication formats include fragmentation of various variants of RSS feed (0.90, 0.91, 0.92, 1.0, 1.1, 2.0), which resulted in difficulty with validation of feeds, limited support from the web feed readers to support all of them, and lack of extensibility—extensibility was addressed by later releases of RSS versions.

---

1 Read "How I Messed up my RSS Feed" (*https://oreil.ly/EWmYq*) by Jake Howard to understand the importance of GUIDs in web feeds.

What Is Atom Feed?

The Atom web feed came into existence as an attempt to address RSS's shortcomings by allowing for metadata extensibility, supporting Unicode for content internationalization, allowing the feed to incorporate various content types as the feed elements (text, HTML, and XML), and, most importantly, by becoming an official web feed specification. In 2005, it was standardized by the IETF as the Atom syndication format, RFC 4287 (*https://oreil.ly/5F8c6*).

Atom is the successor of RSS. The Atom is an XML 1.0–based syndication format (*https://oreil.ly/EkB6f*) for describing web feeds, and a publishing protocol (*https://oreil.ly/KiLTV*). A feed in the Atom syndication format is a human- and machine-readable format built from entity elements, with extensible metadata describing each entity.

The Atom feed was designed to syndicate web content (web logs, podcasts, news headlines, etc.) in such a way that it can be distributed to other websites or platforms. Its origins (*https://oreil.ly/L1y5j*) point toward Sam Ruby's blog post, "Anatomy of a Well-Formed Log Entry" (*https://oreil.ly/390Jk*).

Example 7-2 lists a single-entry Atom feed.

Example 7-2. Single-entry Atom feed

```
<?xml version="1.0" encoding="utf-8"?> ❶
<feed xmlns="http://www.w3.org/2005/Atom"> ❷
  <id>https://example.com/</id>
  <title>Captain's log</title>
  <updated>2024-03-13T08:30:00Z</updated>
  <link rel="self" href="/captainslog"/>
  <author>
    <name>Jack Sparrow</name>
    <uri>https://example.com/</uri>
    <email>jack.sparrow@example.com</email>
  </author>
  <entry xml:lang="en"> ❸
    <id>https://example.com/captainslog/2024/03/13</id>
    <title>Copenhagen vs Warsaw Mermaid</title>
    <updated>2024-03-13T08:30:00Z</updated>
    <link rel="alternate" href="captainslog/2024/03/13"/>
    <summary>The are different</summary>
  </entry>
</feed>
```

❶ The feed starts with an XML declaration in the 1.0 version and the encoding used to encode the document.

❷ The root element of the Atom feed is the feed element that defines the XML namespace (xmlns) that uses the Atom syndication format (*https://oreil.ly/T7OgS*). Required elements (*https://oreil.ly/UdwCO*) of the Atom feed are id, title, and updated, whereas, link and author are recommended elements.

❸ The entry element contains the content of the feed. The required item elements (*https://oreil.ly/IAlTd*) are id, title, and updated, and recommended elements are link and summary.

The Atom feeds are identified by the application/atom+xml media type and are usually read by feed aggregators. Feeds can be combined. A new web feed can be composed of other feeds; for example, basketball news from many sports websites can be combined into one feed. Atom syntax was designed for modularity, and some of its elements are required according to the specification. Compared with the RSS feed, the Atom feed allows specifying an individual language for every entry, the date format follows the RFC 3339 specification (*YYYY-MM-DDTHH:MM:SSZ*) (*https://oreil.ly/W886O*), and its elements can be reused outside of the context of an Atom feed document.

Example 7-3 shows reuse of the Atom feed <*author*> entry from Example 7-2 in an XML document containing Atom's <*entry*> element, which, for example, could be sent via an HTTP POST request to a server that supports the AtomPub protocol (*https://oreil.ly/nAwyP*) to create or update web resources. The CDATA (character data) is a special XML section that allows clients to render content without the need to escape special characters such as "<", "/", "&", etc.

Example 7-3. XML document containing the Atom entry

```
<?xml version="1.0" encoding="utf-8"?>
<entry xmlns="http://www.w3.org/2005/Atom">
  <title>The Atom draft is finished</title>
  <id>urn:uuid:550e8400-e29b-41d4-a716-446655440000</id>
  <updated>2025-01-30T12:34:59Z</updated>
  <author>
    <name>John Sparrow</name>
    <uri>https://example.com/</uri>
    <email>jack.sparrow@example.com</email>
  </author>
  <content type="html">
    <![CDATA[
      <h1>The Atom draft is finished</h1>
      <p>This is an example of submitting a blog post using AtomPub.</p>
    ]]>
  </content>
</entry>
```

Although the Atom feed was created as a successor to the RSS feed (nearly three decades ago) and is an official standard backed by IETF, both web feeds are still used. The lack of a governing organization that would unify and deprecate older versions of RSS led to the RSS feed being forked by individual developers and branched out, resulting in two versions (v1.* and v2.*). RSS 2.0 is the most used version of all RSS versions. The survival of RSS is likely attributed to its early dominance as the first web feed. RSS regained popularity after Google Reader was discontinued,[2] a move attributed to declining usage and a broader shift toward centralized social networks.[3]

After an introduction to the web feed format, now it's time to proceed with the implementation. In the next section, we'll create an Atom feed for our WFS.

Implementation

The WFS we are building exists to provide weather forecasts and historical weather data for a given city. Naturally, we'd like to provide weather forecasts to a wide range of clients, including web feed readers. To do that, we'll add an Atom web feed that points to a web page containing the weather forecast. The Atom feed will allow us to broadcast weather updates to clients who follow the feed.

Our implementation takes advantage of the Django web framework Feed classes (*https://oreil.ly/MM3EE*). Figure 7-2 shows the end goal of web feed exercises.

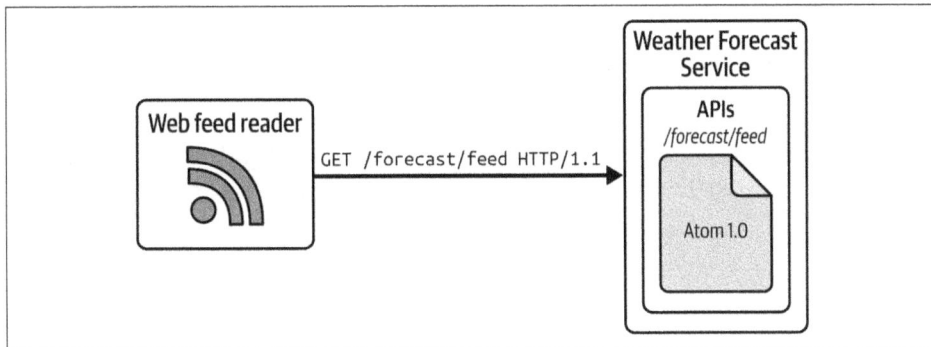

Figure 7-2. WFS forecast feeds

> Every city in our database is identified by a unique identifier (UUID) to prevent collisions between cities with the same name.

---

2 See the Google Reader entry on Wikipedia (*https://oreil.ly/Mcf7U*).

3 Read "Who Killed Google Reader?" (*https://oreil.ly/zHKyL*) by David Pierce.

We'll need to add two API endpoints to the WFS to fulfill the requirements mentioned previously: the first endpoint to render an HTML page containing weather forecasts for a given city, and the second endpoint to render an Atom feed that lists cities and redirects the reader to the first endpoint. This is what Example 7-4 demonstrates: it contains two API endpoints for the WFS's Atom feeds.

Example 7-4. Atom feed URLs

```
# src/django/app/config/urls.py

from core.api.atom.feed import CityAtomFeedView
from core.api.atom.views import WeatherForecastFeedListView
...

urlpatterns = [
    ...
    path("forecast/feed", CityAtomFeedView(), name="city_feed"),   ❶
    path("forecast/<uuid:city_uuid>", WeatherForecastFeedListView.as_view(),   ❷
      name="city_forecast"
    ),
    ...
]
```

❶ The */forecast/feed* endpoint renders an Atom feed. The `CityAtomFeedView` class (see Example 7-5) is responsible for rendering the Atom feed. The rendered-by-class feed contains a list of cities and a link pointing to the HTML web page displaying the forecast (second endpoint).

❷ The */forecast/<uuid:city_uuid>* endpoint renders an HTML page containing a weather forecast for a city identified by UUID (`city_uuid`).

Let's have a look into the */forecast/feed* endpoint and explain the implementation listed in Example 7-5.

Example 7-5. Atom feed view

```
# src/django/app/core/api/atom/feed.py

from django.contrib.syndication.views import Feed as FeedView
from django.utils.feedgenerator import Atom1Feed
...

class CityAtomFeedView(FeedView):   ❶
    feed_guid = "WFS weather feed"   ❷
    feed_type = Atom1Feed   ❸
    language = "en-us"   ❹
    ...
```

```
    def items(self, city):  ❺
        return CityRepository.get_all()

    def item_title(self, city):  ❺
        return city.name

    def item_description(self, city):  ❺
        return f"{city.name}, {city.country}, {city.region}"

    def item_link(self, city):  ❺
        return reverse("city_forecast", args=[city.uuid])

    def item_lastupdated(self, city):  ❺
        return city.updated_at
```

❶ The `CityAtomFeedView` class inherits from Django's syndication views. The Feed (`FeedView`) view is a high-level framework for generating RSS and Atom feeds.

❷ The `feed_guid` uniquely identifies the feed to prevent feed data mixing.

❸ The `feed_type`, which is set to `Atom1Feed`, is a feed generator that makes this view generate the Atom feed.

❹ The `language` indicates that the feed uses the American English dialect.

❺ The `items()` method returns a list of cities that will be included as entries in the feed. The individual `item_()` methods exist to set values for the entry in the feed. The values being set are the entry's title, description, link, and last updated date.

Example 7-6 shows a fragment of an Atom feed generated with the `CityAtomFeedView()` class described in Example 7-5. The document can be downloaded by visiting *http://localhost:8000/forecast/feed*,[4] after starting WFS as described in Example 7-7.

Example 7-6. WFS's weather forecast Atom feed

```
<?xml version="1.0" encoding="utf-8"?>
<feed xmlns="http://www.w3.org/2005/Atom" xml:lang="en-us">
  <title>City Weather Forecast</title>
  <link href="http://localhost:8000/forecast/feed" rel="alternate" />
  <link href="http://localhost:8000/forecast/feed" rel="self" />
  <id>http://localhost:8000/forecast/feed</id>
  <updated>2024-03-15T09:43:02.062628+00:00</updated>
  <subtitle>One week forecast</subtitle>
```

---

4 When working with GitHub Codespaces, you'll use a unique URL containing the Codespace's name instead of the *localhost* URL. The expected URL is bound to port 8000 and can be found in VS Code's PORTS tab.

```
  <entry>
    <title>Cairo</title>
    <link href="http://localhost:8000/forecast/05666603-d357-48bd-a554-5a5db5a67624"
      rel="alternate" />
    <id>http://localhost:8000/forecast/05666603-d357-48bd-a554-5a5db5a67624</id>
    <summary type="html">Cairo, Egypt, Africa</summary>
  </entry>
  ...
</feed>
```

The link in the entry element points toward the */forecast/city_uuid* endpoint resolved by the `item_link()` method in the `WeatherForecastFeedListView` class, which generates an HTML page containing the weather forecast for a given city. The generated page is illustrated in Figure 7-3.

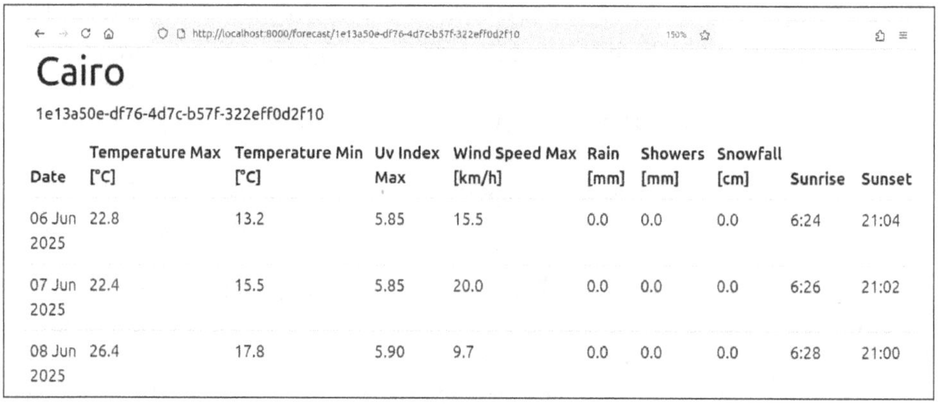

Cairo

1e13a50e-df76-4d7c-b57f-322eff0d2f10

Date	Temperature Max [°C]	Temperature Min [°C]	Uv Index Max	Wind Speed Max [km/h]	Rain [mm]	Showers [mm]	Snowfall [cm]	Sunrise	Sunset
06 Jun 2025	22.8	13.2	5.85	15.5	0.0	0.0	0.0	6:24	21:04
07 Jun 2025	22.4	15.5	5.85	20.0	0.0	0.0	0.0	6:26	21:02
08 Jun 2025	26.4	17.8	5.90	9.7	0.0	0.0	0.0	6:28	21:00

Figure 7-3. City weather forecast page

Being able to implement an Atom feed is one thing, but if no one can read it, then it has no value. In the next section, we'll talk about web feed readers (aggregators) and how to use them.

Reading Feeds

Feed readers allow users to follow the web feeds and aggregate these feeds into one place. A typical feed reader allows users to mark feeds as read, search the feeds for keywords, organize feeds into categories, etc. A feed reader can be a desktop, mobile, web browser plug-in, or a web-based application. Some popular feed readers are Feedly (*https://feedly.com*), Inoreader (*https://www.inoreader.com*), Newsboat (*https://newsboat.org*), and NewsBlur (*https://newsblur.com*).

When choosing a feed reader, you might consider whether it's cloud-based (web service), if it supports your smartphone, or if you want it to be self-hosted.

Receiving updates about new content being published on the web feed requires pasting the title or URL of the feed into the feed reader. The feed reader will then fetch the feed and display the content to the user. In Example 7-7, we'll use the text-based Newsboat command-line program (*https://newsboat.org*) to read our WFS feed.

Example 7-7. WFS Atom feed read using Newsboat

```
# Setup lab environment ❶
cd src/django
docker compose build --build-arg UID=$(id -u) --build-arg GID=$(id -g)
docker compose up --detach --wait

# Get Atom feed ❷
docker compose exec app bash -c \
        "mkdir --parents ~/.newsboat && \
        echo http://localhost:8000/forecast/feed > ~/.newsboat/urls"

# Read the feed ❸
docker compose exec app bash -c \
        "newsboat --refresh-on-start --execute=reload --execute=print-unread"
6 unread articles
```

❶ Execute the lab setup instructions. Navigate to the lab's directory, build Docker images, and start containers.

❷ Add the implemented feed URL to the list of feeds known by newsboat.

❸ Execute newsboat to print the number of unread articles.

You can also start the reader in interactive mode using **docker compose exec app bash -c "newsboat"**, and browse the feed as illustrated in Figure 7-4.

```
newsboat 2.21.0 - Articles in feed 'City Weather Forecast' (6 unread, 6 total)
   1 N  Mar 30     18    Cairo
   2 N  Mar 30     20    Istanbul
   3 N  Mar 30     32    Mexico City
   4 N  Mar 30     30    Sao Paulo
   5 N  Mar 30     24    Sydney
   6 N  Mar 30     16    Tokyo
q:Quit ENTER:Open s:Save r:Reload n:Next Unread A:Mark All Read /:Search ?:Help
```

Figure 7-4. WFS Atom feed read interactively using Newsboat

You might think that an unsophisticated technology like Atom or RSS poses no risks. However, this is far from being true. In the next section, we'll cover common security attacks to which web feeds are exposed.

Security

Usually, a web feed is created with the intention of being exposed to the general public, where anyone with the link can read the feed. But when a web feed has restricted or sensitive content, an authentication method is implemented to control access.

You could use the *basic authentication* method (*https://oreil.ly/uuL5y*), which requires providing a username and password with the request. Nowadays, this method is not recommended since it includes long-lived credentials in every request. An alternative approach is *token-based authentication*. This method addresses problems of credentials exposure, but it requires frequent token regeneration (since a token has an expiration date).

The web feed content is carried over an HTTP GET endpoint, which makes the feed vulnerable to several attacks involving HTTP (even in its encrypted form). An example attack that can be used with the feed's endpoint is the DoS attack. An attacker can overload the feed's server by flooding the feed's endpoint with many HTTP requests. To reduce the impact of a DoS attack, you could address it at several layers of the OSI model (see "TCP/IP and the OSI Model" on page 80).

At the network layer (layer 3 in the OSI model), you could block the requests sent from a single IP address or geographical region (*geo-blocking*). You could also use firewalls or routers (or both) to enforce limits such as the number of packet-per-second, bytes-per-second, or too many SYN packets.

At the application layer (layer 7 in the model), you could suppress excessive requests coming from an IP by setting quotas on requests per second, minute, hour, or day.

Furthermore, to reduce the direct impact of a DoS attack on a server, you could use load-balancing that would reduce the load on the server and distribute requests over multiple servers, which would also lower the possibility of a single point of failure.

RSS feed injection is another type of attack on web feeds. Here, the attacker can inject malicious content into the document containing the feed with XSS or manipulate existing content. The attack aims to edit the content of the feed so that it redirects a user to a different website, or includes a malicious JavaScript code. The attack is possible because the client and the server do not validate the feed's content. The consequences of the attack include risks to the person who clicked the malicious link and a damage to the trustworthiness of the feed's owner. To protect against RSS feed injection, sanitize the feed content, and keep RSS feed software (client and server) updated with security patches.

Most email providers supply tools that can detect malicious content in emails, sometimes resulting in important emails being sent to the spam folder. RSS clients do not have such tools, so the user is responsible for curating the content and vetting the link before clicking it. The same applies to the feed's owner, who should monitor the feeds for malicious content and remove it.

Trade-Offs

Web feeds allow you to build APIs that clients (feed readers or aggregators) periodically pull to obtain new content. In this section, we'll look at the advantages and disadvantages of web feeds. The advantages of web feeds make them an attractive choice for content distribution and consumption for the following reasons:

Broadcasting
> Web feed clients periodically request updates from the web feed API. Whenever the content of a web feed changes, the clients are aware of it, as if the information were being broadcast directly to them.

Timely updates
> The pull frequency of web feeds can be adjusted to a short period (seconds), allowing users to get the latest updates as soon as they are published.

Content aggregation
> A web feed reader aggregates multiple feeds, making it easier for the user to read the content from multiple sources in one place—rather than having to visit each site individually.

Content syndication
> A web feed allows the feed owner to syndicate content such as blog posts, podcasts, or videos to other websites or platforms, expanding the reach of the content beyond the original platform.

Privacy
> Login-less readers can offer increased anonymity by enabling users to access content without direct interaction with the original platform, thereby potentially reducing the amount of personal data that can be collected.

While web feeds provide numerous benefits, they also come with disadvantages:

Lack of contract
> A web feed is not a contract between the feed provider and the consumer. If the provider stops creating or updating the feeds, then the consumer does not know if a feed is no longer updated. Thus, the client relies on the provider to keep the feed updated.

Low user engagement online

The lack of engagement by users of web feeds on online platforms poses a challenge for content creators, publishers, and social platforms, particularly in terms of revenues from advertising. Following a web feed doesn't necessarily mean that a user will be spending time on your platform. For the platform owner, this is problematic because the platform prioritizes prolonged user engagement to maximize advertising and data collection, and web feeds undermine these efforts.

Security challenges

The contents of the web feed are exposed over an HTTP GET endpoint. This makes the web feed vulnerable to a number of attacks involving HTTP, such as a DoS attack or RSS feed injection. Therefore, keep the feed software up-to-date (client and server) to stay on top of security patches.

Information overload

The advantage of web feed aggregation can simultaneously be a disadvantage. A user reading too many web feeds can be overwhelmed with information. This can lead to the user not reading the content at all.

Fragmentation

The web feed format is fragmented among various versions. This means a feed reader is required to support different syndication feeds and their versions and extensions.

Lack of user activity tracking

As a content creator, you'd like to know how users engage with your web feed. It's cumbersome to track metrics such as who's accessing the feed, how often they read articles, or from where they arrive. Tracking web feed metrics is possible but often requires techniques such as these:

- Server log analytics— Counting the number of HTTP calls to the web feed URL, and parsing the log for timestamps, user agent, or IP addresses.

- Query parameters—Adding query parameters such as *?source=blog* to obtain information about where clients come from.

- Redirect link—Providing the user with an intermediate link used for tracking that redirects the user to web feed content.

Exercises

1. If you are interested in software architecture, visit the Developer to Architect website (*https://oreil.ly/2kxDW*) and follow its RSS feed. The URL to the feed can be found at the bottom of the page. For this lab, you could use a web feed reader of your choice, or use instructions from Example 7-7.

2. To stay updated with videos by Modern Software Engineering (*https://oreil.ly/ f2EbJ*), follow its YouTube channel's Atom feed. For this exercise, you need two pieces of information. The first is the YouTube channel's ID, and the second is the YouTube channel's URL of the Atom feed. The YouTube channel's ID can be found in the source code of the YouTube channel page—visit *https:// www.youtube.com/@ModernSoftwareEngineeringYT*, right-click, select "View page source", and search for *youtube.com/channel/* (the channel's ID should be *UCCfqyGl3nq_V0bo64CjZh8g*). The channel's Atom feed URL can be constructed by adding the channel's ID to the following URL: *https://www.youtube.com/ feeds/videos.xml?channel_id=UCCfqyGl3nq_V0bo64CjZh8g*. For this exercise, you could use a web feed reader of your choice, or use instructions from Example 7-7.

3. In this exercise, your task is to read an Atom feed from the *forecast/feed* endpoint implemented in this chapter. GitHub Codespaces has a preinstalled web feed reader program called Newsboat (*https://newsboat.org*), which you'll use to read the feed. To complete this exercise, you'll need to start the Django project with the command `docker compose up --detach --wait`, change the Codespace's port visibility to Public, and configure the `newsboat` reader to read the feeds from the project's Codespaces URL. To change the Codespaces URL visibility to Public, in the Codespaces PORTS tab, right-click on port 8000, and from the Port Visibility menu, choose Public. The solution to this exercise can be found in this book's code repository (see the *src/django/docs/solutions/web-feeds-exercise.md* file).

Summary

This chapter covered the origins and evolution of web feeds. It described RSS and Atom web feeds and their trade-offs. Furthermore, accompanying labs and exercises guided you through the implementation of an Atom web feed and interaction with it using a feed reader (aggregator).

gRPC

RPC stands for *Remote Procedure Call*. As the name suggests, the RPC API style focuses on interaction with APIs by invoking remote procedures (functions). RPC APIs are characterized by intent-oriented interfaces, where an intent describes specific actions (operations), such as "CreateUser" or "GenerateReport." This approach lies on the opposite side of the spectrum compared to REST. REST focuses on retrieval and modification of resources,[1] like "User" and "Report," using standardized HTTP methods like GET, POST, PUT, and DELETE.

gRPC[2] may currently be the most widely adopted RPC implementation.[3] It describes itself as a "high performance, open source universal RPC framework." The project was created by Google, and in 2017, it was donated to the Cloud Native Computing Foundation, which hosts it at *https://grpc.io*.

After describing the overall goals of RPCs, this chapter introduces you to gRPC and its features. You'll explore Protocol Buffers (the binary serialization format) and the HTTP/2 protocol (the transport mechanism used by gRPC; see "HTTP/2" on page 133). Using an implementation of an ECHO service, you'll become familiar with the four RPC types supported by gRPC: unary, server streaming, client streaming, and bidirectional streaming. Next, using gRPC, you'll enrich the WFS's web feed from Chapter 7, with the content generated by a locally running LLM. The chapter ends with a discussion of gRPC security aspects, documentation, and trade-offs.

---

1 See "API Maturity Models" on page 159.

2 The meaning of "g" playfully changes in every release. See the gRPC GitHub repository document, *doc/g_stands_for.md* (*https://oreil.ly/QTdMM*), for the list of meanings.

3 Besides gRPC, several other RPC-based technologies exist, including Apache Thrift (*https://oreil.ly/3llo2*), tRPC (*https://oreil.ly/A8n2b*), and JSON-RPC (*https://www.jsonrpc.org*).

Remote Procedure Call

Fortran II, released in 1958,[4] was the first high-level programming language that introduced a notion of procedures. *Procedures* (also referred to as *subroutines*, *functions*, or *methods*) are chunks of code designed to perform specific tasks. They help developers understand and organize their programs. The use of procedures to facilitate developers' work was extended to the domain of distributed systems, operating on early networks like ARPANET in the 1970s,[5] when the notion of RPC was introduced. Bruce Jay Nelson further detailed RPCs in his doctoral dissertation in the early 1980s.[6]

Apart from resembling the local (single-machine) procedure calls, the main goals of RPCs were to address two particular challenges of distributed systems:[7]

- Communication among services that internally use different data formats
- Communication over unreliable networks

The design of RPCs by Nelson doesn't deal with other challenges, like service failures, or the lack of global time. Nevertheless, modern RPC implementations may address some of these challenges—for example, by supporting call timeouts.

Origins of gRPC

gRPC originates from *Stubby*, an internal RPC framework that Google developed and utilized since the early 2000s. Stubby was tied to Google's name resolution and load-balancing infrastructure, which made it unfit for Google's plans for an open source RPC framework. Therefore, gRPC was started from scratch in 2013,[8] and it evolved around the time when the HTTP/2 specification was finalized. The first stable release of gRPC was made in 2016.

---

4 See page 78 in Gerard O'Regan's *A Brief History of Computing* (Springer, 2008).

5 James E. White, "A High-Level Framework for Network-Based Resource Sharing" (*https://oreil.ly/B1mGW*), *AFIPS '76: Proceedings of the June 7-10, 1976 National Computer Conference and Exposition* (1976): 561–570.

6 Andrew D. Birrell and Bruce J. Nelson, "Implementing Remote Procedure Calls" (*https://oreil.ly/vZUwd*), *ACM Transactions on Computer Systems (TOCS)* 2, no. 1 (1984): 39–59.

7 See the "Remote Procedure Call" section in *Computer Networks: A Systems Approach* (*https://oreil.ly/CKCd5*) by Larry Peterson and Bruce Davie.

8 See "Ten Years of gRPC" on YouTube (*https://oreil.ly/RtehX*) by Jung-Yu (Gina) Yeh and Richard Belleville for more gRPC history.

The design goals of gRPC are similar to the ones described by Nelson; however, they also include features such as health-checking, load-balancing, and failover, to facilitate the building of distributed systems.[9] In the following sections, you'll become familiar with the main gRPC features.

Protobuf Serialization

Data formats can vary in attributes such as endianness (the order in which bytes are stored in computer memory), data sizes (e.g., 32- or 64-bit), or character encoding (e.g., ASCII or Unicode). When dealing with network services that internally use different data formats, three approaches exist: sender-makes-right, receiver-makes-right, and canonical intermediate.[10]

The *sender-makes-right* approach is to make every sending service aware of every format used by receiving services. This requires the sender to send the message in the right format to be used by the receiver.

An opposite approach is to send messages in the sender's internal format and make the receiver convert the message to its internal format. This approach, called *receiver-makes-right*, requires the receiver to be aware of all formats used by the senders.

The third approach makes both the sender and receiver use a single, common format called a *canonical intermediate*. It places the task of conversion on both the sending and receiving sides, but reduces the number of supported conversion formats to one. A practical realization of this approach is serialization and deserialization (see "Encoding Versus Serialization" on page 53).

gRPC adopts the canonical intermediate approach and uses *Protocol Buffers* (*https:// protobuf.dev*), called *protobuf* for short, as the default serialization format.[11] Protocol Buffers are also used by gRPC as the IDL, to describe the API by defining the RPC methods and their request/response messages. Protobuf definitions are stored in human-readable *.proto* files. The data structures in these files are compiled into a binary format, which, compared to text, improves storage size and parsing performance. The use of this compact format to exchange messages over the network contributes to gRPC's high performance.

Example 8-1 shows a complete example of a protobuf definition of an RPC. This file is to be written by you, and it demonstrates an RPC consisting of a single request and

---

9 See "gRPC Motivation and Design Principles" (*https://oreil.ly/WwH61*) by Louis Ryan.

10 See the "Presentation Formatting" section in *Computer Networks: A Systems Approach* (*https://oreil.ly/y6Flc*) by Larry Peterson and Bruce Davie.

11 The main goal of Protocol Buffers as a standalone technology is to provide data serialization mechanisms. gRPC is also designed to support other serialization formats, including JSON.

response, called by gRPC *unary*. This term indicates that both the request and response consist of a single message. This type of RPC corresponds to the request-response model known from HTTP-based APIs. gRPC also supports other RPC types, based on streaming, which we'll discuss in "The Four RPC Types" on page 258.

A gRPC service contains one or more RPC method definitions. In our case, EchoService includes a single DemoUnary RPC. The DemoUnary RPC is invoked by the client using the DemoUnaryRequest message and is executed on the server. The server echoes the content of the received request back to the client as the DemoUnaryRes ponse message.[12] Based on this protobuf definition, gRPC will generate a starter code to be used by you to implement the gRPC client and server. gRPC code generation will be discussed in detail in Example 8-4, but for now let's try to get more familiar with protobuf itself.

Example 8-1. gRPC unary RPC protobuf file

```
// src/grpc/src/echo/echo/proto/echo/v1/echo.proto

syntax = "proto3"; ❶

package echo.v1; ❷

message DemoUnaryRequest { ❸
  // The text content of the request. ❹
  string content = 1; ❺
}

message DemoUnaryResponse { ❻
  // The text content of the response.
  string content = 1;
}

// The service echoes back the content received from the client. ❼
service EchoService { ❽
  // This method demonstrates unary RPC.
  rpc DemoUnary(DemoUnaryRequest) returns (DemoUnaryResponse); ❾
}
```

❶   This protobuf uses the latest Protocol Buffers version.

❷   To help convey changes made to the protobuf definition, Protocol Buffers have built-in support for versioning. Here the echo package is assigned version v1.

---

12 The concept of an ECHO service was introduced in "Implementing TCP ECHO Service" on page 83.

❸ This block defines the request message. Protobufs are designed for evolution; therefore, for the flexibility of making future modifications, it's recommended to separately define the request and response message for every RPC.[13] The common naming convention is to append the RPC name with the Request and Response suffix.

❹ Lines starting with "//" are treated by protobuf as comments. The protobuf files serve as your API documentation, written as comments. This example comment is redundant in the sense that it could be guessed from the code surrounding it, but it's left here to remind you to document protobufs.[14]

❺ The request message uses the string type named content as the first field. The field numbers, like 1 here, must not be reused within the given message.

❻ This block defines the response message. Both the request and response messages consist of a single string type field, yet they are defined as separate messages to facilitate future changes. An alternative approach, which is sometimes seen in gRPC tutorials but discouraged from the perspective of protobuf evolution, would be to define a single message, DemoUnaryMessage, instead of separate DemoUnaryRequest and DemoUnaryResponse messages.

❼ The comment lines present above the service and RPC method definitions will be included in the autogenerated service documentation.

❽ This block defines the gRPC service. A service may contain multiple RPCs.

❾ Lines starting with rpc define RPC methods. An RPC represents an action, and its name typically starts with a verb. Any RPC method accepts and returns only a single argument (a message). However, a message can contain many fields; messages can be nested and use other message types as fields.

---

13 See "Create Unique Protos per Method" in the Protocol Buffers documentation (*https://oreil.ly/6Ex2v*) for more details about this recommendation. Furthermore, it's also recommended to place every message in a separate file (*https://oreil.ly/Q6jWQ*), but this recommendation is not followed here for readability.

14 See "Precisely, Concisely Document Most Fields and Messages" in the Protocol Buffers documentation (*https://oreil.ly/7ik1M*).

Protobufs are designed for evolution. Without going into details about making backward- or forward- compatible protobuf changes, let's mention that adding a new field to the request won't cause the server to fail; the server will ignore any unknown fields. When a field expected in the request is missing, this field will be assigned a default value. To remove a field from a protobuf message, the field can be *deprecated* first. After it's no longer used by the client code, it can be removed from the protobuf, but the removed field's number must be reserved to prevent its reuse.[15]

If you want to know more about protobuf evolution, consult the "Language Guide" (*https://oreil.ly/8Ywtm*) and "API Best Practices" (*https://oreil.ly/l9jq9*) pages, and Eric Anderson's talk, "Modifying gRPC Services Over Time" (*https://oreil.ly/hjtgQ*). Consider also using the formatter, linter, and breaking change detector provided by *buf* (*https://oreil.ly/D5EiI*).

Before continuing our discussion on how gRPC implements RPC, you need to set up the lab environment by following instructions in Example 8-2. The commands need to be executed starting from the root of the book's code repository.

Example 8-2. gRPC lab setup

```
cd src/grpc ❶
docker compose build --build-arg UID=$(id -u) --build-arg GID=$(id -g) ❷
docker compose up --detach --wait ❸
```

❶ Enter the *src/grpc* directory. All commands in this chapter are to be issued from this directory, unless instructed otherwise.

❷ Build container images.

❸ Start two containers: client and server. Also create keys and certificates for TLS.

The request/response functionality of the unary RPC, analogous to a REST-style request-response model, is performed in Example 8-3. To follow along, you'll need a three-pane window. The panes can be opened with tmux. For an introduction to tmux, see Example P-2.

---

15 See "Deleting Fields" in the protobuf documentation (*https://oreil.ly/HqsyX*).

Example 8-3. Unary RPC demo execution flow (requires setup from Example 8-2)

```
# In a terminal run ❶
tmux new-session \; split-window -v \; split-window -v \;

# In the top pane run ❷
SECURITY=insecure
docker compose exec server bash -ci \
      "PYTHONPATH=./src/echo python src/echo/echo/server.py ${SECURITY}"

# In the middle pane run ❸
RPC=unary SECURITY=insecure
PCAP_FILE=/tmp/echo_rpc_${RPC}_${SECURITY}.pcap
docker compose exec client bash -c \
      "sudo rm -f ${PCAP_FILE} && \
      sudo tcpdump -w ${PCAP_FILE} 'port 50051' && \
      cp ${PCAP_FILE} tests"

# In the bottom pane run ❹
RPC=unary SECURITY=insecure
docker compose exec client bash -ci \
      "PYTHONPATH=./src/echo python src/echo/echo/client.py ${RPC} ${SECURITY}"

# Output:
Client request: Hello, Serialized message: 0a0548656c6c6f
Server response: Hello
```

❶ Create three panes with tmux.

❷ Start the gRPC server. This demonstration sets the SECURITY=insecure environment variable to disable TLS encryption, for the purpose of further analysis of the captured network traffic. The code of the server is discussed further in Example 8-6.

❸ Start a packet capture by using tcpdump on the client. The captured traffic will be saved into the *echo_rpc_unary_insecure.pcap* file under the *tests* directory.[16]

❹ Invoke the gRPC client. Its code is discussed in Example 8-7. The client sends "Hello" text to the server, which responds by echoing this content back to the client. The hexadecimal value 0a0548656c6c6f contains the bytes of the request message serialized using protobuf, and will be explained in detail in "Protobuf Wire Format" on page 262.

---

16 The generated packet capture isn't of interest yet, but it will be used in "Protobuf Wire Format" on page 262 to explore the binary format of protobuf messages exchanged over the network during the RPC call.

The `protoc` protobuf compiler, taking the protobuf file as an input, generates a source code used as the base to implement the gRPC client and server used in the demo. You'll see more details about code generation in the next section.

Code Generation

Generating code from an existing API specification (automatically or manually) characterizes the API-first approach.[17] In the case of gRPC API, the protobuf is the API interface specification. The code generated from the protobuf is not to be modified by the developer. Instead, it's used by the developer as a base that is extended to implement the actual application functionality.

Example 8-4 illustrates the protobuf compiler, called `protoc`, generating code from the *echo.proto* file. A programming language may have its own `protoc` wrapper, as in the case of Python's `grpcio-tools` package, which exposes `protoc` through the `grpc_tools.protoc` module.[18] Otherwise, the generic `protoc` compiler can be used.

> The names and locations of the generated files differ across programming languages.[19] The recommendation by gRPC developers from Google is to treat the generated files as a build artifact, place them in a separate directory, and not to store them under version control. This is what Google's Bazel (*https://bazel.build*) tool does. However, for smaller Python gRPC projects, storing the generated files under version control, along with the rest of the application code, and packaging the generated files in a Python native way, may facilitate project maintenance.[20] The `--proto_path` argument, with its unusual looking value, can be used to place the generated files into the directory where the protobuf files are located.

---

17 *API-first* was described in "API-First Approach" on page 24.

18 Note the difference between the package and the module name. Be vigilant when installing software from the internet to avoid typosquatting security attacks.

19 For an overview, see the official protobuf documentation at "What's Generated from Your .proto?" (*https://oreil.ly/M0EP3*) and the gRPC documentation (*https://oreil.ly/Beo04*). Note that for several languages, it's also possible to avoid static code generation and use the protobuf files directly from the application client and server, but this type of use is less common.

20 This approach avoids the operational overhead from the introduction of additional build tools, hinted at in Alex Eagle's quote from his "Building Monorepo gRPC Services with Bazel" talk (*https://oreil.ly/QoArk*): "Bermuda Triangle of Google dev tools: Bazel, Protobuf, gRPC. Looks like a tropical paradise. You fly in there, your instruments all go berserk, everything is errors, you get really disoriented, the developer never comes out again."

Example 8-4. Code generation with `protoc` (requires setup from Example 8-2)

```
docker compose exec client bash -ic \
    "cd src/echo && \
    python -m grpc_tools.protoc \
    --proto_path=echo/proto/echo/v1=echo/proto/echo/v1 \
    --python_out=. --grpc_python_out=. \
    echo/proto/echo/v1/echo.proto"
```

The code generation will produce two files, chosen here to be located in the same directory as the *echo.proto* file:

echo_pb2.py

Contains the binary data structure and metadata for messages, service, and RPC methods.

echo_pb2_grpc.py

Contains so-called stub code, for both the gRPC client and server, and additional code to facilitate the creation of the gRPC server. A part of this file is shown in Example 8-5.

> gRPC stubs serialize and deserialize messages and provide an interface for invoking RPCs.

Example 8-5. Autogenerated echo_pb2_grpc.py *file*

```
# src/grpc/src/echo/echo/proto/echo/v1/echo_pb2_grpc.py

import grpc  ❶
import echo_pb2  ❷

class EchoServiceStub(object):  ❸
    """The service echoes back the content received from the client."""

    def __init__(self, channel):
        self.DemoUnary = channel.unary_unary(
            '/echo.v1.EchoService/DemoUnary',  ❹
            request_serializer=echo_pb2.DemoUnaryRequest.SerializeToString,  ❺
            response_deserializer=echo_pb2.DemoUnaryResponse.FromString)

class EchoServiceServicer(object):  ❻
    def DemoUnary(self, request, context):  ❼
        """This method demonstrates unary RPC."""
        context.set_code(grpc.StatusCode.UNIMPLEMENTED)
        context.set_details('Method not implemented!')
        raise NotImplementedError('Method not implemented!')
```

```
def add_EchoServiceServicer_to_server(servicer, server):  ❽
  rpc_method_handlers = {
    'DemoUnary': grpc.unary_unary_rpc_method_handler(
        servicer.DemoUnary,
        request_deserializer=echo_pb2.DemoUnaryRequest.FromString,  ❾
        response_serializer=echo_pb2.DemoUnaryResponse.SerializeToString)
  }
```

❶ The grpc module comes from the grpcio (*https://oreil.ly/SCGqw*) Python package and provides core gRPC features, such as channel, server, or thread support.

❷ The echo_pb2 module was generated from the protobuf definition file, using the protoc compiler. This module contains data structures used when serializing and deserializing protobuf messages and calling the gRPC services.

❸ The purpose of the EchoServiceStub class is to construct the client stub. The Python class name reflects this by using the Stub suffix. Most languages supported by gRPC include the word *stub* in their generated client stub code.

❹ The URI path of the given RPC service contains the method served by the gRPC server, to be called by the client stub. gRPC hides the details of the network call from the developer by hardcoding the URI in the autogenerated code.

❺ In the client stub, the request is serialized and response deserialized, using the SerializeToString() and FromString() methods, respectively. These methods are provided by protobuf and operate on the entire request and response messages, not individual fields of the message. Contrary to what the String name suggests, it denotes a sequence of bytes— Python's <class *bytes*>, not <class *str*>. See Example 8-7 for more details about this serialization.

❻ A servicer class contains all RPC methods belonging to a single gRPC service. A single gRPC server can serve multiple servicers.

❼ The DemoUnary method is to be implemented by you. It's responsible for generating a response to a client request. In this method, the server-side application logic will be performed.

❽ The implemented servicer is registered with the server, to handle RPC calls.

❾ Analogously to the client stub, the server stub (called generically a *handler*) deserializes incoming requests and serializes outgoing responses.

gRPC ECHO Server and Client

Using the code generated by the `protoc` compiler, we proceed to implement a gRPC server and client for `EchoService`. Figure 8-1 shows an overview of the gRPC data flow. The core of the gRPC client runtime is the so-called *Channel*, started by the *Client application*. The channel represents an abstraction over a connection to a gRPC *Server*. The server is the main component of the gRPC server *Runtime*, and it's started by the *Server application*.

The client application passes the request message to the *Client stub*, which serializes the message and initiates the RPC call. The channel is responsible[21] for creating a *Transport* and sending the RPC call over it to the appropriate gRPC server. The listening gRPC server, after receiving the initial connection, creates its server-side transport, and passes the message to the *Server stub* (handler). The server stub deserializes the message and locally calls the server application. The server application performs the server-side application logic and passes the response message to the server stub for serialization. The response message traverses the transport, is deserialized by the client stub, and is returned to the client application.

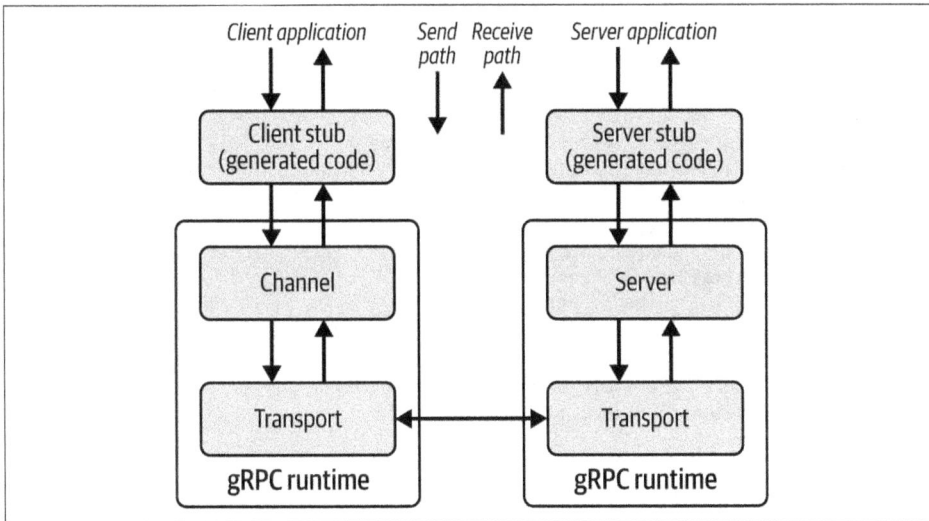

Figure 8-1. gRPC data flow

---

21 For a more detailed description of the channel functionality, including client-side load-balancing, see the Google talks "Deep Dive: gRPC" by Yuxuan Li (*https://oreil.ly/RKc3e*) and "Load Balancing in gRPC" by Easwar Swaminathan (*https://oreil.ly/TNLn0*). Note also that gRPC keeps long-lived TCP connections to improve latency, and this tends to result in load imbalance on the backends of the load-balancer—for example, in the case of the pods behind the Kubernetes ClusterIP service.

Example 8-6 contains the full implementation of a gRPC server, consisting of a unary RPC. The client implementation is provided in Example 8-7. Both the server and client implementations are based on the autogenerated code. The overall structure of the server and client is the same, whether unary or streaming RPCs are used. Streaming RPCs are discussed later, in "The Four RPC Types" on page 258.

Example 8-6. gRPC server unary RPC implementation (written by you)

```python
# src/grpc/src/echo/echo/server.py

import concurrent
import sys

import grpc
from grpc_reflection.v1alpha import reflection

import echo.proto.echo.v1.echo_pb2 as pb2
import echo.proto.echo.v1.echo_pb2_grpc as pb2_grpc

class EchoServiceServicer(pb2_grpc.EchoServiceServicer):  ❶
    def DemoUnary(self, request, context):  ❷
        content = request.content  ❸
        return pb2.DemoUnaryResponse(content=content)  ❹

def get_ssl_server_credentials(use_custom_ca=True, use_mtls=True):
    private_key = open("src/server.key", "rb").read()
    certificate_chain = open("src/server.crt", "rb").read()
    root_certificates = open("src/ca.crt", "rb").read() if use_custom_ca else None
    return grpc.ssl_server_credentials(
        [(private_key, certificate_chain)],
        root_certificates=root_certificates,
        require_client_auth=use_mtls)

server = grpc.server(concurrent.futures.ThreadPoolExecutor())  ❺
pb2_grpc.add_EchoServiceServicer_to_server(  ❻
    EchoServiceServicer(), server)

SERVICE_NAMES = (reflection.SERVICE_NAME,  ❼
    pb2.DESCRIPTOR.services_by_name["EchoService"].full_name)
reflection.enable_server_reflection(SERVICE_NAMES, server)  ❼

credentials = get_ssl_server_credentials(use_mtls=True)
server.add_secure_port("0.0.0.0:50051", credentials)  ❽

server.start()  ❾
server.wait_for_termination()  ❿
```

❶ The servicer class is based on the autogenerated `pb2_grpc.EchoService Servicer` class. The servicer contains all RPC methods belonging to a single gRPC service. A single gRPC server can serve multiple servicers.

❷ The unary RPC method has access to the server-side application logic. In this case, the unmodified `content` of the request is returned as the response. The `request` contains the deserialized request from the client, and `context` allows you to retrieve and interact with the gRPC runtime. The deserialization is performed by the handler, part of the autogenerated server stub code, shown in Example 8-5. gRPC supports both synchronous and asynchronous communication types, but in our chapter we focus on the former.

❸ As expected from an ECHO service, the server's response echoes the content of the original request.

❹ The response is returned to the client. Note that the server stub handler serialized the response.

❺ This line defines the server, but doesn't start it yet, since its configuration is not completed. It's common for gRPC servers to use multiple threads.

❻ The servicer is added to the server.

❼ The `SERVICE_NAMES` variable stores the service names for which reflection is enabled. Reflection allows the client to programmatically query the server for the available services, RPC methods, and message formats. It also provides a human-readable documentation, and is enabled per service. `reflection.SERVICE_NAME` is the built-in name of the gRPC reflection service itself.

❽ The server configuration is completed by defining the IPv4 address and the TCP port on which the server will listen. The `0.0.0.0` IP address instructs the server to listen on all its local network IPv4 addresses, including the IP address of the server on the network created by Docker. This allows the client to reach the server over this network.

To reduce the amount of code here, there's only an example of a connection secured with TLS. The book's code repository also contains an insecure (unencrypted) connection configuration, used for the purpose of packet capture analysis.

The `get_ssl_server_credentials()` function provides an example of the mutual TLS (mTLS) configuration of the server. mTLS, enabled with require_client_auth=True, provides encryption and server authentication as in TLS, and additionally authenticates the client to the server.

❾ The server is started in the background and begins to listen for client connections. Only when the first connection arrives does the server finish the creation of the transport.

❿ The purpose of the wait_for_termination() method is to block the main program, so it keeps the server running and exits only at server termination.

Example 8-7. gRPC client unary RPC implementation (written by you)

```python
# src/grpc/src/echo/echo/client.py

import sys
import time

import grpc

import echo.proto.echo.v1.echo_pb2 as pb2
import echo.proto.echo.v1.echo_pb2_grpc as pb2_grpc

def unary(stub):  ❶
    request = pb2.DemoUnaryRequest(content="Hello")  ❷
    request_serialized = request.SerializeToString()  ❸
    print(f"Client request: {request.content}, "  ❹
          f"Serialized message: {request_serialized.hex()}")
    response = stub.DemoUnary(request)  ❺
    print(f"Server response: {response.content}")  ❻

def get_ssl_channel_credentials(use_custom_ca=True, use_mtls=True):
    root_certificates = open("src/ca.crt", "rb").read() if use_custom_ca else None
    private_key = open("src/client.key", "rb").read() if use_mtls else None
    certificate_chain = open("src/client.crt", "rb").read() if use_mtls else None
    return grpc.ssl_channel_credentials(
        root_certificates=root_certificates,
        private_key=private_key,
        certificate_chain=certificate_chain)

credentials = get_ssl_channel_credentials(use_mtls=True)
channel = grpc.secure_channel("server:50051", credentials)  ❼

stub = pb2_grpc.EchoServiceStub(channel)  ❽

try:
    unary(stub)  ❾
except grpc.RpcError as rpc_error:
    print(f"gRPC call error: {rpc_error}")
    raise
```

```
finally:
    channel.close()  ❿
```

❶ The purpose of the `unary()` helper function is to demonstrate a gRPC client obtaining a response to a request it issues to the server.

❷ The protobuf request message is created, with the `content` field set to the string "Hello".

❸ The serialization of the protobuf request message is included here in order to print the message. For this purpose, the `SerializeToString()` method, provided by protobuf, is used to serialize the protobuf request message to its Python `bytes` representation, a sequence of bytes. This same call to `SerializeToString()` is performed on the request protobuf message implicitly, as part of the client stub gRPC functionality.

❹ The request message `content` (the "Hello" string) is printed, together with the type and the hexadecimal representation of the serialized request message.

❺ The client stub's `DemoUnary()` method performs the RPC call.

❻ The `content` (the "Hello" string) of the response message is printed.

❼ Creation of a gRPC client starts by defining a channel, which is an abstraction over a connection to the gRPC `server` on TCP port 50051. It's an abstraction because gRPC supports client-side load balancing, where `server` can resolve to multiple IP addresses. Every connection between the client and the actual server is handled by a *subchannel*, but this functionality isn't discussed in this book.

This example shows only a configuration of the channel secured with TLS, but the book's code repository also contains an insecure (unencrypted) example.

❽ The next step is to associate the client unary stub with the defined channel. For efficiency, one channel can handle multiple client stubs.

❾ This line uses the `unary()` helper function to perform the RPC call.

❿ The channel is closed before exiting the main program. In a more realistic example, the channel wouldn't be closed immediately, but reused during the life of the client to perform multiple calls across different stubs, to avoid the repeated cost of the channel creation.

The Four RPC Types

Using the code structure of the server and client for the unary RPC, this section introduces you to the remaining gRPC RPC types: server streaming, client streaming, and bidirectional streaming.

Unary RPC
> Consists of a single client request followed by a server response.

Server streaming RPC
> Consists of the server sending one or more responses following a single client request.[22] A typical use case for server streaming is to provide update notifications. The client sends a request to the server to start watching a resource for changes (e.g., configuration changes), and the server responds with a stream of updates.[23] An example of a file download/upload can be used to further clarify this RPC type. Using server streaming, you could implement a file download out of the box, but it would lack resume support, for which application retry logic would be needed.

Client streaming RPC
> Consists of one or more client requests followed by a single response from the server. An example use case for client streaming is pushing logs to a server. You could use out-of-the-box client streaming for uploading a file in chunks, without the resume functionality.

Bidirectional streaming RPC
> Consists of an arbitrary number of client requests and server responses. Bidirectional streaming facilitates use cases such as chat applications or file downloads/ uploads with resume support.

Example 8-8 shows a *.proto* file that defines the ECHO service, which implements these four RPC types. Note how the streaming side of the RPC is marked by the *stream* keyword. This file is an extended version of Example 8-1, which specified the unary RPC, demonstrating the extensibility of protobufs.

---

22 Streaming RPCs come with challenges. In his "Using gRPC for Long-Lived and Streaming RPCs" talk (*https:// oreil.ly/mHwxe*), Eric Anderson advises that "most RPCs should be unary RPCs." Recall also that, just like unary RPCs, streaming RPCs can be implemented as both synchronous and asynchronous.

23 The server uses the End Stream flag of HTTP/2 to indicate that no more data will be sent. See "Protobuf Wire Format" on page 262 for more details about HTTP/2 use in gRPC.

Example 8-8. The four RPC types supported by gRPC

```
// src/grpc/src/echo/echo/proto/echo/v1/echo.proto

syntax = "proto3";

package echo.v1;

message DemoUnaryRequest {
  string content = 1;
}

message DemoUnaryResponse {
  string content = 1;
}

message DemoServerStreamingRequest {
  string content = 1;
}

message DemoServerStreamingResponse {
  string content = 1;
}

// Analogous Request and Response messages follow for the remaining RPC types,
// which we skipped for readability ...

// The service echoes back the content received from the client.
service EchoService {
  // This method demonstrates unary RPC.
  rpc DemoUnary(DemoUnaryRequest) returns (DemoUnaryResponse);

  // This method demonstrates server streaming RPC.
  rpc DemoServerStreaming(DemoServerStreamingRequest)
      returns (stream DemoServerStreamingResponse);

  // This method demonstrates client streaming RPC.
  rpc DemoClientStreaming(stream DemoClientStreamingRequest)
      returns (DemoClientStreamingResponse);

  // This method demonstrates bidirectional streaming RPC.
  rpc DemoBidirectionalStreaming(stream DemoBidirectionalStreamingRequest)
      returns (stream DemoBidirectionalStreamingResponse);
}
```

Example 8-9 shows the output of four RPC types produced by the EchoService executed by the client.

To experiment with the code, execute every RPC type analogously to the unary example in Example 8-3, using the following environment variable settings: RPC=unary, RPC=server_streaming, RPC=client_streaming, RPC=bidirectional_streaming (adjust them accordingly).

Example 8-9. Client output of gRPC's four RPC types

```
# RPC=unary
Client request: Hello
Server response: Hello

# RPC=server_streaming
Client request: Hello
Server response: H
Server response: e
Server response: l
Server response: l
Server response: o

# RPC=client_streaming
Client request: H
Client request: e
Client request: l
Client request: l
Client request: o
Server response: Hello

# RPC=bidirectional_streaming
Client request: H
Server response: H
Client request: e
Server response: e
Client request: l
Server response: l
Client request: l
Server response: l
Client request: o
Server response: o
```

To facilitate visual comparisons, the server implementations of the four RPC types are presented in Example 8-10, followed by the client implementations in Example 8-11. All four RPC types are implemented in the same ECHO service, with the streaming RPCs designed to operate on individual characters of the "Hello" string.

Example 8-10. Server implementations of gRPC's four RPC types

```
# src/grpc/src/echo/echo/server.py

class EchoServiceServicer(pb2_grpc.EchoServiceServicer):
    def DemoUnary(self, request, context):
        content = request.content
        return pb2.DemoUnaryResponse(content=content)

    def DemoServerStreaming(self, request, context):
        for content in request.content:
            yield pb2.DemoServerStreamingResponse(content=content)

    def DemoClientStreaming(self, request_iterator, context):
        content = ""
        for request in request_iterator:
            content += request.content
        return pb2.DemoClientStreamingResponse(content=content)

    def DemoBidirectionalStreaming(self, request_iterator, context):
        for request in request_iterator:
            content = request.content
            yield pb2.DemoBidirectionalStreamingResponse(content=content)
```

Example 8-11. Client implementations of gRPC's four RPC types

```
# src/grpc/src/echo/echo/client.py

def unary(stub):
    request = pb2.DemoUnaryRequest(content="Hello")
    print((f"Client request: {request.content}")
    response = stub.DemoUnary(request)
    print(f"Server response: {response.content}")

def server_streaming(stub):
    request = pb2.DemoServerStreamingRequest(content="Hello")
    print(f"Client request: {request.content}")
    responses = stub.DemoServerStreaming(request)
    for response in responses:
        print(f"Server response: {response.content}")

def client_streaming(stub):
    def requests():
        for content in "Hello":
            yield pb2.DemoClientStreamingRequest(content=content)
            print(f"Client request: {content}")
    response = stub.DemoClientStreaming(requests())
    print(f"Server response: {response.content}")

def bidirectional_streaming(stub):
    def requests():
        for content in "Hello":
```

```
                yield pb2.DemoBidirectionalStreamingRequest(content=content)
                print(f"Client request: {content}")
                time.sleep(1)
    responses = stub.DemoBidirectionalStreaming(requests())
    for response in responses:
        print(f"Server response: {response.content}")
```

There are some additional points to clarify about the server and client implementation. First, gRPC streams in Python require the use of iterators. The `yield` keyword,
which creates a Python generator, is a way to implement an iterator, since every generator is an iterator. Second, the `bidirectional_streaming()` method makes use of
`time.sleep(1)`, to sleep for one second between the requests in the client stream.
The purpose of this sleep is to slow down the client so that the individual letters in
the client and server stream appear consecutively. This is possible because bidirectional streaming follows a full-duplex transmission mode (see Figure 1-4).

Protobuf Wire Format

This section explains the main features of gRPC at the network level, using the example of a unary request captured in Example 8-3. Understanding gRPC at this level is
helpful when planning its adoption, performing benchmarks against other RPC
implementations,[24] or debugging communication failures.[25]

Figure 8-2 illustrates the packet capture loaded in the Wireshark GUI (*https://
www.wireshark.org*), with the highlighted request packet number 10, which is the
subject of the explanation. Additionally, the regions containing interesting protocol
details are labeled with numbers 1 to 4.

---

24 Connect RPC (*https://connectrpc.com*) is an alternative implementation that aims to be compatible
   with gRPC.

25 The main way of troubleshooting gRPC services (*https://oreil.ly/Bj0JW*) is to increase the amount of logging.

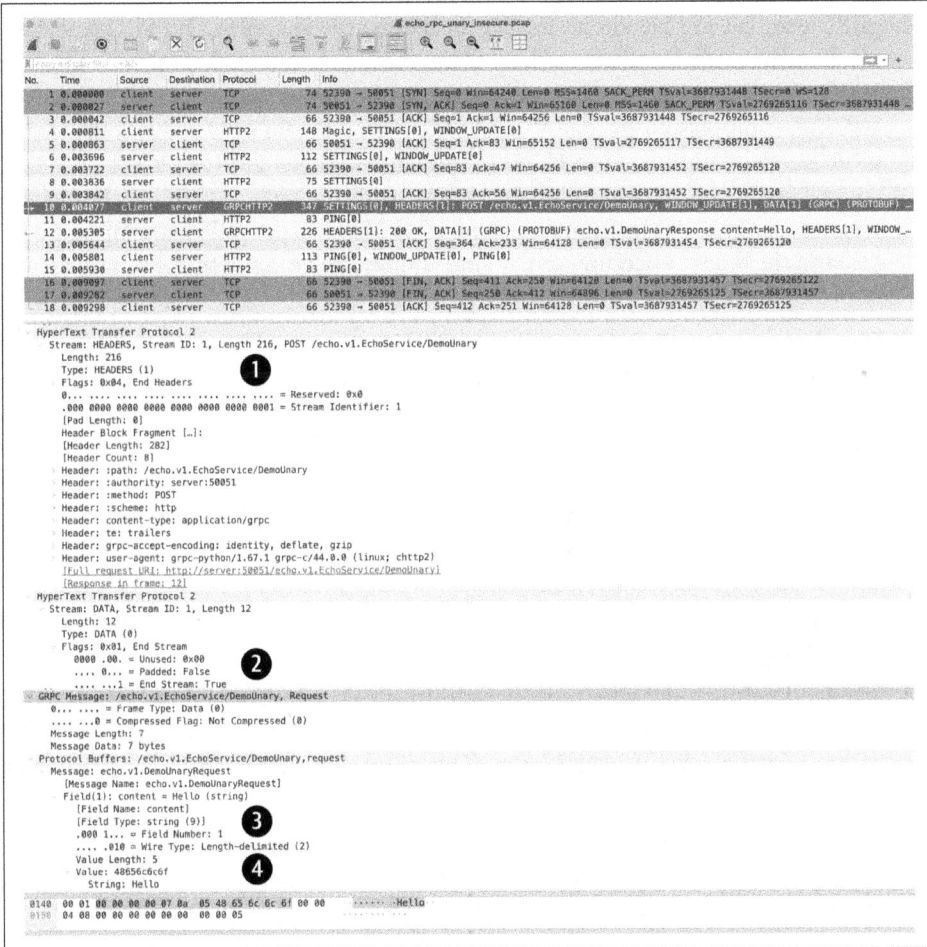

Figure 8-2. gRPC transport mechanism with HTTP/2[26]

---

26 See the full-sized screenshot in the book's code repository in the *src/grpc/README.md* file.

1. gRPC uses HTTP/2 as the transport mechanism.[27] The gRPC HTTP/2 transport mechanism is to be distinguished from the TCP transport protocol, used by HTTP/2 itself. A gRPC request is sent to the server as an HTTP POST. The HPACK compression format of the headers used by HTTP/2 reduces the size of gRPC requests compared to HTTP/1 implementations. gRPC uses HTTP/2 flow control, and achieves several other features with the help of HTTP/2. For example, independent, bidirectional streams of HTTP/2 make gRPC streaming possible, and the binary encoding of HTTP/2 frames integrates with the binary format of protobuf.

2. The client uses the End Stream flag of HTTP/2 to notify the server that no more data is expected from the client. The client enters a so-called *half-closed* state, where the server will continue sending the response but reject further client data. Since this gRPC request is unary, the client sends End Stream immediately. In the case of client or bidirectional streaming, the client would send End Stream only at the end of its stream. The server uses End Stream as well, to notify the client about the end of its response (not shown on this image). Additionally (not shown on the image either), the server uses HTTP *trailers* to provide the gRPC response status information to the client. Trailers are like HTTP headers, but sent after the HTTP message body.[28]

3. The field number and wire type (hexadecimal 0a), together with the length of the value in bytes (hexadecimal 05), and the value itself (hexadecimal 48656c6c6f) compose the protobuf *wire format*. This format is discussed in the remaining part of this section.

4. The 48656c6c6f value is the hexadecimal representation of the 7-bit ASCII string "Hello" (same as its UTF-8 encoding). Protobuf uses a length-prefixed encoding for strings, where the UTF-8 encoded string follows its length.

Packet number 10 contains the bit stream expressed in hexadecimal as 0a0548656c6c6f, which is an example of the protobuf wire format. This format can be decoded using the protoc compiler, as shown in Example 8-12. Its output confirms that the wire format corresponds to field number 1 with the "Hello" string.

---

27 See "HTTP/2" on page 133 for an introduction to HTTP/2. The proposal to Support gRPC over HTTP/3 (*https://oreil.ly/QNQ8k*) is completed, but at the time of this writing, not many implementations exist.

28 Trailers are part of the "Hypertext Transfer Protocol—HTTP/1.1" specification (*https://oreil.ly/gWBpi*). The lack of their implementation in the JavaScript fetch API is one of the reasons gRPC isn't supported by web browsers; see "Why Does gRPC Insist on Trailers?" (*https://oreil.ly/V4Qlb*) by Carl Mastrangelo and this MDN GitHub issue (*https://oreil.ly/y7JFU*).

> The protobuf wire format uses field numbers instead of names, and this contributes to the reduction of the amount of data transferred over the network by gRPC.

Example 8-12. Protobuf wire format decoded using xxd and `protoc` *(requires setup from Example 8-2)*

```
docker compose exec client bash -ci \
    "echo -n 0a0548656c6c6f | \
    xxd -plain -revert | \
    python -m grpc_tools.protoc --decode_raw"
1: "Hello"
```

To further explain this wire format,[29] let's separate the components identified in our example by spaces: `0a 05 48656c6c6f`. This type of representation is called tag-length-value (*https://oreil.ly/RhUQD*). The tag in the protobuf wire format is composed of the *field number* and the *wire type*, following the formula (`field_number << 3`) | `wire_type`, with << denoting the binary shift-left by three positions. This means the lowest (the rightmost) three bits denote the wire type, as defined in Table 8-1, and the rest denote the field number.

Table 8-1. Protobuf wire types

ID	Name	Used for
0	VARINT	int32, int64, uint32, uint64, sint32, sint64, bool, enum
1	I64	fixed64, sfixed64, double
2	LEN	string, bytes, embedded messages, packed repeated fields
3	SGROUP	group start (deprecated)
4	EGROUP	group end (deprecated)
5	I32	fixed32, sfixed32, float

In our example the tag is 1 byte long and equals `0a` in hexadecimal (`10` in decimal). In Example 8-13, using Python's read, evaluate, print loop (REPL), you can arrive at this value by following the protobuf tag formula. You need to use the following values of the field number and wire type:

---

29 You can find additional information in "Encoding" in the protobuf documentation (*https://oreil.ly/r5rEL*).

1. Our protobuf, shown in Example 8-1, sets the content field number to 1, and its type to string.

2. In Table 8-1, you find that the string type corresponds to the wire type numerical ID of 2.

> You can start Python's REPL with **docker compose exec client python**, and stop by typing **exit()** followed by Enter.

Example 8-13. Protobuf wire format tag encoded using Python

```
>>> field_number = 1
>>> wire_type = 2
>>> tag = (field_number << 3) | wire_type
>>> print(tag)
10
>>> print(f"{tag:02x}")
0a
```

Table 8-1 shows several other protobuf wire types, in particular *VARINT*. This type, as the name suggests, represents integers using a variable length. Such representation is space efficient for small integers. The protobuf wire format uses varints not only to represent the value of the message but also for the tag and length. In our example, the decimal number 10 requires 1 byte of storage, instead of a common 64-bit (8-byte) fixed-length representation. Both the 0a tag and the 05 length of the "Hello" string, encountered in our example, are 1-byte-long varints.

Implementation

The main use case of gRPC is for service-to-service communication. This section guides you through implementing such a use case by building an enricher service for the WFS's Atom feed. You'll extend the Atom feed, implemented in Chapter 7, to include a summary of the current weather conditions in a city, and recommendations for tourists. This enrichment is generated by an LLM. Additionally, you'll explore some of the more advanced gRPC features: use of other message types as protobuf field types (*https://oreil.ly/cE261*), server-side caching of responses using interceptors (*https://oreil.ly/ozsUP*), error (*https://oreil.ly/liYsd*) status codes, and client-defined deadlines (*https://oreil.ly/Qg2wG*). More features can be found in the official gRPC guides (*https://oreil.ly/tsE2b*) and in the gRPC repository code examples (*https://oreil.ly/i7D3V*).

gRPC Atom Feed Enricher Service

If you start reading from here and are following hands-on, make sure the lab environment is initiated as shown in Example 8-2. Also have a look at the usage of tmux in Example 8-3, and open two panes. Start the enricher gRPC server as shown in Example 8-14. If the ECHO server is still running in one of the panes, it can be stopped by pressing Ctrl+C.

Example 8-14. Start the enricher gRPC server (requires setup from Example 8-2)

```
docker compose exec server bash -ci \
    "PYTHONPATH=./src/enricher python src/enricher/enricher/server.py"
```

Consider performing the warm-up request in Example 8-15 in any available pane, shortly after starting the server, using a city of your choice.

Example 8-15. Warm up the LLM model (requires setup from Example 8-14)

```
docker compose exec client grpcurl -plaintext \
    -d '{"weather_forecast": {"city": {"name": "A city"}}}' \
    server:50051 enricher.v1.EnricherService/Enrich
```

You are encouraged to make this request already now, because the first invocation of a gRPC client, such as grpcurl (*https://oreil.ly/fdBUa*), against the enricher gRPC server may take several minutes, depending on the internet connection speed of the machine running the lab. This is due to the LLM weights being downloaded on first use. The model also needs time to generate the output in response to the prompt. By making this request, you can also check the quality of the LLM response for your city of choice.

After getting the server running and the LLM downloaded, let's proceed to discussing the server's implementation. You'll interact with the server using grpcurl as the client to demonstrate the implemented gRPC features.

Example 8-16 shows the protobuf of `EnricherService`. The `Enrich()` unary RPC method accepts a `WeatherForecast` custom message type as the request, and responds with a `content` string containing the summary of the weather forecast and recommendations for tourists generated by the LLM.

Example 8-16. Protobuf definition of the gRPC Enricher service

```
// src/grpc/src/enricher/enricher/proto/enricher/v1/enricher.proto

syntax = "proto3";
package enricher.v1;

import "google/protobuf/timestamp.proto"; ❶

message City { ❷
  // Universal Unique Identifier of the city.
  string uuid = 1;
  // City name.
  string name = 2;
  // The country name where the city is located.
  string country = 3;
  // The continent name where the country is located.
  string region = 4;
}

message WeatherForecast {
  // The city this weather forecast is for.
  City city = 1; ❸
  // Seconds of UTC time since Unix epoch 1970-01-01T00:00:00Z.
  google.protobuf.Timestamp timestamp = 2; ❹
  // Amount of rain forecasted for today.
  double rain_sum_mm = 3;
  // Amount of showers forecasted for today.
  double showers_sum_mm = 4;
  // Amount of snow forecasted for today.
  double snowfall_sum_cm = 5;
  // Maximum temperature forecasted for today.
  double temperature_max_celsius = 6;
  // Minimum temperature forecasted for today.
  double temperature_min_celsius = 7;
}

message EnrichRequest {
  // The weather forecast details for a city.
  WeatherForecast weather_forecast = 1;
}

message EnrichResponse {
  // Text content of the enriched weather forecast.
  string content = 1;
}

// The service enriches request information.
service EnricherService {
  // This method returns the enriched content of the request.
  rpc Enrich(EnrichRequest) returns (EnrichResponse);
}
```

❶ This line demonstrates a protobuf `import` feature. The definitions are imported from *google/protobuf/timestamp.proto*. This file originates from the protobuf source code repository (*https://oreil.ly/7LR1m*), but for Python it's distributed as part of the `grpcio-tools` package (*https://oreil.ly/mF4DS*). The import functionality enables composability (combination and reuse) of protobufs.

❷ This block defines the `City` message.

❸ The custom `City` message, defined above, is used as a field in the `WeatherForecast` message.

❹ The imported `google.protobuf.Timestamp` message is used as a message field. The `Timestamp` message itself is composed of two fields: `message Timestamp {int64 seconds = 1; int32 nanos = 2;}`, showing it has a nanosecond resolution. It should be noted that protobuf fields have default values, with the default value of 0 for both `int64` and `int32`. For our application, the `nanos` field is left at its default value, and therefore the `timestamp` field represents seconds of UTC time since the Unix epoch 1970-01-01T00:00:00Z.

The implementation of the gRPC server for `EnricherService`, shown in Example 8-17, differs from the gRPC server used for `EchoService` and described in Example 8-6, by the addition of a `CachingInterceptor` interceptor. A gRPC interceptor is similar to middleware, discussed in Example 10-7. As the name suggests, an interceptor intercepts every RPC to perform a functionality, then passes the RPC further in the chain of interceptors. Interceptors can be implemented by clients (on the channel) and servers. The common use cases for interceptors include caching, logging, or authentication.

Example 8-17. gRPC server and interceptor implementation

```
# src/grpc/src/enricher/enricher/server.py

class CachingInterceptor(grpc.ServerInterceptor):
    def __init__(self):
        self.cache = {}  ❶

    def intercept_service(self, continuation, handler_call_details):  ❷
        rpc_method = handler_call_details.method
        logger.info("Intercepting", extra={"rpc_method": rpc_method})

        if rpc_method.startswith("/grpc.reflection.v1"):  ❸
            logger.info("Bypassing interceptor")
            return continuation(handler_call_details)

        next_handler = continuation(handler_call_details)  ❹
```

```
        def return_cached_response(request, context):
            cache_key = request.SerializeToString()  ❺
            if cache_key not in self.cache:  ❻
                response = next_handler.unary_unary(request, context)
                self.cache[cache_key] = response
            return self.cache[cache_key]  ❼

        return grpc.unary_unary_rpc_method_handler(  ❽
            return_cached_response,
            request_deserializer=next_handler.request_deserializer,
            response_serializer=next_handler.response_serializer)
server = grpc.server(
    concurrent.futures.ThreadPoolExecutor(),
    interceptors=(CachingInterceptor(),),)
pb2_grpc.add_EnricherServiceServicer_to_server(
    EnricherServiceServicer(), server)

SERVICE_NAMES = (reflection.SERVICE_NAME,
    pb2.DESCRIPTOR.services_by_name["EnricherService"].full_name)
reflection.enable_server_reflection(SERVICE_NAMES, server)

server.add_insecure_port("0.0.0.0:50051")
server.start()
logger.info("gRPC server is ready to serve requests")
server.wait_for_termination()
```

❶ For the purpose of caching the server's responses, a Python dictionary is used as the class instance attribute. It is initialized as an empty, in-memory cache. A more realistic cache would be limited in size and have a TTL feature to purge old items.

❷ The `intercept_service()` method is required to be implemented by any server interceptor.

❸ This condition is used to skip the interceptor if the client's request RPC is a reflection. Reflection is an optional feature of the gRPC server that can be enabled per service to expose to clients the protobuf definitions of the services and messages as a gRPC API.

❹ The `continuation()` function gets `next_handler` in the chain. This could be another interceptor or the actual RPC method handler. In this case, there is only one interceptor, so `next_handler` is an RPC method handler.

❺ The protobuf `SerializeToString()` method serializes the request to Python's bytes (not string, as the name suggests). The result is used as the cache key.

❻ If the response isn't cached yet, the appropriate RPC method on the handler is called to obtain the response. Here, the unary_unary() method of the next_han dler is called. The response is then saved in the cache.

❼ The cached response is returned.

❽ The RPC handler that uses the return_cached_response() method to perform caching of the response is returned.

The CachingInterceptor could be written to be general-purpose, to cache responses of various unary RPC methods, and to be reused across different gRPC servicers. For our servicer, shown in Example 8-18, the next_handler is the handler for Enricher ServiceServicer, and the unary_unary() method is the Enrich() unary method. EnricherServiceServicer makes use of two more gRPC features: error status codes and deadlines.

Example 8-18. gRPC EnricherServicer implementation

```
# src/grpc/src/enricher/enricher/server.py

class EnricherServiceServicer(pb2_grpc.EnricherServiceServicer):
    def Enrich(self, request, context):
        if not (-90 <= request.weather_forecast.temperature_max_celsius <= 60):
            context.abort(  ❶
                grpc.StatusCode.INVALID_ARGUMENT,
                "Allowed temperature_max_celsius range is [-90, 60].")

        if not (-90 <= request.weather_forecast.temperature_min_celsius <= 60):
            rich_status = create_field_validation_error_status(
                field="temperature_min_celsius",
                description="Allowed range is [-90, 60].")
            context.abort_with_status(rpc_status.to_status(rich_status))  ❷

        deadline = context.time_remaining()  ❸
        logger.info("Remaining deadline", extra={"deadline": deadline})

        weather_forecast = get_weather_forecast(request)  ❹
        summary = summarize_weather_forecast(weather_forecast)  ❺
        enriched_content = weather_forecast + (
            f"<br>\n"
            f"<br>\n"
            f"\nLanguage Model says:\n"
            f"<br>\n"
            f"{summary}")
        return pb2.EnrichResponse(content=enriched_content)  ❻
```

❶ This range validation of the maximum temperature is used to illustrate a basic type of error status returned by a gRPC server to abort the RPC with an Invalid Argument gRPC status Code, and the specified Message. The error can be triggered by providing an invalid value for the maximum temperature.

```
docker compose exec client grpcurl -plaintext \
       -d '{"weather_forecast": {"temperature_max_celsius": 100.0}}' \
       server:50051 enricher.v1.EnricherService/Enrich
ERROR:
  Code: InvalidArgument
  Message: Allowed temperature_max_celsius range is [-90, 60].
```

❷ This range validation of the minimum temperature is the same as for the maximum temperature example above, but an RPC abort provides a rich error status. The rich error status additionally contains a Details field. Only the example output of a rich error status is shown; the implementation itself is available in the book's code repository.

```
docker compose exec client grpcurl -plaintext \
       -d '{"weather_forecast": {"temperature_min_celsius": 100.0}}' \
       server:50051 enricher.v1.EnricherService/Enrich
ERROR:
  Code: InvalidArgument
  Message: Field validation error
  Details:
  1) { "@type": "type.googleapis.com/google.rpc.BadRequest",
       "field_violations": [
       { "field": "temperature_min_celsius",
         "description": "Allowed range is [-90, 60]."
       }]
     }
```

❸ The remaining time left from the deadline specified by the client is obtained from the context. A deadline defines a point in time after which the client won't wait for the server response, and it will terminate the RPC with the DEAD LINE_EXCEEDED gRPC status code.

In microservices architectures, a gRPC server may act as a client of another gRPC server. For this reason, gRPC supports propagation of the initial deadline. Even if the initial RPC request triggers more RPCs on the way, the original deadline will be obeyed, including retries. This behavior is useful to avoid unnecessarily tying up resources, like memory, while waiting for responses that most likely won't arrive. See the gRPC guide for more information about deadlines (*https://oreil.ly/ kCwd7*).

```
docker compose exec client grpcurl -plaintext \
       --max-time 1 server:50051 enricher.v1.EnricherService/Enrich
ERROR:
```

```
Code: DeadlineExceeded
Message: context deadline exceeded
```

❹ The get_weather_forecast() function prepares the weather forecast in a text format, suitable as an input to an LLM. The implementation of the function isn't discussed further here, but it combines the fields present in the WeatherForecast message of EnrichRequest to produce a string such as, "This is today's weather forecast for Tokyo in Japan in the beginning of June: No rain. No showers. No snowfall. Maximum temperature 24 degrees Celsius. Minimum temperature 17 degrees Celsius."

❺ Taking the text of the weather forecast, the LLM summarizes this forecast and enriches it with recommendations for tourists visiting the city. The implementation of this function isn't discussed here, but its result can be seen in Figure 8-3.

❻ The enriched content is returned to the client.

Before discussing the implementation of the Atom feed enrichment, let's see it in action. After making sure the enricher gRPC server is running in one of the panes, as shown in Example 8-14, in another pane configure and start the newsboat reader using the commands provided in Example 8-19.

Example 8-19. Enriched Atom feed read using Newsboat (requires setup from Example 8-14)

```
# Start Django app ❶
cd src/django
docker compose build --build-arg UID=$(id -u) --build-arg GID=$(id -g)
docker compose up --detach --wait

# Configure newsboat reader ❷
docker compose exec app bash -c \
    "mkdir --parents ~/.newsboat && \
    echo 'download-timeout 600' > ~/.newsboat/config && \
    echo http://app:8000/forecast/feed_enriched > ~/.newsboat/urls"

# Read the feed ❸
docker compose exec app bash -c "newsboat --refresh-on-start"
```

❶ Navigate to the Django app directory, build Docker images, and start containers.

❷ Configure the newsboat feed reader. Increase the feed download time to a value sufficient for the LLM to produce its output, and provide the URL of the enriched feed.

❸ Start the newsboat reader in interactive mode.

The first invocation of the LLM may take several minutes, depending on the internet connection speed of the machine executing the commands, because the model weights are downloaded on first use. The locally running model also needs time to generate the output in response to the prompt, and this depends on the machine speed. It can take up to several minutes on an older machine.

After some time (seconds or minutes, depending on the speed of the LLM), press Enter in `newsboat` to access the *City Weather Forecast Enriched* feed, and then press Enter again to select the feed for your city of choice. You'll see the weather forecast information enriched by the summary generated by the model, as in Figure 8-3. Press Q to back off to the cities menu, browse other cities with Enter, or continue pressing Q to ultimately quit `newsboat`.

```
newsboat 2.21.0 - Article 'Tokyo' (5 unread, 6 total)
Feed: City Weather Forecast Enriched
Title: Tokyo
Date: Fri, 06 Jun 2025 23:43:00 +0000
Link: http://app:8000/forecast/cf945356-8cf0-4baf-9177-bcc9b3e4a561

This is today's weather forecast for Tokyo in Japan in the beginning of June:
No rain.
No showers.
No snowfall.
Maximum temperature 24 degrees Celsius.
Minimum temperature 17 degrees Celsius.

Language Model says:
Yes, this weather is typical for early June in Tokyo, Japan. The absence of
precipitation suggests clear skies with mild temperatures suitable for outdoor
activities. For tourists interested in exploring traditional Japanese culture during
this time, consider visiting Ueno Park or Asakusa to experience the vibrant atmosphere
and historical sites.
q:Quit s:Save n:Next Unread o:Open in Browser e:Enqueue ?:Help           Top
```

Figure 8-3. Atom weather forecast feed enriched by an LLM

The remaining part of this section discusses the integration of the gRPC client into the Atom feed served by the Django app, shown in Example 8-20.

Example 8-20. Enriched Atom weather forecast feed implementation

```python
# src/django/app/core/api/atom/feed_enriched.py

class CityAtomFeedEnrichedView(FeedView):
    feed_type = Atom1Feed
    title = "City Weather Forecast Enriched"
    link = "/forecast/feed_enriched"

    channel = grpc.insecure_channel("grpc-server:50051")  ❶
    stub = pb2_grpc.EnricherServiceStub(channel)  ❶
```

```
def item_description(self, city):
    forecast = WeatherForecastRepository.filter(city=city).first()  ❷
    city_proto = pb2.City(  ❸
        uuid=str(city.uuid),
        name=city.name,
        country=city.country,
        region=city.region,
    )
    forecast_timestamp = datetime.datetime.combine(  ❹
        forecast.date, datetime.datetime.min.time()
    )
    timestamp_proto = Timestamp()  ❹
    timestamp_proto.FromDatetime(forecast_timestamp)  ❹
    weather_forecast_proto = pb2.WeatherForecast(  ❺
        city=city_proto,
        timestamp=timestamp_proto,
        rain_sum_mm=forecast.rain_sum_mm,
        showers_sum_mm=forecast.showers_sum_mm,
        snowfall_sum_cm=forecast.snowfall_sum_cm,
        temperature_max_celsius=forecast.temperature_max_celsius,
        temperature_min_celsius=forecast.temperature_min_celsius,
    )
    request = pb2.EnrichRequest(weather_forecast=weather_forecast_proto)  ❻
    try:
        response = self.stub.Enrich(request, wait_for_ready=True)  ❼
    except grpc.RpcError as rpc_error:
        logger.exception(f"gRPC call error: {rpc_error}")
        raise

    return response.content  ❽
```

❶ This block creates a gRPC client channel and stub. A gRPC client channel is created to connect to the gRPC server at `grpc-server:50051`. The connection is insecure (unencrypted) to limit the amount of code discussed in this section. The stub for the `EnricherService` is created on this channel. It's recommended to reuse channels and stubs to limit resource utilization, so here they are created as class attributes.

❷ The latest weather forecast for the given city is retrieved from the database.

❸ The protobuf `City` message is constructed. Note that `str(city.uuid)` ensures that the `uuid` field of the message has the expected type.

❹ The value for the `timestamp` protobuf field is populated. Since `forecast.date` contains only a date, it's extended to represent the timestamp at midnight on that day. Then this `forecast_timestamp` is used to construct a protobuf of the built-in `Timestamp` type.

❺ The `WeatherForecast` protobuf message is constructed, using the messages created above and other primitive type values present in `forecast` database model.

❻ At this point, the protobuf request message can be created, using the protobuf of the `WeatherForecast` message. Recall that gRPC RPC methods accept only a single argument.

❼ The RPC call is made using the `Enrich()` method of the client stub. This call makes the stub wait for the gRPC server to become available before sending the request, using the wait-for-ready gRPC feature (*https://oreil.ly/b68ML*). If the client uses a deadline (*https://oreil.ly/HUJB0*) (in our example it doesn't), the deadline applies to the waiting time as well. This block catches the `grpc.RpcError` exception, logs the error information, and reraises the exception (bubbles it up), assuming the error is nonrecoverable. A more realistic example would be trying to recover from recoverable errors.[30]

❽ The string value of the `content` field is returned, deserialized from the RPC response.

This implementation of RPC may give you a flavor of the convenience provided by local calls. With an additional development effort,[31] it may be possible to expand this convenience to operational domains such as creation of API documentation, encryption and authentication, resiliency, or observability, but these features aren't available in gRPC out of the box.

Security

gRPC is based on the HTTP/2 protocol, so it inherits the security risks associated with it. These generic risks were discussed in "OWASP Top 10 API Security" on page 69 and can be classified into three categories: authentication and authorization, inventory management, and resource management.

The most common gRPC use case is for service-to-service communication, happening usually within a private network. In such setups, there is an incentive for adopting less secure practices, known from the management of perimeter-based computer networks.

---

30 See "The Ultimate Guide to Error Handling in Python" (*https://oreil.ly/IbTFa*) by Miguel Grinberg for an introduction to exception handling in Python.

31 See the "How Netflix Makes gRPC Easy to Serve, Consume, and Operate" talk (*https://oreil.ly/NqgA9*) by Benjamin Fedorka. Many enhancements mentioned during this talk exist as proprietary extensions of gRPC made internally by Netflix.

> The security of perimeter-based computer networks relies on controlling access on the network boundaries, with less scrutiny of the network traffic within the perimeter. This approach contrasts with a zero-trust network, where no traffic is trusted by default.

For example, in terms of authentication, a perimeter model may assume that standard TLS encryption and server authentication are sufficient, often combined with the use of a long-lived certificate. As a result, this opens the system to client insider attacks.

Adopting mTLS is a step forward, but it results in operational challenges due to the additional key and certificate management required. The SPIRE project (*https://oreil.ly/ukU61*) provides a means of automating mTLS; however, its primary focus is on systems hosted in the cloud. In addition to mTLS, gRPC also supports token-based client authentication, which offers another layer of security but requires an extra operational effort as well.[32]

A particular security risk of gRPC is associated with the reflection feature (*https://oreil.ly/Wi1hF*), which can be enabled on gRPC servers. Reflection allows clients to discover information about the API provided by the server. Leaving reflection enabled is a security risk, as it allows enumerating services, RPC methods, and message types. Exposing this information can potentially lead to targeted attacks.

Documentation

At the time of this writing, there is no official gRPC support for generating developer-facing, HTML-based documentation similar to Swagger UI (*https://oreil.ly/70qwo*) or GraphiQL (*https://oreil.ly/oW3JN*). Tools that aim to achieve this goal appear and fade away, and larger gRPC projects use unofficial tools, or, like Kubernetes, maintain custom generators.

For small projects, the protobuf file itself can be treated as static gRPC documentation. Additionally, reflection provides online documentation as shown in Example 8-21. It features the discovery of services, RPC methods, and messages. Reflection is disabled by default and can be enabled on a per-service basis.

Example 8-21. gRPC reflection as online documentation (requires setup from Example 8-2)

```
# List available services
docker compose exec client grpcurl -plaintext server:50051 list
```

---

32 For more details about authentication, see the gRPC auth guide (*https://oreil.ly/pLFeC*).

```
# Output:
enricher.v1.EnricherService
grpc.reflection.v1alpha.ServerReflection

# Describe a service
docker compose exec client grpcurl -plaintext \
      server:50051 describe enricher.v1.EnricherService

# Output:
enricher.v1.EnricherService is a service:
service EnricherService {
  rpc Enrich ( .enricher.v1.EnrichRequest )
      returns ( .enricher.v1.EnrichResponse );
}

# Provide a message template containing default values
docker compose exec client grpcurl -plaintext \
      -msg-template server:50051 describe enricher.v1.EnrichRequest

# Output:
enricher.v1.EnrichRequest is a message:
message EnrichRequest {
  .enricher.v1.WeatherForecast weather_forecast = 1;
}

Message template:
{ "weather_forecast": {
    "city": { "uuid": "", "name": "", "country": "", "region": "" },
    "timestamp": "1970-01-01T00:00:00Z",
    "rain_sum_mm": 0, "showers_sum_mm": 0, "snowfall_sum_cm": 0,
    "temperature_max_celsius": 0, "temperature_min_celsius": 0
  }
}
```

Trade-Offs

gRPC is associated with advantages, such as the following:

Performance
> The use of Protocol Buffers as a binary serialization format, combined with HTTP/2 header compression, results in smaller payloads transferred over the network, compared to JSON/XML- and HTTP/1-based APIs. gRPC controls both the client- and server-side implementations, which facilitates optimizations. The core gRPC library used by the Python implementation is written in C++. This makes it possible to mitigate performance limitations caused by Python's Global Interpreter Lock (GIL), and is one of the reasons gRPC is used for back-ends of machine learning systems.

Distributed systems support

Historically, one of the goals of RPCs is to address challenges resulting from the unreliability of networks. gRPC is a modern implementation of the concepts used for building distributed systems, such as request deadlines, request cancellation, client-side load balancing, flow control, server health checks, caching, or retries. This makes gRPC suitable for systems composed of many services communicating over a network, as in the case of microservices architectures.

API contract

The Protocol Buffers messages and services define a typed API contract between the client and the server, enforced by using an autogenerated code as the base for the custom application logic implementation. Additionally, protobuf files may be extended by the use of `protoc` plug-ins, such as Protovalidate (*https://oreil.ly/Z9nI2*), used to include field validation logic. Working with gRPC is an API-first approach that requires planning before making breaking changes.

Streaming support

gRPC, in addition to the *unary* RPC type, supports three streaming types: *server streaming, client streaming,* and *bidirectional streaming*. Bidirectional streaming in gRPC allows for full-duplex transmission mode, offering full control over messages exchanged over the network. This enables developers to build custom application layer protocols using gRPC.

Multilanguage support

gRPC tends to focus first on Java (*https://oreil.ly/TFXbN*) and Go (*https://oreil.ly/HvNa2*) implementations when adding new features. The features then make their way into the C++ (*https://oreil.ly/EMlr4*) implementation, which is the base library used for supporting other languages, such as C++, Python, Ruby, Objective-C, or PHP. There also exist .NET (*https://oreil.ly/5Zwme*), Node.js (*https://oreil.ly/lwyNL*), and a few other language-specific implementations. Thanks to protobufs, clients and servers written in different programming languages can communicate, but functional differences tend to exist.

However, gRPC is not free of disadvantages, like these:

Limited browser support

Web browsers don't support gRPC natively.[33] Limited support for browsers exists, e.g., through *grpc-web* (*https://oreil.ly/gbSmS*) or *grpc-Gateway* (*https://oreil.ly/Xx4PX*) involving a proxy, or using Connect Protocol (*https://oreil.ly/DBnAB*), a modified version of HTTP for RPC, which doesn't require HTTP trailers (HTTP trailers are described in "Protobuf Wire Format" on page 262).

---

33 See "The State of gRPC in the Browser" on the gRPC website (*https://oreil.ly/TrM6u*).

Code generation challenges

Code generation creates operational challenges in terms of generating code using the right version of `protoc`, which is the approach recommended by gRPC developers from Google, or distributing the generated code to the clients and servers. In both cases, the protobuf directory structure and the definitions of protobuf messages and services need to be organized to support the evolution of the project. Specialized CI/CD processes are needed for deployments of gRPC projects. Moreover, the generated code may introduce programming conventions that otherwise wouldn't be used by your project.

Limited documentation support

At the time of this writing, there is no official gRPC support for generating developer-facing, HTML-based documentation similar to Swagger UI (*https:// oreil.ly/lX7UK*) or GraphiQL (*https://oreil.ly/eMaz7*). The protobuf files serve as a static gRPC documentation, and reflection provides an online documentation. Examples of using reflection as documentation are shown in Example 8-21.

Lack of official tools

Challenges in the tools space originate from Protocol Buffers and gRPC itself. The recommended gRPC usage of protobufs requires specialized code dependency management tools, like Bazel (*https://bazel.build*). Editors/IDEs tend to lack support for gRPC. Production-related features are provided by third-party tools, for example, protobuf formatting, linting, and breaking change detection by *buf* (*https://oreil.ly/qwsTr*), or load-testing by *ghz* (*https://oreil.ly/Br8rL*).

Unfamiliarity

The RPC approach to building an API, used by gRPC, tends to be less familiar compared to REST. The binary format of Protocol Buffers requires new skills when building and debugging gRPC-based services.

In addition to these gRPC advantages and disadvantages, consult the series of blog posts under "gRPC: The Good and the Bad" (*https://oreil.ly/qjcld*) by Kevin McDonald for more discussion about gRPC trade-offs.

When to Use gRPC

gRPC is suitable for service-to-service communication, such as among the services in microservices architectures. However, a decision about gRPC adoption is to be made after evaluating its trade-offs.

The performance gains in service-to-service communication from efficient, binary messaging and the advantages of a typed API contract may, in certain cases, outweigh the operational challenges introduced by gRPC. Teams that have adopted microservices architectures may also already possess the technical capabilities needed to overcome these challenges. Additionally, in multilanguage environments, when the use of services written in multiple programming languages cannot be avoided, gRPC offers a communication mechanism among them.

Applications such as chat, data streaming, mobile apps, or live system updates may benefit from gRPC because it offers low latencies thanks to the use of the HTTP/2 protocol and native support for data streaming.

Exercises

1. Manually encode decimal 150 into 9601 protobuf varint in hexadecimal. See the example in the documentation (*https://oreil.ly/v4IYX*) for help. You can find the solution in the book's code repository, in the *src/grpc/README.md* file.

2. Modify the server implementation code from Example 8-6 to use standard TLS instead of mTLS. Use the provided grpcurl command to confirm that the communication is still secured (encrypted), without the need for the client certificate and key (`--cert src/client.crt --key src/client.key`) required for mTLS. Hint: recall the role of the `require_client_auth` argument.

   ```
   docker compose exec client bash -ci \
       "SSLKEYLOGFILE=tests/SSLKEYLOGFILE.client grpcurl \
       --cacert src/ca.crt \
       -d '{ \"content\": \"Hello\" }' \
       server:50051 echo.v1.EchoService/DemoUnary"
   ```

3. Use of interceptors requires an understanding of their interactions with RPCs. Consider the following implementation of the basic error status in Example 8-18. Does it change the server behavior? Hint: remember caching.

   ```
   if not (-90 <= request.weather_forecast.temperature_max_celsius <= 60):
       context.set_code(grpc.StatusCode.INVALID_ARGUMENT)
       context.set_details("Allowed temperature_max_celsius range is [-90, 60].")
       return pb2.EnrichResponse()
   ```

Summary

This chapter introduced gRPC as an example of an RPC API style. To become familiar with the main features of gRPC, such as protobufs, code generation, and the four RPC types (unary, server streaming, client streaming, and bidirectional streaming), you implemented a gRPC ECHO service and secured the client and server with mTLS, which mutually authenticated them and provided encryption.

You also implemented some of the more advanced gRPC features, such as server-side caching, status codes, and client deadlines. For this purpose, you extended the implementation of the WFS Atom feed with a summary generated by an LLM.

We hope that the discussion of gRPC trade-offs in the chapter, along with the references to advanced materials, will encourage you to further explore this technology.

## CHAPTER 9

Webhooks

Before talking about webhooks, we need to explain the callback concept. In real life, you might experience a callback when calling a friend who is currently busy, and they promise to call you back. For APIs, a callback is an application's interface (e.g., an HTTP endpoint) that is used to receive messages (calls).

The communication flow in callback APIs goes like this: a destination service that wishes to be notified registers its callback within the source service responsible for producing events. In callback APIs, every message sent by the source service is expected to be acknowledged by the destination service through a response.

Figure 9-1 shows the architecture of callback APIs.

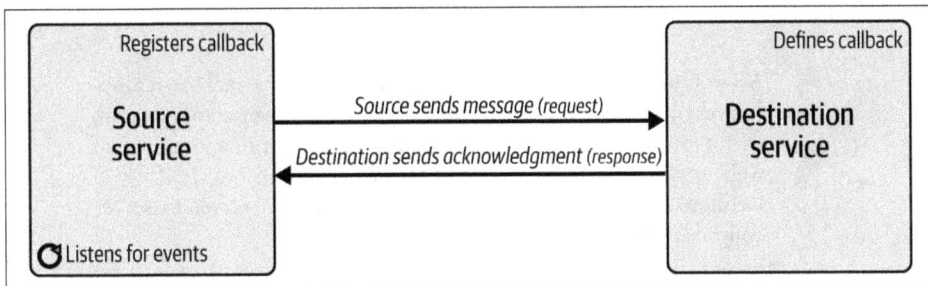

Figure 9-1. Callback architecture

A *webhook* is an HTTP request triggered by an event in the source service and sent to a callback URL defined in the destination service. The webhook payload data contains information about the event. The destination service then processes the data and responds to the event's occurrence.

In this chapter, you'll be introduced to webhooks, their origins, classification, and trade-offs. Completing this chapter will help you determine whether webhooks are the right choice for your use case. Besides conceptual knowledge, you'll gain practical skills to implement, secure, and document webhook APIs.

What Are Webhooks?

Webhooks go by many names, such as *HTTP push APIs*, *HTTP callbacks*, or *reverse APIs*. The purpose of a webhook is to send a message from a source to a destination service without the destination service explicitly requesting the message. The destination service exposes an endpoint (callback) that acts as an open door through which messages funnel in. In the most common implementation, a webhook uses the HTTP POST method, but you could also have a webhook that uses the HTTP GET method, which is less common.

With webhooks, destination services receive notifications about events known by the source service only after registering to them (subscribing to the source). This registration can be set up manually through configuration (out-of-band), or automatically via an HTTP POST request containing the destination service's callback URL, sent to the source service.

The webhook messages are serialized (usually text-based, encoded as JSON or XML) and are sent after the occurrence of an event in the source service. The destination service receives the message, and acknowledges it by an HTTP response with a success status code. Note that the destination service doesn't request the message (apart from the potential initial registration request sent to the source service); instead, the message is pushed to it by the source service.

> A webhook's source and destination services are machines (servers), and direct human interaction, apart from configuration, is not involved. In the context of the intuitive understanding of web applications, servers are identified as machines, leading to webhooks sometimes being referred to as server-to-server communication.
>
> However, this way of speaking about servers is informal. The server, according to the client-server definition from "Socket API" on page 78, is the one who awaits the connection. To avoid confusion, we use the more general terms *source* and *destination*.

Origins of Webhooks

The term *web hook* (with the space between two words) is attributed to Jeff Lindsay, who in 2007 shared it in his blog, "Web Hooks to Revolutionize the Web" (*https://oreil.ly/VhF8d*). The inspiration for webhooks came from thinking about websites as data sources that can be reused and remixed, similarly to how programs are combined via Unix's pipes.[1] A pipe in Unix allows a series of programs to be chained together by their standard streams, where the output of one program (program A) becomes an input to the other program (program B). Jeff imagined passing web data between services similarly to the way Unix pipes pass data between processes, using stdout and stdin. In webhooks, an HTTP POST request can act like a pipe, sending data from one system to another when specific events occur, thereby connecting various services in an event-driven way.

Webhooks became an alternative to polling (*https://oreil.ly/op4yf*). In polling, a client repetitively requests the server to check for the availability of new data. The server responds, providing the new data, if available. The client receives the response from the server, and the cycle repeats.

Incoming and Outgoing Webhooks

Webhooks are classified into incoming and outgoing webhooks. *Incoming webhooks* allow a service to receive messages from a source, while *outgoing webhooks* enable sending messages to the destination. To distinguish which one is which, you need to choose one service as the frame of reference.

To illustrate this concept, in Figure 9-2 we'll focus on the message flow from the perspective of Service B (central service). Service B is integrated with Service A via an incoming webhook because Service B receives the message from Service A. Meanwhile, Service B and Service C are integrated via an outgoing webhook because Service B sends the message to Service C.

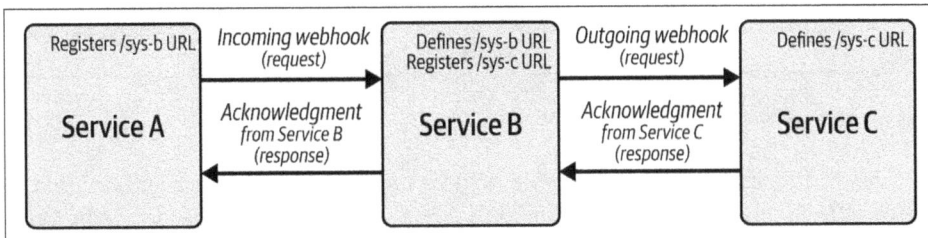

Figure 9-2. Incoming versus outgoing webhooks

---

1 In "Annotate the Web, Then Rewire It" (*https://oreil.ly/1NEnd*), Jon Udell expressed a vision of websites as data sources that could be reused.

One way to think about incoming versus outgoing webhooks is to look at the message flow to and from a service. If a message arrives at the service, it's an incoming webhook, whereas if a message leaves the service, it's an outgoing webhook.

Integration and Data Flow

Let's recall the diagram from Figure 9-2 and apply thinking about the webhook to a fictitious online bookstore named *books.example.com* that is integrated with a fictitious supplier of books, *warehouse.example.com*. As you can imagine, *books.example.com* is selling books online, and its strategic partner is distribution center *warehouse.example.com*. Figure 9-3 shows webhook integration between these two services and the flow of messages.

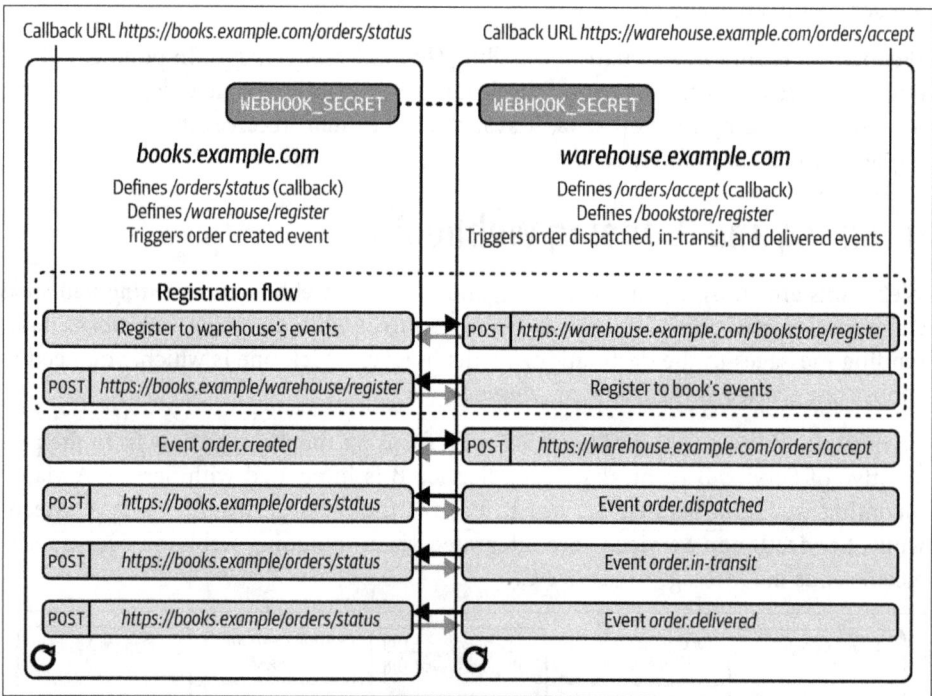

Figure 9-3. Webhooks integration between two services

As shown in Figure 9-3, each service defines its callback URL that will be used to receive the webhooks. The service *books.example.com* defines the */orders/status* callback, and the service *warehouse.example.com* defines the */orders/accept* callback. Integration starts with both services registering to each other by sending a callback URL to the appropriate service registration endpoint. The *books.example.com* service registers to the *warehouse.example.com* service to be able to receive a webhook about order status from the warehouse, and the *warehouse.example.com* service registers to the *books.example.com* service to be notified about the bookstore's newly created order. When the *order.created* event occurs in the *books.example.com* service, that event triggers a webhook (POST request) to the *warehouse.example.com* service, which accepts the order and starts processing it. While the order is being processed by the warehouse, it generates events *order.dispatched*, *order.in-transit*, and *order.delivered*, which are sent over as a webhook to the *books.example.com* service. Additionally, both services are in possession of a WEBHOOK_SECRET that is used to sign and verify the message's payload, ensuring that the message is authentic and has not been tampered with (more on this in "Security" on page 291).

Independently of which service you'll work with, the procedure for integrating webhooks will follow these steps:

1. Destination service:
   a. Implements a callback URL (HTTP endpoint) through which it will receive a webhook (request) from the source service.
   b. Contains a shared secret (symmetric key) also known by the source service.[2]
   c. Registers its callback URL in the source service (performs subscription).

2. Source service:
   a. Integrates the destination service's callback URL.
   b. Contains the shared secret that is also known by the destination service. This shared secret is used to sign the request's payload.
   c. Triggers a webhook (HTTP request) against the destination service's callback URL.

3. Destination service:
   a. Verifies the received webhook by checking its payload, using the shared secret.
   b. Processes the webhook.
   c. Returns an acknowledgment (an HTTP response) to the source service.

---

2 This example discusses only the scenario of symmetric cryptography using HMAC, as opposed to digital signatures based on asymmetric cryptography.

Implementation

In this section, we'll integrate our WFS using a webhook. To accomplish this, two services are necessary. The first service will act as a source that generates events, and the second as a consumer that receives a webhook.

Figure 9-4 shows the overview of WFS that uses webhooks for integration. On the left, we have a source service, which is WFS's `app_event` CLI program that creates `dummy.event`, which triggers an HTTP POST to the destination service's callback URL. On the right, we have a destination service (API producer) that implements callback URL endpoints (*/webhooks/v1/echo* and */webhooks/v2/echo*).

The OpenAPI document that appears on the left describes the webhook's request and response, which both services must follow to be successfully integrated. The document ensures that the source and destination services involved in communication understand the structure and behavior of the webhook. The document describes the behavior and expectations of the webhook request initiated by the source and the expected responses from the destination.

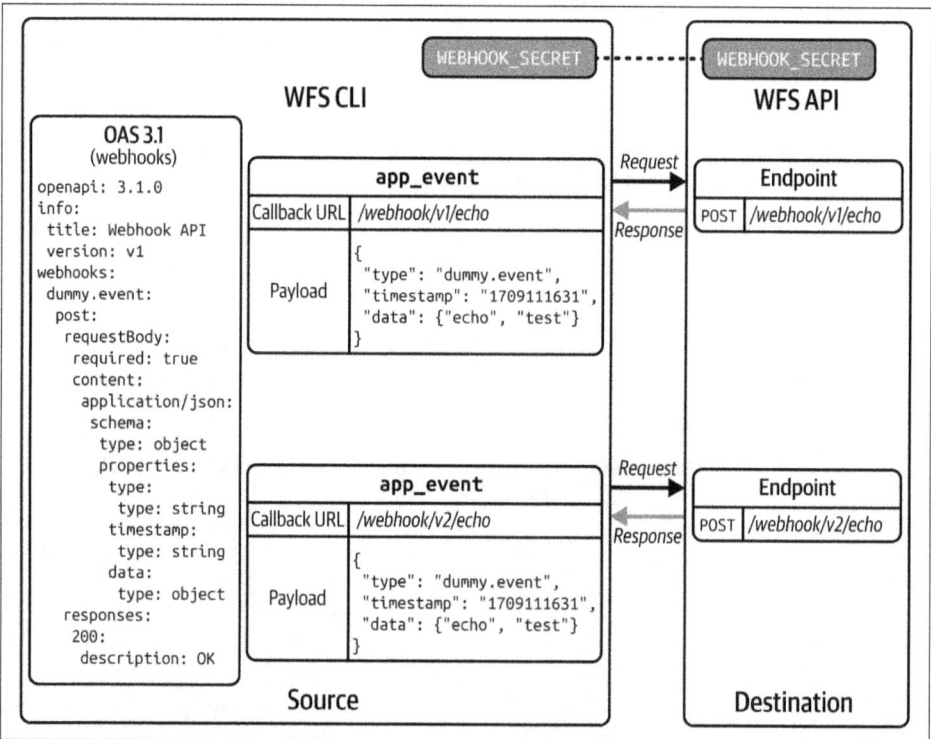

Figure 9-4. WFS webhooks

Both webhook implementations (v1 and v2) will follow the webhooks specification proposed by the standard-webhooks (*https://www.standardwebhooks.com*). The callback endpoint will perform the same functionality in both v1 and v2 cases—that is, to receive a webhook from a source service and return an acknowledgment response. The objectives of these two examples are to practice the implementation of the standard-webhooks specification by using its library, as well as implementing the webhook manually, to understand the underlying concepts.

Standard-Webhooks Specification

Standard-webhooks (*https://oreil.ly/137po*) is a project that aims to normalize the implementation of webhooks across the IT industry by defining a webhook specification (*https://oreil.ly/pO9P6*). The project proposes a set of guidelines that should be followed when implementing webhooks, including security, reliability, interoperability, simplicity, and backward and forward compatibility. The standard-webhooks project provides reference implementations of the guidelines in various programming languages—including C#, Elixir, Go, Java/Kotlin, JavaScript/TypeScript, PHP, Python, Ruby, and Rust.

The callback URLs (webhook endpoints) are defined in Example 9-1.

Example 9-1. Webhook endpoints (callback URLs) definition

```
# src/django/app/config/urls.py

from core.api.webhook.v1.views import WebhookStandardView
from core.api.webhook.v2.views import WebhookCustomView

...
urlpatterns = [
    ...
    path("webhook/v1/echo", WebhookStandardView.as_view()),   ❶
    path("webhook/v2/echo", WebhookCustomView.as_view()),     ❷
    ...
]
```

❶ The WebhookStandardView class takes an easy approach to implementing webhooks by using Python's standardwebhooks package (*https://oreil.ly/ksYiD*), which follows the standard-webhooks specification that also includes a built-in functionality of HMAC (*https://oreil.ly/mxw5n*).

❷ The WebhookCustomView class takes a harder approach to webhooks and implements the standard-webhooks specification manually.

After defining the endpoints, let's proceed to implement the logic that processes the incoming HTTP requests. The implementation of `WebhookStandardView` is shown in Example 9-2.

Example 9-2. ECHO webhook implementation using Python's standardwebhooks *package*

```
# src/django/app/core/api/webhook/v1/views.py

from standardwebhooks import Webhook
from django.utils.decorators import method_decorator
from django.views import View
from django.views.decorators.csrf import csrf_exempt

from config.constants import WEBHOOK_SECRET_B64


@method_decorator(csrf_exempt, name="dispatch")  ❶
class WebhookStandardView(View):
    wh = Webhook(WEBHOOK_SECRET_B64)  ❷

    def post(self, request):  ❸
        try:
            payload = self.wh.verify(request.body, request.headers)  ❹
        except Exception as e:
            return JsonResponse({"errors": [str(e)]}, status=400)

        return JsonResponse(payload)  ❺
```

❶ The `WebhookStandardView` class is a class-based view (*https://oreil.ly/QjxI3*), whose input by default is validated because the Django framework treats it as an HTML form. Django checks all incoming HTTP POST data against CSRF attacks. If the request doesn't have a CSRF token, the request is rejected by Django. Adding the `csrf_exempt` decorator bypasses validation of the CSRF token when receiving HTTP requests. This is an undesirable weakening of security, which may, however, be necessary when integrating with third-party services over which you have no control.

❷ The `Webhook` class comes from the `standardwebhooks` package and is instantiated with a Base64-encoded secret (`WEBHOOK_SECRET_B64`) that is used to verify the message's payload. The webhook instance is assigned to a class attribute `wh` variable.

❸ The `post()` method aggregates the logic that is executed every time a destination service receives the HTTP POST request.

❹ The webhooks `verify()` method verifies the message's payload. If the verification fails, an exception is raised, and a JSON response with the error message and 400 (Bad Request) status code is returned to the source service.

❺ If the verification is successful, the acknowledgment is returned to the source service as an HTTP response with the JSON payload and a 200 (OK) status code.

Security

Common security measures used to protect webhooks include TLS (*https://oreil.ly/ u9rEh*), for encrypting and providing integrity and authenticity of data in transit, and HMAC (*https://oreil.ly/uMOPR*), to additionally verify message integrity and authenticity. This section demonstrates how to apply HMAC, which standard-webhooks specification relies on.

> HMAC is not unique to webhooks and can be applied as a general security mechanism. Unlike typical HTTP-based API authentication using tokens or API keys, webhooks commonly use HMAC so the HTTP server can verify that incoming POST requests come from the expected client. HMAC assumes communication is already encrypted with TLS, providing integrity and authenticity but not encryption.

HMAC uses a cryptographic hash function and a shared secret to sign and verify the message's payload, providing both integrity and authenticity. The shared secret is known by both the source and destination services, which use it to verify payload. Figure 9-3 shows the WEBHOOK_SECRET being used by both services.

Example 9-3 shows how to implement webhook verification following the standard-webhooks signature scheme, which includes calculating HMAC.

Example 9-3. ECHO webhook implementation using manual request verification

```
# src/django/app/core/api/webhook/v2/views.py

...
class WebhookCustomView(View):
    def post(self, request):
        """
        Method echoes the request body
        """
        if len(request.body) > 20480:   ❶
            return JsonResponse({"errors": ["Payload is too big."]}, status=413)

        wh_id = request.headers.get("Webhook-Id")   ❶
```

```
    if not wh_id:
        err = "Missing Webhook-Id header."
        return JsonResponse({"errors": [err]}, status=400)

    wh_received_signature = request.headers.get("Webhook-Signature")   ❶
    if not wh_received_signature:
        err = "Missing Webhook-Signature header."
        return JsonResponse({"errors": [err]}, status=400)

    wh_timestamp = request.headers.get("Webhook-Timestamp")   ❶
    if not wh_timestamp:
        err = "Missing Webhook-Timestamp header."
        return JsonResponse({"errors": [err]}, status=400)

    timestamp = datetime.fromtimestamp(int(wh_timestamp), tz=timezone.utc)
    offset = (datetime.now(timezone.utc) - timestamp).total_seconds()
    wh_expired = (int(offset) >= 5)
    if wh_expired:   ❷
        return JsonResponse({"errors": ["Request is too old."]}, status=400)

    # Create standard-webhooks signature   ❸
    payload = request.body.decode("utf-8")
    secret = WEBHOOK_SECRET.encode("utf-8")
    sig_scheme = f"{wh_id}.{int(wh_timestamp)}.{payload}".encode("utf-8")
    signature = hmac.new(secret, msg=sig_scheme, digestmod="SHA256").digest()
    signature_b64 = base64.b64encode(signature).decode("utf-8")
    wh_expected_signature = f"v1,{signature_b64}"

    # Compare signatures
    if wh_received_signature != wh_expected_signature:   ❹
        return JsonResponse({"errors": ["HMAC mismatch."]}, status=401)
    ...
```

❶ These statements check whether the payload is within the 20 kB recommendation (*https://oreil.ly/SG6FZ*), and for the presence of Webhook-Id, Webhook-Signature, and Webhook-Timestamp headers required by the standard-webhooks specification. If the check fails, an appropriate HTTP response with a 413 (Content Too Large) or 400 (Bad Request) status code is returned.

❷ The incoming request is checked for expiration. If the request timestamp is older than five seconds, then it's considered expired, and the response with an HTTP 400 (Bad Request) status code is returned. Note that checking for an expiration date prevents a replay (repeat) attack (*https://oreil.ly/D2IuK*).

❸ This code block generates the request's signature according to the standard-webhooks specification (*https://oreil.ly/dPaGl*) signature scheme. The procedure involves the calculation of the HMAC from the signature scheme (sig_scheme) and secret. An important element of this procedure is sig_scheme, which consists of the webhook's ID, timestamp, and payload. The timestamp in a signature is used to prevent bypassing the expiration check, and the webhook ID is used to verify the identity of the webhook. The signature is then converted to a Base64 string (`signature_b64`), and concatenated with the version number reflected in `wh_expected_signature`.

❹ This check ensures that the message's payload is not tampered with by verifying that the received and expected signatures match. If signatures don't match, the response with the HTTP 401 (Unauthorized) status code is returned.

Webhooks Security

While writing this code, we made a few assumptions that impacted implementation. First, we treat the webhook endpoint as an internal one that is to be consumed within an organization. Because of that, we decided to expose detailed error messages. However, if the webhook was designed to be consumed publicly, we would not expose detailed error messages.

Second, to prevent the message from being tampered with, we're using a shared secret to sign and verify the message's payload. Sharing secrets might be a security risk if it's not handled properly.

Finally, we're using the timestamp to check the message's age. The timestamp prevents the message from being replayed in a replay (repeat) attack (*https://oreil.ly/H7K1i*). Our implementation calculates the timestamp after checking for the presence of the timestamp header. However, it should start at the moment of request handling.

Now we'll test service integration using both webhook implementations.

Example 9-4 simulates webhooks that are sent from the source to the destination service. Each implementation is chosen based on the command line's `--callback-url` argument. The command line provides a payload that is sent to the webhook's destination callback URL using the HTTP POST method. A successful test prints the response payload to the console, which is the acknowledgment received from the destination service.

> To see implementation details of the `app_event` CLI, look into the *src/django/app/core/management/commands/app_event.py* file.

Example 9-4. Webhook implementations testing

```
# Setup lab environment ❶
cd src/django
docker compose build --build-arg UID=$(id -u) --build-arg GID=$(id -g)
docker compose up --detach --wait

# Set environment variables ❷
EPOCH=$(date +%s)
PAYLOAD='{"type":"dummy.event", "timestamp":'$EPOCH', "data":{"echo":"test"}}'

# Execute v1 endpoint test ❸
docker compose exec app bash -c \
        "python manage.py app_event \
        --callback-url webhook/v1/echo \
        --payload '$PAYLOAD'"

POST webhook/v1/echo
{"type":"dummy.event","timestamp":1709111631,"data":{"echo":"test"}}

# Execute v2 endpoint test ❹
docker compose exec app bash -c \
        "python manage.py app_event \
        --callback-url webhook/v2/echo \
        --payload '$PAYLOAD'"

# Output:
POST webhook/v2/echo
{"type":"dummy.event","timestamp":1709111631,"data":{"echo":"test"}}
```

❶ Execute the lab setup instructions. Navigate to the lab's directory, build Docker images, and start containers.

❷ Set the EPOCH environment variable, which is the timestamp of the occurred event, measured in seconds of UTC time since the Unix epoch 1970-01-01T00:00:00Z. This timestamp is conceptually different from the timestamp of emitting the webhook. Create the PAYLOAD environment variable that uses EPOCH.

❸ Run the first test (*/webhook/v1/echo*), which uses the webhook implemented with the help of the standard-webhooks library.

❹ Run the second test (*/webhook/v2/echo*), which uses the webhook implemented manually following the standard-webhook specification.

Documentation

In Example 5-19, we introduced the OpenAPI specification (OAS). In this section, we'll continue with OAS but look at it from a webhooks perspective.

> OAS has a dedicated vocabulary that supports webhooks using the webhooks and `callbacks` fields.

Webhooks can be documented with OAS, starting from version 3.0, which added the `callbacks` field (*https://oreil.ly/NOXRq*). The `paths` field contains `callbacks`, which encapsulates OAS's path item object (*https://oreil.ly/Y4Fae*) that can be used to document the webhooks in-band registration process. The process requires the destination service to send an HTTP request to the source service, with the request containing the destination callback URL.

OAS version 3.1 added the `webhooks` field (*https://oreil.ly/JK5nE*), which can be used to describe events that trigger webhooks, in the case when webhooks are registered using an out-of-band method (e.g., by hard-coding the callback URL in the source code or by providing it through a web interface).

Our command-line tool (`app_event`), which acts as a source service used to emit webhooks, is not an API, so it does not support HTTP-based, in-band webhook registration. However, OAS can still be used to document its functionality.

Example 9-5 shows an OpenAPI document that describes our webhook.

Example 9-5. ECHO webhook v1 OpenAPI specification

```
# src/django/docs/api/webhook/v1-schema.yaml

openapi: 3.1.0 ❶
info:
  title: WFS CLI's webhooks
  description: Webhooks (events) triggered by WFS's CLI.
  version: v1
webhooks: ❷
  dummy.event: ❷
    post: ❷
      summary: Dummy event created in source service
      description: |
        Webhook initiated by the source service (API provider),
        and expected responses from the destination service (API consumer).

        **Warning:** Response from destination services other than 2XX
        status code is treated as failed webhook.
```

```
      parameters: ❸
        - $ref: '#/components/parameters/WebhookId'
        - $ref: '#/components/parameters/WebhookSignature'
        - $ref: '#/components/parameters/WebhookTimestamp'
      requestBody: ❹
        $ref: '#/components/requestBodies/Event'
      responses: ❺
        200:
          $ref: '#/components/responses/OK'
        400:
          $ref: '#/components/responses/BadRequest'
components:
  parameters: ❸
    WebhookId:
      name: Webhook-Id
      in: header
      required: true
      schema:
        type: string
    WebhookSignature:
      name: Webhook-Signature
      in: header
      required: true
      schema:
        type: string
    WebhookTimestamp:
      name: Webhook-Timestamp
      in: header
      required: true
      schema:
        type: string
  requestBodies: ❹
    Event:
      description: Event's JSON payload
      required: true
      content:
        application/json:
          schema:
            $ref: '#/components/schemas/Event'
          examples:
            dummy.event:
              value:
                type: dummy.event
                timestamp: 1709111631
                data:
                  echo: test
  responses: ❺
    OK:
      description: Webhook was accepted by the destination service
      content:
        application/json:
          schema:
```

```
          $ref: '#/components/schemas/Event' ❻
    BadRequest:
      description: Webhook rejected by the destination service
      content:
        application/json:
          schema:
            $ref: '#/components/schemas/Error'
  schemas: ❻
    Event:
      type: object
      properties:
        type:
          type: string
          description: The type of the event
        timestamp:
          type: string
          description: The timestamp of the event
        data:
          type: object
          description: The data associated with the event
    Error:
      type: object
      properties:
        errors:
          type: array
          description: The error message!
          items:
            type: string
```

❶ The openapi (required) field holds the version of OAS used for the API.

❷ The webhooks field lists the API provider's webhooks (each webhook has a unique name). In this case, it's only one webhook, which corresponds to dummy.event. This webhook describes an HTTP POST request (the post field) and expected responses from the destination service.

❸ The parameters field uses a reference ($ref.) to locate reusable headers: Webhook-Id, Webhook-Signature, and Webhook-Timestamp. The # (hash or pound) sign tells OAS to search for a component field (e.g., #/components/parameters/), starting at the root of the OpenAPI document.

❹ The requestBodies field describes the body of the request. In this case, it's a JSON object that contains type, timestamp, and data keys. The data key is an object type, and the other keys are string types.

❺ The responses field describes the webhook responses. In this case, it can return OK or BadRequest.

❻ The schemas field describes a payload that has type (string), timestamp (string), and data (object) fields.

Presented in Example 9-5, OAS allows developers to document their APIs using machine language formats like YAML or JSON. However, from the perspective of a person using an API, human readability of the specification is also important.

A tool like Swagger Editor (*https://editor-next.swagger.io*) lets you write and validate OAS online. What we like about Swagger Editor is the live preview of the OAS. To try it on your own, copy the specification from Example 9-5 and paste it into the editor. The outcome of this exercise should produce a result that looks like Figure 9-5.

> Be cautious when using online tools. While they are convenient, they may be unsafe. Online tools may not be suitable for handling sensitive data. Always consider using local alternatives first.

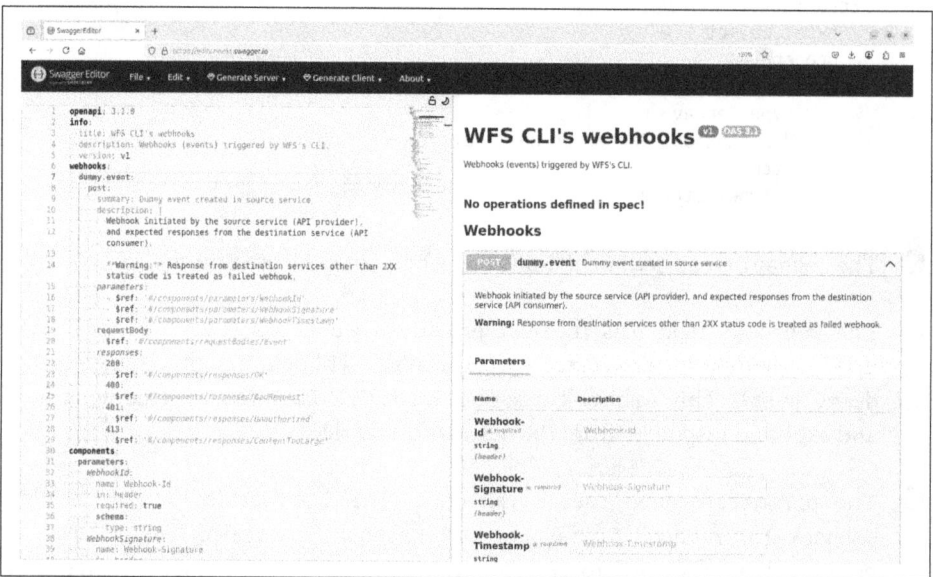

Figure 9-5. Online Swagger Editor

Trade-Offs

Webhooks are event-driven APIs in which the destination service that defines a callback receives a message, and the source service that registers the callback produces an event and sends the message to the destination. This section describes the advantages and disadvantages of webhooks.

Let's look at the advantages of webhooks:

Message acknowledgment

Contrary to broker-based APIs (Chapter 11) that allow sending messages without acknowledgment, in webhooks, the destination service acknowledges every message. Message acknowledgment strengthens service integration because failed messages may be resent. This feature makes webhooks more resilient to failures because when the destination service is down, delivery of the message will be attempted later.

No polling

In polling, a service sends periodical requests to get data; in other words, the service is actively polling for new data on a timely basis, increasing the amount of data transferred over the network and introducing delays between the occurrence of an event and the moment the destination service receives a notification about the event. In webhooks, messages are sent to the destination service (on an event basis) without the service polling them.

Event-driven

Sending the message is triggered by the occurrence of an event. This characteristic allows webhooks to send a message to the destination service instantly.

Asynchronous processing

Webhooks are sometimes described as inherently asynchronous. This interpretation originates from treating the initial HTTP POST performing the callback URL registration as the request, and the emitted webhooks as responses. This definition of webhooks asynchronicity does not apply in the case of out-of-bound configuration of the callback URL, since such configuration is not really a "request." Therefore, while being familiar with this interpretation of asynchronicity, consider following the definition of asynchronous communication from "Synchronous and Asynchronous Communication Types" on page 9.

Message broadcasting

Webhooks are point-to-point HTTP POST requests that operate in a *one-to-one* (one source and one destination) or *one-to-many* (one source and many destinations) configuration, whereas broker-based APIs mostly operate in a *many-to-many* configuration, having multiple sources (producers) and destinations (consumers). Implementing webhooks in a many-to-many configuration is possible, but such an arrangement would require extra work that would spill over to both source and destination services. In broker-based APIs, this work is handled by the broker.

Payload integrity

The message's payload may be tampered with, and the message may be sent from an untrusted source. To mitigate these risks, you can use HMAC with a shared secret to sign and verify the message's payload, and use the timestamp to check the message's age. Finally, you can use an IP address allowlist to limit the message only to the IP addresses of a trusted source.

On the other hand, the disadvantages of webhooks are as follows:

Versioning challenges

Services in webhooks are coupled by the message address and payload, and a change to either could break the webhook integration. If it's desirable to keep the callback URL unchanged, we can version webhooks by using two methods, HTTP headers or message body (see Table 2-6). In the following example, we're focusing on message body versioning.

For every existing event, the source service creates a separate message containing the old and new payload—for example, `{"version": "v1", "first_name": "John", "last_name": "Doe"}` for the old message, and `{"version": "v2", "full_name": "John Doe"}` for the new message. The advantage of this approach is that both versions are sent to the destination service, allowing it to choose the appropriate message and gradually migrate to the new message format. The disadvantage is that the destination service has to receive two messages for the same event, and the source service has to maintain two versions of the payload and send two requests.

Another approach is not to version the message payload but to add a new field to it—for example, adding `full_name` to the payload `{"first_name": "John", "last_name": "Doe"}`, so it becomes `{"first_name": "John", "last_name": "Doe", "full_name": "John Doe"}`, and send only the message with the new payload. When a new field is added, it's generally considered optional to consume. In this approach, both the new and the old fields are available in the message, and the destination service decides which one to use.

Often these two approaches are combined with a switch-over date communicated to the destination service in advance, indicating when the source service will stop sending the old payload. The time preceding the switch-over date is the time when a destination service must migrate to the new payload.

Lack of message-delivery guarantees

Webhooks are used in service-to-service integration, where each message is acknowledged. Suppose a message is not acknowledged because the destination service was down or the network had an issue. In that case, a failed message must be resent, which adds complexity to the source service because you need to add components for message storage, queuing, and scheduling, and the destination service needs to know how to handle potential duplicates.

Lack of standards

Although webhooks were introduced in 2007, they are still not standardized. The standard-webhooks project tried to create a consistent protocol by offering its specification and providing libraries for popular programming languages.

When to Use Webhooks

Webhooks are used for service-to-service integration, when one service needs to act upon events coming from an external service. For example, when a new order is created in an e-commerce service (like the bookstore described earlier), a webhook can be used to notify the warehouse service to start processing the order.

Another use case for webhooks is process automation. For example, a deployment pipeline is triggered when a new commit is pushed to the repository.

Additionally, webhooks are used for notifications, when one service needs to notify the other about events. For example, when you update the monitoring page of your services, a webhook can be used to notify users about the change.

Last but not least, webhooks are suitable for long-running asynchronous processes, when a service provides the status of the process progress—for example, when finishing archiving data, converting video, or synchronizing files between systems.

Exercises

1. In "Integration and Data Flow" on page 286, we described the webhook integration process. Now, it's your turn to implement it. You'll implement webhooks that come from GitHub (*https://github.com*). Fork this book's code repository and create a webhook that notifies the destination endpoint (*/webhook/v3/echo* callback) about any event that happens to the repository such as a push or repository description update. Hint: to solve this exercise, use the `ngrok` command-line program (*https://ngrok.com*) to expose the local server, which is the destination of the webhook accessible from the internet. The solution to this exercise can be found in this book's code repository (see the *src/django/docs/solutions/callbacks-exercise.md* file).

2. In the custom implementation of webhooks, we manually created the HMAC signature in Python. Now, the task is to implement the webhook's HMAC signature but as a shell script. Once you have the signature, compose a `curl` command that sends `POST` data to the */webhook/v1/echo* and */webhook/v2/echo* endpoints. The solution to this exercise can be found in this book's code repository (see the *src/django/docs/solutions/callbacks-exercise.md* file).

Summary

This chapter introduced you to webhooks, which enable services to exchange information through a callback-based process. In this process, the service that registers the callback (the source service) sends a message to the service that defines the callback (the destination service).

Webhooks are callbacks that use the HTTP `POST` method, and looking at them from the service perspective, they can be perceived as incoming or outgoing. They are commonly used in service-to-service integration, process automation, and notifying or logging.

Finishing this chapter gave you insights into webhooks' origins and their integration process. In the chapter's labs, you implemented webhooks following the standard-webhooks specification, used HMAC to provide message integrity and authenticity, and documented the webhook using OpenAPI.

Knowing the advantages and disadvantages of webhooks will help you determine whether they are a suitable solution for your challenges.

## CHAPTER 10

WebSocket

The APIs based on HTTP operate following the request-response model, where the client sends a request to the server and waits for the corresponding response. In HTTP, a server can't initiate a connection or send a response to a client without the client making a prior request. A server *can* "push" information to the client multiple times, using methods like server-side events (*https://oreil.ly/sDPnx*) or HTTP streaming (*https://oreil.ly/ETuMx*), but these methods still require an initial request from the client. Alternatively, a client can poll the server (send requests) for new information, using *short-polling* (a new TCP connection is established for each request) or *long-polling* (a single, long-lived TCP connection is reused for multiple requests).

The goal of WebSocket is to provide simultaneous bidirectional communication. In WebSocket, both the client and server can send messages to each other independently, without adhering to the request-response model. This is achieved by switching from HTTP to a custom, TCP-based protocol (WebSocket), which supports a full-duplex transmission mode.

When discussing WebSocket, asynchronous communication is often mentioned.[1] WebSocket is not inherently asynchronous.[2] Synchronous implementations of Web-Socket clients and servers exist,[3] but using WebSocket asynchronously has benefits like efficiently managing multiple connections and improving responsiveness.[4]

---

[1] See "Synchronous and Asynchronous Communication Types" on page 9 for more details about synchronous and asynchronous communication types.

[2] The WebSocket standard (*https://oreil.ly/VEGhC*) is agnostic to synchronicity.

[3] See, for example, the simple WebSocket server and client for Python (*https://oreil.ly/W3E1D*).

[4] Responsiveness means that the system responds in a timely manner. See the definition of *responsiveness* in "The Reactive Manifesto" (*https://www.reactivemanifesto.org*).

In this chapter, you'll be exposed to the WebSocket protocol, its opening handshake process, and how to implement the WebSocket API on both the backend and frontend. You'll expand our WFS with weather notification alerts, using WebSocket in a secure way. At the end of the chapter, you'll have the skills to document the WebSocket API and know its advantages and disadvantages.

WebSocket and WebSocket API

WebSocket is a communication protocol that was created to allow for bidirectional communication without relying on methods that involve sending multiple HTTP requests such as XMLHttpRequest (*https://oreil.ly/OePtl*) or long polling (*https://oreil.ly/JYxQX*).[5] The WebSocket protocol was standardized by RFC 6455 (*https://oreil.ly/PSNLg*) in 2011 and offers a bidirectional communication channel over a single long-lived TCP connection.

Figure 10-1 shows the difference between the data flow of messages between client and server when using HTTP and WebSocket protocols. In HTTP/1, messages flow in one direction from sender to receiver (from client to server, and vice versa) at a time. Meanwhile, in WebSocket, messages can flow in both directions between the client and the server simultaneously.

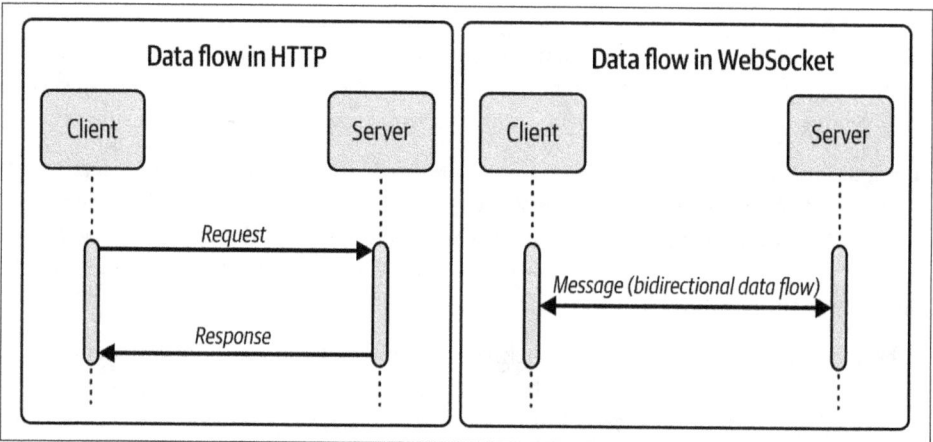

Figure 10-1. Comparison of HTTP and WebSocket data flow

It's worth mentioning that while HTTP is used for the initial opening handshake, the WebSocket protocol does not use HTTP afterward. Moreover, the design of the WebSocket protocol also allows for non-HTTP handshakes.

---

5 To learn more about applications of WebSocket, we recommend reading *The WebSocket Handbook* (*https://oreil.ly/4o8tV*) by Alex Diaconu.

To use the WebSocket protocol in a web browser, the web browser implements Web-Socket API according to the WebSocket Web interface description language (*Web-Sockets Web IDL*) (*https://oreil.ly/a5quQ*).[6]

WebSocket Opening Handshake

To establish bidirectional communication between the client and the server with the WebSocket protocol, the client and the server undergo a three-step protocol altera-tion process (*https://oreil.ly/611PH*), known as the WebSocket opening handshake illustrated in Figure 10-2.

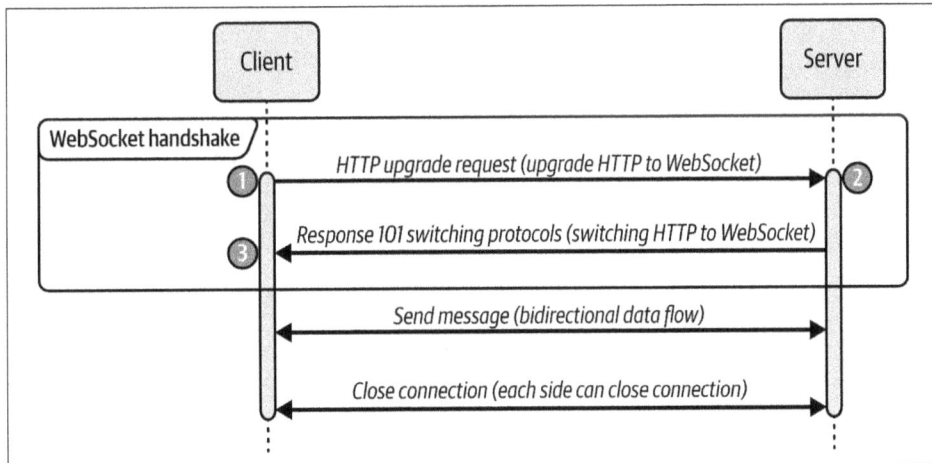

Figure 10-2. WebSocket connection overview

The opening handshake proceeds as follows:

1. The client sends an HTTP GET request containing the Upgrade, Connection, and Sec-WebSocket-Key headers.

2. The server receives the client's request and returns an HTTP response containing the Upgrade, Connection, and Sec-WebSocket-Accept headers, with status code 101 (Switching Protocols) indicating that it's ready to switch the underlying HTTP connection to WebSocket.

3. The client receives the server's response and switches to a WebSocket connection from the HTTP connection.

---

6 The *Web IDL* (*https://oreil.ly/0qz3P*) is an interface description language that emerged to address the interop-erability of web programming interfaces. It allows the expression of web APIs with JavaScript-compatible constructs. Example 10-4 shows the WebSocket Web IDL API implemented in the browser.

After a successful opening handshake, both the client and the server will be able to send WebSocket data frames.

To understand the aforementioned WebSocket handshake process, let's see it in action. For this purpose, you'll need to set up the lab according to the instructions listed in Example 10-1.

> In this chapter, when working in GitHub Codespaces, you need to change the visibility of WebSocket server port 8001 to Public, and disable TLS by setting the TLS_ENABLE variable to 0 (*src/django/compose.yaml*). TLS in GitHub Codespaces comes out of the box.

Example 10-1. WebSocket lab setup

```
cd src/django ❶
docker compose build --build-arg UID=$(id -u) --build-arg GID=$(id -g) ❷
docker compose up --detach --wait ❸
```

❶ Navigate to the lab's directory.

❷ Build Docker images.

❸ Start Docker containers.

After executing these instructions, follow the next steps to see the WebSocket opening handshake in action:

1. Open a new tab in a web browser.
2. Open the web browser's developer tools (use the keyboard shortcut Ctrl+Shift+I on Windows/Linux, or Option+Cmd+I on macOS), and click the Network tab.
3. Visit *http://localhost:8000/websocket/echo*.[7] Executing these steps should present a page that looks like the one illustrated in Figure 10-3.

---

7 When working with GitHub Codespaces, you'll use a unique URL containing the Codespace's name instead of the *localhost* URL. The expected URL is bound to port 8000 and can be found in VS Code's PORTS tab.

Name	Scheme
🔲 echo	http
🔳 echo.js	http
⟷ echo	ws
☐ echo	http

▼ General

Request URL: ws://localhost:8001/ws/v1/echo
Request Method: GET
Status Code: ● 101 Switching Protocols

▼ Response Headers ☐ Raw

Connection:	Upgrade
Date:	Thu, 06 Mar 2025 10:22:54
Sec-Websocket-Accept:	bKccWvWtA1+Gt1AOMs6LQU
Server:	uvicorn
Upgrade:	websocket

▼ Request Headers ☐ Raw

Cache-Control:	no-cache
Connection:	Upgrade
Host:	localhost:8001
Origin:	http://localhost:8000
Pragma:	no-cache
Sec-Websocket-Key:	iWLHxqNHUFhbA63N/7+fAw=:
Sec-Websocket-Version:	13
Upgrade:	websocket

⋮ Console Issues
```
Connected to ws://localhost:8001/ws/v1/echo
Sent 'Hello WebSocket!' message
Received 'Hello WebSocket!' message
Closed connection to ws://localhost:8001/ws/v1/echo
```

Figure 10-3. WebSocket opening handshake inspected using a web browser

Figure 10-3 shows the ECHO WebSocket Application (EWA). We confirm that the application is working by seeing the Hello WebSocket! message displayed in the main browser window. The headers listed in the Response Headers and Request Headers sections describe the server and the client headers used in the opening handshake. The client's log is presented in the web browser's console, and shows the sequence of steps that goes like this:

1. A client tries to establish a WebSocket connection to the *ws://localhost: 8001/ws/v1/echo* endpoint. The client sends the HTTP request with headers appropriate to the client's opening handshake.

2. The server receives and validates the client's request. It then returns an HTTP response with status code 101 (Switching Protocols) and with headers appropriate to the server's opening handshake. The response's 101 (Switching Protocols) status code tells the client to switch the connection from HTTP to WebSocket.

3. The client receives the server's response and switches the connection to WebSocket.

    a. Next, the client sends to the server a text data frame containing the JSON-encoded "Hello WebSocket!" message.

    b. The server receives the text data frame and sends (echoes) it back to the client.

    c. Upon receiving the text data frame, the client prints the message to the console and closes the WebSocket connection.

The term *message* is associated with the OSI or TCP/IP model application layer data. A message in the WebSocket protocol is called a *data frame* (not to be confused with *Ethernet frame*), and such a frame can carry text or binary data.

After understanding EWA's flow, let's have a detailed look at the WebSocket opening handshake's headers illustrated in Figure 10-3.

Example 10-2 shows mandatory HTTP headers, which compose the client's handshake. The server needs to understand HTTP because the server will use its headers to validate the client, and switch the protocol from HTTP to WebSocket.

EWA uses a JavaScript client (Django's generated website), which automatically sends a request to the server upon loading. Example 10-2 and Example 10-3 were trimmed for brevity and consist of only mandatory headers, so don't be surprised if you see more headers when inspecting them in the browser.

Example 10-2. WebSocket opening handshake (client's request)

```
GET /ws/v1/echo HTTP/1.1                         ❶
Origin: http://localhost:8000                    ❷
Host: localhost:8001                             ❸
Connection: keep-alive, Upgrade                  ❹
Upgrade: websocket                               ❺
Sec-WebSocket-Key: zLsL2bD4QARLOTXv0vI1Ig==      ❻
Sec-WebSocket-Version: 13                        ❼
```

❶ The client sends an HTTP GET request to the */ws/v1/echo* server endpoint.

❷ The Origin header assigns an identity to the client. The client is identified by request scheme, hostname, and port number.

❸ The Host header identifies the location of the WebSocket server, its hostname, and port number.

❹ The Connection header with a keep-alive directive indicates that the client wants to reuse the TCP connection established during the initial HTTP request and keep it open, allowing subsequent messages to propagate. The Upgrade directive tells the server that the client wants to switch the existing protocol to the protocol controlled by the Upgrade header.

❺ The Upgrade header tells the server that the client wants to switch the application protocol to websocket.

❻ The `Sec-WebSocket-Key` header (*https://oreil.ly/YW5W5*) is sent by the client and used by the server to validate the handshake. The value of the header is a random Base64-encoded 16-byte value.

❼ The `Sec-WebSocket-Version` header version (*https://oreil.ly/taO5a*) must be set to 13. If the server doesn't support this version of the WebSocket protocol, then the connection will not be established.

> Notice that port 8001 in the `Host` header (the server) differs from port 8000 in the `Origin` header (the client). The reason is that in our setup, the server handles all WebSocket requests with the Starlette framework (*https://oreil.ly/T0BkU*) on port 8001, whereas the Django server application (*https://www.djangoproject.com*) running on port 8000 sends a request to the WebSocket server. In other words, we have two applications run by two different processes, where each application is bound to a specific port due to the technological stack and how it is deployed. However, if a server supported handling the relevant protocols (HTTP, TCP, and WebSocket) on the same port, then this setup would not be required.

Once the server validates the headers in the client's request, it responds with status code 101 (Switching Protocols) and the expected headers. WebSocket-related headers in the server's handshake response are listed in Example 10-3.

Example 10-3. WebSocket opening handshake (server's response)

```
HTTP/1.1 101 Switching Protocols          ❶
Upgrade: websocket                        ❷
Connection: Upgrade                       ❸
Sec-WebSocket-Accept: +KhiFov/sM2iO0A+xSQebkTa+0E=  ❹
```

❶ The server informs the client that it's ready to switch protocols by sending an HTTP response with the 101 (Switching Protocols) status code.

❷ The `Upgrade` header indicates that the protocol will be switched to `websocket`.

❸ The `Connection` header indicates that the server will switch to the protocol specified by the `Upgrade` header.

❹ The `Sec-WebSocket-Accept` header (*https://oreil.ly/5f8wY*) indicates that the server accepted the connection. The generated hash nonce is created from the client's `Sec-WebSocket-Key`.

After a successful handshake, the WebSocket connection is established, allowing the client and the server to transfer data in both directions.

Implementation

The WebSocket API requires two components: the client and the server. Figure 10-3 presented a WebSocket opening handshake and the flow of a single WebSocket data frame exchange between the client and the server. In this section, we'll go through the implementation of WebSocket APIs for the EWA's client and server.

WebSocket ECHO Client and Server

Having explained the WebSocket protocol and its opening handshake, we can implement the WebSocket API for the client and the server. Example 10-4 shows an implementation of the WebSocket API by a JavaScript client.

Example 10-4. EWA's client implementation

```
// src/django/app/core/www/static/app/js/echo.js

...
const socket = new WebSocket('ws://localhost:8001/ws/v1/echo'); ❶

socket.onopen = function(e) { ❷
  console.info(`Connected to ${socket.url}`);
  const msg = {'message': 'Hello WebSocket!'};
  socket.send(JSON.stringify(msg));
  console.info(`Sent '${msg.message}' message to ${socket.url}`);
}

socket.onmessage = function(e) { ❸
  const message = JSON.parse(e.data).message;
  document.querySelector('h1').innerText = message;
  console.info(`Received '${message}' message from ${socket.url}`);
  socket.close();
}

socket.onclose = function(e) { ❹
  console.info(`Closed connection to ${socket.url}`);
}

socket.onerror = function(e) { ❺
  console.error(`Encountered an error when talking to ${socket.url}`);
};
...
```

❶ The WebSocket client tries to establish a new WebSocket connection to the server. This line initiates the WebSocket opening handshake.

❷ The `onopen()` function is triggered when a successful WebSocket connection is established. The client sends a JSON-encoded message to the server and then logs the message to the console.

❸ The `onmessage()` function is triggered when the client receives a message from the server. Here, the client does four things: reads the message, updates the web page's `h1` tag, logs the message to the console, and closes the WebSocket connection. Normally, the client wouldn't close the connection after receiving a message; we do it only for demonstration purposes.

❹ The `onclose()` function is triggered when detecting that the WebSocket connection was closed. The client logs information that the connection was closed.

❺ The `onerror()` function logs an error message when it detects an error event during an already-established connection.

> Printing logs to the client's console might expose unnecessary information or impact application performance. We do it only to demonstrate the program flow. In the production environment, you'd log into a log aggregator service instead of a console.

Example 10-5 shows the EWA's server implementation.

Example 10-5. EWA's server implementation

```
# src/django/app/core/api/websocket/v1/endpoints.py

from starlette.endpoints import WebSocketEndpoint

...
class EchoEndpoint(WebSocketEndpoint):   ❶
    encoding = "json"

    async def on_connect(self, websocket):   ❷
        await websocket.accept()

    async def on_receive(self, websocket, data):   ❸
        await websocket.send_json(data)
```

❶ The `EchoEndpoint` class handles incoming WebSocket connections. It inherits from Starlette's `WebSocketEndpoint` (*https://oreil.ly/JwqFN*) that offers three overridable methods for handling WebSocket connections: `on_connect()`, `on_receive()`, and `on_disconnect()`. Our endpoint uses only `on_connect()` and `on_receive()`. The `encoding` attribute validates data as JSON in `on_receive()`.

➋ The on_connect() method is triggered when the client establishes a connection to the WebSocket endpoint. Here, the client connection is accepted, but it could also be rejected if needed.

➌ The on_receive() method is triggered when the client sends a data frame (message) to the server. The ECHO server responds to the client with the exact data it received (it echoes the data back).

WebSocket Protocol

In this section, we'll discuss an example of a WebSocket wire protocol communication and inspect its data frames. By inspecting communication EWA packets, you'll be able to reverse-engineer the application flow as described in "WebSocket Opening Handshake" on page 305. We'll analyze communication traffic using the Wireshark tool (*https://www.wireshark.org*) (network protocol analyzer).

Let's inspect the WebSocket traffic captured when visiting *http://localhost:8000/websocket/echo*. The traffic packet capture, stored in *src/django/docs/assets/websocket-echo-unencrypted.pcap* file, is loaded into Wireshark as shown in Figure 10-4.

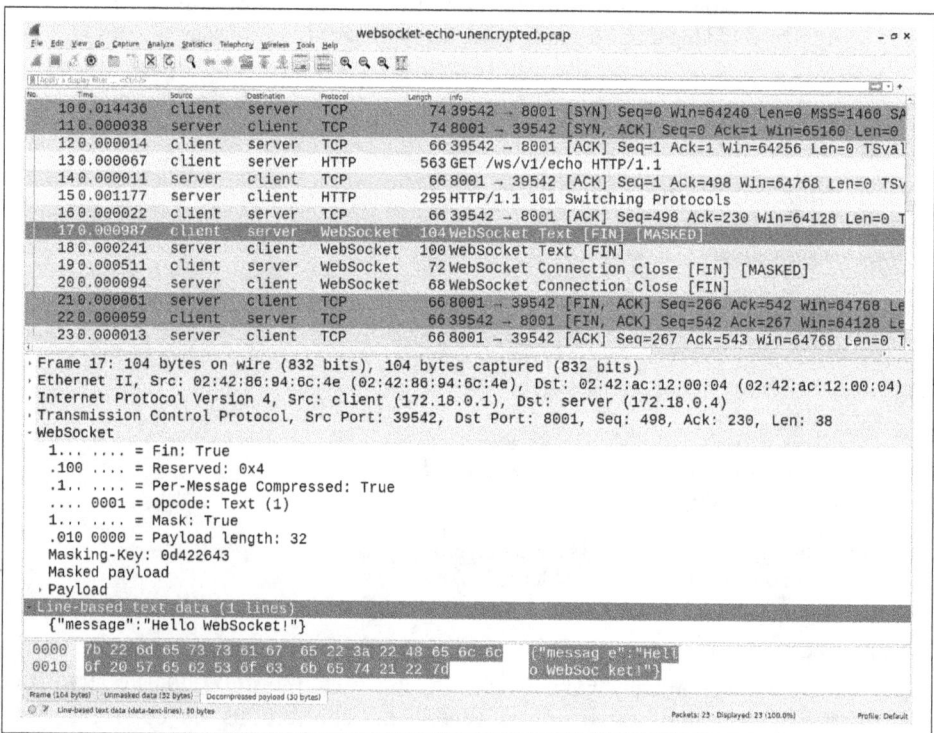

Figure 10-4. EWA's unencrypted WebSocket traffic

- Frame 10 to 12—The client establishes a TCP connection with the server by following a TCP three-way handshake.

- Frame 13—The client initiates the WebSocket opening handshake with the HTTP GET request.

- Frame 15—The server responds to the opening handshake, indicating that it's ready to switch the protocol to WebSocket (101 status code).

- Frame 17—After establishing a WebSocket connection with the server, the client sends a text data frame that contains a JSON-encoded payload with a "Hello WebSocket!" message, using WebSocket protocol. The WebSocket Final Fragment Indicator (FIN) flag (set to 1) tells the server that there will be no more data frames to follow, indicating that the message is contained in a single frame.

- Frame 18—The server echoes the payload that it receives, which can be seen in the bottom half of Figure 10-4.

- Frame 19—The client sends a close frame to terminate the WebSocket connection (closing handshake). This is done by setting the Opcode close frame to Connection Close.

- Frame 20—The server acknowledges the intent and responds with a close frame.

- Frames 21 to 23—The server and the client close the underlying TCP connection.

Having understood the WebSocket protocol, its opening and closing handshakes, and the network packets exchanged between the client and the server, we'll proceed to implement a more advanced WebSocket example.

WebSocket Weather Alert Server

In this section, you'll expand our WFS by adding weather alerts. The program that you'll implement will allow clients to obtain weather alerts for a given city identified by the city's UUID. The city's UUID will be used to identify the city to which the alert messages will be sent after triggering an alert from the CLI. All WebSocket clients connected to the API will receive the alerts.

Figure 10-5 shows the alerting system you'll build, and the message flow between its components.

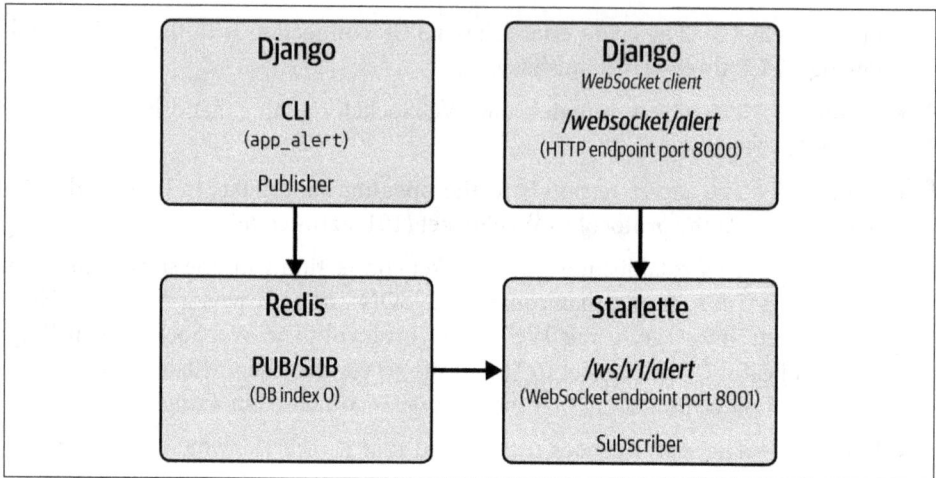

Figure 10-5. Overview and message flow in the WFS's alerting system

Because the WFS runs as two applications (independent processes)—the Django application (WebSocket client) that runs on port 8000, and the Starlette application (WebSocket server) that runs on port 8001—you'll need to find a way of passing messages from the former to the latter. For that, we've chosen to implement the pub/sub messaging pattern, which fits this use case (see "Publish-Subscribe Pattern" on page 342 for more details on pub/sub). The pub/sub pattern will allow you to send data from Django to the Starlette application.

You'll implement pub/sub with Redis, an in-memory key-value database that offers a lightweight implementation of pub/sub message delivery. You'll also implement Django's app_alert CLI, which will create an alert message and publish it to the pub/sub. Next, the Starlette application will subscribe to the pub/sub, consume any messages that arrive on it, and send them as alerts to all connected WebSocket clients.

Before discussing the implementation of alerting, let's try out our system by issuing an alert message. The steps listed in Example 10-6 show how to send an alert. The instructions assume that you are located in the lab's directory as specified in Example 10-1.

Example 10-6. WFS alert sent using CLI (requires setup from Example 10-1)

```
# Get city's UUID ❶
CITY_UUID=$(docker compose exec app python manage.py app_cities | \
  head -n 1 | \
  cut -d' ' -f 2)

# Issue an alert message ❷
docker compose exec app python manage.py app_alert --city-uuid=$CITY_UUID
```

```
# Output:
Alert 'Hail storm is coming!' sent to 'd86962f4-fb28-4b98-bbeb-c9fbec0d0fca' channel.
```

❶ Get the UUID of the first city (CITY_UUID), which is used as a Redis pub/sub channel.

❷ Send the default alert message ("Hail storm is coming!") to all clients listening on the --city-uuid Redis pub/sub channel.

Figure 10-6 illustrates the flow of alert messages pushed from the WebSocket server to the client. The bottom part of the image shows a terminal in which a user executes the app_alert command from Example 10-6. The top part of the image shows the web browser, receiving a default alert message. Notice the order of console log messages (in the middle part of the image), which indicates that the connection to the WebSocket endpoint was established, and that a message was received. Knowing the flow of the alert message, we'll proceed to the implementation of WebSocket server.

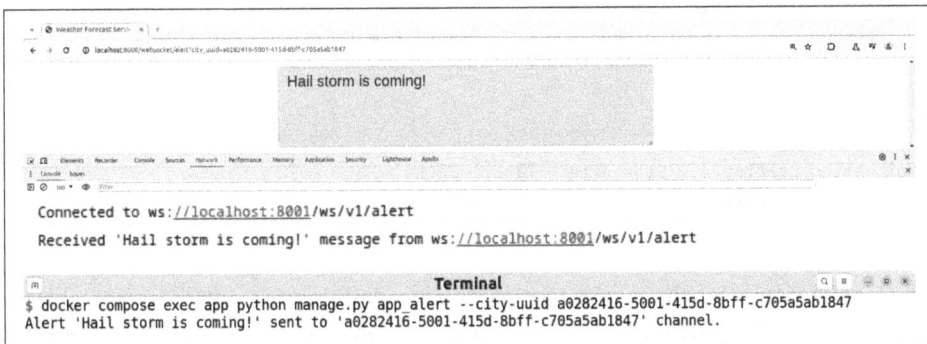

Figure 10-6. WFS alert end-to-end testing

We start by choosing technology that will allow us to implement a WebSocket server. For this purpose, we choose the Starlette framework (*https://www.starlette.io*), which supports the WebSocket API (*https://oreil.ly/82kVk*) and can process requests asynchronously due to Asynchronous Server Gateway Interface (ASGI) (*https://oreil.ly/USGcA*).

Example 10-7 shows the configuration of the Starlette's application.

> The Asynchronous Server Gateway Interface allows Python web servers to process requests asynchronously.

Example 10-7. Starlette configuration

```python
# src/django/app/config/asgi.py

...
from starlette.applications import Starlette
from starlette.middleware import Middleware
from starlette.middleware.authentication import AuthenticationMiddleware
from core.helpers.middleware import WebSocketOriginValidatorMiddleware
from core.helpers.middleware import WebSocketTrustedHostMiddleware
...
from config.constants import APP_STARLETTE_AUTHENTICATE_ENDPOINTS
from config.urls import routes
from core.helpers.auth import auth_error
from core.helpers.auth import StarletteJWTAuthBackend
...

middleware = [   ❶
  Middleware(WebSocketOriginValidatorMiddleware, allow_origins=["localhost:8000"]),
  Middleware(WebSocketTrustedHostMiddleware, allowed_hosts=["localhost:8001"]),
  Middleware(AuthenticationMiddleware,
    backend=StarletteJWTAuthBackend(APP_STARLETTE_AUTHENTICATE_ENDPOINTS),
    on_error=auth_error
  ),
]

application_starlette = Starlette(   ❷
  debug=True, routes=routes, middleware=middleware
)
```

❶ Configuration of the application starts with defining three Middleware objects: WebSocketOriginValidatorMiddleware, WebSocketTrustedHostMiddleware, and AuthenticationMiddleware, which is extended by the custom StarletteJWTAuthBackend for authenticating the clients. StarletteJWTAuth Backend is explained in Example 10-11.

Middleware is a class whose behavior is applied across the application request-response cycle. Before the request arrives at the specific function within the application, it goes through the stack of middleware in the order specified by the application. After the application generates the response, it goes through the middleware stack in reverse order. The allow_origins list includes the client origins permitted to connect to the server, and the allowed_hosts list specifies the allowed server hosts.

❷ The application_starlette variable is created from the Starlette object, where we pass the middleware list along with WebSocket routes defined in Example 10-8.

Now that the Starlette server application is in place, the next step is to define two endpoints. The first endpoint exposed by the Django server application is used by the browser to fetch a web page. The second endpoint exposed by Starlette is used by the browser's JavaScript code on the web page to establish a WebSocket connection to receive alerts. This is shown in Example 10-8.

Example 10-8. WebSocket endpoints

```
# src/django/app/config/urls.py

...
from rest_framework_simplejwt.views import TokenObtainPairView
from starlette.routing import WebSocketRoute
from core.api.websocket.v1.endpoints import AlertEndpoint
from core.www import ws_alert_view
...

urlpatterns = [  ❶
    ...
    path("websocket/alert", ws_alert_view),
    path("api/jwt/obtain", TokenObtainPairView.as_view()),
    ...
]
routes = [  ❷
    WebSocketRoute("/ws/v1/alert", AlertEndpoint),
    ...
]
```

❶ The `urlpatterns` list contains WFS application endpoints. The */websocket/alert* endpoint is a Django view that renders the WebSocket client (HTML page). The client obtains a JWT and establishes and handles the WebSocket connection with the WebSocket server. The */api/jwt/obtain* endpoint allows you to get JWT (access token) implemented by Simple JWT (*https://oreil.ly/rDMcm*), a package designed to work with DRF (see Example 5-17).

❷ The `WebSocketRoute` object defines the */ws/v1/alert* endpoint, which is handled by the `AlertEndpoint` class that implements WebSocket API server logic.

Let's look into the AlertEndpoint class that handles the */ws/v1/alert* route shown in Example 10-9 and explain its implementation details.

Example 10-9. WebSocket alert server

```
# src/django/app/core/api/websocket/v1/endpoints.py

import asyncio

from asgiref.sync import sync_to_async
from redis import asyncio as redisasyncio
from starlette.endpoints import WebSocketEndpoint

from core.helpers.utils import to_bytes
from core.helpers.utils import to_str
from core.models import CityRepository

class AlertEndpoint(WebSocketEndpoint):          ❶
    clients = dict()
    encoding = "json"
    lock = asyncio.Lock()
    pubsub = redisasyncio.Redis(host="redis", port=6379, db=0).pubsub()   ❷

    async def on_connect(self, websocket):         ❸
        await websocket.accept()
        city_uuid = websocket.query_params.get("city_uuid")
        if not city_uuid:
            reason = "Query parameter city_uuid is missing or is invalid."
            return await websocket.close(code=1008, reason=reason)    ❹

        city = await sync_to_async(CityRepository.get_by_id)(city_uuid)
        if not city:
            reason = f"City with {city_uuid} doesn't exist."
            return await websocket.close(code=1008, reason=reason)    ❹

        await self.pubsub.subscribe(city_uuid)      ❻

        if city_uuid not in self.clients:          ❼
            self.clients[city_uuid] = set()
        self.clients[city_uuid].add(websocket)

        asyncio.create_task(
            self.__msg_watch_and_broadcast(websocket, city_uuid)    ❽
        )

    async def on_disconnect(self, websocket, close_code):      ❺
        city_uuid = websocket.query_params.get("city_uuid")
        clients = self.clients.get(city_uuid)
        if city_uuid and clients:
            for client in clients.copy():
                if websocket == client:
```

```
                     self.clients[city_uuid].remove(client)

    async def __msg_watch_and_broadcast(self, websocket, city_uuid):  ❽
        while to_bytes(str(city_uuid)) in self.pubsub.channels:
            async with self.lock:
                message = await self.pubsub.get_message(
                    ignore_subscribe_messages=False
                )
                msg = message and message["type"] == "message"
                msg_matches_channel = (
                    message and to_str(message["channel"]) == city_uuid
                )
                if msg and msg_matches_channel:
                    data = {"message": to_str(message["data"])}
                    await self.__broadcast(data, city_uuid)  ❾
            await asyncio.sleep(1)

    async def __broadcast(self, city_uuid, data):  ❾
        for client in self.clients.get(city_uuid).copy():
            try:
                await client.send_json(data)
            except Exception as e:
                print(f"Failed to send message due to {e}")
```

Originally, Redis was an in-memory key-value database. With time, it extended its offerings to be a cache, a key-value NoSQL database, and now it supports more features, such as vector search, transactions, and pub/sub messaging.

❶ A WebSocket message (data frame) goes through the /ws/v1/alert route that is handled by the AlertEndpoint class, which inherits from the WebSocketEndpoint Starlette's class.

❷ The pubsub class attribute is a Redis pub/sub object (https://oreil.ly/tS1K9) that is used to consume messages being published to it.

❸ The on_connect() method is called when the client establishes a connection to the WebSocket endpoint. The method accepts a WebSocket connection and reads the city's UUID from the query parameter.

❹ If the city's UUID is absent or the city doesn't exist, the connection is closed with the WebSocket status code 1008 (Policy Violation), triggering a close event.[8]

---

8 See RFC 6455 for WebSocket status codes (https://oreil.ly/eJFCp).

❺ The on_disconnect() method is called whenever detecting a WebSocket connection close event. The method attempts to delete the connected WebSocket client by removing it from the class's clients attribute.

❻ If the city's UUID is provided, and the city exists in our database, then we are using the pubsub object to subscribe and listen for messages. The city's UUID is used to create a Redis pub/sub channel to which the WebSocket client subscribes.[9]

❼ The code block creates a Python dictionary that will hold all WebSocket clients associated with a city.

❽ The private method __msg_watch_and_broadcast() is listening for new messages from the pub/sub messaging channel. The pub/sub messaging pattern is described in detail in "Publish-Subscribe Pattern" on page 342. If a message is of message type, and its channel property matches the city's UUID, then the message is broadcast to all connected WebSocket clients. The self.pubsub.get_message() method continuously listens for messages arriving at the channel because it runs inside the nonblocking loop at a one-second interval. The method runs in an asynchronous task handled by the *asyncio* Python library (*https://oreil.ly/2HPNj*). asyncio.Lock prevents race conditions during the processing of messages from the Redis pub/sub channel.

❾ The private __broadcast() method sends an alert message to all connected WebSocket clients.

Having implemented an alert endpoint, we can proceed with the implementation of the alert command-line program. The alert program is Django CLI, which publishes an alert message to the Redis pub/sub. Example 10-10 shows how to publish a message to the Redis pub/sub.

Example 10-10. Application alert command-line program

```
# src/django/app/core/management/commands/app_alert.py

from asgiref.sync import async_to_sync
from django.core.management.base import BaseCommand
from redis import asyncio
from core.models import CityRepository
...
```

---

9 The Redis channel is used by subscribers to receive messages; see the pub/sub messaging pattern (*https://oreil.ly/411ub*).

```
class Command(BaseCommand):
    city = CityRepository.get_first()
    ...
    redis = asyncio.Redis(host="redis", port=6379, db=0)  ❶

    def add_arguments(self, parser):  ❷
        parser.add_argument("--city-uuid", default=f"{self.city.uuid}", ...)
        parser.add_argument("--message", default="Hail storm is coming!", ...)

    @async_to_sync
    async def handle(self, *args, **options):
        city_uuid = options["city_uuid"]
        message = options["message"]
        ...
        await self.redis.publish(city_uuid, message)  ❸
        await self.redis.close()

        return f"Alert '{message}' sent to '{city_uuid}' channel."
```

❶ The redis class attribute holds an instance of asyncio's Redis, which connects to the Redis database at index 0. The same index is used by the server in Example 10-9.

❷ The add_arguments() method contains two arguments: --city-uuid and --message. Each argument has a default value assigned. An example usage of the --city-uuid flag passed to the app_event CLI is shown in Example 10-6.

❸ The publish() method publishes an alert message to the Redis pub/sub channel identified by the city's UUID.

WebSocket Weather Alert Client

Implemented in Example 10-9 and Example 10-10 is all the backend code for the WebSocket server API. What is missing is the WebSocket client API implementation, which can be found in the *src/django/app/core/www/static/app/js/alert-ws.js* file. We won't describe the client here because it stretches over 100 lines of code and would be difficult to explain in a printed version. Nevertheless, we encourage you to look into the file because it contains an implementation of the back-off algorithm to reconnect the client when a connection is lost. However, what we'll do in this section is explain the WebSocket client API program flow:

1. The program starts with the client obtaining an access token (JWT) for a default application user. The token is obtained from the */api/jwt/obtain* endpoint.

2. The access_token and city_uuid are passed as query parameters to the */ws/v1/ alert* endpoint. The access_token is used to authenticate the user, and the

city_uuid to subscribe to the Redis pub/sub channel. If you wondered why we don't pass the access token as a header, the reason is that the WebSocket API doesn't allow passing headers.[10]

3. After establishing a WebSocket connection, the client starts waiting for alert messages. If an alert message arrives, it is displayed to the user.

4. If the program detects that the connection was terminated unexpectedly (by checking the WebSocket connection close status code in the onclose() function), then it attempts to reconnect by calling the webSocketReconnect() function.

Security

In this section, we'll cover several methods for improving WebSocket security. While these methods are discussed in the context of WebSocket, they are also applicable to most HTTP-based APIs:

Origin validation
> The WebSocket specification defines the use of the client's Origin header as a security measure, allowing the server to decide whether to accept or reject the opening handshake request.

Trusted host security
> This method limits clients' requests to those destined only to a trusted host.

Token-based authentication with JWTs
> Tokens, particularly JWTs, provide a stateless way to authenticate and authorize clients. In the WebSocket context, these tokens can be passed during the handshake as part of the query string and validated by server.

Transport Layer Security (TLS)
> TLS provides encryption confidentiality, integrity, and authenticity to the application data exchanged over the network. For WebSocket, this means using wss:// instead of ws:// to ensure secure communication.

Origin Validation

The security model described in the WebSocket specification is origin-based, similar to *same-origin policy* (SOP) (*https://oreil.ly/YEqyt*). However, the validation is performed by the server. This helps prevent unauthorized resource access across different origins. In the origin validation model, a client can communicate with the server

---

10 More info on implementing WebSocket clients can be found in the MDN WebSockets documentation (*https://oreil.ly/p6ToW*).

only if it shares the same origin (that is, scheme, hostname, and port). The server inspects the origin by checking the `Origin` header in the client's opening handshake HTTP request. Our implementation enforces this by adding `WebSocketOriginValidatorMiddleware`, as seen in Example 10-7.

Trusted Host Security

Another security measure (similar to the origin validation model) that can be used with WebSocket is to check clients' opening handshake HTTP request for the host header as implemented in the `WebSocketTrustedHostMiddleware` listed in Example 10-7. As the name indicates, only client's requests that contain the host header value included in the server's trusted hosts list are accepted by the server. By restricting server hosts to hostname or IP addresses in `allowed_hosts`, we reduce the risk of HTTP host header attack.

JSON Web Token

Implementation of JWT has been described in detail in "JSON Web Token" on page 183. In this section, we'll implement server-side validation of JWT obtained from the WebSocket initial handshake.

The middleware responsible for request authentication in the WebSocket connection is `AuthenticationMiddleware` from Example 10-7. The middleware is extended by the custom `StarletteJWTAuthBackend`, which is responsible for validating JWT and providing user identity. The details of the authentication mechanism are described in Example 10-11.

Example 10-11. Starlette application authentication backend

```
# src/django/app/core/helpers/auth/permissions.py

from starlette.authentication import AuthenticationBackend
...

class StarletteJWTAuthBackend(AuthenticationBackend):    ❶

    def __init__(self, authenticate_endpoints):
        self.authenticate_endpoints = authenticate_endpoints

    async def authenticate(self, conn):
        if conn.scope["path"] not in self.authenticate_endpoints:    ❷
            return

        access_token_b64 = conn.query_params.get("access_token")
        if not access_token_b64:    ❸
            raise AuthenticationError("Query parameter missing `access_token`.")
```

```
try:  ❹
    jwt_token = base64.b64decode(access_token_b64).decode("ascii")
    payload = jwt.decode(
        jwt_token,
        SECRET_KEY,
        algorithms=["HS256"],
        options={"verify_signature": True}
    )
except jwt.ExpiredSignatureError:
    raise AuthenticationError("Provided `access_token` has expired.")
except (Exception, json.JSONDecodeError):
    msg = "Provided `access_token` is not base64 or JSON encoded."
    raise AuthenticationError(msg)

token_expired = datetime.now() >= datetime.fromtimestamp(payload["exp"])
if token_expired:  ❺
    raise AuthenticationError("Provided `access_token` has expired.")

query_set = await sync_to_async(User.objects.filter)(pk=payload["id"])
user = await sync_to_async(query_set.first)()
if not user:  ❻
    raise AuthenticationError("User not found.")

return AuthCredentials(scopes=["authenticated"]), user  ❼
```

❶ The `StarletteJWTAuthBackend` class extends Starlette's `AuthenticationBackend` class.

❷ Authentication starts by checking whether the endpoint is in the set of endpoints that require authentication. If the endpoint is not in the set, then the connection is not intended to be authenticated, and the request proceeds unauthenticated.

❸ A query parameter is checked for the presence of `access_token` during the initial opening handshake request. You might ask why the check is performed only during the initial handshake. This is because after a WebSocket connection is established, it's assumed to be trusted. If `access_token` is missing, then the request is rejected.

❹ The program tries to decode JWT's encoded payload. If anything goes wrong during decoding, then the request will be rejected.

❺ The token expiration date is extracted from the payload and compared with the current date. If the token has expired, then the request is rejected.

❻ The user is extracted from the database based on the user's ID provided in the JWT's payload. If the user is not found, then the request is rejected.

❼ Successful authentication results with an authentication credentials object and a user object being returned.

Transport Layer Security

When dealing with an application layer protocol such as WebSocket, a necessary line of defense is to encrypt its in-transit data. The TLS protocol secures data exchanged between clients and servers by encrypting it during transmission.

This section explains the steps needed to secure the Starlette application (WebSocket API) with TLS using a self-signed SSL certificate. For details, please consult the *src/django/app/scripts/startup.sh* script. Here are the steps:

1. Edit *src/django/compose.yaml* and set `TLS_ENABLE=1`. This environment variable acts as a guard that triggers the creation of a self-signed SSL certificate. The generated certificate is located in the */etc/wfs/ssl/certs/wfs.crt* file, and the private key is in the */etc/wfs/ssl/private/wfs.key* file. These files are provided, respectively, with `--ssl-certfile` and `--ssl-keyfile` flags to the `uvicorn` web server, which fronts the Starlette application that exposes the WebSocket API.

2. Start the WFS service with the **`docker compose up --detach --wait`** command.

> The self-signed certificates may be used for testing but are not recommended for production environments, so when encrypting WebSocket (or any other) connection with TLS in production, use certificates issued by a trusted CA.

Figure 10-7 shows the encrypted EWA. Notice that the schema in the WebSocket protocol is `wss://`, not `ws://`.

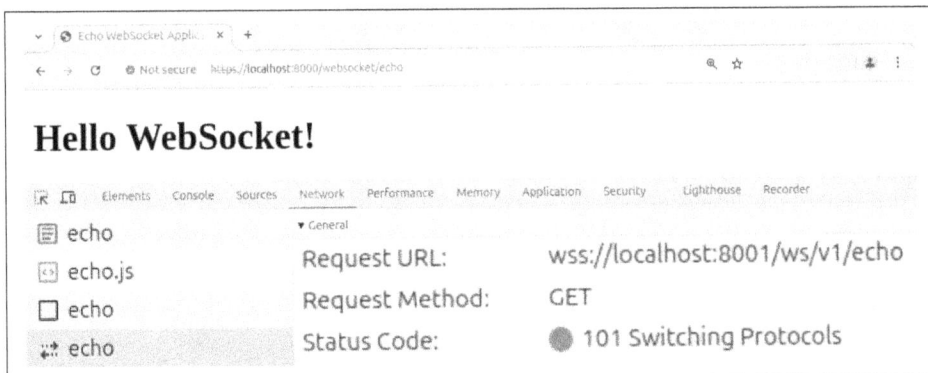

Figure 10-7. Encrypted EWA in a browser

Documentation

Most WebSocket implementations fall into the category of asynchronous APIs, where data is exchanged in a nonblocking manner. We'll document WFS's WebSocket API using the AsyncAPI Specification (*https://www.asyncapi.com*). Although AsyncAPI focuses on documenting applications built in event-driven architectures (EDAs), it supports WebSocket APIs as well.

AsyncAPI is a project complementary to OpenAPI (*https://www.openapis.org*), but its focus is on asynchronous APIs. The AsyncAPI Specification is the most commonly used standard for documenting, testing, and visualizing asynchronous APIs. AsyncAPI contracts are shared with API users (developers, testers, architects, etc.) in a portable (YAML or JSON) format.

AsyncAPI Specification

AsyncAPI is an open source project under the Linux Foundation that helps make EDA easier to work with.

AsyncAPI isn't tied to a specific technology; it provides a way to describe how applications communicate asynchronously, along with tools for testing, monitoring, and managing event-driven systems.

The AsyncAPI Specification is inspired by the OpenAPI Specification (OAS) (*https://oreil.ly/jIEgl*), formerly known as Swagger.

Example 10-12 shows the AsyncAPI Specification for the WFS's WebSocket API. Even though this document is only a fragment of the complete specification, it contains all the information to describe the WebSocket API.

Example 10-12. AsyncAPI Specification for the WebSocket API

```
# src/django/docs/api/websocket/v1-schema.yaml

asyncapi: 3.0.0 ❶
defaultContentType: application/json ❷
info:
  title: Weather Forecast Service - WebSocket API
  version: v1
operations: ❸
  receiveAlert:
    action: receive
    summary: Receive message from alert channel
    channel: ❹
      $ref: '#/channels/alert'
    bindings: ❺
```

```
      ws:
        query:
          type: object
          required:
            - access_token
            - city_uuid
          properties:
            access_token:
              type: string
              description: JWT
            city_uuid:
              type: string
              description: City's UUID
channels:
  alert:
    address: /ws/v1/alert
    messages: ❻
      genericMessage:
        $ref: '#/components/messages/genericMessage'
components:
  messages:
    genericMessage:
      contentType: application/json
      payload:
        type: object
        required:
          - message
        properties:
          message:
            type: string
```

❶ The asyncapi field specifies the version of the AsyncAPI Specification.

❷ The defaultContentType field tells that messages are JSON encoded by default.

❸ The operations field describes operations that can be performed on the Web-Socket API endpoint. The operation with ID receiveAlert is responsible for receiving messages from the alert channel (an addressable component exposed by the server) in our case described by action: receive. A channel, in this case, is the concept that describes AsyncAPI, not Redis.

❹ The channel field contains the WebSocket endpoints that receive messages. In this case, we create an alert channel on the */ws/v1/alert* endpoint.

❺ The bindings field describes the bindings used to establish a connection. In this case, we expect the access_token and city_uuid query parameters.

❻ The `messages` field describes the schema of a message received from the alert endpoint. In our case, we expect a `message` to be present in the JSON payload.

> To see a preview of HTML documentation generated from the AsyncAPI Specification, copy the contents of Example 10-12 and paste it into AsyncAPI Studio (*https://studio.asyncapi.com*). Remember to use only online services that you trust when pasting information online. Prefer a local alternative as in Example 10-13.

If you need to increase the discoverability of your API, you could convert the AsyncAPI schema to HTML documentation and expose it to the users. Example 10-13 shows steps to execute to generate HTML documentation from the AsyncAPI Specification and to serve it using the Nginx web server. The generated documentation will look like the page shown in Figure 10-8.

Example 10-13. WebSocket API documentation generation using `asyncapi/cli`

```
# Change directory location ❶
cd src/django/docs/api/websocket

# Convert AsyncAPI documentation from YAML to HTML ❷
docker run --rm -it --user=root \
      --volume ${PWD}/output:/app/output \
      --volume ${PWD}/v1-schema.yaml:/app/asyncapi.yaml \
      asyncapi/cli generate fromTemplate /app/asyncapi.yaml \
      @asyncapi/html-template@3.0.0 \
      --force-write --use-new-generator --output /app/output

# Serve documentation as HTML web page ❸
docker run --rm --detach --publish 127.0.0.1:8888:80 \
      --volume ${PWD}/output:/usr/share/nginx/html:ro nginx
```

❶ Change the location to the directory that contains the AsyncAPI schema.

❷ Generate HTML documentation using the `asyncapi/cli` (*https://oreil.ly/7V6O4*) Docker image.

❸ Serve the generated HTML documentation using the Nginx web server. The documentation is accessible at *http://localhost:8888*.[11]

---

11 When working with GitHub Codespaces, you'll use a unique URL containing the Codespace's name instead of the *localhost* URL. The expected URL is bound to port 8888 and can be found in VS Code's PORTS tab.

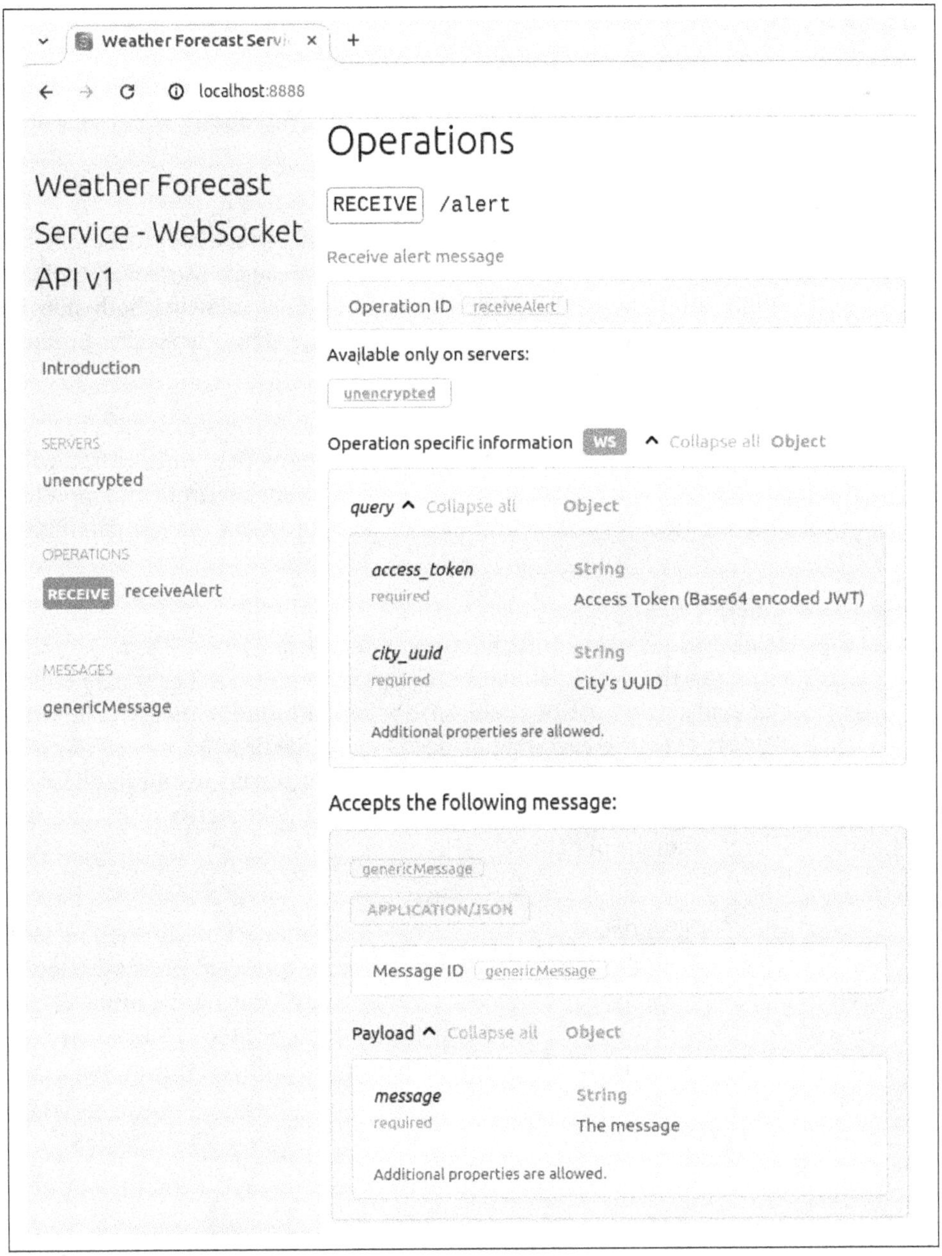

Figure 10-8. WebSocket AsyncAPI documentation

So far, we have covered WebSocket handshakes, implementation, security, and documentation. In the next section, we will present the trade-offs of WebSocket.

Trade-Offs

This section describes WebSocket advantages and disadvantages. With WebSocket, you can build APIs that support bidirectional data flow. WebSocket is advantageous for the following:

Bidirectional communication

WebSocket operates in full-duplex transmission mode, which means that the client and the server can send and receive data simultaneously. Moreover, the data is sent without adhering to the request-response model, allowing both sides to send and receive data without waiting for a response. The WebSocket protocol uses a single TCP connection to transfer the data.

Responsiveness

The WebSocket protocol supports building applications that are constrained to communication at low latencies (responsive applications), such as chat, interactive dashboards, remote shells embedded in web browsers, online gaming, or alerts.

Large data transfer

The WebSocket protocol supports binary and text data frames. The responsibility of interpreting the data is shifted to the application layer. The binary data is useful when transferring various multimedia content (audio, video, or images) because it doesn't require encoding or decoding of the data. However, transferring large amounts of data over WebSocket increases server memory utilization. WebRTC (*https://webrtc.org*) is currently becoming an alternative technology for streaming large amounts of data.

Low latency

Compared to HTTP 1.0, which requires a new TCP connection for each request, and HTTP 1.1, where the connection is kept alive for a limited time, WebSocket establishes a single persistent TCP connection (created during the initial HTTP request), therefore reducing latency because you don't need to create a new connection when new data is sent. Also, WebSocket reduces the message size because it doesn't send HTTP headers with every message (data frame). WebSocket can run with HTTP/2 and take advantage of HTTP/2's multiplexing.[12]

---

12 Read RFC 8441, "Bootstrapping WebSockets with HTTP/2" (*https://oreil.ly/6SL0d*).

Compatibility with HTTP

WebSocket is designed to work over HTTP ports 80 and 443. This allows Web-Socket traffic to usually pass through intermediaries, like proxies (reverse prox-ies, load balancers); however, middleboxes, like some enterprise firewalls that support packet inspection, may reject WebSocket traffic if configured to do so (see "HTTP/2" on page 133).

Extensibility

The WebSocket protocol is designed to be extended (*https://oreil.ly/ykp9D*) by other protocols, which could add new features to the WebSocket protocol such as multiplexing. Usage of extensions happens during the opening handshake, where the client and the server negotiate the extensions they support.

On the other hand, the disadvantages of WebSocket APIs are as follows:

No caching support

WebSocket doesn't support caching. WebSocket is designed for simultaneous bidirectional communication. In this paradigm, every message can be different from another, and the application state can change rapidly. Therefore, caching in such circumstances would be impractical.

State management challenges

WebSocket connections are stateful, and tracking the client's state information can overwhelm the server because it maintains and synchronizes the state for each client. This can impact system performance due to memory utilization. Fur-thermore, interrupting the client's session will more likely require the user to be signed out from the application, forcing the user to rejoin and re-create the state from scratch.

Brittle connections

WebSocket applications are subject to the fallacies of distributed computing (*https://oreil.ly/HGOpB*), including unreliability of the network. Implement a reconnecting mechanism that detects the connection loss and attempts to recon-nect the client in such a way that it will not result in the *thundering herd* problem (see "Request Retry" on page 63).

Authentication challenges

Authentication in WebSocket happens during the opening handshake. Once the client is authenticated and the connection is established, the server assumes all subsequent messages are authenticated. Therefore, if additional post-connection security is needed, authentication needs to be implemented on the application level, where each WebSocket frame would be validated. WebSocket uses an origin-based security model. In this model, the server checks the `Origin` header and allows or denies the connection based on the client's origin. However, malicious users can bypass this model by changing the `Origin` header during the opening handshake.

Unreliable message delivery

WebSocket inherits TCP reliability, ensuring that messages are delivered in order and without corruption as long as the connection remains open. However, WebSocket does not include built-in message acknowledgment or retransmission mechanisms at the application level. If a connection is lost, in-flight messages may not be delivered, and the application needs to handle reconnections and message resending.

Limited scalability

WebSocket applications can consume many resources, leaving you with the challenge of scaling (ability to handle a growing amount of work). WebSocket is a stateful protocol that enforces both the server and the client to maintain the state of the connection. In a stateful connection, the challenge is scaling without compromising the already established connections. One of the solutions is to limit the maximum number of connections each server handles, and have enough servers to handle the connections. In this case, you could use a load balancer to distribute the load among servers.

No application-level backpressure

To handle backpressure at the application level, techniques such as data aggregation (combining multiple messages), compression (reducing data size through encoding), deduplication (eliminating duplicate data), and pruning (removing unnecessary data) can help reduce the amount of transmitted data.[13] This technique is known as *compaction*.

---

13 WebSocketStream (*https://oreil.ly/IpUO7*) addresses WebSocket backpressure using streams (*https://oreil.ly/ytstS*). However, at the moment, this technology is experimental and has limited web browser compatibility.

When to Use WebSocket

If your application profile requires communicating bidirectionally at low latencies, then WebSocket is the technology to choose. Besides alerting, WebSocket is often used for notifications, online chat, multiplayer games, visualization dashboards, and interactive collaboration (e.g., Miro (*https://miro.com*), a company that counts millions of users, uses WebSocket to make its dashboard tool interactive).

Exercises

1. Extend our Weather Forecast Service by adding a chat feature. In the chat, a user should be able to send and receive messages. In this exercise, you'll implement the chat's client and the server. The chat client is fetched by the browser from the *http://localhost:8000/websocket/chat* HTTP endpoint and the WebSocket server is located at the *ws://localhost:8001/ws/v1/chat* endpoint. The latter endpoint requires an authentication token to be passed as an `access_token` in the query parameter.

   To obtain the token, send a JSON-encoded `POST` request to the *http://localhost:8000/api/jwt/obtain* endpoint with the payload values: `username` and `password` set to `admin`. When working with the WebSocket client, think about implementing a reconnecting mechanism in case of connection loss from the server side. When implementing the server, think about a mechanism to broadcast messages to all connected clients.

   This exercise is demanding because you'll implement both the client (frontend) and the server (backend) side. When working with a client, focus on the following functions: `onopen()`, `onmessage()`, `onclose()`, and `onerror()`. The solution to this exercise can be found in the book's code repository (see the *src/django/docs/solutions/websocket-exercise.md* file).

2. In "Transport Layer Security" on page 325, we showed how to encrypt the Starlette application by providing a TLS certificate and private key to the `uvicorn` ASGI web server. In this exercise, you will test that TLS works by using HTTP and WebSocket traffic to interact with the WFS website.

   To enable or disable TLS for the WFS, you need to set the environment variable to `TLS_ENABLE=1` (encrypted traffic) or `TLS_ENABLE=0` (unencrypted traffic), respectively, in the *src/django/compose.yaml* file, and start (or restart) the project with the **docker compose up --detach --wait** command.

   When visiting *https://localhost:8000* locally (not in GitHub Codespaces), the browser will display a warning: "Your connection is not private" in Chrome and "Warning: Potential Security Risk Ahead" in Firefox. To interact with the WFS web page, add the application's self-signed SSL certificate to the browser's exception list. To do this, visit *https://localhost:8000* as well as *https://localhost: 8001*, and depending on what web browser you are using, click "Proceed to localhost (unsafe)" in Chrome or "Accept the risk and continue" in Firefox. Next, visit *https://localhost:8000/websocket/echo* to see the "Hello WebSocket!" message.

Summary

WebSocket APIs allow for simultaneous bidirectional client-server communication. This chapter covered the WebSocket protocol, and the WebSocket client and server APIs.

You implemented the WebSocket ECHO application and inspected WebSocket opening (and closing) handshakes with Wireshark. Familiarity with the WebSocket protocol, as well as WebSocket client and server APIs, allowed you to implement an alerting system. To do so, in our WFS, you implemented a pub/sub pattern with Redis and a WebSocket server-side API with Starlette, and consumed the API with JavaScript WebSocket client. Furthermore, you secured the WFS with various middlewares and encrypted the WebSocket traffic with TLS. In the documentation section, you became familiar with the AsyncAPI Specification. Finally, the trade-offs section exposed you to the advantages and disadvantages of WebSocket APIs.

## CHAPTER 11

Messaging

This chapter discusses APIs in the context of broker-based messaging systems, which we refer to as *broker-based APIs*. The chapter aims to familiarize you with common messaging patterns, and provide you with the skills needed to implement and document them. In particular, you'll work with the RabbitMQ message broker.

Several application architectures that use messaging have been proposed over the past decades. In the early 2000s, a service-oriented architecture (SOA) allowed to exchange messages over an Enterprise Service Bus (ESB), a communication system for interacting software applications. In the mid-2000s, attention was drawn to EDA, which allows systems to respond to each other based on the messages created by events. Both ESB and EDA used message-oriented middleware (MOM) as a component for passing data among applications. In the 2010s, microservices architectures gained adoption and continue to use MOM, such as ActiveMQ (*https:// activemq.apache.org*), Amazon SQS (*https://oreil.ly/DeI6R*), Azure Service Bus (*https://oreil.ly/U0743*), Google Cloud Pub/Sub (*https://oreil.ly/QJ36Q*), Kafka (*https://oreil.ly/2knCH*), RabbitMQ (*https://www.rabbitmq.com*), or Redis (*https:// redis.io*).

> The *MOM* term was created at the end of the 20th century.[1] While it's no longer used in today's discussions, MOM represents the idea of using a component to mediate message exchanges, with or without the broker involved.

---

1 David A. Chappell explains MOM's inner workings in his book, *Enterprise Service Bus* (O'Reilly), first published in 2004.

What Is Messaging?

Messaging is a communication method that allows software applications to exchange data in the form of messages. In "Message" on page 6, we defined a message as a discrete data unit (a self-contained record) sent by a sender to one or many receivers.

In a client-server architecture, a message is sent directly between the client and the server, and it's the client who initiates the communication by sending the first message (a request), and the server responds to it with a counter message (a response).

The MOM is a software or hardware solution that facilitates sending and receiving messages among applications. Contrary to client-server architecture, messages in the MOM are never sent directly among applications. The MOM acts as a middleman, ensuring that the messages are delivered from the producer (also known as a *publisher*, *sender*, or *emitter*) to the consumer (also called *subscriber* or *receiver*). The messages are usually sent and received asynchronously (see "Synchronous and Asynchronous Communication Types" on page 9).

Figure 11-1 illustrates the concept of MOM. The system contains six applications (producers and consumers) that use the MOM's API (client library) to send or receive messages. The applications exchange messages, which funnel through the MOM. Each application sends or receives one message, which flows from the producer to the consumer. The numbers on the envelopes label the messages for tracking purposes.

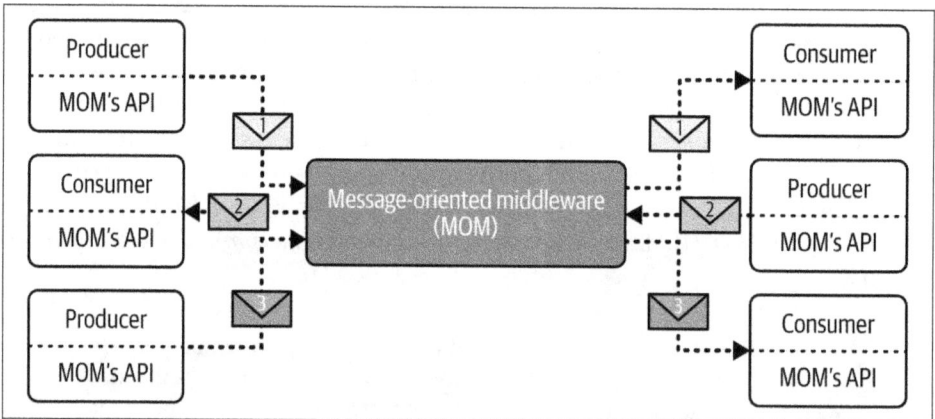

Figure 11-1. Architecture of message-oriented middleware

In broker-based MOMs, messages aren't exchanged directly among applications, but they are sent through an intermediary (a broker). The main task of a broker is to route messages. Moreover, the broker also has auxiliary tasks, such as authentication, monitoring, and logging. An application that connects to a broker-based MOM is called a *client*, and it can act as a message producer or consumer. The *broker* is the server that waits for client connection. An example of a broker from the real world would be a parcel service office that receives packages from senders and passes them for delivery to receivers.

There are several technologies that you could use to implement broker-based message delivery. In this chapter, you'll work with RabbitMQ.

RabbitMQ Broker Configurations

In addition to a single broker configuration, RabbitMQ supports both clustering and federation of brokers.

Clustering allows multiple nodes to operate as a single logical broker within a local network, combining resources for high availability and scalability. This setup requires low-latency connections, since all nodes share metadata and queue state.

On the other hand, *federation* allows for message forwarding between independent brokers across different networks, regions, or even cloud providers. This approach enables hybrid cloud deployments, cross-region communication, and bridging separate administrative domains.

Figure 11-2 illustrates the typical message flow in RabbitMQ.

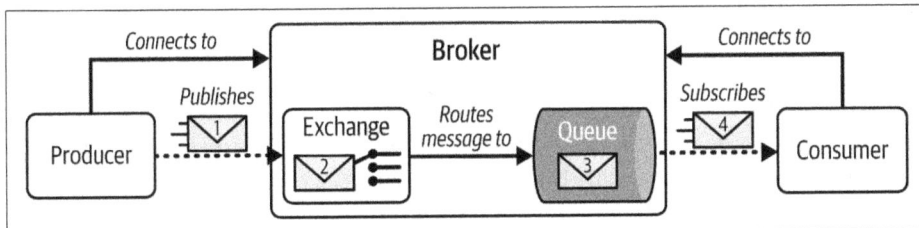

Figure 11-2. Message flow in RabbitMQ

The described flow has four steps:

1. The producer sends a message to the exchange.
2. A message arrives at the exchange, and the exchange routes it to the queue based on exchange type and configuration.
3. The queue (acting as a buffer) stores the message for consumption by the consumer.
4. A consumer consumes the message from the queue.

Note that broker-based messaging systems aren't limited to queues. For example, Apache Kafka uses partitioned logs, MQTT relies on topics, and Redis pub/sub uses channels. While these differ from traditional queues, they serve a similar purpose.

To explain the messaging patterns discussed in this book, we need to define some RabbitMQ vocabulary:

Producer
A client that sends messages to the broker.

Consumer
A client that receives messages from the broker.

Channel
A dedicated connection path at the RabbitMQ's Advanced Message Queuing Protocol (AMQP) application protocol layer. Multiple channels share the same single TCP connection.

Queue
A buffer-like storage that holds messages to be consumed by consumers following a first-in-first-out (FIFO) order. Think of it as a mailbox. On the one end, the mailbox allows the mailman (producer) to drop the mail into, and on the other end, it allows the receiver (consumer) to pick it up from.

Exchange
A router that receives messages from a producer and forwards them to queue(s). Think of it as a relay or dispatcher. There are four types of exchange in RabbitMQ: `direct`, `fanout`, `topic`, and `headers`.

Routing key
A message property that is used by the exchange to route the message to queue(s). Think of the routing key as an address.

Topic
A type of exchange that routes messages to queues based on wildcard patterns ("*" or "#") defined in the bindings between the exchange and queue(s). The message's routing key is a string that the exchange matches against these patterns.

Binding
A link between an exchange and a queue, or an exchange and another exchange. The exchange uses binding to route messages to the queue. The flow of the message goes from the exchange to the queue.

Correlation ID (CID)
A unique identifier carried with the message. It's often used to match the request message with the response message.

Acknowledgment
A message confirmation signal sent from consumer to broker, or broker to producer.[2] The consumer sends a manual acknowledgment to the broker to indicate that it has successfully received or processed the message. Separately, the broker can send an acknowledgment to the producer to confirm receipt of the message, but this depends on the messaging system and its configuration. In RabbitMQ, this requires the producer to enable the "publisher confirms" feature.

What Is a Queue?

In computer science, a *queue* (*https://oreil.ly/5jC3q*) is a collection of data items stored in a FIFO order, where the first item added is the first to be removed. Figure 11-3 illustrates a queue. The data entering the queue is added at the back (enqueued) and removed from the front (dequeued).

Figure 11-3. Queue

In the context of messaging, a *queue* is a placeholder for messages, where the producer publishes messages and consumers consume them. The RabbitMQ broker stores and manages the queues. A message is stored in the queue until the broker deletes it. Acknowledgment tells the broker to delete the message from the queue. A happy queue is an empty queue, says a popular proverb in messaging.

Once a message is in the queue, it is immutable, meaning it cannot be changed. The only way to change the message is to create a new message (republish it). Producers don't track consumers' responses but instead operate in a "fire-and-forget" manner. After sending a message to the queue, the producer doesn't wait for a consumer's response. However, there is an exception to this behavior when using the request-response messaging pattern (see "Request-Response Pattern" on page 344).

---

2 There also exists an automatic acknowledgment type handled internally by the broker; see "RabbitMQ Message Acknowledgment" on page 350.

To discover all the messaging patterns mentioned in this chapter, consult the book's code repository under the *src/rabbitmq* directory.

A queue helps the producers and consumers of messages to become more loosely coupled, meaning that producers and consumers don't need to be constantly aware of each other's presence. This doesn't mean that broker-based messaging systems are completely free of coupling.[3] For example, a producer and a consumer can be coupled to the message protocol (e.g., AMQP or MQTT) and the message format. If the producer sends a message whose payload is JSON encoded, the consumer must be able to decode it. Moreover, if the message changes (field is renamed or removed), the clients must be able to handle this change too.

Coupling is a dependency among system components where a change in one component affects another.

Systems that use queues tend to be more reliable and tolerate faults. For example, when a message consumer is unavailable, the message remains in the queue until the consumer is back online and can retrieve it. Moreover, in the case of a sudden influx of messages, you could scale out the system by adding more consumers.

In RabbitMQ, queues and exchanges can be durable or transient. Durable queues and exchanges survive broker restart, but transient ones don't. Transient ones must be redeclared manually when the broker returns online.

RabbitMQ's durable queue doesn't make messages persistent. It only ensures queue continuity. It means that the queue will be re-created after the broker restarts, not the messages it contains. To make the message persistent, you need to set the `delivery_mode` property, as shown in Example 11-4.

---

3 To understand coupling more, read Vlad Khononov's *Balancing Coupling in Software Design* (Addison-Wesley, 2023). If you'd like to know more about coupling in the context of messaging-based systems, read "The Many Facets of Coupling" blog (*https://oreil.ly/X2doC*) by Gregor Hohpe.

Messaging Patterns

This section will familiarize you with common messaging patterns used in broker-based messaging systems. The examples are based on RabbitMQ Tutorials (*https://oreil.ly/rI0Ip*).

Work Queue Pattern

A *work queue* is a messaging pattern (also known as *competing consumers*) that allows a messaging system to handle multiple messages in parallel. In a work queue, messages are delivered to a single queue, and a broker delivers messages from the queue to the next consumer. On average, every consumer receives the same number of messages. In a work queue, consumers compete for each message because every consumer consumes messages from the same queue. The queue ensures that each message is delivered to only one consumer (this removes the need for consumers to coordinate with one another).

Figure 11-4 illustrates how the work queue works. In our example, there are three messages, and each message is delivered to exactly one consumer.

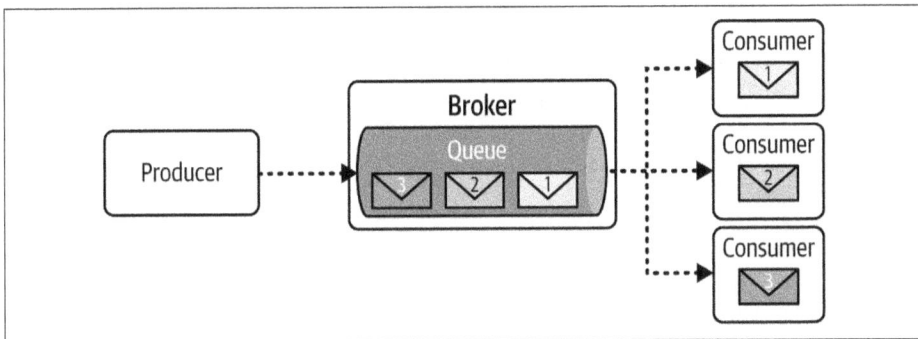

Figure 11-4. Work queue pattern delivers each message to exactly one consumer

The messages illustrated in Figure 11-4 are distributed among consumers in a round-robin fashion, where each consumer receives one message. However, this behavior is specific to RabbitMQ, and other messaging systems could distribute messages differently.

> The implementation of the work queue pattern is located in the book's code repository in the *src/rabbitmq/2.WorkQueue* directory.

Publish-Subscribe Pattern

Publish-subscribe (pub/sub) is a messaging pattern that fans out each message to multiple consumers, ensuring one-to-many message delivery. This pattern is commonly used for alerting or notifications when each message is sent to multiple consumers. When a new consumer is added to the pub/sub queue, it receives all messages that are published to the queue from the moment the new consumer joins the queue. Figure 11-5 illustrates how a pub/sub works. Note that the diagram shows an exchange sending the same message to three separate queues.

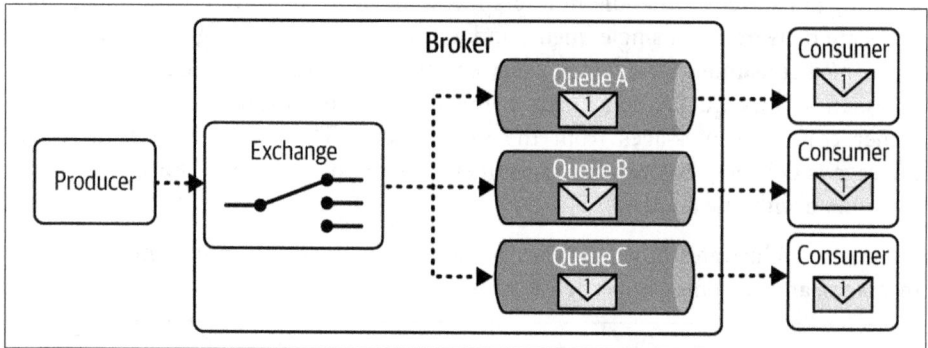

Figure 11-5. Pub/sub pattern delivers each message to all consumers

> The implementation of the pub/sub pattern is located in the book's code repository in the *src/rabbitmq/3.PubSub* directory.

Routing Pattern

The *routing* pattern is a variation of the pub/sub messaging pattern. In the routing pattern, consumers receive messages selectively based on a routing key. Figure 11-6 illustrates two messages sent by the producer and then going via the exchange (router), which relays them into the appropriate queue. Two consumers consume the first message, and the second message is consumed by one consumer.

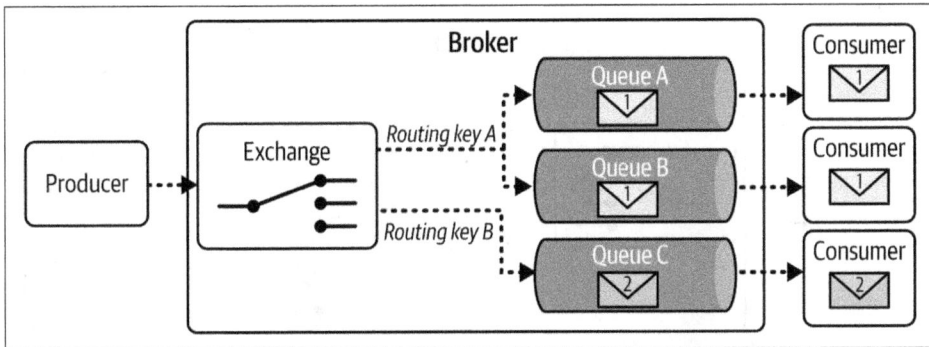

Figure 11-6. Routing pattern delivers message based on a routing key

The implementation of the routing pattern is located in the book's code repository in the *src/rabbitmq/4.Routing* directory.

Topics Pattern

A limitation of the routing pattern is that it can deliver messages based only on a specific routing key. The *topics* pattern addresses the limitation of the routing pattern by allowing consumers to subscribe to messages based on the routing key pattern. Figure 11-7 illustrates two messages sent by the producer and then going via the exchange (router), which relays them into the appropriate queue. Two consumers consume the first message, and the second message is consumed by one consumer. Note that the difference between the routing pattern and topics is subtle. In routing, the routing key is one word, whereas in topics, the routing key uses a pattern containing a dot and a wildcard ("*").

The routing pattern and the topics pattern can be considered a special case of the *content-based routing* pattern.

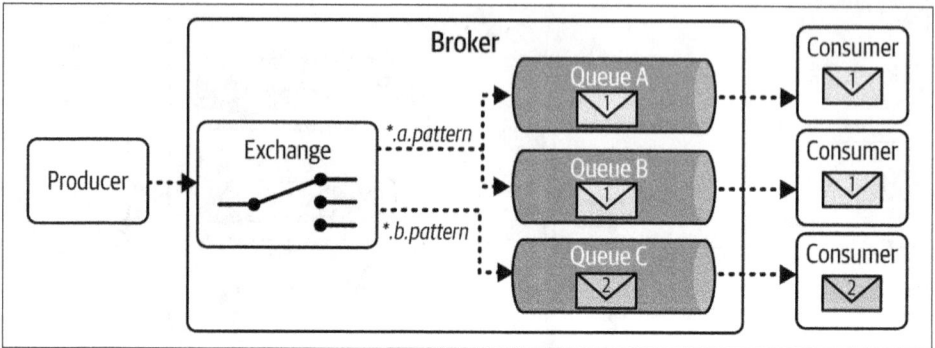

Figure 11-7. Topics pattern delivers message based on a pattern in the routing key

The implementation of the topics pattern is located in the book's code repository in the *src/rabbitmq/4.Topics* directory.

Request-Response Pattern

The *request-response* messaging pattern originates from client-server architecture. Figure 11-8 illustrates how a request-response model can be implemented with RabbitMQ. Notice that both client applications act as message producer and consumer. In the request-response pattern, two queues are created, one for the request and one for response messages.

In our setup, the responder declares the request queue, and the requester declares the response queue. The request message sent by the requester to the request queue contains a CID. The CID is used to match the request message with the response message.

After sending a request message, the requester waits for a response message by listening on the response queue. The responder receives the request message, and sends a response message along with the CID to the response queue. The requester receives a response message. If the CID of the request and the CID of the response message match, the requester knows it received the expected response from the responder. If the CIDs don't match, the requester can either ignore the response message, log the mismatch incident as an error, or send the response message to the dead letter queue (DLQ) (*https://oreil.ly/J3GNH*), for further investigation, ensuring they don't block the main response queue.

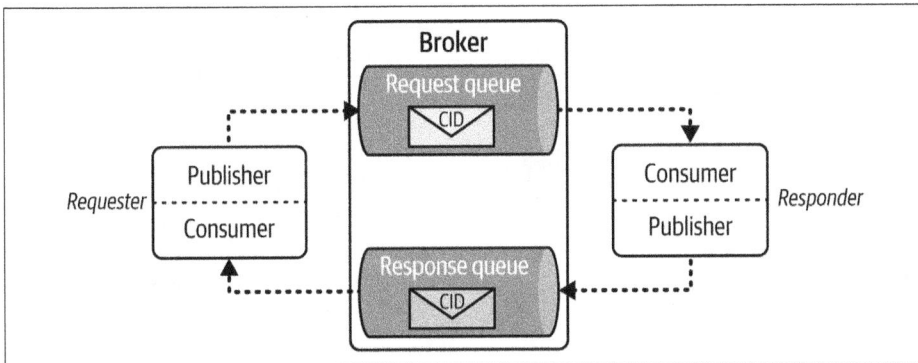

Figure 11-8. Request-response pattern

> The implementation of the request-response pattern is located in
> the *src/rabbitmq/6.RequestResponse* directory in the book's code
> repository.

Implementation

This section explains the implementation of the work queue messaging pattern. All
messaging patterns included in this book have a similar folder structure. This way,
after becoming familiar with this section, you can proceed with other messaging patterns on your own.

> The implementation of the work queue pattern, among other mes-
> saging patterns, is located in the book's code repository under the
> *src/rabbitmq* directory.

Work Queue

To become familiar with the work queue messaging pattern, you'll use a die-rolling
example. Figure 11-9 illustrates the overview of the setup.

The producer simulates rolling a die. The result of a single roll is a random number
from 1 to 6, and every such result creates a new message. This message is sent to the
die queue. A consumer pulls one message from the die queue at a time.

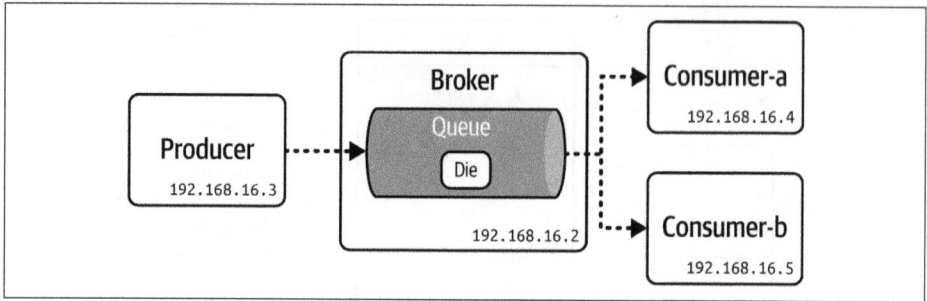

Figure 11-9. Topology of the work queue example

Notice that the components in the diagram contain IP addresses. These IP addresses are static, so you can more easily identify them and experiment with the solution.

Start by executing commands from Example 11-1. They are expected to produce an output similar to Figure 11-10.

```
$ for i in {1..6}; do docker compose exec producer python /usr/src/producer.py; done
[x] Sent '{'data': {'message': 'Rolling 1', 'count': 1}, 'version': '1.0.0'}' message to 'die' queue.
[x] Sent '{'data': {'message': 'Rolling 3', 'count': 3}, 'version': '1.0.0'}' message to 'die' queue.
[x] Sent '{'data': {'message': 'Rolling 5', 'count': 5}, 'version': '1.0.0'}' message to 'die' queue.
[x] Sent '{'data': {'message': 'Rolling 3', 'count': 3}, 'version': '1.0.0'}' message to 'die' queue.
[x] Sent '{'data': {'message': 'Rolling 4', 'count': 4}, 'version': '1.0.0'}' message to 'die' queue.
[x] Sent '{'data': {'message': 'Rolling 2', 'count': 2}, 'version': '1.0.0'}' message to 'die' queue.

$ docker compose exec consumer-a python /usr/src/consumer.py  $ docker compose exec consumer-b python /usr/src/consumer.py
[*] Waiting for messages from 'die' queue.                    [*] Waiting for messages from 'die' queue.
[x] Received 'Rolling 1' message.                             [x] Received 'Rolling 3' message.
[x] Received 'Rolling 5' message.                             [x] Received 'Rolling 3' message.
[x] Received 'Rolling 4' message.                             [x] Received 'Rolling 2' message.
```

Figure 11-10. Expected output of the work queue example

Example 11-1. Sequence of commands for the work queue example

```
# Setup lab environment ❶
cd src/rabbitmq/2.WorkQueue
docker compose up --detach --wait
tmux new-session \; split-window -v \; split-window -h \; select-pane -U \;

# In the bottom left pane run ❷
docker compose exec consumer-a python /usr/src/consumer.py

# In the bottom right pane run ❷
docker compose exec consumer-b python /usr/src/consumer.py

# In the top pane run ❸
for i in {1..6}; do docker compose exec producer python /usr/src/producer.py; done

# In the top pane run ❹
docker compose down --volumes && docker network rm -f rabbitmq
```

❶ Execute the lab setup instructions. Navigate to the lab's directory, start the Docker containers, and create a new tmux session that splits the terminal window into three panes.

❷ Make the two consumers listen for messages.

❸ Make the producer send six messages within a for-loop. The queue distributes the messages among consumers in a round-robin fashion, where each consumer receives one message.

❹ Terminate the example by stopping and deleting its containers, volumes, and network.

Example 11-2 and Example 11-3 show the implementation details of the producer and consumer. The order of explanations follows the order of program execution: instantiate producer and consumer classes, connect to the broker, declare a channel and a queue, and send or receive messages.

Example 11-2. Message producer implementation

```
# src/rabbitmq/2.WorkQueue/src/producer.py

...
class RabbitMQProducer:
  ...
  queue = os.getenv("RABBITMQ_QUEUE", "die")
  ...

  def __init__(self):  ❸
    self.__connect()  ❹
    self.__declare_channel()  ❺
    self.__declare_queue()  ❻

  def __connect(self):  ❹
      ...
      self.connection = BlockingConnection(params)
      ...

  def __declare_channel(self):  ❺
    self.channel = self.connection.channel()

  def __declare_queue(self, durable=True):  ❻
    self.channel.queue_declare(queue=self.queue, durable=durable)

  def publish(self, msg: dict):  ❼
    ...
    self.channel.basic_publish(
      exchange="",
```

```
      routing_key=self.queue,
      body=to_json(msg),
      ...
  )


if __name__ == "__main__":  ❶
  ...
  number = random.randrange(1, 6)
  msg = {
    "data": {
      "message": f"Rolling {number}",
      "outcome": number
    },
    "version": "1.0.0"
  }

  producer = RabbitMQProducer()  ❷
  producer.publish(msg)  ❼
```

Example 11-3. Message consumer implementation

```
# src/rabbitmq/2.WorkQueue/src/consumer.py

...
class RabbitMQConsumer:
  ...
  queue = os.getenv("RABBITMQ_QUEUE", "die")
  ...

  def __init__(self):  ❸
    self.__connect()  ❹
    self.__declare_channel()  ❺
    self.__declare_queue()  ❻

  def __connect(self):  ❹
      ...
      self.connection = BlockingConnection(params)
      ...

  def __declare_channel(self):  ❺
    self.channel = self.connection.channel()

  def __declare_queue(self, durable=True):  ❻
    self.channel.queue_declare(queue=self.queue, durable=durable)

  def __callback(self, channel, method, properties, msg):  ❽
    msg = json_to_dict(msg, properties.content_encoding)["data"]["message"]
    print(f"[x] Received '{msg}' message.")
    channel.basic_ack(delivery_tag=method.delivery_tag)

  def consume(self):  ❼
```

```
self.channel.basic_qos(prefetch_count=1)
self.channel.basic_consume(
  queue=self.queue,
  auto_ack=False,
  on_message_callback=self.__callback
)
self.channel.start_consuming()


if __name__ == "__main__":   ❶
  ...
  consumer = RabbitMQConsumer()   ❷
  consumer.consume()   ❼
```

❶ __main__ is the program entry point that allows the code to be executed only
   when the script is run from the command line rather than when it is imported as
   a module. This is where program execution starts.

❷ The producer and consumer instances are created from the RabbitMQProducer
   and RabbitMQConsumer classes, respectively.

❸ The program moves to the init() method (a class constructor), which is responsible for creating a connection to the RabbitMQ broker.

❹ The __connect() method creates two TCP connections. One TCP connection
   connects the producer with the broker, and the other connects the consumer
   with the broker.

❺ The __declare_channel() method creates a messaging *channel*, a virtual connection inside a TCP connection that all published or consumed AMQP messages go through.

❻ The __declare_queue() method creates a queue. By setting the durable parameter to True, we ensure that the queue will be retained even after the RabbitMQ
   broker restarts.

   Notice that both *producer.py* and *consumer.py* execute the __declare_queue()
   method. The method ensures that the queue exists before we start consuming its
   messages. This prevents situations such as consumers failing to read messages
   from the queue that doesn't exist.

❼ The publish() method enqueues a message to the queue, and the consume()
   method dequeues a message from the queue.

❽ The consumer has an extra __callback() method executed when a message is received. This method is responsible for processing and manually acknowledging the message to the broker with basic_ack(delivery_tag=delivery_tag).

RabbitMQ Message Acknowledgment

In RabbitMQ, there are different types of acknowledgments. The acknowledgment can be sent from consumer to broker, or broker to producer. Moreover, there exists an automatic acknowledgment local to the broker that is not sent to any client.

RabbitMQ messages can be acknowledged by the consumer in two ways: *manual*, sent by the consumer at will, or *automatic*, where the broker assumes that every message is successfully delivered.

In manual acknowledgment, the consumer can acknowledge the message either at the moment of receiving the message or after finishing the operation that the message triggered. The consumer-to-broker acknowledgment ensures that the broker removes messages from the queue only after receiving an acknowledgment from the consumer. Usually, the consumer acknowledgment is executed as the last step within the program (indicating a successful operation). Be aware that acknowledging a message too early puts the operation at risk of not being completed when an error occurs.

If you decide to acknowledge messages manually, remember to invoke the basic_ack() method. The consequences of not acknowledging a message will cause the broker to consume memory and storage increasingly without releasing unacknowledged messages, and that behavior may eventually crash the broker. Be aware that if a consumer doesn't send an acknowledgment (while being in manual acknowledgment mode, using auto_ack=False), the broker will mark the message for redelivery. An acknowledgment can be seen at the AMQP level as the AMQP frame containing the Basic.Ack flag.

The downside of manual acknowledgment is reduced throughput. To achieve higher message throughput, the consumer can use automatic message acknowledgment, often referred to as "fire-and-forget." This method offers the highest message throughput at the cost of reduced safety of delivery.

Automatic message acknowledgment (auto_ack=True) is unsafe because a message is removed from the queue immediately after it's sent by the broker (without consulting the consumer).[4] When the automatic acknowledgment mode is used, the broker doesn't know, or care, what happens to the message after it's removed from the queue.

---

4 In RabbitMQ's automatic acknowledgment mode, a message is considered delivered when it's written to the consumer's TCP connection, and AMQP sends the Basic.Deliver frame, without waiting for any TCP acknowledgment.

An acknowledgment can also be sent by the broker to the producer. The broker-to-producer acknowledgment informs the producer that the broker has received the message. This method is called "publisher confirms" and must be explicitly enabled by the producer.

Let's publish (enqueue) a message to the queue. This is done by executing the publish() method in the *producer.py* script as shown in Example 11-4.

Example 11-4. Producer message publishing implementation

```python
# src/rabbitmq/2.WorkQueue/src/producer.py

...
from pika import BasicProperties
from pika.spec import PERSISTENT_DELIVERY_MODE

class RabbitMQProducer:
    ...
    queue = os.getenv("RABBITMQ_QUEUE", "die")
    properties = BasicProperties(
      ...
      delivery_mode=PERSISTENT_DELIVERY_MODE,  ❺
      ...
    )
    ...

    def publish(self, msg: dict):  ❶
      ...
      self.channel.basic_publish(  ❶
        exchange="",                    ❷
        routing_key=self.queue,          ❸
        body=to_json(msg),               ❹
        properties=self.properties       ❺
      )
      self.disconnect()  ❻

    def disconnect(self):  ❻
        if self.channel.is_open:
            self.channel.close()

        if self.connection.is_open:
            self.connection.close()
```

❶ In the publish() method, a message is published to the queue by executing the basic_publish() method.

❷ The exchange option set to an empty string forces a message to be sent to a default exchange.

❸ The `routing_key` specifies the binding name that is used to route the message to the queue.

❹ A `msg` is encoded as a JSON string.

❺ Message `properties` are set by reading them from class attributes. In this case, the message delivery mode is set to `PERSISTENT_DELIVERY_MODE`. This ensures that the message is saved to the filesystem to survive broker restart.

❻ The `disconnect()` method closes the channel and the connection.

Having both a queue marked as `durable` and messages set to `PERSISTENT_DELIV ERY_MODE` makes the queue survive the broker restart. The messages are delivered after the broker recovers from the restart.

> Remember that marking a queue and message *persistent* doesn't guarantee that a message won't be lost. There is a risk associated with a time window when the broker accepts a message but hasn't saved it yet on disk. When the broker crashes, messages can be lost during this time window. Strong guarantees of producer message delivery are provided by the "producer confirms" technique (*https://oreil.ly/TaEqy*).

Another thing worth mentioning is the risk of message loss during message recovery. After you spin up a crashed broker, it will start recovering the queue and messages from the filesystem, but this procedure takes time. Suppose the broker is restarted during the recovery process. In that case, messages, queues, and exchanges might be lost because the recovery process has yet to fully reestablish the durable state of the broker's data. Therefore, the durability settings we configure reduce the risk of message loss in the event of a broker crash but do not guarantee complete message preservation, especially if multiple failures occur during recovery.

Message Delivery

Generally, a message in distributed systems can be delivered in three ways:

At-least-once delivery
> You are certain that a message will be delivered, but possibly more than once.

At-most-once delivery
> A message is delivered once or never. This method prevents message duplication at the risk of message loss.

Exactly-once delivery
> A message is delivered exactly once.[5]

Be aware that exactly-once message delivery is hard to achieve natively at the protocol level.[6] In most cases, exactly-once delivery requires message coordination among producers and consumers at the application level.[7] The exactly-once delivery can be achievable through at-least-once delivery with message deduplication.

Using manual acknowledgment, described in "RabbitMQ Message Acknowledgment" on page 350, RabbitMQ provides an at-least-once delivery guarantee because messages remain in the queue until the broker receives the consumer's acknowledgment. If the consumer fails before sending acknowledgment, the unacknowledged messages are requeued for redelivery.

In contrast, using automatic acknowledgment, the message is removed from the queue as soon as it is sent to the consumer, independently of whether it was delivered to the consumer or not. This leads to an at-most-once delivery guarantee and an increased risk of message loss.

Additionally, without "publisher confirms" on the producer side, messages may be lost during publishing, also leading to at-most-once delivery. Thus, trying to achieve at-least-once delivery requires manual consumer acknowledgments and "publisher confirms." In the absence of these mechanisms, there is a risk of message loss during publishing or consumption, resulting in at-most-once delivery.

---

[5] Exactly-once message delivery is a challenging problem. Read the "You Cannot Have Exactly-Once Delivery" (*https://oreil.ly/bjDo7*) and "Exactly-Once Message Delivery" (*https://oreil.ly/lfz2g*) blogs on this topic.

[6] Kafka (*https://oreil.ly/CKiRE*) claims to achieve exactly-once semantics through its transactional APIs.

[7] If you want to know how message delivery in RabbitMQ fares against Kafka, read the "RabbitMQ versus Kafka—Message Delivery Semantics and Guarantees" blog post (*https://oreil.ly/L4QE3*) by Jack Vanlightly.

Let's look at message consumption in the *consumer.py* script in Example 11-5.

Example 11-5. Consumer message consumption implementation

```
# src/rabbitmq/2.WorkQueue/src/consumer.py

...
class RabbitMQConsumer:
    ...

    def __callback(self, channel, method, properties, msg):  ❻
        ...
        delivery_tag = method.delivery_tag
        channel.basic_ack(delivery_tag=delivery_tag)
        ...
    ...

    def consume(self):  ❶
        ...
        self.channel.basic_qos(prefetch_count=1)  ❷
        self.channel.basic_consume(                ❸
          queue=self.queue,                        ❹
          auto_ack=False,                          ❺
          on_message_callback=self.__callback      ❻
        )
        self.channel.start_consuming()  ❼
        ...
...
```

❶ The consume() method is responsible for consuming messages from the queue.

❷ The basic_qos() method with parameter prefetch_count=1 limits message consumption to only one message from a channel. This ensures that messages will be evenly distributed among consumers, making each consumer process only one message at a time and not sending a new message to that consumer until it has acknowledged the previous one. This creates a more balanced workload distribution among consumers.

❸ The basic_consume() method configures parameters for message consumption.

❹ The queue argument controls from which queue a message will be consumed.

❺ The auto_ack argument controls automatic message acknowledgment. Here, the automatic acknowledgment is disabled in favor of manual acknowledgment (step 6). You control the consumer's message acknowledgment. There could be a setup where some consumers use manual acknowledgment and others automatic, but consistent acknowledgment for all consumers of a queue is recommended.

❻ The `on_message_callback` argument binds the consumer's `__callback()` method to be executed whenever a new message is received. The message is uniquely identified by the `delivery_tag` parameter that RabbitMQ automatically assigns. The message is acknowledged by calling the `basic_ack()` method.

❼ The `start_consuming()` method starts message consumption from the queue.

Security

In this section, you'll secure RabbitMQ communication with TLS, and authenticate clients with Simple Authentication and Security Layer (SASL) (*https://oreil.ly/VMMdb*).

Before looking at the encryption in RabbitMQ, let's introduce RabbitMQ's Advanced Message Queuing Protocol. AMQP (*https://oreil.ly/10LlL*) is a binary application layer protocol that uses TCP as the transport protocol. AMQP is intended to support messaging applications that use various communication and message delivery patterns.

The demonstrations in this section compare the unencrypted and encrypted AMQP communication, captured while performing Example 11-1. Encryption is controlled by the `TLS_ENABLE` environment variable in the *compose.yaml* file and set by default to 1 to encrypt the messages in transit, both between the producer and the broker, and between the broker and the consumer.

Instructions on how to capture the network traffic aren't presented in this chapter (consult Chapter 3 for examples). Instead, you'll open the provided *.pcap* files using Wireshark (*https://www.wireshark.org*), a network protocol analyzer.

> In order to see hostnames instead of IP addresses in Wireshark, add the following lines near the top of the */etc/hosts* file on the machine running Wireshark (modifying this file requires `sudo` permissions):[8]
>
> ```
> 192.168.16.2  broker
> 192.168.16.3  producer
> 192.168.16.4  consumer-a
> 192.168.16.5  consumer-b
> ```
>
> Then, in Wireshark, go to Edit > Preferences > Name Resolution, and select "Resolve network (IP) addresses."

---

8 The location of the *hosts* file may differ for different operating systems.

Unencrypted Messages in Transit

Figure 11-11 shows a screenshot of unencrypted AMQP traffic loaded in Wireshark. If you work in a terminal, you could also use `tshark -r src/rabbitmq/2.Work Queue/docs/assets/amqp-unencrypted.pcap` to list the traffic. By looking at the order of packets in the *amqp-unencrypted.pcap* file, you'll deduce the program flow and analyze the content of the exchanged messages.

> The AMQP messages are called *frames* and differ from Ethernet frames discussed in "TCP/IP and the OSI Model" on page 80.

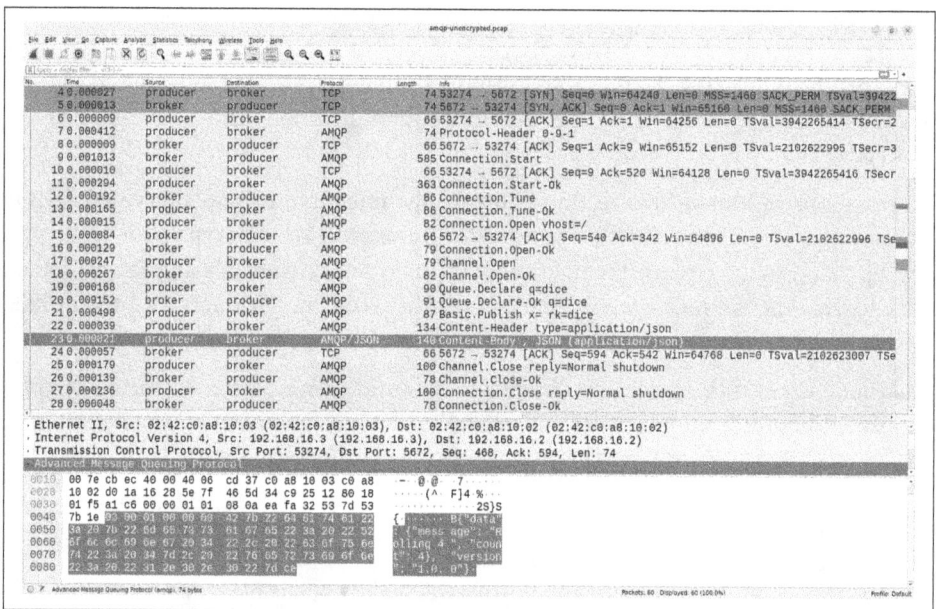

Figure 11-11. AMQP unencrypted traffic

- Frames 4 to 6—The `producer` opens the TCP connection with the `broker`. For more details about the TCP three-way handshake, see Example 3-5, or watch the few-minutes-long summary video "TCP Connection Walkthrough" (*https://oreil.ly/b2CNg*) by Ben Eater.

- Frames 7 to 16— After opening the TCP connection, the `producer` opens an AMQP connection with the `broker`.

- Frames 17 and 18—After creating the AMQP connection, a RabbitMQ channel is created.

- Frames 19 and 20—The producer declares the die queue, and the broker confirms the creation of the queue.

- Frame 21—The producer declares the settings of the message it is about to send. Setting x= to empty selects the default exchange, and rk=die (routing key) carries the message directly to the queue based on the routing key.

- Frames 22 and 23—The producer publishes a message to the queue. The message is split across two AMQP frames: one with the message header, and another with the 66-byte message body containing "Rolling 4." This second AMQP frame contains the JSON-encoded unencrypted payload. The payload is plain-text readable to anyone who can watch the network traffic.

- Frames 25 to 28—The AMQP channel and connection are closed.

Message consumption has a similar flow to message publishing. The difference is that a consumer (e.g., consumer-a) reads the message from the broker. This is captured by frames 52 and 53 (not shown on the screenshot).

Messages Encrypted in Transit

When AMQP is encrypted using TLS, it is referred to as *AMQPS*. Note that AMQPS isn't an officially defined, standalone protocol. AMQPS refers to AMQP over TLS, in the same way as HTTPS refers to HTTP over TLS. For more information about TLS, see Example 3-12.

Let's compare the unencrypted AMQP traffic shown in Figure 11-11 with the encrypted AMQPS traffic in Figure 11-12 (file *src/rabbitmq/2.WorkQueue/docs/assets/amqp-encrypted.pcap*). The difference is that this time, the communication between the broker and the producer (as well as the consumer) is encrypted with TLS.

> To discover the details of TLS for RabbitMQ, consult the book's code repository file *src/rabbitmq/README.md*.

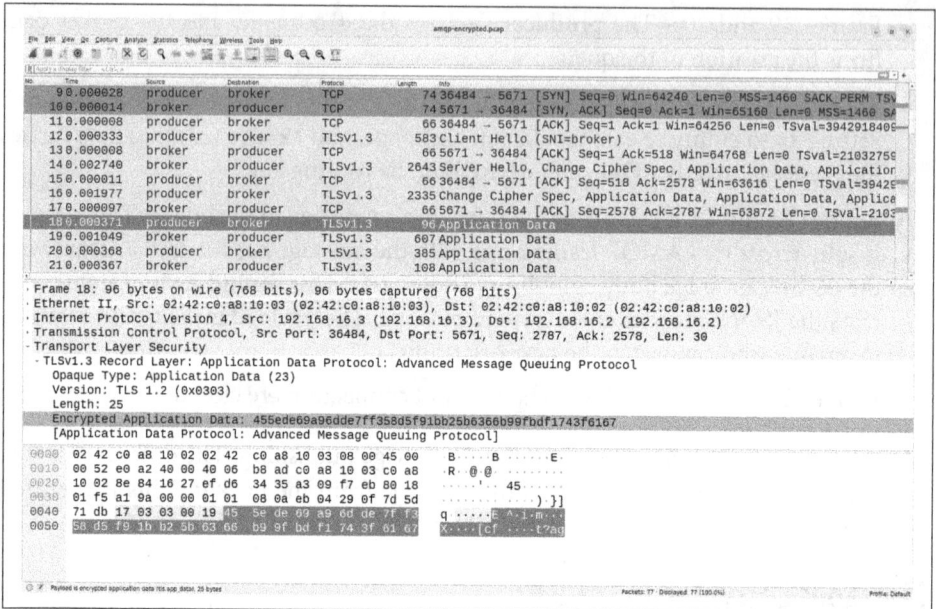

Figure 11-12. AMQPS encrypted traffic

After the TLS handshake is completed, starting from frame 18, you see encrypted `Application Data` inside TCP segments. The highlighted text at the bottom right of the screenshot, "E^.i.m…X….[cf….t?ag", shows the encrypted payload.

Let's look at the RabbitMQ broker's TLS configuration, given in Example 11-6.

Example 11-6. RabbitMQ broker's TLS configuration

```
# src/rabbitmq/2.WorkQueue/src/config/etc/rabbitmq/conf.d/10-defaults.conf

# Set ports for unencrypted and encrypted communication ❶
listeners.tcp.default = 5672
listeners.ssl.default = 5671

# Enable SSL/TLS support ❷
ssl_options.cacertfile = /etc/rabbitmq/ssl/certs/ca_certificate.pem
ssl_options.certfile = /etc/rabbitmq/ssl/certs/server_certificate.pem
ssl_options.fail_if_no_peer_cert = true
ssl_options.keyfile = /etc/rabbitmq/ssl/private/server_key.pem
ssl_options.verify = verify_peer
...
```

❶ The `listeners` settings specify application ports for unencrypted (5672) and encrypted (5671) communication.

❷ The block describes the broker's TLS configuration. It uses the server-side certificates by setting the `ssl_options` properties, such as the location of the *ca_certificate.pem*, *server_certificate.pem*, and *server_key.pem* files. The `verify=verify_peer` option instructs a `broker` (server) to validate the client's certificate, if the client presents its TLS certificate.

In an mTLS setup, the client and broker (server) verify each other's certificates to authenticate each other.

You can proceed now to implementing the secure communication on the client's side (producer and consumer). Let's look at the implementation shared by *producer.py* and *consumer.py* in Example 11-7.

Example 11-7. Producer (and consumer) TLS implementation

```
# src/rabbitmq/2.WorkQueue/src/producer.py

...
broker = os.getenv("RABBITMQ_BROKER")
user = os.getenv("RABBITMQ_USER")
password = os.getenv("RABBITMQ_PASS")
tls_enable = to_bool(os.getenv("TLS_ENABLE", True))  ❸
...

def __init__(self):
    self.__connect()  ❶

def __connect(self):  ❶
    """Establishes a connection to the RabbitMQ broker."""
    credentials = PlainCredentials(self.user, self.password)  ❷
    if self.tls_enable:  ❸
        port = 5671
        context = create_default_context(
          cafile="/etc/rabbitmq/ssl/certs/ca_certificate.pem"
        )
        context.load_cert_chain(  ❹
            "/etc/rabbitmq/ssl/certs/client_certificate.pem",
            "/etc/rabbitmq/ssl/private/client_key.pem"
        )
        ssl_options = SSLOptions(context)  ❺
        params = ConnectionParameters(  ❻
          self.broker, port, ssl_options=ssl_options, credentials=credentials
        )

    ...
    try:
      self.connection = BlockingConnection(params)  ❼
    except Exception:
        print(f"Error: Cannot connect to '{self.broker}' host.")
        exit(1)
```

❶ The __connect() method holds settings for establishing a connection to the broker service.

❷ The PlainCredentials class creates a credentials object to authenticate the clients (producers and consumers) against the broker service, using a username and password.

❸ The tls_enable setting controls encryption. If set to true, the encrypted connection will use port 5671, and create a secure context using create_default_context() method, which reads the *ca_certificate.pem* file. This CA certificate is used on the client side to verify the broker's certificate. In an mTLS setup, the broker uses this CA certificate to validate the client certificate.

❹ The load_cert_chain() method loads the client certificate (*client_certificate.pem*) and key (*client_key.pem*) into the context variable.

❺ The ssl_options variable holds various SSL options based on the context variable.

❻ ConnectionParameters creates a params object that takes broker, port, ssl_options, and credentials as its arguments.

❼ BlockingConnection establishes a blocking connection to the broker service using the settings contained in params.

Authentication and Authorization

Authentication and authorization are other aspects to be addressed in the context of RabbitMQ's security. In this section, you'll look at RabbitMQ's authentication with SASL and how to use access control lists (ACLs) (*https://oreil.ly/S1dGy*) to control authorization.

SASL, a framework for authentication, separates application protocols (e.g., AMQP, LDAP, SMTP) from authentication methods with the goal of letting any application protocol that supports SASL use the SASL-supported authentication methods. RabbitMQ supports the following SASL authentication mechanisms: PLAIN, AMQPLAIN, ANONYMOUS (not to be used in production), RABBIT-CR-DEMO (used to demonstrate challenge-response authentication), and EXTERNAL (available as a plug-in).

This section uses the PLAIN mechanism, which is enabled by default in the RabbitMQ clients (consumers and producers) and server (broker). The PLAIN mechanism uses credentials (username and password) to authenticate. This method needs to be combined with TLS encryption, since PLAIN credentials are sent in plaintext.

Let's look at code handling for authentication, split across three files: Example 11-8, Example 11-9, and Example 11-10.

Example 11-8. Authentication settings in the compose.yaml *file*

```
# src/rabbitmq/2.WorkQueue/compose.yaml

services:
  broker:
    ...
    environment:
      - RABBITMQ_USER=bugs ❶
      - RABBITMQ_PASS=${RABBITMQ_PASS:-bunny} ❷
    ...

  producer:
    ...
    environment:
      - RABBITMQ_USER=bugs ❶
      - RABBITMQ_PASS=${RABBITMQ_PASS:-bunny} ❷

  consumer-a:
    ...
    environment:
      - RABBITMQ_USER=bugs ❶
      - RABBITMQ_PASS=${RABBITMQ_PASS:-bunny} ❷
```

Example 11-9. RabbitMQ's broker SASL configuration

```
# src/rabbitmq/2.WorkQueue/src/config/etc/rabbitmq/conf.d/10-defaults.conf

default_user = $(RABBITMQ_USER) ❶
default_pass = $(RABBITMQ_PASS) ❷
```

Example 11-10. Producer (and consumer) SASL implementation

```
# src/rabbitmq/2.WorkQueue/src/producer.py

...
broker = os.getenv("RABBITMQ_BROKER")
user = os.getenv("RABBITMQ_USER")        ❶
password = os.getenv("RABBITMQ_PASS")    ❷
...

def __init__(self):
    self.__connect()
    ...

def __connect(self):
    credentials = PlainCredentials(self.user, self.password)  ❸
```

```
...
params = ConnectionParameters(self.broker, port, credentials=credentials)
...
self.connection = BlockingConnection(params)
...
```

❶ The `RABBITMQ_USER` environment variable stores the username.

❷ The `RABBITMQ_PASS` environment variable stores the password.

❸ A client (producer or consumer) is authenticated when connecting to the server (broker). If the credentials are invalid, the broker rejects the connection.

> Remember to change the default credentials of your services. Default credentials lead to risks recognized by the OWASP Top 10 (*https://oreil.ly/lqDLe*).

RabbitMQ is a multitenant system. The system allows sharing the same infrastructure among many tenants (users) while ensuring security and strict data isolation among tenants. To support multitenancy, RabbitMQ uses a virtual host mechanism. The virtual host allows logical grouping and separation of RabbitMQ's resources (e.g., exchanges, bindings, and queues).

A user can be bound to only three categories of permissions in RabbitMQ: `read`, `write`, and `configure`. The `read` permission allows users to consume messages from resources. The `write` permission allows users to create messages that will propagate through resources. The `configure` permission allows users to declare, remove, or set resources permissions. Regular expression patterns are used to describe permissions. For example, the ".*" pattern means that a user has access to all resources within the assigned category (`read`, `write`, and `configure`).

Using the commands listed in Example 11-11, let's investigate default permissions assigned by RabbitMQ to the `bugs` user.

Example 11-11. RabbitMQ users' permissions inspection

```
# Enter the exercise directory ❶
cd src/rabbitmq/2.WorkQueue

# Start the containers ❷
docker compose up --detach --wait

# List RabbitMQ's users ❸
docker compose exec broker rabbitmqctl list_users --formatter pretty_table
```

```
Listing users ...
┌───────┬───────────────┐
│ user  │ tags          │
├───────┼───────────────┤
│ bugs  │ administrator │
└───────┴───────────────┘

# List RabbitMQ's vhosts ❹
docker compose exec broker rabbitmqctl list_vhosts --formatter pretty_table
Listing vhosts ...
┌───────┐
│ name  │
├───────┤
│ /     │
└───────┘

# List users permissions ❺
docker compose exec broker rabbitmqctl list_permissions --formatter pretty_table
Listing permissions for vhost "/" ...
┌───────┬───────────┬───────┬──────┐
│ user  │ configure │ write │ read │
├───────┼───────────┼───────┼──────┤
│ bugs  │ .*        │ .*    │ .*   │
└───────┴───────────┴───────┴──────┘
```

❶ Enter the exercise directory.

❷ Wait for the containers to start in detached mode.

❸ List RabbitMQ users.

❹ List RabbitMQ virtual hosts.

❺ List the users' permissions. As you can see, the bugs user has read, write, and configure permissions for all (".*") resources within the "/" virtual host, allowing bugs to do administrative work. That's needed for an admin user but not for a nonadmin user. To control access to the individual resources, you'd have to create a nonadmin user and assign the desired resource permissions.

Documentation

So far, we have covered the implementation and security of RabbitMQ. Now, it's time to change our hat and adopt the user perspective. In this section, you'll become familiar with documenting messaging APIs using AsyncAPI (*https://www.asyncapi.com*).

AsyncAPI Specification

Example 11-12 shows an AsyncAPI Specification used to describe the messaging API of the work queue from Figure 11-9.

> If you're familiar with the OpenAPI Specification (OAS) (*https://oreil.ly/Ke7WN*), but not with the AsyncAPI Specification, then reading "Coming from OpenAPI" on the AsyncAPI website (*https://oreil.ly/33mBQ*) provides an overview of the differences between the two specifications.

Example 11-12. Work queue AsyncAPI Specification

```
# src/rabbitmq/2.WorkQueue/docs/api/v1.0.0/work_queue.yaml

asyncapi: 3.0.0 ❶
defaultContentType: application/json ❷
info: ❸
  title: Work Queue
  version: 1.0.0
  description: Work queue lab documentation.
channels: ❹
  Die:
    description: Die Queue
    address: die
    bindings:
      amqp:
        is: queue
        queue:
          contentEncoding: utf-8
          durable: true
          name: die
          vhost: /
    messages:
      RollDie:
        $ref: '#/components/messages/RollDie'
operations: ❺
  Roll:
    action: send
    channel:
      $ref: '#/channels/Die'
    bindings:
      amqp:
        deliveryMode: 2 # 1 - transient, 2 - persistent
  Pick:
    action: receive
    channel:
      $ref: '#/channels/Die'
    bindings:
      amqp:
```

```
        ack: true
components: ❻
  messages:
    RollDie:
      name: Roll Die
      title: Roll Die
      headers:
        type: object
        properties:
          version:
            type: string
            default: 1.0.0
      payload:
        type: object
        properties:
          data:
            type: object
            properties:
              outcome:
                type: string
              message:
                type: string
          version:
            type: string
            default: 1.0.0
```

❶ The `asyncapi` required field holds the AsyncAPI Specification version.

❷ The `defaultContentType` field describes the default content type of the message payload (JSON).

❸ The `info` required field holds metadata about the documented API.

❹ The `channels` required field describes pathways for sending and receiving messages. A pathway could be topics, routing keys, queues, event types, or paths (depending on the messaging system). In this example, a channel is defined with the `Die` ID as an AMQP queue (`die`) along with the queue's properties (`durability`, etc.).

❺ The `operations` field describes operations that the application must implement over the channels. This example has two operations, `Roll` (`send`) and `Pick` (`receive`), that describe the intent of sending and receiving messages over the channel (`Die`). The `Roll` operation says that the producer uses `deliveryMode` of 2 (persistent delivery). The `Pick` operation says that the consumer must acknowledge the message. Note that it doesn't tell which acknowledgment the consumer should use (automatic or manual).

The operation names Roll and Pick are figurative names used in our example. The name Roll conveys that rolling a die publishes a message to the die queue, and the name Pick indicates consuming the message from the queue.

❻ The components field defines reusable structures (or definitions) applicable across the document—in this case, a specification describing a message (Roll Die) sent and received via channels. The properties describe the headers and payload.

> By looking at the specification, you can notice that some fields use the lowercase camel notation (e.g., defaultContentType), and others uppercase camel case notation (e.g., RollDie). The lowercase fields are specific to the AsyncAPI Specification, whereas the uppercase fields are ID fields specific to your application. We choose to use uppercase notation for our application, but you are free to use lowercase notation too.

AsyncAPI Documentation

Let's look at the tooling provided by AsyncAPI. Example 11-13 shows asyncapi/cli, which is used to convert the AsyncAPI Specification to HTML. asyncapi/cli is run in the container created from the asyncapi/cli Docker image. Alternatively, you could execute the asyncapi program as a standalone CLI.

> You can also generate a preview of AsyncAPI as HTML documentation online by pasting the AsyncAPI Specification into AsyncAPI Studio (https://studio.asyncapi.com). However, consider using local alternatives first, to avoid exposing sensitive information online.

Example 11-13. Work queue documentation generation using asyncapi/cli

```
# Enter the exercise directory ❶
cd src/rabbitmq/2.WorkQueue/docs/api/v1.0.0

# Generate HTML documentation ❷
docker run --rm -it --user=root \
        --volume ${PWD}/output:/app/output \
        --volume ${PWD}/work_queue.yaml:/app/asyncapi.yaml \
        asyncapi/cli generate fromTemplate /app/asyncapi.yaml \
        @asyncapi/html-template@3.0.0 \
        --use-new-generator --force-write --output /app/output

# Serve documentation with Nginx ❸
docker run --rm --detach --publish 127.0.0.1:8888:80 \
        --volume ${PWD}/output:/usr/share/nginx/html:ro nginx
```

❶ Enter the directory containing the *work_queue.yaml* AsyncAPI Specification file.

❷ Convert the AsyncAPI Specification into HTML documentation. The `asyncapi` program takes the *work_queue.yaml* file as input, along with `@asyncapi/html-template`. The resulting HTML documentation is saved in the container's filesystem, in the directory specified by the `--output` option. The `--force-write` flag ensures that documentation is generated, even if files are already present.

❸ Start the Nginx server to serve the generated HTML documentation. The `--volume` flag mounts the documentation present in the *output* directory at the Docker host, into the */usr/share/nginx/html* location in the container filesystem. The `--publish` flag exposes container port 80 to the Docker host port 8888.[9]

When *http://localhost:8888* is opened in a browser, it will show the documentation, as in Figure 11-13.

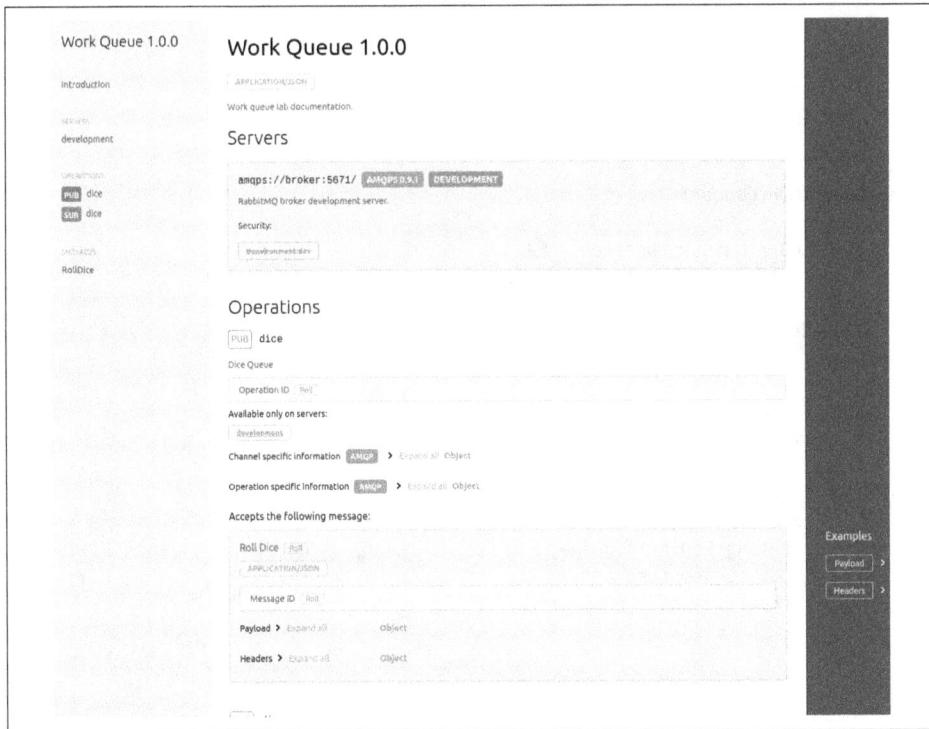

Figure 11-13. HTML documentation generated from the AsyncAPI Specification

---

9 When working with GitHub Codespaces, you'll use a unique URL containing the Codespace's name instead of the *localhost* URL. The expected URL is bound to port 8888 and can be found in VS Code's PORTS tab.

Message Versioning

In REST APIs, versioning happens at the API's endpoint or resource level. But how do we version messaging APIs?

One approach is to version the message itself. Another approach is to version a resource (exchange or queue) by adding a version to the resource name.

Message versioning can be implemented by adding a version field to the message header, payload, or both, as shown in Example 11-14.

> A version of the message in both the headers and the payload is shown here for educational purposes. In reality, you would separate the message payload from its metadata, by removing the version from the msg and keeping it only in the header. However, this would make versioning harder to debug, since the header isn't visible in the message body.

Example 11-14. Message payload versioning

```
# src/rabbitmq/2.WorkQueue/src/producer.py

...
class RabbitMQProducer:
    ...
    properties = BasicProperties(  ❷
        content_type='application/json',
        ...
        headers={"version": "1.0.0"}
    )
    ...

    def publish(self, msg: dict):
        self.properties.headers["version"] = msg["version"]  ❸
        self.channel.basic_publish(
            exchange="",
            routing_key=self.queue,
            body=to_json(msg)
            properties=self.properties
        )
        ...

if __name__ == "__main__":
    ...
    msg = {  ❶
        "data": {
            "message": f"Rolling {number}",
            "outcome": number
        },
        "version": "1.0.1"
```

```
  }
  ...
  publisher = RabbitMQProducer()  ❷
  publisher.publish(msg)  ❸
```

❶ The `msg` Python dictionary holds a message, which contains `data` and a message version (`1.0.1`).

❷ The `producer` object holds `BasicProperties`, including the message `con tent_type` (`application/json`) and the `headers` Python dictionary containing a default `version` field (`1.0.0`).

❸ The default version in the properties header is overridden by the value specified by the message payload.

Trade-Offs

Let's look at the advantages of messaging-based APIs:

Message delivery

Depending on what messaging technology you will work with, in general, messaging systems provide a means to deliver messages at least once, at most once, or exactly once.

High throughput and low latency

Messaging systems are designed to handle high throughput of messages at low latencies. RabbitMQ claims to handle messages of 1,024 bytes (1 KB) at the rate of around 26 thousand messages per second (*https://oreil.ly/U1vz7*) when publishing or consuming them from the broker. In an informal test, we achieved a throughput of 67 thousand messages per second when testing on a Lenovo ThinkPad P17 G1 (16 CPUs, 32 GB memory). On the other hand, Apache Kafka claims to handle 2 million writes per second (*https://oreil.ly/QKaWj*). In general, the benchmarking of any system is complex and depends on many parameters. However, what this benchmark shows is the order of magnitude of messages they can handle.

Scalability

Messaging systems are designed to scale (to handle a growing amount of work). If you are in a situation where the system can't catch up with the influx of incoming messages created by producers, then you could scale consumers vertically or horizontally.

When the broker isn't able to handle the load, scale it vertically by adding more resources, or use clustering for horizontal scaling.[10] You could even hybrid scale by scaling horizontally and vertically simultaneously. Physically decoupling producer and consumer applications facilitates scaling.

Be aware that each scaling technique has its trade-offs. For example, scaling horizontally increases system complexity, because you need to configure and manage more applications. Scaling vertically requires system downtime, and you may be eventually limited by hardware capacity.

Resilience

Queues act as a buffer between producers and consumers of the messages. In case of a consumer failure, the broker will keep receiving messages from the producer and will keep storing them. This way, the consumer can catch up with the messages when it's up again. To prevent message loss in the case of a failed producer, you could make the channel transactional for each published message, and by doing this, you'll assure message delivery to the broker. However, this solution will reduce message throughput.

Alternatively, you could use the publisher confirms (*https://oreil.ly/KMwTg*) pattern to ensure message delivery to the broker without paying the toll of reduced throughput due to transactions. While these mechanisms protect against producer and consumer failures, ensuring resilience against broker failures requires additional measures. For instance, deploying a RabbitMQ broker in a high-availability (HA) configuration (e.g., a cluster with mirrored queues) mitigates the worst-case scenario where a broker node fails.

Loose coupling

In a broker-based architecture, clients are loosely coupled because they interact only with the broker and not with each other directly. This decoupling allows clients to be independently deployable, scalable, and maintainable. For example, clients can be deployed on different machines, in separate datacenters or cloud environments (such as AWS, Azure, or Google Cloud), or written in different programming languages. As long as each client can connect to the broker, they can exchange messages.

Responsiveness

Messaging systems are designed to be responsive. For example, Kafka claims to deliver messages with latencies as low as 2 milliseconds.[11]

---

10 Read ScaleGrid's "Best Practices for Scaling RabbitMQ" (*https://oreil.ly/G69UV*), as well as RabbitMQ's "Cluster Sizing and Other Considerations" (*https://oreil.ly/ll0Ge*).

11 This is the official claim taken from Kafka (*https://kafka.apache.org*).

Let's consider the disadvantages of messaging-based APIs:

Complexity

Messaging APIs aren't the simplest to implement. Architects and developers need to understand the details of the messaging system, such as queues, topics, messages, when to use appropriate acknowledgment methods, and what message delivery guarantees to choose. Additionally, service integration may be difficult to implement, if other services use a different messaging technology.

Coupling

Being loosely coupled leads systems to be independently deployable, but it doesn't mean the components are fully decoupled. Producers and consumers are coupled by the message, so if a breaking change occurs in the message schema, the system is left in a state of failure that makes deployment potentially impossible. The producer and consumer are also coupled by the broker, which acts as a single point of failure. Without the broker, the communication between the producer and consumer is broken.

Message duplication and lack of ordering guarantees

Message duplication is a common problem in messaging-based systems that could potentially slow down message processing and increase storage space if consuming applications don't make their processing idempotent.[12] The duplicated messages could be caused by the applications being restarted unexpectedly.

Another disadvantage of messaging systems is issues with message ordering. Although queues enforce FIFO order, some applications require different order guarantees—for example, last-in-first-out (LIFO), or even more complex ordering based on application logic. This mismatch can introduce additional complexity in ensuring that the messages are processed in the intended order, especially when consumers restart or when duplicate messages occur.

Cumulative latency

It takes time for a message to propagate from the producer via the broker to the consumer. If the flow that the message must follow several hops, then the latency increases with each hop. For example, online payment processing is better suited for synchronous APIs, where the request is blocked until it receives the response (e.g., confirming a successful transaction). In contrast, sending a purchase notification (e.g., email or SMS) is better handled asynchronously since the response can be processed without blocking the client.

---

12 RabbitMQ provides a message deduplication plug-in (*https://oreil.ly/sK65V*) and streams message deduplication (*https://oreil.ly/9as6b*) to remediate this problem.

Debugging challenges

> Tracking messages as they traverse a system composed of several components is challenging. A common solution is to create a CID for every message and search for the CID in the system logs. Another challenge is the order of events that in asynchronous systems may be nondeterministic.

Error-handling challenges

> In synchronous communication, you know immediately when an error occurs, either by the application indicating it (4xx, 5xx errors) or by a timeout. In asynchronous communication, you don't know when an error occurs, forcing you to implement additional error handling. For example, in the case of an application error, identifying the error in the sequence of events associated with the call is a challenging task. To store failed messages, you could implement a DLQ. Additionally, you may attempt to recover from certain errors by retrying the messages. RabbitMQ provides a dead letter exchange (DLX) pattern (*https://oreil.ly/MQJhf*) to handle messages that fail delivery.

High cost

> Messaging systems are known for their high costs. The costs are associated with staff training, infrastructure, operations, testing, and integration with other systems. However, some companies that have adopted messaging systems claim that the benefits outweigh the costs (*https://oreil.ly/eSUgB*).

When to Use Messaging

After discovering the advantages and disadvantages of messaging, the question arises of when to use it.

Messaging is suitable in scenarios where message delivery must be ensured. In scenarios such as financial transactions or healthcare communications, losing even a single message can lead to significant economic losses or endanger lives. Therefore, the system design must account for failures to guarantee that messages are reliably transmitted even under adverse conditions.

Messaging-based systems are used for building resilient, scalable systems intended to handle decoupled, asynchronous workflows. This is needed to handle varying and increasing levels of traffic, to maintain high availability, and to ensure that messages are reliably delivered even during peak loads or failures. Scaling these components, either by adding more instances (horizontal scaling) or by upgrading resources (vertical scaling), enables the system to remain elastic and resilient as demand fluctuates.

Messaging can serve as an alternative when synchronous interaction with a system results in a poor user experience, such as when triggering specific application flows makes the user wait without an indication of progress. For example, video conversion implemented in REST will force the user to wait for a response, blocked until video conversion is over. The same task implemented in a messaging-based system would improve perceived user experience because one message would be created to start the conversion process, and a second message would be sent to notify the user that video conversion is completed. The user is nonblocked and proceeds with the application flow while the video is being converted.

Additionally, messaging can be used when the system's responsiveness (*https:// oreil.ly/l5IBE*) is desired. For example, a system shall respond promptly to the input provided to it, such as in high-frequency trading systems.

Finally, messaging can be used for interservice communication. You could use synchronous REST API calls to trigger a certain application workflow. Once a service receives the REST request, it pushes a message into a message broker that then asynchronously communicates with other services. This converts the synchronous action into asynchronous interservice communication.

Exercises

1. Use Shodan (*https://shodan.io*) to create a query that scans for RabbitMQ servers that use the PLAIN SASL mechanism. What is the number of servers that could be potentially breached? Hint: create an account on Shodan, and figure out the RabbitMQ default port.

Shodan

Shodan (*https://www.shodan.io/dashboard*) is a search engine for internet-exposed systems (e.g., routers, servers, and webcams). Because the engine scans and indexes publicly open systems, it's called a "search engine for hackers."

With Shodan, you can write a query that scans the internet for systems exposing a specific port, technology, or even a system owned by an organization. A detailed filter list (*https://oreil.ly/VKZsw*) allows you to do that.

For example, if you want to find webcams in Denmark, you could use a `webcam country:DK` query. If you would like to find web servers globally, you would use a query with a port filter (e.g., `port:80`).

---

2. Using `rabbitmqctl`, create a new user called `roger`, tag the user as a `developer` (metadata describing a user role), and restrict the user access only to the `die` queue on the "`/`" vhost with `write` and `read` permissions. Hint: to complete this exercise, use the `rabbitmqctl` subcommands `add_user`, `set_user_tags`, and `set_permissions`.

3. Spin up the work queue example from this chapter, and test RabbitMQ broker messages throughput with the *perf-test* program (*https://oreil.ly/w7JzM*). Hint: What throughput do you get when you execute the following command?

```
docker run -it --rm --name perf-test --network rabbitmq \
    pivotalrabbitmq/perf-test:latest \
    --uri amqp://bugs:bunny@broker \
    --time 10 --json-body --size 1024
```

Summary

Messaging-based APIs can be used to build scalable, resilient, and responsive systems. However, they aren't the simplest to design, implement, and monitor.

This chapter started by introducing generic concepts of messaging systems, such as a message, a queue, and content-based routing. Using a specific messaging technology, RabbitMQ, you implemented a work queue. Furthermore, you discovered other common messaging patterns such as publish-subscribe, routing, topics, and request-response. In addition, you documented the API using AsyncAPI, including message versioning. You also explored the security aspects of RabbitMQ, by securing the messages with TLS, SASL, and restricting user access with ACL.

The chapter ended with a discussion of the trade-offs of messaging-based APIs.

Index

X.509 certificates and, 97
CDC (consumer-driven contract), 28
certificate authorities (see CAs)
chunked transfer coding, 128, 148
CI/CD (continuous integration/continuous
    delivery and deployment) pipelines, 30-31
CIDs (Correlation IDs), 339, 344, 372
client complexity, in RESTful APIs, 163
client streaming RPCs, 258-262
client, defined, 79
client-server architecture, 4
    (see also ECHO service)
    backward compatibility, 47
    HTTP, 154
    messaging, 336, 344
    REST, 158
    web applications, 4
client-side caching, 66
cloud vendor feeds, 229
code injection attacks, 70
code-on-demand, 159, 195
Common Object Request Broker Architecture
    (CORBA) standard, 12
compaction, 332
compression
    API performance, 75
    encoding versus, 51
    HTTP headers, 116, 134
connection migration, QUIC, 139, 141, 143
consumer-driven contract (CDC), 28
content negotiation, 129
continuous integration/continuous delivery
    and deployment (CI/CD) pipelines, 30-31
contracts
    CDC and PDC, 28
    contract testing and fuzzing, 27
    protobufs, 279
    versioning, 47
CORBA (Common Object Request Broker
    Architecture) standard, 12
corrective maintenance, 34
Correlation IDs (CIDs), 339, 344, 372
counting records, 58
coupling
    defined, 340
    loose, 370
Create operation, CRUD
    GraphQL, 213-216
    REST APIs, 169-172
cross-site scripting, 70

CRUD operations
    Create operation
        GraphQL, 213-216
        REST APIs, 169-172
    Delete operation
        GraphQL, 213-216
        REST APIs, 175-177
    Read operation
        GraphQL, 208-213
        REST APIs, 173-175
    Update operation
        GraphQL, 213-216
        REST APIs, 168
cryptography, 96
cryptology, 96
cursor-based pagination, 60
cybersecurity web feeds, 229

D

data link layer, 81, 82
data transmission modes (transmission
    modes), 7
DDoS (Distributed Denial of Service) attacks,
    66
dead letter queues (DLQs), 344, 372
decapsulation, 82
declarative APIs, 43
declarative programming languages, 199
defensive programming approach, 28, 172
Delete operation, CRUD
    GraphQL, 213-216
    REST APIs, 175-177
deletion of resources, 67
Denial of Service (DoS) attacks, 65, 70, 238
deprecation, 35-36
deprecation banners, 35
deserialization, 53, 56
design by contract, 27
developers, benefits of APIs for, 14
DevOps, 30-32
DevSecOps, 31
Distributed Denial of Service (DDoS) attacks,
    66
Django REST Framework (DRF), 151
DLQs (dead letter queues), 344, 372
DNS (Domain Name System) protocol
    browser connections and loading times,
        117-119
    defined, 83
documentation

About the Authors

Lukasz Dynowski is an independent consultant with over 10 years of expertise in IT. He has held numerous positions and responsibilities, including full-stack developer, DevOps engineer, software architect, and many others. Lukasz has a scientific background; he spent several years in academia as a coauthor and contributor to scientific papers. Lukasz won and judged O'Reilly's Software Architectural Katas and ranks among the top 0.1% developers on Stack Overflow. He is a Docker Captain and the biggest geek you'd ever meet. He is a devoted husband and father to two lovely kids.

Marcin Dulak has over 20 years of experience in IT. He developed quantum modeling algorithms, including porting code to high-performance computing architectures. He acquired expertise in implementing and operating on-premises and cloud infrastructure, focusing most recently on web applications. When at home, he enjoys time with his family and cats.

Colophon

The animal on the cover of *Learning API Styles* is the Patagonian mockingbird (*Mimus patagonicus*), native to Patagonia (Argentina and Chile).

Despite their name, which suggests vocal mimicry, Patagonian mockingbirds actually tend to sing their own unique tunes (with slight undertones of mimicry). Their designation as mockingbirds stems from their place within the *Mimidae* family, a group known for its vocal abilities.

The Patagonian mockingbird's most striking physical feature is its pale eyebrows. While there isn't a definite evolutionary purpose for this, the pale streaks may help in identifying other members of the species and in camouflaging themselves from predators. They are ground-based more often than other birds, although they still utilize their wings for flitting about, and they forage for most of their food on the ground. During mating season, their diet shifts from fruits and berries to higher-protein insects, to provide better nutrients for their young. Patagonian mockingbird families exhibit strong bonds, tending to stay together much longer than typical bird families. It should come as no surprise, then, that they are relatively territorial in nature.

Many of the animals on O'Reilly covers are endangered; all of them are important to the world. The cover illustration is by Karen Montgomery, based on an antique line engraving from Lydekker's *Royal Natural History*. The series design is by Edie Freedman, Ellie Volckhausen, and Karen Montgomery. The cover fonts are Gilroy Semibold and Guardian Sans. The text font is Adobe Minion Pro; the heading font is Adobe Myriad Condensed; and the code font is Dalton Maag's Ubuntu Mono.

O'REILLY®

Learn from experts.
Become one yourself.

60,000+ titles | Live events with experts | Role-based courses
Interactive learning | Certification preparation

**Try the O'Reilly learning platform
free for 10 days.**

©2025 O'Reilly Media, Inc. O'Reilly is a registered trademark of O'Reilly Media, Inc. 718900_7x9.1875

www.ingramcontent.com/pod-product-compliance
Lightning Source LLC
Chambersburg PA
CBHW080654220326
41598CB00033B/5202